I

ALL ABOU

1995

HARRY SHAY, EDITOR

This is the third edition of this unique Michigan book. This 1995 edition is completely updated, enlarged and revised. Since first published (1989), it has grown into a series of similar books which now cover Ohio, California and Florida

User-friendly, it is completely indexed (starting on the next page), to provide instant answers to a multitude of questions. It is useful to everyone, from the student to the senior citizen, from alert residents to informed leaders. And it is indeed a "pathfinder" for new arrivals to the state.

A delight to the trivia buff too, a browse through its pages is both entertaining and informative. The multitude of statistics and facts are arranged to focus on the significant aspects. Brief commentary brings much of the information to "life".

Your comments and suggestions are sincerely welcome. We want it to be the reference resource that you want.

Instant Information Company
P.O. Box 202
Hartland, MI 48353

Available at leading bookstores $17.95, or by mail to the above address. To order by mail, please send $17.95, plus $2.75 shipping/handling.

Associate Editors & Specialists:
Susan Shay (M.L.S.), Teresa Dryer, Kathryn Guzowski, Lee Hickey, Kathleen Imre, Jodie Kleymeer, Barbara Loggins and Donna Sisson.

ISBN 1-883351-03-0
Printed in the United States of America

Dedicated to the Memory
of the Publisher
Vonda Shay
1926 - 1990

INDEX

A

AGING - AREA AGENCIES, 226-229
AGRICULTURE, 256-259
AIDS, 194-200
Age
Cases
Deaths
Gender
Map by County
Races
Transmission
AIRPORTS / AIRLINES/ 800 PHONES, 74-75
AMERICAN NATIVE INDIANS
Casinos - Gaming, 64
Population, 160, 239-240, 234
ANCESTRY OF POPULATION, 165
ARTS, 69
ASIANS, 160, 239-240, 234
ASSOCIATIONS, 283-288
ATTRACTIONS - MAJOR, 65
AUTO BARONS - HOMES OF THE 75-77
AUTOMOTIVE PIONEERS - TOP 10 139
AWARDS
Hall of Fame, 133-134
Sports Hall of Fame, 135
Womens Hall of Fame, 137-138

B

BIRTHS, 279-282
BLACKS, 160, 239-240, 234
BOOKS ABOUT MICHIGAN 270-273

C

CAPSULE FACTS OF MICHIGAN, 23-28
CHRONOLOGY OF MICHIGAN HISTORY 202-212
CIRCLE TOURS OF LAKES, 59
CHAMBERS OF COMMERCE, 70
CITIES & PLACES, 144-161
County Location
Population
Zip
Population by Race, 234
CITIES BY COUNTY AND S.E.V. (TAX), 260-269
CITIES - 10 LARGEST AT STATEHOOD & NOW, 143
CITIES- LARGEST, 233-238
Area
Population
Racial
Language
Age
Education
Social Security
Public Assistance
Income
Goverment Employment
Finances
Housing
CITIZEN PARTICIPATION IN GOVERMENT, 98
CITY MAPS, 222-225
CONVENTION & VISITOR CENTERS, 78-80
COLLEGES, 170-177
City
Telephone
Year Founded
Enrollment
Student Costs
CONGRESS, 87
CONSTITUTION - STATE BILL OF RIGHTS, 116-118
COUNTIES, 29-51
Population
% Change 1980-1992
Area
Density
Map Locator
Phone Area Code

COUNTIES - MI IN TOP 25 IN U.S., 52-53
COUNTIES - HIGHEST RANKING IN MI, 54
COUNTIES - S.E.V. (TAX), 260-269
COUNTIES - TOP TEN IN PROPERTY VALUE, 269
COUNTIES, 239-246
Area
Population
Racial
Language
Age
Education
Social Security
Public Assistance
Income
Goverment Employment
Fiances
Housing
CRIME, 253-255
Offenses by County
Offenses & Arrests by Year-State

D

DEATHS, 279-282
DIVORCES, 279-282

E

EDUCATION, 166-168
Adult, 162
Attainment by County, 234-244
Financial Facts, 166-168
MEAP, 169
Non- Public Schools & Enrollment K-12, 168
Blue Ribbon Schools, 140
Statistics - Mi Schools, 166-168
Student Enrollment, K-12, 166
Teacher of The Year, 140
ELECTIONS
Attorney General By County, 84
Congress 1994, 87
Governor - 1835-1994, 95-96
Governor By County 1990 & 1994 81-82
Legislature 1994, 88-92
President - 1928-1992, 97
President By County - 1988 & 1992 93-94
Proposals, 87
Secretary of State by County 1944, 83
U.S. Senate by County 1994, 85
State-Wide 1994, 86
Supreme Court 1994,87
ENTERTAINERS - FAMOUS BORN IN MI 141-142

F

FAIRS - STATE & COUNTIES, 67-68
FALL COLORS IN REGIONS, 63
FESTIVALS - ANNUAL, 66
FISHING RECORDS, 275
FORTUNE 500 COMPANIES IN MI, 213

G

GOVERMENT
Departments, 109-110
Elections, 81-97
Executive - Description, 111-112
Judicial - Description, 114
Legislative - Description, 113
Legislative Committees, 105-108
Letter Writing & Lobbying, 98
Organization, 111-114
GOVERNORS - VOTE 1835-1994 95-96

H

HALLS OF FAME
Michigan,133-134
Sports, 135
Women's, 137-138
HISPANICS, 160, 239-240
HISTORICAL CENTER, 123-132
HISTORICAL MARKERS, 201
HISTORY
Counties - Year Organized, 31-57
Chronology State, 202-212
Population - 1810-1990, 162
Vote For President - 1928-1992, 97

Vote Fot Governor - 1835-1994, 95-96
HOLIDAYS 201
HOME PRICES BY REGION, 277
HOUSE OF REPRESENTATIVES, 89-92
HUNTING, 278

I

INCOME - PLACES WITH HIGHEST MEDIAN, 214
INDIANS
Population, 160, 239-240
INTERNATIONAL VISITORS INFO, 72

L

LABOR 230-231
Employment - State & Metro Areas
Employment by Major Industry, 233
LAKES & WATERWAYS 232
LAW
Driving, 274
Hunting, 274
Constitution, State Bill of Rights 116-118
Legal Public Info System by Phone 121-122
LEGISLATURE
Description, 113
District Maps, 102-105
House of Representatives, 89-92
State Senate, 88
House Senate Committees, 106-108
House & Senate Leaders, 108
Letter Writing & Lobbying, 99
Telephones, 99-100
LIBRARY - STATE, 123-132
LIGHTHOUSES, 63
LOTTERY, 215-217
Prizes
Revenue
Winners

M

MAPS
Aids by County, 195
Cities, 222-225
Congressional Districts, 101
Counties, 29-51
Legislative Districts, 102-105
Metro Areas, 55-57
Mileage, 71
Telephone Area Codes, 219-220
Zip Areas, 221
MARRIAGES, 279-282
MASON, STEVENS, 133
MEAP, 169
MEDIA, 250-252
METRO AREAS, 55-56, 230-233
MICHIGAN HALL OF FAME, 132-133
MICHIGAN & U.S. OVERVIEW, 9-22
MILEAGE BETWEEN SELECT CITIES, 71

N

NEWSPAPERS, 250-252

O

ORGANIZATIONS, 283-288
OVERVIEW OF MICHIGAN & U.S. RANK, 9-22

P

PARK - RIDE, 276
POPULATION
Age, 241-242, 235
Ancestry, 165
Asian, 160, 239-240, 234
Black, 160, 239-240, 234
Cities & Places, 144-161
Counties, 31-51
Indian, 160, 239-240, 234
State 1810-1990
Townships-Largest, 163
Villiages-Largest, 163
White, 234

R

REVENUE & EXPENDITURES STATE, 115

S

SCHOOLS
Blue Ribbon, 140
SENATE - STATE, 88

SENIOR CITIZENS
Area Agencies, 226-229
S.E.V. (TAX), 260-269
State
Cities
Townships
SPORT HALL OF FAME, 135
SPORTS CHAMPIONS, 178-193
College 136
Lions
Pistons
Professional
Prep All Sports
Prep Basketball Boys
Prep Basketball Girls
Prep Football
Red Wings
STADIUM - SPORT
Joe Louis Arena
Palace of Auburn Hills
Sliverdome
Tiger Stadium
STATE STATS, 239-246
Area
Population
Racial
Language
Age
Education
Social Security
Public Assistance
Income
Goverment Employment
Finances
Housing
STATE POLICE POSTS, 122
SUPREME COURT
SYMBOLS, 27-28

T

TAXES
Appeal, 119-120
City Income
Revenue - Expenditures, 115
S.E.V. by County, City,
Township, 260-269
TEACHER OF THE YEAR, 140
TELE - COURT, 121-122
TELEPHONE AREA CODES
REVISED (313) AND (810), 219-220
TOWNSHIPS
S.E.V. (Tax), 260-269
THEATERS, 86-87
TRAVEL Airline / Airport /
800 Phones, 73-74
Attraction - Major, 65
Chambers of Commerce Phones, 78
Circle Tour Lakes, 59
Convention & Visitor Center, 79-80
Fairs - County, 67-68
Fall Colors, 63
Festivals - Annual, 66
Information - Travel, 80
International Visitors Info, 72
Lighthouses, 62-63
Mileage Map, 71
Park - Ride, 276
Theaters, 69
Welcome Centers & Info, 60
TRIVIA, Random Pages
TV STATIONS, 247-249

V

VETERANS, 244-245
VITAL STATISTICS
STATE & COUNTIES, 279-282
Births
Deaths
Marriages
Divorces

W

WEATHER, 58
WELCOME CENTERS & INFO, 60
WOMEN'S HALL OF FAME, 137-138

Z

ZIP CODES, 144-161
ZOOS, 61

HELPFUL EXPLANATION ABOUT "RATE" and 'RANK"

RATE is sometimes more significant than total numbers. For example, if there are 500 farmers in County A and 1,500 in County B, and if the total population is 25,000 in County A and 90,000 in County B, the **rate** of farmers per 10,000 population is 200 for County A and 166 for County B. Thus, although County B would have three times the number of farmers, County A would have more farmers in relation to population.

NOTE: The formula for this calculation: 500 farmers, multiplied by the given "'per 10,000 population" (equals 5,000,000), divided by the actual population of 25,000 (equals 200).

RANK refers to the position of the subject in relation to others. For example, Michigan is the the eighth largest state in population and is therefore ranked No. 8 in population among the 50 states. It produces more tart cherries than any other state, and it is therefore ranked No. 1 in that category.

Trivia

Q The U.S. Bureau of the Census ranked the top 25 counties in the nation in select subjects, and found 7 Michigan counties among the 25 in one category. What was the subject?

A The highest percentage of workers driving alone to work (The counties are Macomb, Oakland, Midland, Bay, Monroe, Genesee and Saginaw, and the percentage of lone drivers ranged from 87.4% to 84.8%).

Q Which two Michigan cities did U.S. News report among the top ten cities of more than 100,000 people in the nation with the lowest crime rate per capita?

A Sterling Heights and Livonia (Macomb and Wayne counties).

OVERVIEW OF

MICHIGAN & RANK IN U.S.

The data in this overview is the latest available at the start of 1995.

Additional detailed data on most of these overview subjects appear on other pages of this Almanac (please see Index).

Quantities are noted with the subject. For example, "actual" indicates the full number is shown, and "thousands" indicates the number shown is given in thousands ("9,576" in thousands reads "9,576,000").

Michigan, based on population, is ranked the 8th largest state. For comparative purposes this rank form is used here to indicate Michigan's position on other subjects in relation to the other states.

"Rate" indicates the quanity out of a specific total.

Source: Compiled by the Almanac from multiple sources, including the U.S. Stat. Abst., and U.S. Bureau of the Census

SUBJECT	MICHIGAN	US
PEOPLE		
Population 1995 (THOUSANDS)	9,576	263,436
Rank (among 50 states)	8	
Percentage change		
1990-1995	+3%	+5.9%
Rank	37	
Population		
1980 (Thousands)	9,262	226,546
1990 (Thousands)	9,295 (+0.3)	248,709 (+9%)
Projected 2000 (Thousands)	9,759 (+5%)	276,242 (11%)

SUBJECT	MICHIGAN	US
Density, per sq. mile (Actual) 1993	166.8	72.9
Rank	14	
White 1995 (Thousands)	7,958	218,333
Rank	8	
Black	1,417	33,118
Rank	8	
American Indian	61	2,229
Rank	10	
Asian	140	9,756
Rank	13	
Hispanic	242	26,797
Rank	15	
Age (1993) (thousands)		
Under 5 years	705	19,759
5 - 17 years	1,801	47,428
18-24 years	967	25,659
25 - 34 years	1,487	41,907
35 - 44 years	1,511	40,830
45 - 44 years	1,067	28,666
55 - 64 years	770	20,923
65 - 74 years	676	18,652
75 - 84 years	378	10,769
85 and older	166	3,369
% 65 and older	12.4%	12.7%
Total	9,478	252,908
Urban 1990 (thousands)	6,556	187,053
Rank	9	
%	70.5%	75.2%
Rural	2,739	61,656
Rank	6	
%	29.5%	24.8%
Metro Areas 1992 (thousands)	7,799	203,908
Percent	82.7%	79.7%
Rank	8	
Net change (1980-1992)	0.08	26,270
% Total	1%	14.8%
Non Metro 1992 (thousands)	1,635	51,905
Percent	16.7%	20.3%
Rank	10	
Net change (1980-1992)	0.92	2,256
% Total	5.9%	4.5%

SUBJECT	MICHIGAN	US
Households 1993 (thousands)	3,497	95,133
% change (1990 - 1993)	+2.3%	+3.5%
Families	2,439*	68,144
Persons per household	2.65	2.64
Married couple	1,883*	53,171
Married w/children	875*	25,157
One parent w/children	317*	10,901
Non-family	980*	28,247
One person	809*	23,642
* = Michigan 1990		
Non Households 1990 (thousands)	211	6,697
Correctional Institutions	42	1,115
Nursing homes	57	1,772
College dormitories	73	1,953
Shelters, homeless	3	178
Religious, Adherents (thousands)		
Christian (1990)	4,580	131,084
Jewish (1992)	107	5,828
Muslim (est.)	N/A	8,000
Others	N/A	N/A
Vital Statistics 1992		
Births (in thousands)	194.2	4,110.9
Rate per 1,000 pop.	16.0	16.3
% low birth weight	7.8%	7.1%
% teenage mothers	13.2%	12.9%
% unmarried mothers	26.6%	29.2%
Abortions 1992	56	1,529
Rate per 1,000 women	25.2	25.9
Ratio to live births	393	379
Deaths 1992 (thousands)	79	2,177
Rate per 1,000 pop.	8.4	8.5
Infant mortality, per 1,000 live births (1991)	10.4	8.9
white (1990)	7.9	7.7
black (1990)	21.	17.0
Marriages 1992 (thousands)	70.7	2,362
Rate per 1,000 pop.	7.5	9.3
Divorces 1992 (thousands)	39.4	1,215
Rate per 1,000 pop.	4.2	4.8

SUBJECT	MICHIGAN	US
<u>HEALTH</u> 1992		
Physicians (non-federal) (thousands)	18.2	568
Rate per 100,000 pop. (actual)	194	224
Dentists (thousands)	6	155
Rate, per 100,000 pop (actual)	63	61
Nurses (thousands)	65	1,853
Rate, per 100,000 pop. (actual)	694	731
Community Hospitals (actual)	170	5,292
Hospital Beds (thousands)	31.6	921
Rate per 100,000 pop.	262	276
Occupancy rate	64.8%	65.6%
Patients, average daily (thousands)	1,061	31,033
Outpatient visits, millions	17.1	348.5
Personnel (thousands)	142.7	3,619
Daily cost, average	$847	$820
Rank	17	
Per stay	$5,899	$5,794
Rank	12	
Medicare 1992		
Enrollment (thousands)	1,282	34,853
Pymt., $ millions	$4,642	$128,520
Medicaid 1992 (thousands)		
Recipients	1,129	30,251
Pymt., $ millions	2,802	91,317
<u>EDUCATION 1993</u>		
Public school students		
K-8th grade (thousands)	1,166	31,091
Rank	8	
9 - 12 grade (thousands)	449	11,880
Rank	8	
Teachers (thousands)	82.4	2,464
Rank	9	
Salary (thousands) average	$43.6	$35
Rank	4	
Revenue, Publ. School, in $ millions 1991	$11,409	$250,966
Rank	6	
Expenditures, Public schools $ millions	$10,896	$251,703
Rank	7	
Per capita, dollars (actual)	$1,155	$987
Per Student (actual)	$6,402	$5,574
Rank	13	
Public High School Graduates, 1994 (thousands)	83.7	2,209
Rank	8	

SUBJECT	MICHIGAN	US
Colleges, 1994		
Numbers, actual	102	3,638
Rank	11	
Students (thousands) 1992	560	14,491
Rank	8	
Crime, 1992		
Rate per 100,000 people		
Total	5,611	5,660
Rank	19	
Violent	770	758
Rank	12	
Murder	9.9	9.3
Rank	16	
Rape, Forcible	80	43
Rank	3	
Robbery	221	264
Rank	12	
Aggravated Assault	459	442
Rank	15	
Property Crime	4,841	4,903
Rank	18	
Theft-motor vehicle	626	631
Rank	13	
Police, full-time per 10,000 pop. (1991)	23.1	28
Rank	38	
Correction employees, per 10,000 pop. (1991)		
Full-time, actual	19.8	
Rank	18	
Police & Corrections Expenditures, $ Millions	$2,838	$75,506
Rank	6	
Expenditures, Per Capita	$303	$299
Rank	13	
Adults under correctional supervision 1990 (thousands)	190	2,670
Rank	6	
GOVERNMENT, 1993		
Black Elected Officials		
Actual	333	7,984
Rank	10	
Hispanic Public Officials	8	4,202
1991, actual		
Women Public Officials		
Actual	10	5,170
Rank	12	
Women Public Officials	2,823	17,921
Rank		

SUBJECT	MICHIGAN	US
Registered Voters % of Voting Age population 1992	74.6%	68.2%
Rank	17	
Votes cast % of registered voters 1992	65.9%	61.3%
Rank	22	
Federal aid to state & local government, $ millions	$6,654	$195,201
Rank	8	
Per Capita, $ actual	$702	$746
Rank	25	
Federal Aid for education of the disadvantaged, millions	$256	$6,582
Rank	7	
Federal Aid for waste treat-ment facilities construction, $ millions	$89	$2,126
Rank	7	
Federal Aid for family support, including AFDC, incentives, refugees assistance, etc., $ millions	$1,343	$28,347
Rank	3	
Federal Aid for Medicaid (millions)	$2,547	$75,774
Rank	9	
Federal Aid for low income housing, $ millions	$343	$12,457
Rank	13	
Federal Aid for community development, $ millions	135	$3,198
Rank	7	
Federal Aid for job training, $ millions	$326	$6,811
Rank	5	
Federal Aid, Highway Trust Fund, $ millions	$435	$16,152
Rank	10	
Revenue State Gov't (1992) $ millions	$26,298	$741,853
Rank	9	
Per capita, $ actual	$2,340	$2,379
Rank	24	
Taxes, State $ millions	$11,279	$327,822
Rank	9	
Expenditures, State $ millions	$25,522	$700,891
Rank	9	
Education, $ millions	$7,416	$211,570
Rank	8	
Public Welfare, $ millions	$5,575	$156,364
Rank	8	
Highways, $ millions	$1,482	$48,747
Rank	9	
Health & Hospitals $ million	$2,447	$48,123
Rank	4	
Tax Collections, State $ millions	$11,279	$328,370
Rank	9	

SUBJECT	MICHIGAN	US
Sales & gross receipts, general $ millions	$4,989	$107,757
Rank	9	
Income Tax, Individual $ millions	$3,242	$104,609
Rank	9	
Corporation net income tax, $ millions	$1,730	$21,566
Rank	3	
Per capital, $ actual	$2,392	$2,188
Rank	15	
VETERANS, 1993 (thousands)		
Wartime total	748	20,575
Rank	8	
World War I	0.7	25
Rank	11 (tied)	
World War II	284	8,124
Rank	8	
Korean	156	4,656
Rank	8	
Vietnam	293	8,251
Rank	8	
Persian Gulf War	39	1,021
Rank	8	
SOCIAL SERVICES		
Social Security (1992)		
Number of beneficiaries (thousands)	1,546	41,497
Rank	8	
Annual pymts. $ millions	$11,478	$285,980
Rank	8	
Avg. monthly benefit, retired workers $ actual	$697	$653
Rank	4	
Food stamp recipients (1993)		
Households	419	10,791
Rank	8	
Expenditures, $ millions	$837	$22,009
Rank	7	
School lunch program (1993)		
Persons (thousands)	747	25,334
Rank	10	
Aid to families with dependent children (AFDC) (1992)		
Recipients	684	14,035
Rank	6	
Expenditure, $ millions	$837	$22,009
Rank		
Avg. monthly pymt. per family, $ actual	$431	$381
Rank	13	
Supplemental Security Income (SSI) 1992		
Recipients (thousands)	143	5,566

SUBJECT	MICHIGAN	US
Rank	10	
Expenditure, $ millions	$667	$21,682
Rank	6	
Public aid recipients as % of population (AFDC and FSSI)	9%	7.6%
Rank	5 (tied)	
LABOR		
State Unemployment Insurance $ millions (1992)	$1,288	$26,153
Rank	6	
Average weekly	$211	$174
Rank	6 (tied)	
Civilian Labor Force (1993)		
Total (thousands)	4,702	128,040
Rank	8	58,407
Female (thousands)	2,111	58,407
Rank	8	
Employees, non farm (1993)		
Total, (thousands)	3,982	110,178
Rank	8	
Construction 1993 (thousands)	133	4,574
Rank	10	
Manufacturing	902	17,802
Rank	7	
Transportation & Public Utilities	156	5,708
Rank	11 (tied)	
Wholesale & Retail Trade	935	25,857
Rank	8	
Finance, Insurance & real estate	192	6,604
Rank	10	
Services	1,016	30,192
Rank	8	
Government	640	18,842
Rank	8	
Average Annual Pay $ actual (1992)	$27,463	$25,903
Rank	8	
GROSS STATE PRODUCT 1990		
Current dollars, $ billions	$188	$5,499
Rank	9	
INCOME 1993		
Disposable personal income per capita		
$ current (actual)	$17,886	$18,177
Rank	18	
Personal Income		
$ billions	$152	$4,220
Rank	+10	

SUBJECT	MICHIGAN	US
Personal Income		
per capita, $ current (actual)	$20,453	$20,817
Rank	15	
Median Income household, actual $ (1992)	$32,347	$430,786
Rank	16	
Percent of persons below poverty level	13.5%	14.5%
Rank	24	
BANKING, FINANCE & INSURANCE (1993)		
Banks		
Number (actual)	208	10,957
Rank	22	
Assets, $ billions	$106	$3,705
Rank	8	
Deposits, $ billions	81	2,753
Rank	9	
Banks closed or assisted	0	41
BUSINESS ((1992)		
New Corporations (thousands)	24.7	666.8
Rank	7	
Failures	2.5	97.0
Rank	8	
Bankruptcy petitions	23.3	972.5
Rank	14	
Patents, total, actual	3,028	58,694
Rank	6	
COMMUNICATIONS (1992)		
Newspapers		
Daily, number, actual	52	1,570
Rank	7	
Circulation, paid (thousands)	2,195	60,164
Rank	9	
Per capita	0.23	0.24
Rank	19 (tied)	
Sunday, number, actual	27	891
Rank	10	
Circulation, paid (thousands)	2,422	62,160
Rank	8	
ENERGY (1992)		
Gas Utility Industry		
Customers, total (thousands)	2,852	56,132
Rank	6	
Residential	2,640	51,525
Rank	6	
Revenues, $ millions total	$2,332	$46,178
Rank	8	

SUBJECT	MICHIGAN	US
Electric Energy Sales		
Total, billions of kilowatt hours	83	2,763
Rank	10	
Nuclear Power Plants		
Units (actual)	5	109
Rank	4 (tied)	
Net generation, billion kilowatts	18.8	618.7
Rank	15	
Energy Consumption (1991)		
Total, trillions of BTU	2,754	81,119
Rank	9	
Per capita, millions BTU	293	321
Rank	31	
Residential, trillions BTU	697	16,377
Rank	8	
Commercial, trillions of BTU	442	13,020
Rank	9	
Industrial, trillions of BTU	927	29,601
Rank	8	
Transportation, trillions of BTU	689	22,121
Rank	10	
Expenditures, End use (1991)		
Total, $ millions	$16,754	$467,132
Rank	8	24%
Per Capita, $ actual	$1,786	$1,853
Rank	35	
Residential, $ millions	$4,340	$114,740
Rank	8	
Commercial, $ millions	$2,789	$81,488
Rank	9	
Industrial, $ millions	$4,201	$99,701
Transportation $ millions	$3,008	$171,203
Rank	1	
RESEARCH & DEVELOPMENT (1991)		
Total, $ millions	$8,851	$145,385
Rank	3	
Federal Government	$92	$15,238
Rank	24 (tied)	
Industry	$8,116	$102,246
Rank	3	
Universities & College	$601	$22,701
Rank	9	
TRANSPORTATION (1993)		
Federal Grants		
Highways, $ millions	$437	$16,060
Rank	6	

SUBJECT	MICHIGAN	US
Per capita, $ actual	46.1	62.3
Rank	47	
State Gasoline Tax, per gallon, (1993)	15¢	18.4¢
Rank (tied)	42 (tied)	
Motor Vehicle Registrations (1992) thousands	7,311	190,362
Rank	8	
Miles traveled, billions	84	2,240
Rank	8	
Drivers licenses (thousands)	6,481	173,125
Rank	8	
Motor Vehicle Deaths actual (1992)	1,295	40,300
Rank	8	
Per million vehicle miles, actual	1.5	1.8
Rank (tied)	36 (tied)	
<u>STATE LAW, ROAD SAFETY</u>		
Alcohol, 21 years	yes	all
Open containers prohibited	yes	27 states
% blood alcohol	0.10	all (.08- 1.2)
seat belt, mandatory	yes	43 states
<u>AGRICULTURE</u> (1993)		
Farms, thousands	52	2,068
Rank	16	
Acreage, millions	11	978
Rank (tied)	28 (tied)	
Acreage per farm (actual)	206	473
Rank	36	
Value of land & bldgs., $ millions	$12,000	$684,554
Rank	23	
Average value, per acre		
$ actual	$1,130	$700
Rank	18	
Farm assets, $ million (1992)	$15,567	$861,497
Rank	21	
Farm Debt, $ millions	$2,602	$138,645
Rank	21	
Farm Debt/Asset Ratio	16.7%	16.1%
Rank (tied)	20	
Farm Gross Income $ millions	$3,787	$197,741
Rank	22	
Farm Net Income, $ millions	$581	$48,647
Rank	30	
Farm Mrkt. $ millions (1992)		
Total	$3,286	$171,168
Rank	20	
Crops, $ millions	$1,962	$84,810

SUBJECT	MICHIGAN	US
Rank	14	
Livestock & products $ millions	$1,325	$86,358
Rank	25	
Government pymts.	$143	$9,169
Rank	22	
Principal Commodities	1.Dairy Pro. 2. Corn 3.Greenhouse 4. Cattle	1.Cattle 2. Dairy Pro. 3. Corn 4. Soybean
Crops, Acres harvested, (1993) thousands	6,751	295,918
Rank	16	
Farm value, of production millions	$2,220	$83,715
Rank	13	
MINING & MINERALS (1993)		
Value of nonfuel mineral production		
$ millions	$1,408	$31,556
Rank	5	
Minerals in order of value	1. Iron Ore 2. Cement (Portland 3. Sand & Gravel	
CRUDE PETROLEUM (1992)		
Millions of barrels	16	2,625
Rank	16	
Value, $ millions	$296	$41,968
Rank	16	
Natural gas		
Billions of cubic feet	195	712
Rank	11	
Value, $ millions	$528	$32,571
Rank	11	
CONSTRUCTION & HOUSING (1993)		
Total Value, construction, $ millions	$7,952	$267,262
Rank	10	
Residential, $ millions	$3,656	$121,942
Rank	11	
Existing Home Sales (thousands)	170.6	3,802
Rank	8	
Housing Units, owner occupied (thousands) (1990)	1,916	44,918
Rank	8	
Renter occupied	966	32,170
Rank	9	
Median rent,$ actual	$423	$447
Rank	21	
MANUFACTURERS, (1991)		
Employees, total (thousands)	858	18,062
Rank	7	
Payroll, total, $ millions	$30,752	$529,019

SUBJECT	MICHIGAN	US
Rank	4	
Value added, mfg.$ millions	$63,351	$1,313,829
Rank	7	
Value of shipments, $ millions	$143,103	$2,826,207
Rank	6	
Avg. hourly earnings, mfg. production workers (1993)	$15.36	$11.76
Rank	1	
Export , 1989		
Mfg., shipment value, $ billions	423.7	$460.8
Rank	5 (tied)	
% of total mfg. value	15.1%	16.5%
Rank	25 (tied)	
Employment, export related (thousands)	154.8	2,948.7
Rank	6	
Retail Trade Establishments (thousands) 1991	54	1,547
Rank	7	
Annual payroll, $ millions	$8,974	$247,001
Rank	8	
Employees (thousands)	746	19,600
Rank	8	
Sales, retail total $ millions 1992	$73,197	$1,964,022
Rank	8	
Food Stores, $ millions	$11,591	$384,574
Rank	9	
General Merchandise, $ millions	$10,857	$247,448
Rank	6	
Automobile dealers, $ millions	$16,664	$398,768
Rank	8	
Eating & drinking places, $ millions	$7,474	$202,079
Rank	8	
Gasoline service stations, $ millions	$4,824	$133,722
Rank	8	
Building materials and hardware dealers, $ millions	$3,893	$103,134
Rank	8	
Apparel & accessory stores, $ million	$3,781	$105,050
Rank	8	
Furniture & appliance stores, $ millions	$4,011	$104,906
Rank	8	
Shopping Centers, 1993 number, actual	958	39,633
Rank	12	
Retail sales, $ billions	$20	$814
Rank	12	
Foreign investment in U.S., book value of property, plant & equipment, $ millions (1991)	$13,767	$634,688
Rank	13	

SUBJECT	MICHIGAN	US
Total employment (thousands)	139	4,809
Rank	11	
% of all business	4.1%	5.1%
Rank	34 (tied)	
Manufacturing Employment (thousands) total	70.9	2,024
Rank	10	
% of all manufacturing	7.9	10.8
Rank	36	
U.S. Exports, $ millions (1993)	$23,196	$464,767
Rank	5	

Note: Imports by state N/A. U.S. exports/imports by selected countries, $ millions (1992):

Exports

1. Canada, $90,584
2. Japan, $47,813
3. Mexico, $40,592
4. U. K., $22,800
5. Germany, $21,249
6. S. Korea, $14,639
7. France, $14,593
8. Italy, $8,721

Imports

1. Canada $98,630
2. Japan, $97,414
3. Mexico, $35,211
4. Germany, $28,820
5. U.K., $20,093
6. S. Korea, $16,682
7. France, $14,797
8. Italy, $12,314

is commonly termed a geologic basin; that is, an area of slow and intermittent downward movement where sediments collect over millions of years. Michigan's basin structure began forming over 500 million years ago when large, shallow inland seas covered much of the state. These seas left thousands of feet of sand, clay, lime, and salt formations before receding completely. The Michigan Basin has accumulated almost 14,000 feet of sediment at its deepest point.

Source - Michigan Manual 1993-1994
MI Legislative Service Bureau

During the Pleistocene Period, or Ice Age, continental glaciers repeatedly advanced over the Great Lakes' region. The advance and retreat of the ice resulted in large deposits of unsorted sediments, cobbles, and boulders, collectively known as glacial drift or debris. Perhaps of greatest importance, however, is the effect the ice had in shaping Michigan's landscape. As the glaciers advanced over North America, they scoured the earth's surface, transporting rock materials for hundreds of miles. Under the weight of the ice, hills were flattened and the glacial scouring removed large amounts of sediment, pushing rocks ahead of the advancing ice sheet like snow before a plow. Linearly shaped mounds of rock material were left behind when the glaciers retreated and are now represented by the many regions of rolling hills across the state.

The glaciers also helped build and shape the Great Lakes. Prior to the Pleistocene glaciation, the sites of the present-day Great Lakes basins were probably stream valleys. Following the pre-cut paths of these stream valleys, the glaciers scoured them to greater depths and filled these depressions with thick ice lobes. A warming of the global environment caused the ice to melt, slowly shrinking the glacier. Scientists believe that this cyclic pattern of cooling and warming occurred at least four times during Michigan's geologic history, each time carving wider and deeper basins. When the last glacial ice retreated (about 10,000 years ago), great volumes of "melt waters" filled the remnant basins forming lakes even larger than the current Great Lakes. The ancient lakeshores can be seen in the form of beach ridges and eroded bluffs located high above present Great Lakes' shorelines.

Due to the diversity of the state's geology, Michigan has a wide variety of mineral resources. Some of the more important resources that have played a role in Michigan's economic development include copper ore, iron ore, sand, gravel, salt, oil, and gas.

Michigan copper deposits exist in two distinctly different forms, metallic or "native" copper ore and a nonmetallic copper mineral called chalcocite. Although native copper occurs in other parts of the world, the quantity of Michigan's native ore was unsurpassed. From 1845 to 1887, Michigan's Keweenaw Peninsula mines produced more native copper ore than any other mining area in North America. As native copper resources were depleted, large reserves of chalcocite or copper sulphide began to be mined near White Pine in the Upper Peninsula's Ontonagon County. However, these easily mined near-surface copper deposits have been largely exhausted. In 1982, only two companies located in the Upper Peninsula were producing copper.

Michigan's Lake Superior region also includes geologic formations containing large concentrations of iron. Although most of the iron in these formations is not pure, many techniques are available to separate the ore from the non-iron materials. In addition, naturally concentrated iron deposits have been discovered and mined in the past. However, most near surface iron deposits have been exhausted, requiring the use of underground mines. In recent

years, subsurface mining has become too costly for many of Michigan's companies. Today, two companies still extract iron from formations located in the Upper Peninsula.

Sand and gravel formations are found in varying thicknesses across much of the Michigan Basin. Some of these materials were left by the ancient inland seas that once covered the state. Sand and gravel were also deposited by wind and glacial processes. Perhaps the most noteworthy deposits are the large accumulations of wind-blown sand, or sand dunes, that occur in western Michigan. Sands and gravels deposited beneath and around the margins of glaciers are also common in Michigan. In many cases, these deposits represent unique recreational resources. In others, sand and gravel are important resources for construction and industrial uses.

The Michigan Basin includes one of the world's largest salt accumulations. The thickest salt beds, known as the Salina Formation, underlie most of Michigan's Lower Peninsula. The Salina Formation's maximum thickness of 3,100 feet is composed of layers of salts and other minerals. These deposits were important in the state's early development. Michigan ranked first or second in national salt production from 1880 through 1926. The bulk of the salt production was from natural brines which were pumped from six salt formations. Salt was also produced from artificial brines that were derived by injecting freshwater into salt formations and retrieving the resulting brine. During the peak year of 1919, almost 18,000,000 barrels of brine were produced. The old Detroit salt mine produced rock salt using the room and pillar method from 1910 until 1983. In general, the salt was mined from a layer approximately 30 feet thick and 1,135 feet below the surface of Detroit. The mined space encompasses approximately 1,100 acres of subsurface land. Since the Detroit salt mine closed, the room and pillar method has not been used to produce salt in Michigan. However, salt is still produced from brines extracted at locations within the Michigan Basin.

Geographically, oil and gas are produced from fields scattered across 61 counties in the Lower Peninsula. Between 1925 and 1992, about 40,846 oil and gas wells were drilled in Michigan. Of this total, approximately 20,670 have produced oil or gas. To date 1.146 billion barrels of crude oil and 3.585 trillion cubic feet of gas have been withdrawn from Michigan's rock formations. 1992 was a record year for natural gas production in Michigan.

Forests cover 49% (18.2 million acres) of Michigan's total land base. These vast forests provide Michigan with the largest state-owned forest system in the nation. Michigan's forests are used for both industry and recreation. The total *timberland*, or forest lands capable of producing commercial timber, covers 95% of Michigan's total forested lands. The timberlands support 4.2 million acres of softwoods and 13.1 million acres of hardwoods. Michigan has the fifth largest timberland acreage in the continental United States.

Michigan's forests contribute significantly to our state's economy. Forest-based industries (wood products industry, tourism, and recreation) support nearly 180,000 jobs statewide while contributing over $18 billion to the state's economy. The wood products industry provides 75% of the economic value of our forests while forest-based tourism and recreation make up the remaining 25%.

Michigan residents currently use 770 million cubic feet of wood products annually. This is nearly equal to the 753 million cubic feet of timber grown each year of the total timberland base. Annual timber harvests are approximately 356 million cubic feet, or just less than one-half of annual timber growth and resident consumption of wood products.

Michigan borders four of the five Great Lakes, which collectively comprise the largest body of fresh water in the world. In addition, Michigan has over 10,000 inland lakes, and 36,000 miles of rivers and streams. Approximately, 1.6 million individuals, including nearly 400,000 nonresidents purchase licenses to sport fish in Michigan each year. Anglers under the age of 17, who fish for free, increase the total number of anglers in the state to 2 million. About one-third of Michigan anglers fish on the Great Lakes, while 45% fish inland lakes and 20% fish rivers and streams. Spending by sport fishermen in Michigan amounts to $1.2 billion, not including investments in boats, cottages, and real estate. The Great Lakes, Lake St. Clair, Houghton Lake, and Higgins Lake are intensively fished. Michigan is third in the nation in fishing licenses sold and first in the number of nonresidents fishing.

Each year Michigan commercial fishermen take nearly 16 million pounds of fish from the Great Lakes, worth $10 million. Whitefish account for approximately 75% of the total landed value. Native Americans, fishing under federal treaty rights, produce 50% of the catch, by weight, and 55% of the landed value. Most Native Americans fish in the northern parts of Lakes Michigan and Huron and eastern Lake Superior. State-licensed fishermen are primarily restricted to northern Green Bay in Lake Michigan and Saginaw Bay in Lake Huron.

According to 1992 estimates, approximately 10.8 million acres in the state are used for farming, supporting about 54,000 farmers. More than 50 major commercial crops are produced each season. The state ranks among the top five nationwide producers of over 30 different types of crops. Michigan's "number one" crops include black turtle beans, cranberry beans, small white beans, navy beans, cucumbers for pickles, geraniums, and red tart cherries. Michigan is the second largest producer of bedding plants, all dry beans, flowering hanging baskets, gladioli, and Easter lilies; third largest producer of apples, celery, carrots, snap beans for processing, dark red kidney beans, prunes and plums, and asparagus; fourth in Concord grapes, light red kidney beans, mushrooms, tomatoes for processing, trout, fresh sweet corn, and sweet cherries; and fifth in cauliflower, mohair, strawberries, sugar beets, floriculture, and all varieties of grapes.

Michigan's livestock and poultry industry accounts for just under 50% of total cash receipts from farming. In 1992, the state's inventory of livestock and poultry included 1.2 million head of cattle, 1.1 million hogs and pigs, 103,000 sheep and lamb, 6.3 million chickens. Michigan's 338,000 head of dairy cows contributed 5.4 billion pounds of milk to the market in 1992.

Located in the Great Lakes Region, Michigan is surrounded by the world's largest bodies of fresh water. The lakes affect our weather, providing a semi-marine type climate. The lakes slow the oncome of both winter and summer because the lake water responds slowly to temperature change. The cooler spring temperatures and the warmer fall temperatures are a boon to agriculture in the state, preventing new growth until the threat of frost is over and extending the summer to allow for a longer harvesting season.

During July, the mean temperature in Michigan ranges from 63-73°F. January mean temperatures range from 13-25°F. It is not unusual, however, to see temperatures much colder or warmer than the averages. The coldest temperature recorded in Michigan as of 1985 was -51°F in February 1934. The warmest was 112°F in July 1936.

Average annual precipitation in the state is about 31 inches. Michigan experiences a number of thunderstorms and showers during the summer, and steadier, lighter rainfalls other times of the year. Snowfall varies around the state with a maximum average snowfall of 180 inches in the western Upper Peninsula. The northwestern Lower Peninsula receives snow in excess of 120 inches while the rest of the state averages 30-90 inches annually.

Origin of Name: The name "Michigan" is derived from the Indian word "*Michigama,*" meaning great or large lake.

Nickname: The Wolverine State.

State Motto: *Si quaeris peninsulam amoenam circumspice* (If you seek a pleasant peninsula, look about you).

State Bird: Robin. *State Flower:* Apple blossom.
State Tree: White pine. *State Fish:* Brook trout.
State Gem: Chlorastrolite. *State Stone:* Petoskey Stone.
State Soil: Kalkaska Soil Series.

History: First permanent French settlement by Father Jacques Marquette at Sault Ste. Marie, 1668; French forces surrendered Detroit to British at close of French and Indian War, 1760; became part of the Northwest Territory, 1787; became Michigan Territory, 1805; admitted into the Union as the twenty-sixth state, 1837.

State Capital: Moved to Lansing, 1847; State Capitol designed by Elijah E. Myers, dedicated January 1, 1879.

State Government: Under the *Constitution of Michigan of 1963* the legislative power is vested in a senate (38 members) and a house of representatives (110 members); the executive power is vested in the governor; and the judicial power is vested exclusively in one court of justice, which is divided into one supreme court (7 justices), one court of appeals (24 judges), one trial court of general jurisdiction known as the circuit court (179 judges), one probate court (107 judges), and courts of limited jurisdiction, such as the district court created by the state legislature.

Salaries:

	1993	1994
Governor	$106,690	$112,025
Lieutenant Governor	80,300	84,315
Secretary of State	109,000	109,000
Attorney General	109,000	109,000
State Legislators	45,450	47,723
Justices of the Supreme Court	106,610	111,941
Court of Appeals Judges	102,346	107,463

Local Government: Michigan ranks 14th among the 50 states in the number of local governments. The state has 83 counties, 1,241 townships, 271 cities, 263 villages, 564 school districts, 54 intermediate school districts, 14 planning and development regions, and 250 special districts and authorities.

U.S. Congress: The state has two senators - one Democrat and one Republican - and 16 representatives - 9 Democrats and 7 Republicans - in the 1995-96 Congress.

Population: 9,437,000 *(1992 estimate)*; ranks 8th among the 50 states.

Area: 58,110 square miles of land, 1,305 square miles of inland water, and 38,575 square miles of Great Lakes water area; there are 10,083 inland lakes of over 5 acres in surface area and 3,288 miles of Great Lakes' shoreline.

Elevation: Highest point in state is Mt. Arvon in Baraga County, 1,981 feet above sea level; lowest point is along the Lake Erie shoreline, 572 feet above sea level.

THE WHITE PINE

The white pine (Pinus strobus, L.) was adopted as the official state tree in 1955. *(Act 7 of 1955)*

CHLORASTROLITE

Chlorastrolite, commonly known as greenstone, was adopted by the legislature in 1972 as the official gem of Michigan. *(Act 56 of 1972)*

THE PETOSKEY STONE

The Petoskey Stone, believed to be found only in Michigan, was adopted by the legislature as the state stone in 1965. *(Act 89 of 1965)*

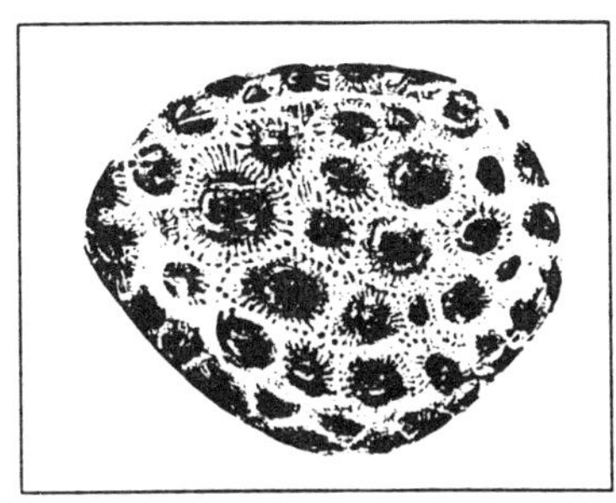

THE KALKASKA SOIL SERIES

The Kalkaska Soil Series was adopted by the legislature as the official soil of the state in 1990. *(Act 302 of 1990)*

THE STATE FLAG

The state flag, which is "blue charged with the arms of the state," was adopted by the legislature in 1911. *(Act 209 of 1911)*

THE APPLE BLOSSOM

Noting that "at least one of the most fragrant and beautiful flowered species of apple, the pyrus coronaria, is native to our state," the legislature adopted the apple blossom as the state flower in 1897. *(Joint Resolution No. 10, 1897)*

THE ROBIN

The Robin was adopted by the legislature as the state bird in 1931. *(House Concurrent Resolution No. 30, 1931)*

THE BROOK TROUT

By Act 5 of 1988, the legislature designated the brook trout as the official fish of the State of Michigan. Prior to the enactment of Act 5, the trout was the state fish. *(Act 58 of 1965)*

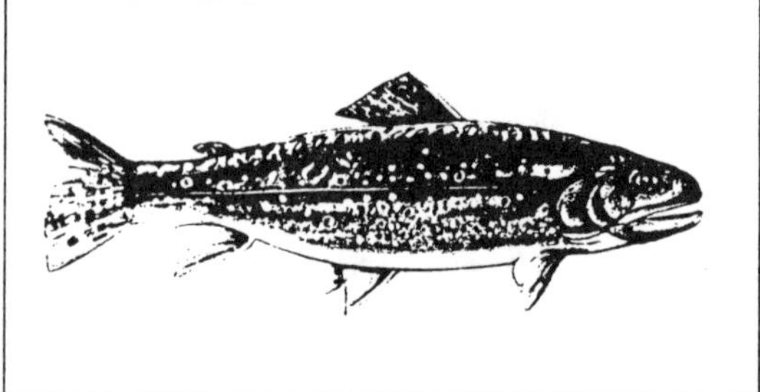

MICHIGAN COUNTIES

NOTE: Michigan has 83 counties. According to the 1990 federal decennial census, they range in population from 1,701 persons in Keweenaw County in the Upper Peninsula to Wayne County's 2,111,687 persons (approximately 48% of whom reside in the city of Detroit) in the southeastern part of the state.

COUNTY LOCATOR MAP
Please use with locator numbers
on adjoining pages to locate county.

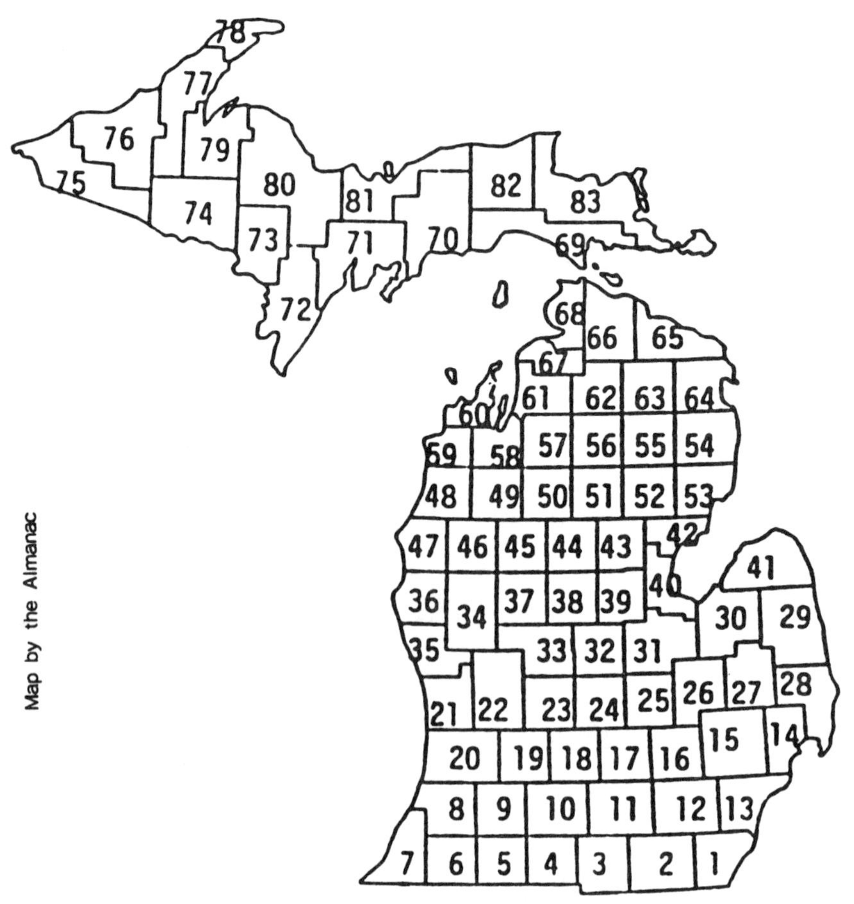

ALCONA

County Seat: Harrisville 48740. The name is an Indian word meaning a fine or excellent plain. Organized in 1869.

Population (1990)	10,145
Population (1992)	*10,254*
Net change (1980-1992)	*+5.3%*
Area	*54*
Density	*675*
Map location number	*15*
Phone Area Code	*517*

ALGER

County Seat: Munising 49862. Named for the Hon. Russell A. Alger, Governor of the State, 1885-1886. Organized in 1885.

Population (1990)	8,972
Population (1992)	*9,349*
Net change (1980-1992)	*+1.3%*
Area	*918*
Density	*10*
Map location number	*81*
Phone Area Code	*906*

ALLEGAN

County Seat: Allegan 49010. It was named for the Indian tribe of "Allegawi" or "Allegans" believed by some to have been identical with the mound builders. Organized in 1835.

Population (1990)	90,509
Population (1992)	*93,078*
Net change (1980-1992)	*+141%*
Area	*828*
Density	*112*
Map location number	*20*
Phone Area Code	*616*

ALPENA

County Seat: Alpena 49707. The name of the county is an Indian word meaning "a good partridge country." Organized in 1857.

Population (1990)	30,605
Population (1992)	*31,000*
Net change (1980-1992)	*-4.1%*
Area	*574*
Density	*54*
Map location number	*64*
Phone Area Code	*517*

ANTRIM

County Seat: Bellaire 49615. Named for County Antrim in Ireland. Organized in 1863.

Population (1990)	18,185
Population (1992)	18,897
Net change (1980-1992)	+16.7%
Area	477
Density	40
Map location number	61
Phone Area Code	616

ARENAC

County Seat: Standish 48658. Arenac is a derivation of the Latin "arena" and the Indian "ac." The combined words mean "sandy place." Organized in 1883.

Population (1990)	14,931
Population (1992)	15,625
Net change (1980-1992)	+6.2%
Area	367
Density	43
Map location number	42
Phone Area Code	517

BARAGA

County Seat: L'Anse 49946. Bishop Frederic Baraga, a missionary, was honored in the naming of this county. Organized in 1875.

Population (1990)	7,954
Population (1992)	7,828
Net change (1980-1992)	-7.7%
Area	904
Density	9
Map location number	79
Phone Area Code	906

BARRY

County Seat: Hastings 49058. Named for the Hon. William T. Barry, Postmaster General under President Andrew Jackson. Organized in 1839.

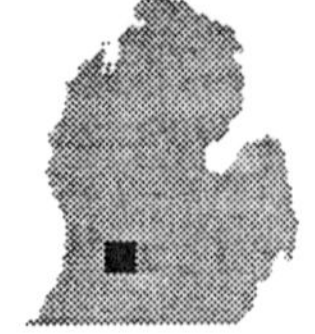

Population (1990)	50,057
Population (1992)	51,196
Net change (1980-1992)	+11.8%
Area	556
Density	92
Map location number	19
Phone Area Code	616

BAY

County Seat: Bay City 48706. Obtained its name because it encircles Saginaw Bay. Organized in 1857.

Population (1990)	111,723
Population (1992)	112,131
Net change (1980-1992)	-6.5%
Area	444
Density	252
Map location number	40
Phone Area Code	517

BENZIE

County Seat: Beulah 49617. This is a derivative of the French "aux-Bec-Scies." The name was first applied to the river, changed to Betsey and finally Benzie. Organized in 1869.

Population (1990)	12,200
Population (1992)	12,612
Net change (1980-1992)	+12.6%
Area	321
Density	39
Map location number	59
Phone Area Code	616

BERRIEN

County Seat: St. Joseph 49085. Named for the Hon. John M. Berrien, Attorney General under President Andrew Jackson. Organized in 1831.

Population (1990)	161,378
Population (1992)	161,466
Net change (1980-1992)	-5.7%
Area	571
Density	283
Map location number	7
Phone Area Code	616

BRANCH

County Seat: Coldwater 49036. Hon. John Branch, Secretary of the Navy under President Andrew Jackson, was honored in the naming of this county. Organized in 1833.

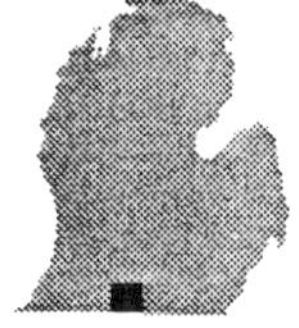

Population (1990)	41,502
Population (1992)	41,871
Net change (1980-1992)	+4.2%
Area	507
Density	83
Map location number	4
Phone Area Code	517

CALHOUN

County Seat: Marshall 49068. Named for the Hon. John C. Calhoun, Vice President of the United States. Organized in 1833.

Population (1990)	135,982
Population (1992)	*138,381*
Net change (1980-1992)	*-2.3%*
Area	*709*
Density	*195*
Map location number	*10*
Phone Area Code	*616*

CASS

County Seat: Cassopolis 49031. Named in honor of Lewis Cass, a Governor of the Territory. Organized in 1829.

Population (1990)	49,477
Population (1992)	*49,112*
Net change (1980-1992)	*-0.8%*
Area	*492*
Density	*100*
Map location number	*6*
Phone Area Code	*616*

CHARLEVOIX

County Seat: Charlevoix 49720. Pierre F. de Charlevoix, a Jesuit missionary, was honored in this naming. Organized in 1869.

Population (1990)	21,468
Population (1992)	*22,225*
Net change (1980-1992)	*+11.6%*
Area	*417*
Density	*53*
Map location number	*67*
Phone Area Code	*616*

CHEBOYGAN

County Seat: Cheboygan 49721. The word is Indian and was first applied to the river. Organized in 1853.

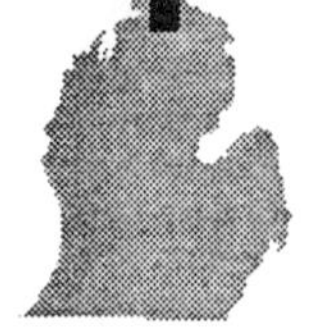

Population (1990)	21,398
Population (1992)	*21.780*
Net change (1980-1992)	*+5.5%*
Area	*716*
Density	*30*
Map location number	*66*
Phone Area Code	*616*

CHIPPEWA

County Seat: Sault Ste. Marie 49783. The county was named for the Indian tribe of the same name. Organized in 1826; boundaries changed in 1843.

Population (1990) 34,604

Population (1992)	*35,640*
Net change (1980-1992)	*+22.8%*
Area	*1,561*
Density	*23*
Map location number	*83*
Phone Area Code	*906*

CLARE

County Seat: Harrison 48625. Named for County Clare in Ireland. Organized in 1871.

Population (1990) 24,952

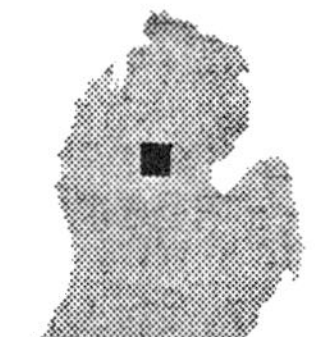

Population (1992)	*16,384*
Net change (1980-1992)	*+10.8%*
Area	*567*
Density	*47*
Map location number	*44*
Phone Area Code	*517*

CLINTON

County Seat: St. Johns 48879. Hon. DeWitt Clinton, Governor of New York and builder of the Erie Canal, was honored in this naming. Organized in 1839.

Population (1990) 57,883

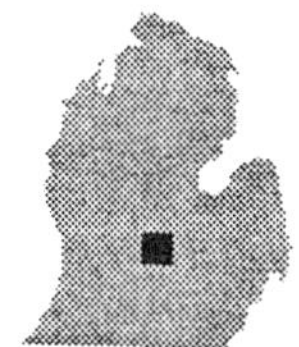

Population (1992)	*59,397*
Net change (1980-1992)	*+6.3%*
Area	*572*
Density	*104*
Map location number	*24*
Phone Area Code	*517*

CRAWFORD

County Seat: Grayling 49738. Col. Wm. Crawford was recognized in the naming of this county. Organized in 1879.

Population (1990) 12,260

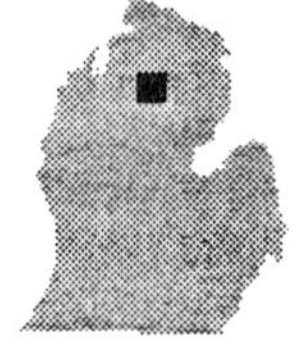

Population (1992)	*12,972*
Net change (1980-1992)	*+37.1%*
Area	*558*
Density	*23*
Map location number	*56*
Phone Area Code	*517*

DELTA

County Seat: Escanaba 49829. Name taken from the Greek letter "Delta" referring to the triangular shape of the original county which included parts of Menominee, Dickinson, Marquette and Iron Counties. Organized in 1861.

Population (1990)	37,780
Population (1992)	38,206
Net change (1980-1992)	-1.9%
Area	1,170
Density	33
Map location number	71
Phone Area Code	906

DICKINSON

County Seat: Iron Mt. 49801. Named for the Hon. Donald M. Dickinson, Postmaster General under President Grover Cleveland. Organized in 1891.

Population (1990)	26,831
Population (1992)	27,014
Net change (1980-1992)	+6.6%
Area	766
Density	35
Map location number	73
Phone Area Code	906

EATON

County Seat: Charlotte 48813. Named for the Hon. John H. Eaton, Secretary of War under President Andrew Jackson. Organized in 1837.

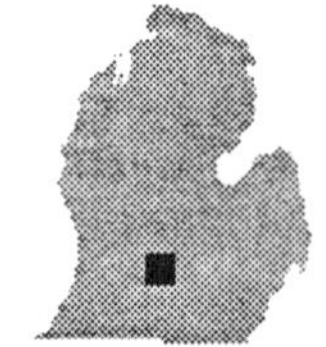

Population (1990)	92,879
Population (1992)	95,253
Net change (1980-1992)	+7.8%
Area	577
Density	165
Map location number	18
Phone Area Code	517

EMMET

County Seat: Petoskey 49770. Robert Emmet, the Irish patriot, was honored by this naming. Organized in 1853.

Population (1990)	25,040
Population (1992)	26,057
Net change (1980-1992)	+13.3%
Area	468
Density	56
Map location number	68
Phone Area Code	616

GENESEE

County Seat: Flint 48502. The settlers of this part of the state came from a county in western New York by the same name. Organized in 1836.

Population (1990) 430,459

Population (1992)	433,508
Net change (1980-1992)	-3.8%
Area	640
Density	678
Map location number	26
Phone Area Code	810

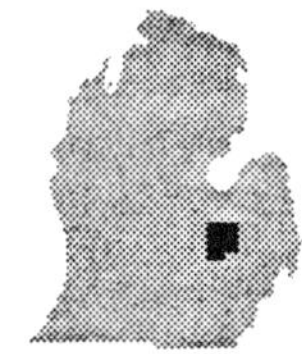

GLADWIN

County Seat: Gladwin 48624. Named for Major Henry Gladwin, English Commandant at Detroit in 1763. Organized in 1875.

Population (1990) 21,896

Population (1992)	23,007
Net change (1980-1992)	+15.3%
Area	507
Density	45
Map location number	43
Phone Area Code	517

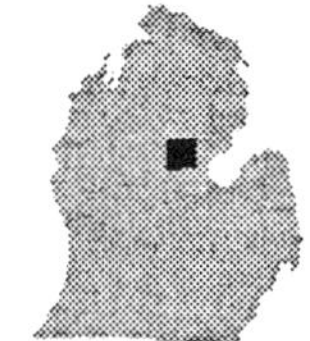

GOGEBIC

County Seat: Bessemer 49911. The county was named for a lake in the territory called Lake Agogebic but was changed to Gogebic. Agogebic is an Indian word. Organized in 1887.

Population (1990) 18,052

Population (1992)	17,891
Net change (1980-1992)	+15.3%
Area	1,102
Density	16
Map location number	75
Phone Area Code	906

GRAND TRAVERSE

County Seat: Traverse City 49684. The name of the county is a French phrase "grande traverse" meaning long crossing. Organized in 1851; boundaries changed in 1865.

Population (1990) 64,273

Population (1992)	67,290
Net change (1980-1992)	+22.6%
Area	465
Density	145
Map location number	58
Phone Area Code	616

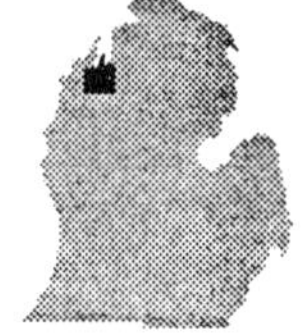

GRATIOT

County Seat: Ithaca 48847. Named for Capt. Charles Gratiot, who supervised the building of Fort Gratiot at the present site of Port Huron. Organized in 1855.

Population (1990)	38,982
Population (1992)	*39,450*
Net change (1980-1992)	*-2,5%*
Area	*570*
Density	*69*
Map location number	*32*
Phone Area Code	*517*

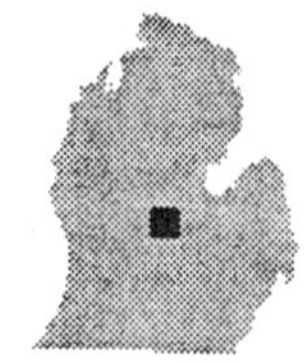

HILLSDALE

County Seat: Hillsdale 49242. The rolling terrain of the area served as the basis for the name of the county. Organized in 1835.

Population (1990)	43,431
Population (1992)	*44,407*
Net change (1980-1992)	*+5.6%*
Area	*599*
Density	*74*
Map location number	*3*
Phone Area Code	*517*

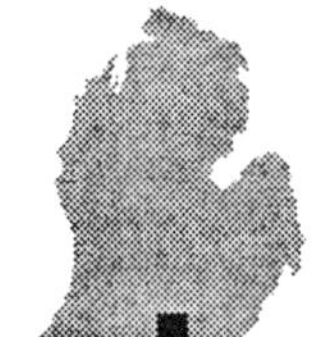

HOUGHTON

County Seat: Houghton 49931. Named for Prof. Douglass Houghton, a geologist in Michigan. Organized in 1846 and reorganized in 1848.

Population (1990)	35,446
Population (1992)	*35,831*
Net change (1980-1992)	*-5.4%*
Area	*1,012*
Density	*35*
Map location number	*77*
Phone Area Code	*906*

HURON

County Seat: Bad Axe 48413. Named for the Indian tribe of the same name. Organized in 1859.

Population (1990)	34,951
Population (1992)	*34,977*
Net change (1980-1992)	*-4.1%*
Area	*837*
Density	*42*
Map location number	*41*
Phone Area Code	*517*

INGHAM

County Seat: Mason 48854. Named for the Hon. Samuel D. Ingham, Secretary of the Treasury under President Andrew Jackson. Organized in 1838.

Population (1990) 281,912

Population (1992)	*281,798*
Net change (1980-1992)	*+2.3%*
Area	*559*
Density	*504*
Map location number	*17*
Phone Area Code	*517*

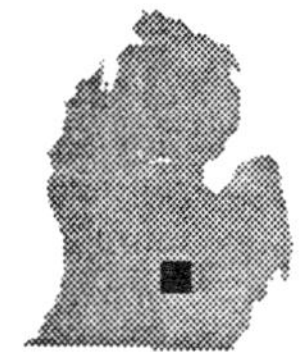

IONIA

County Seat: Ionia 48846. Named for a province in Greece. Organized in 1837.

Population (1990) 57,024

Population (1992)	*57,986*
Net change (1980-1992)	*+11.9%*
Area	*573*
Density	*101*
Map location number	*23*
Phone Area Code	*616*

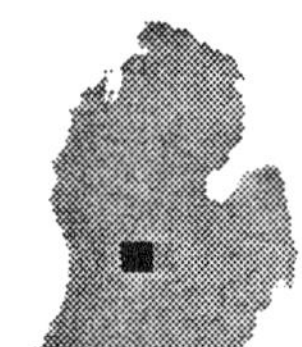

IOSCO

County Seat: Tawas City 48763. An Indian word meaning "water of light." Organized in 1857.

Population (1990) 30,209

Population (1992)	*30,211*
Net change (1980-1992)	*+6.6%*
Area	*549*
Density	*55*
Map location number	*53*
Phone Area Code	*517*

IRON

County Seat: Crystal Falls 49920. The mineral product of the county served as the reason for this name. Organized in 1885.

Population (1990) 13,175

Population (1992)	*13,136*
Net change (1980-1992)	*-3.7%*
Area	*1,167*
Density	*11*
Map location number	*74*
Phone Area Code	*906*

ISABELLA

County Seat: Mt. Pleasant 48858. Queen Isabella of Spain was honored in this designation. Organized in 1859.

Population (1990) 54,624

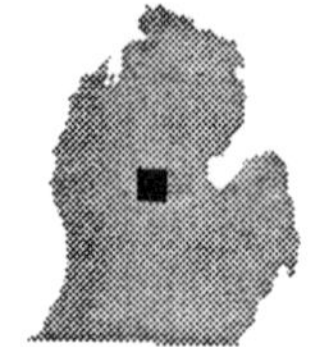

Population (1992)	56,212
Net change (1980-1992)	+3.0%
Area	574
Density	96
Map location number	38
Phone Area Code	517

JACKSON

County Seat: Jackson 49201. Named for President Andrew Jackson. Organized in 1832.

Population (1990) 149,756

Population (1992)	151,740
Net change (1980-1992)	+0.2%
Area	707
Density	215
Map location number	11
Phone Area Code	517

KALAMAZOO

County Seat: Kalamazoo 49007. The name supposedly means "the mirage or reflecting river" and the original Indian name was "Kikalamazoo." Organized in 1830.

Population (1990) 223,411

Population (1992)	225,648
Net change (1980-1992)	+6.2%
Area	562
Density	402
Map location number	9
Phone Area Code	616

KALKASKA

County Seat: Kalkaska 49646. This is an Indian word of uncertain meaning. Organized in 1871.

Population (1990) 13,497

Population (1992)	14,038
Net change (1980-1992)	+28.2%
Area	561
Density	25
Map location number	57
Phone Area Code	616

KENT

County Seat: Grand Rapids 49503. Chancellor James Kent, a celebrated jurist of New York, was honored by this naming. Organized in 1836.

Population (1990)	500,631
Population (1992)	511,997
Net change (1980-1992)	+15.2%
Area	856
Density	598
Map location number	22
Phone Area Code	616

KEWEENAW

County Seat: Eagle River 49924. This is an Indian word meaning "portage or place where portage is made." Organized in 1861.

Population (1990)	1,701
Population (1992)	1,706
Net change (1980-1992)	-13.1%
Area	541
Density	3
Map location number	78
Phone Area Code	906

LAKE

County Seat: Baldwin 49304. There is no special appropriateness to this name other than the fact that the county has numerous small lakes. Organized in 1871.

Population (1990)	8,583
Population (1992)	9,029
Net change (1980-1992)	+17.1%
Area	568
Density	16
Map location number	46
Phone Area Code	616

LAPEER

County Seat: Lapeer 48446. This is supposedly a derivation of the French words "La Pierre." Organized in 1835.

Population (1990)	74,768
Population (1992)	78,526
Net change (1980-1992)	+12.1%
Area	654
Density	120
Map location number	27
Phone Area Code	810

LEELANAU

County Seat: Leland 49654. This is an Indian word meaning "delight of life." Organized in 1863.

Population (1990)	16,527
Population (1992)	17,292
Net change (1980-1992)	+23.5%
Area	349
Density	50
Map location number	60
Phone Area Code	616

LENAWEE

County Seat: Adrian 49221. An Indian word meaning "male" was used for this naming. Organized in 1826.

Population (1990)	91,476
Population (1992)	94,132
Net change (1980-1992)	+4.7%
Area	751
Density	125
Map location number	2
Phone Area Code	313

LIVINGSTON

County Seat: Howell 48843. Named for the Hon. Edward Livingston, Secretary of State under President Andrew Jackson. Organized in 1836.

Population (1990)	115,645
Population (1992)	122,658
Net change (1980-1992)	+22.3%
Area	568
Density	216
Map location number	16
Phone Area Code	810 (313/517)

LUCE

County Seat: Newberry 49868. The county was named for the Hon. Cyrus G. Luce, Governor of Michigan, 1887-1890. Organized in 1887.

Population (1990)	5,763
Population (1992)	5,604
Net change (1980-1992)	-15.8%
Area	930
Density	6
Map location number	82
Phone Area Code	906

MACKINAC

County Seat: St. Ignace 49781. The county was laid out under the name of Michilimackinac in 1818. Organized in 1849.

Population (1990)	10,674
Population (1992)	10,752
Net change (1980-1992)	+5.6%
Area	1,022
Density	11
Map location number	69
Phone Area Code	906

MACOMB

County Seat: Mt. Clemens 48043. Named for General Alexander Macomb, an officer in the War of 1812. Organized in 1818.

Population (1990)	717,400
Population (1992)	726,220
Net change (1980-1992)	+4.8%
Area	480
Density	1,516
Map location number	14
Phone Area Code	810

MANISTEE

County Seat: Manistee 49660. The name is Indian and was first applied to the principal river of the county. Organized in 1855.

Population (1990)	21,265
Population (1992)	21,925
Net change (1980-1992)	-48%
Area	544
Density	40
Map location number	48
Phone Area Code	616

MARQUETTE

County Seat: Marquette 49855. Father Marquette, the Jesuit missionary, was honored in this naming. Organized in 1846 and reorganized in 1848.

Population (1990)	70,887
Population (1992)	71,428
Net change (1980-1992)	-3.6%
Area	1,821
Density	39
Map location number	80
Phone Area Code	906

MASON

County Seat: Ludington 49431. The county was named for the Hon. Stevens T. Mason, Governor of Michigan, 1835-1840. Organized in 1855.

Population (1990) 25,537
Population (1992) 26,420
Net change (1980-1992) -0.2%
Area 495
Density 53
Map location number 47
Phone Area Code 616

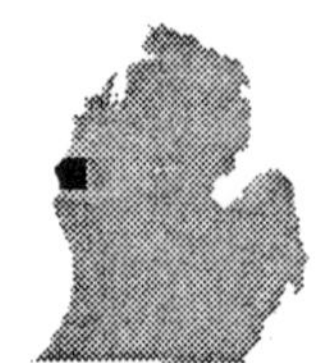

MECOSTA

County Seat: Big Rapids 49307. Chief Mecosta, an Indian chief, was recognized in this naming. Organized in 1859.

Population (1990) 37,308
Population (1992) 38,553
Net change (1980-1992) +4.3%
Area 556
Density 69
Map location number 37
Phone Area Code 616

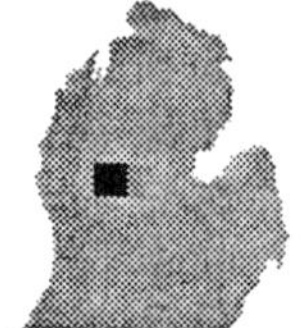

MENOMINEE

County Seat: Menominee 49858. Named for the Menominee tribe of Indians who lived in the county. Organized under the name of Bleeker in 1861 and reorganized in 1863.

Population (1990) 24,920
Population (1992) 24,593
Net change (1980-1992) -6.1%
Area 1.044
Density 24
Map location number 72
Phone Area Code 906

MIDLAND

County Seat: Midland 48640. The county is located not far from the geographical center of the Lower Peninsula and thus was named. Organized in 1850.

Population (1990) 75,651
Population (1992) 77,950
Net change (1980-1992) +5.9%
Area 521
Density 150
Map location number 39
Phone Area Code 517

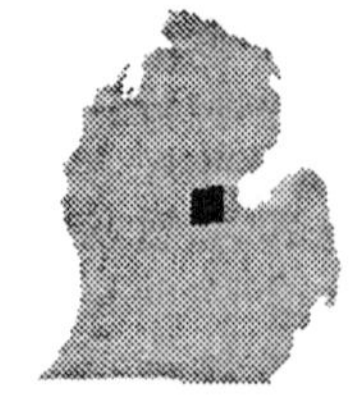

MISSAUKEE

County Seat: Lake City 49651. Named for a prominent Indian chief of that region who was better known as "Nesaukee." Organized in 1871.

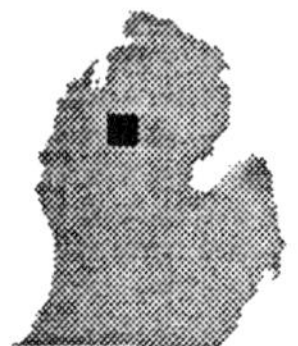

Population (1990)	12,147
Population (1992)	12,739
Net change (1980-1992)	+27.3%
Area	567
Density	22
Map location number	50
Phone Area Code	517

MONROE

County Seat: Monroe 48161. It was named in honor of President James Monroe. Established in 1817.

Population (1990)	133,600
Population (1992)	135,962
Net change (1980-1992)	+1.0%
Area	551
Density	247
Map location number	1
Phone Area Code	313

MONTCALM

County Seat: Stanton 48888. A French officer, General Marquis de Montcalm, was recognized in the naming of this county. Organized in 1850.

Population (1990)	53,059
Population (1992)	55,445
Net change (1980-1992)	+16.6%
Area	708
Density	78
Map location number	33
Phone Area Code	517

MONTMORENCY

County Seat: Atlanta 49709. Named in honor of Count Morenci, who aided the united colonies in the war with England. Organized in 1881.

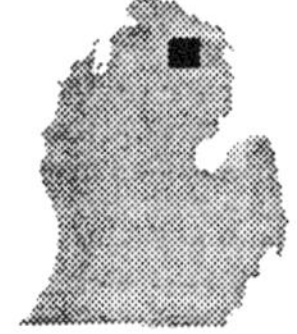

Population (1990)	8,936
Population (1992)	9,355
Net change (1980-1992)	+24.9%
Area	548
Density	17
Map location number	63
Phone Area Code	517

MUSKEGON

County Seat: Muskegon 49440. This is a derivation of the Indian word "river with marshes." Organized in 1859.

Population (1990)	158,983
Population (1992)	*161,980*
Net change (1980-1992)	*+2.8%*
Area	*509*
Density	*318*
Map location number	*35*
Phone Area Code	*616*

NEWAYGO

County Seat: White Cloud 49349. This county was named for Chief Newaygo, a Chippewa chief. Organized in 1851.

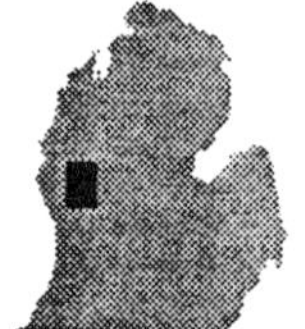

Population (1990)	38,202
Population (1992)	*40,756*
Net change (1980-1992)	*+16.7%*
Area	*842*
Density	*35*
Map location number	*34*
Phone Area Code	*616*

OAKLAND

County Seat: Pontiac 48053. The prevalence of oak trees in the area was the reason for this name. Organized in 1820.

Population (1990)	1,083,592
Population (1992)	*1,118,611*
Net change (1980-1992)	*+10.6%*
Area	*873*
Density	*1,282*
Map location number	*15*
Phone Area Code	*810*

OCEANA

County Seat: Hart 49420. Traditional explanation is that it derives its name from its proximity to Lake Michigan; more recent deduction attributes the name to the title of a book (*Oceana*, James Harrington, 1656). Organized in 1851 and reorganized in 1855.

Population (1990)	22,454
Population (1992)	*22,954*
Net change (1980-1992)	*+4.3%*
Area	*541*
Density	*42*
Map location number	*36*
Phone Area Code	*616*

OGEMAW

County Seat: West Branch 48661. Named in honor of the Ogemaw tribe of Indians. Organized in 1875.

Population (1990)	18,681
Population (1992)	*19.640*
Net change (1980-1992)	*+19.5%*
Area	*564*
Density	*35*
Map location number	*52*
Phone Area Code	*517*

ONTONAGON

County Seat: Ontonagon 49953. This is a derivation of the Indian word "Nondon-organ" meaning "hunting river." Organized in 1846, reorganized in 1848 and legalized by the legislature in 1853.

Population (1990)	8,854
Population (1992)	*8,761*
Net change (1980-1992)	*-11.2%*
Area	*1,312*
Density	*7*
Map location number	*76*
Phone Area Code	*906*

OSCEOLA

County Seat: Reed City 49677. Chief Osceola, a Seminole Indian, was honored. Organized in 1869.

Population (1990)	20,146
Population (1992)	*20,638*
Net change (1980-1992)	*+9.0%*
Area	*566*
Density	*36*
Map location number	*45*
Phone Area Code	*616*

OSCODA

County Seat: Mio 48647. The name is supposedly an Indian word meaning "pebbly prairie." Organized in 1881.

Population (1990)	7,842
Population (1992)	*8,222*
Net change (1980-1992)	*19.9%*
Area	*565*
Density	*15*
Map location number	*55*
Phone Area Code	*517*

OTSEGO

County Seat: Gaylord 49735. The county was named for the Otsego tribe of Indians. Organized in 1875.

Population (1990)	17,957
Population (1992)	19,096
Net change (1980-1992)	+27.4%
Area	515
Density	37
Map location number	62
Phone Area Code	517

OTTAWA

County Seat: Grand Haven 49417. Named for the Indian tribe of the same name. Organized in 1837.

Population (1990)	187,768
Population (1992)	197,297
Net change (1980-1992)	+25.5%
Area	566
Density	349
Map location number	21
Phone Area Code	616

PRESQUE ISLE

County Seat: Rogers City 49779. This is a derivation of the French, meaning "narrow peninsula." Organized in 1871; reorganized in 1875.

Population (1990)	13,743
Population (1992)	13,865
Net change (1980-1992)	-2.8%
Area	660
Density	21
Map location number	65
Phone Area Code	517

ROSCOMMON

County Seat: Roscommon 48653. The name was taken from the county of the same name in Ireland. Organized in 1875.

Population (1990)	19,776
Population (1992)	20,861
Net change (1980-1992)	+27.4%
Area	521
Density	40
Map location number	51
Phone Area Code	517

SAGINAW

County Seat: Saginaw 48602. Takes its name from the Indian words "Sac-e-nong" or "Sac-town" having reference to the story that a tribe of Sacs lived at the mouth of the river. Organized in 1835.

Population (1990) 211,946

Population (1992)	*212,085*
Net change (1980-1992)	*-6.8%*
Area	*809*
Density	*263*
Map location number	*31*
Phone Area Code	*517*

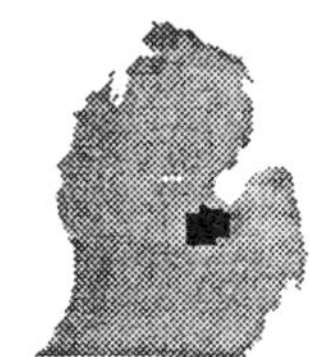

ST. CLAIR

County Seat: Port Huron 48060. Named for General Arthur St. Clair, the first Governor of the Northwest Territory. Organized in 1821.

Population (1990) 145.607

Population (1992)	*150,085*
Net change (1980-1992)	*+8.1%*
Area	*725*
Density	*207*
Map location number	*28*
Phone Area Code	*810*

ST. JOSEPH

County Seat: Centreville 49032. This county honored St. Joseph, the patron saint of New France. Organized in 1829.

Population (1990) 58,913

Population (1992)	*59,388*
Net change (1980-1992)	*+5.9%*
Area	*504*
Density	*118*
Map location number	*5*
Phone Area Code	*616*

SANILAC

County Seat: Sandusky 48471. Named for Sanilac, an Indian chieftain. Organized in 1848.

Population (1990) 39,928

Population (1992)	*40,810*
Net change (1980-1992)	*+0.1%*
Area	*964*
Density	*42*
Map location number	*29*
Phone Area Code	*810*

SCHOOLCRAFT

County Seat: Manistique 49854. The county was named for Henry R. Schoolcraft, who served as mediator between the United States and the Indians, and who was also a member of the Territorial Council of Michigan. Organized in 1846.

Population (1990)	8,302
Population (1992)	8,478
Net change (1980-1992)	-1.1%
Area	1,178
Density	7
Map location number	70
Phone Area Code	906

SHIAWASSEE

County Seat: Corunna 48817. This is an Indian word meaning "river that twists about," supposedly refers to the stretch of the Shiawassee River. Organized in 1837.

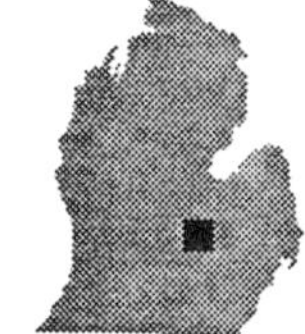

Population (1990)	69,770
Population (1992)	70,832
Net change (1980-1992)	-0.4%
Area	539
Density	131
Map location number	25
Phone Area Code	517

TUSCOLA

County Seat: Caro 48723. The name is Indian but there is no record of the meaning of the word. Organized in 1850.

Population (1990)	55,498
Population (1992)	56,130
Net change (1980-1992)	-1.5%
Area	813
Density	69
Map location number	30
Phone Area Code	517

VAN BUREN

County Seat: Paw Paw 49079. The Hon. Martin Van Buren, then Secretary of State and later President of the United States, was honored in the naming of this county. Organized in 1837.

Population (1990)	70,060
Population (1992)	72,331
Net change (1980-1992)	+8.3%
Area	611
Density	118
Map location number	8
Phone Area Code	616

WASHTENAW

County Seat: Ann Arbor 48107. The original word was "wash-ten-ong" meaning at or on the river. Organized in 1826 and reorganized in 1829.

Population (1990)	282,937
Population (1992)	*288,025*
Net change (1980-1992)	*+8.8%*
Area	*710*
Density	*406*
Map location number	*12*
Phone Area Code	*313*

WAYNE

County Seat: Detroit 48226. The first county to be organized was named for General Anthony Wayne. Organized in 1815.

Population (1990)	2,111,687
Population (1992)	*2,096,179*
Net change (1980-1992)	*-10.3%*
Area	*614*
Density	*3,413*
Map location number	*13*
Phone Area Code	*313*

WEXFORD

County Seat: Cadillac 49601. Named for County Wexford in Ireland. Organized in 1869.

Population (1990)	26,360
Population (1992)	*27,099*
Net change (1980-1992)	*+8.0%*
Area	*566*
Density	*48*
Map location number	*49*
Phone Area Code	*616*

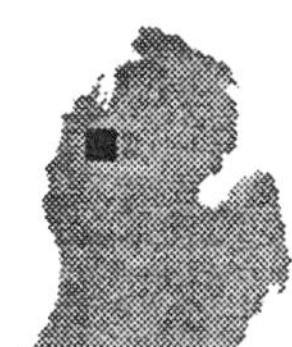

MICHIGAN COUNTIES AMONG THE TOP 25 COUNTIES RANKED IN U.S. BY SELECT SUBJECTS

Source; U.S. Bureau of the Census

NOTE; All years, except as noted, are 1990.

RANK IN U.S.	COUNTY	SUBJECT
8	Wayne	Largest population (1992) / 2,096,179
4	Wayne	Largest population (1980) / 2,337,843
25	Oakland	Largest population (1980) / 1,011,793
1	Wayne	Largest population decline (1980-1992) / - 241,664
20	Genesee	" " " " / - 16,941
25	Saginaw	" " " " / - 15,562
25	Wayne	Most people per square mile / 3,413,400
4	Wayne	Largest black population / 849,109
10	Keweenaw	Highest percentage of persons 65 years and older / 29.4
8	Wayne	Most households / 780,535
14	Keweenaw	Highest percentage of one-person households / 34.5%
12	Crawford	Highest infant death rate per 1,000 live births (1988) / 32.4
19	Charlevoix	Highest infant death rate per 1,000 live births (1988) / 28.3%
10	Washtenaw	Highest physician rate per 100,000 residents population (1990), AMA report / 773
16	Washtenaw	Highest percentage of people 25 years or older with college bachelors's degree or higher / 41.9%
25	Oakland	Highest money income per capita (1989) / $21.125
7	Keweenaw	Highest percentage of owner-occupied housing units / 86.5%
18	Oakland	Largest number of new private housing units authorized by building permits (1990-1992) / 16,352
2	Macomb	Highest percentage of workers driving alone to work / 87.4%
3	Oakland	" " " / 87.4%
7	Midland	" " " / 85.8%

RANK IN U.S.	COUNTY	SUBJECT
12	Bay	Highest percentage of workers driving alone to work / 85.4%
13	Monroe	" " / 85.4%
20	Genesee	" " / 85.0%
24	Saginaw	" " / 84.8%
8	Cheboygan	Highest unemployment rate (1991) / 22.6%
14	Mackinac	" " / 19.8%
19	Montmorency	" " / 19.2%
4	Wayne	Highest manufacturing earning in $1,000 / $10,704,073
12	Macomb	" " / $ 5,079,373
19	Oakland	" " / $ 4,602,973
7	Wayne	Highest amount of Federal funds and grants (1992) / $ 9,595,919
13	Luce	Highest State and local goverment employment per 10,000 population / rate 2,143
23	Washtenaw	" " / rate 1,953

HIGHEST RANKING COUNTY IN MICHIGAN BY SELECT SUBJECT

Source: U.S. Bureau of the census

Note : Years, unless otherwise noted, are for 1990.

COUNTY	SUBJECT
Wayne	Largest population (1992) / 2,096179
Keweenaw	Smallest population (1992) / 1,706
Oakland	Largest population growth (1980-1992) / 106,816
Crawford	Highest population growtrh rate (1980-1992) / 37.1
Keweenaw	Highest percentage of persons 65 years and over / 29.4%
Oakland	Highest percentage of movers (1985-1990) / 58%
Wayne	Highest percentage of one-parent family households / 35.9
Kent	Highest birth rate per 1,000 residents populations / 18.6
Crawford	Highest infant death rate per 1,000 live births (1988) / 32.4
Washtenaw	Highest physician rate per 100,000 resident population, from AMA / 773
Kent	Lowest percentage of elementary and high school enrollment in public schools / 81.6%
Washtenaw	Highest percentage of persons 25 years or older who are high school graduates or higher / 87.2%
Washtenaw	Highest percentage of persons 25 years or older with a college bachelor's degree or higher / 41.9%
Oakland	Highest money income per capita (1989) / $21,125
Lake	Lowest money income per capita (1989) / $8,195
Lake	Highest percentage of persons below the poverty level (1989) / 26.4%
Keweenaw	Highest percentage of owner-occupied housing units / 86.5%
Livingston	Highest median value of specified owner-occupied housing units / $97,300
Oakland	Largest number of new private housing units authorized by building permits (1990-1992) / 16,352
Cheboygan	Highest unemployment rate (1991) / 22.6
Washtenaw	Lowest unemployment rate (1991) / 6.0
Washtenaw	Highest female civilian labor force participation rate / 64.8
Iosco	Highest amount of Federal funds and grants per capita (1992) / $6,054
Oakland	Highest personal income per capita / $ 26,884
Huron	Highest percentage of earning in agriculture / 24.5%
Midland	Highest percentage of earning in manufacturing / 53.9%
Emmet	Highest percentage of earning in service / 42.4%

METROPOLITAN AREAS

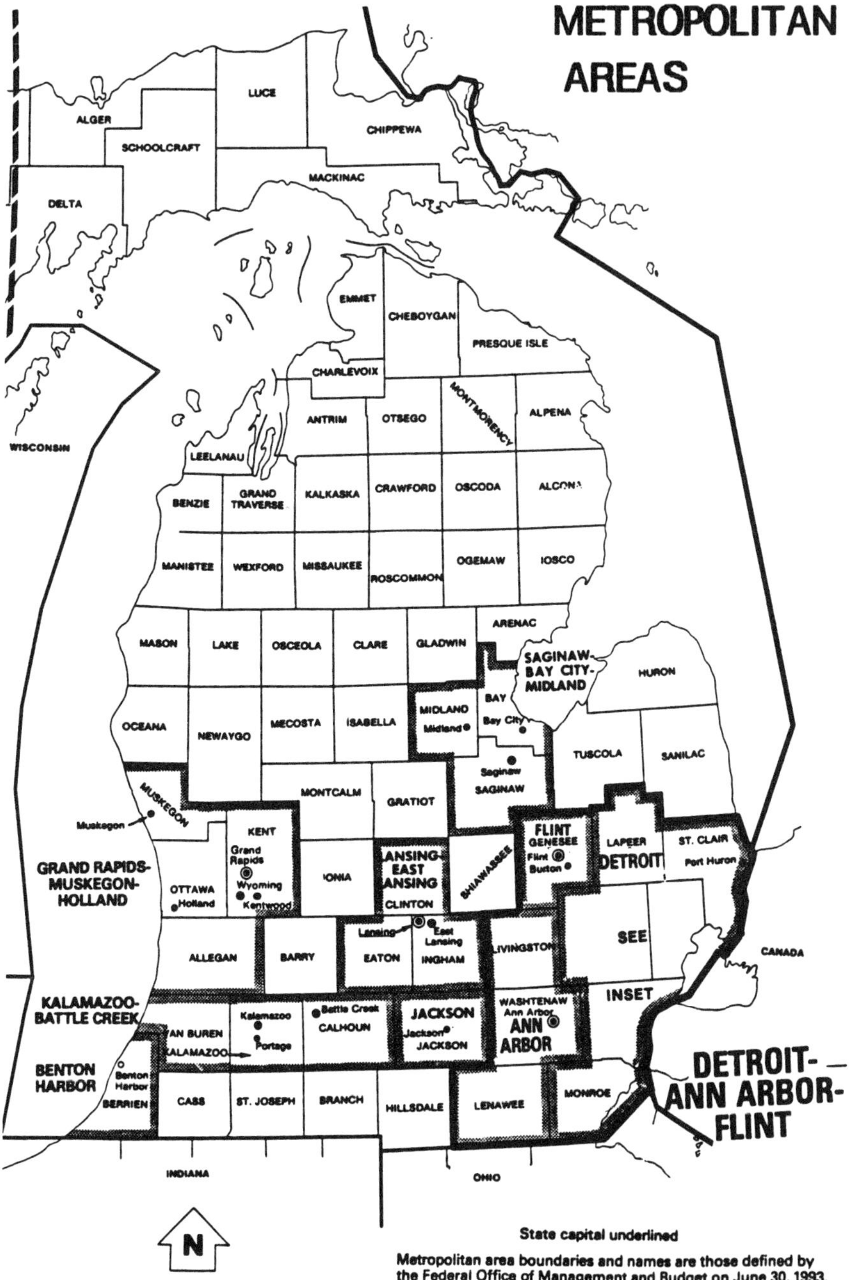

State capital underlined

Metropolitan area boundaries and names are those defined by the Federal Office of Management and Budget on June 30, 1993. All other boundaries and names are as of January 1, 1990.

SCALE

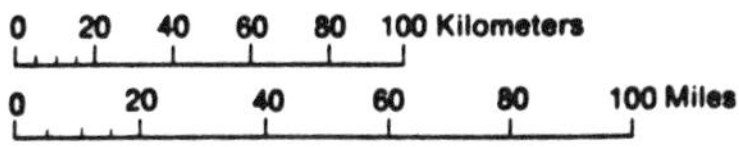

Source; U.S. Dept of Commerce

METROPOLITAN AREAS IN MICHIGAN

Source - U.S. Bureau of the Census and U.S. Office of Mgt. & Budget

Michigan has nine metro areas. 'Metro areas,' or 'Metropolitan Statistical Areas,' are defined by the U.S. Office of Management & Budget as one or more central cities with a high degree of economic and social integration with the surrounding communities. Three of Michigan's are combined into a 'Consolidated Metropolitan Statistical Area' consisting of Metro Detroit-Ann Arbor-Flint.

The state's metro areas cover 25 of the 83 counties, all located in the southern half of the Lower Peninsula.

Note: Please see pages 230-233 for data about labor, by industry, in the metro areas, and other metro data.

METRO AREAS	AREA Sq Miles	POPULATION 1992 (IN 1,000)
METRO DETROIT-ANN ARBOR-FLINT		5,246
METRO DETROIT		4,308
LAPEER COUNTY	654	78
MACOMB COUNTY	480	726
MONROE COUNTY	551	155
OAKLAND COUNTY	873	1,118
ST CLAIR COUNTY	725	150
WAYNE COUNTY	614	2,096
METRO ANN ARBOR		
LENAWEE COUNTY	751	94
LIVINGSTON COUNTY	568	122
WASHTENAW COUNTY	710	288
METRO FLINT		
GENESEE COUNTY	640	434
METRO GRAND RAPIDS-MUSKEGON-HOLLAND		
ALLEGON COUNTY	828	93
KENT COUNTY	856	511
MUSKEGON COUNTY	509	161
OTTAWA COUNTY	566	197

METRO KALAMAZOO-BATTLE CREEK		**436**
CALHOUN COUNTY	709	138
KALAMAZOO COUNTY	562	225
VAN BUREN COUNTY	611	72
METRO LANSING-EAST LANSING		
CLINTON COUNTY	572	59
EATON COUNTY	577	95
INGHAM COUNTY	559	281
METRO SAGINAW-BAY CITY-MIDLAND		
BAY COUNTY	444	112
MIDLAND COUNTY	521	77
SAGINAW COUNTY	809	212
METRO BENTON HARBOR		
BERRIEN COUNTY	571	161
METRO JACKSON		
JACKSON COUNTY	707	151

Sault Ste. Marie
Detroit

Michigan

Weather

Source: U.S. Natl. Oceanic & Atmospheric Admin.
Notes: (1) Period of record 1961 through 1990.
(2) Period of record through 1992.

(DETROIT station)	Jan.	Feb.	March	April	May	June	July	Aug.	Sept.	Oct.	Nov.	Dec.	Annual	note
Normal Daily Mean Temp.	22.9°	25.4°	35.7°	47.3°	58.4°	67.6°	72.3°	70.5°	63.2°	51.2°	40.2°	28.3°	48.6°	(1)
Normal Daily High Temp.	30.3°	33.3°	44.4°	57.7°	69.6°	78.9°	83.3°	81.3°	73.9°	61.5°	48.1°	35.2°	58.1°	(1)
Normal Daily Low Temp.	15.6°	17.6°	27.0°	36.8°	47.1°	56.3°	61.3°	59.6°	52.5°	40.9°	32.2°	21.4°	39.0°	(1)
Highest Temp. of Record	62°	65°	81°	89°	93°	104°	102°	100°	98°	91°	77°	68°	102°	(2)
Lowest Temp. of Record	-21°	-15°	-4°	10°	25°	36°	41°	38°	29°	17°	9°	-10°	-21°	(2)
Normal Precipitation, "	1.76"	1.74"	2.55"	2.95"	2.92"	3.61"	3.18"	3.43"	2.89"	2.10"	2.67"	2.82"	32.62"	(1)
Average Number of Days With Precipitation, .01"+	11	13	13	13	11	10	9	9	10	10	12	14	136	(2)
Snow & Ice Pellets, "	10.2"	8.9"	6.7"	1.6"	Trace	-	-	-	Trace	0.2"	3.0"	10.4"	41.0"	(2)

(SAULT STE. MARIE station)	Jan.	Feb.	March	April	May	June	July	Aug.	Sept.	Oct.	Nov.	Dec.	Annual	
Normal Daily Mean Temp.	12.9°	14.0°	24.0°	38.2°	50.5°	58.4°	63.8°	62.6°	55.1°	45.3°	33.0°	19.0°	39.7°	(1)
Normal Daily High Temp.	21.1°	23.2°	32.8°	48.0°	61.6°	70.5°	76.3°	73.8°	65.9°	54.3°	40.0°	26.2°	49.6°	(1)
Normal Daily Low Temp.	4.6°	4.8°	15.3°	28.4°	38.4°	45.5°	51.3°	54.3°	44.3°	36.2°	25.9°	11.8°	29.8°	(1)
Highest Temp. of Record	45°	47°	75°	85°	89°	93°	97°	98°	95°	80°	67°	60°	98°	(2)
Lowest Temp. of Record	-36°	-35°	-24°	- 2°	18°	26°	36°	29°	25°	16°	-10°	-25°	-36°	(2)
Normal Precipitation,"	2.42"	1.74"	2.30"	2.35"	2.71"	3.14"	2.71"	3.61"	3.69"	3.23"	3.45"	2.88"	34.23"	(1)
Average Number of Days With Precipitation, .01"+	19	15	13	11	11	11	10	11	13	13	17	19	166	(2)
Snow & Ice Pellets, "	28.7"	19.0"	15.1"	5.5"	0.5"	T	-	-	0.1"	2.4"	15.4"	30.0"	116.7"	(2)

Source: *Michigan Travel Bureau*

Circle Tours

Motorists can take scenic tours along the Great Lakes by following routes that are marked by distinctive green-and-white signs displaying a different design for each of the lakes. The tours in Michigan guide travelers to countless communities and attractions and natural beauty areas along 3,200 miles of shoreline in the state. The 2- by 2-foot signs appear at least every 10 miles along the designated routes, as well as at points where highways deviate from a straight course. The complete Great Lakes Circle Tour, totaling about 6,500 miles, extends into eight states and Canadian provinces that border the largest system of freshwater lakes in the world.

Lake Huron Circle Tour

The Michigan leg of this two-nation, two-peninsula, three-bridge tour starts at the American end of one international bridge and ends at the approach to another some 345 miles away.

Much of this well-marked tour puts the traveler within view of the second largest of the Great Lakes—Lake Huron. This inland sea is 206 miles long and 183 miles wide and covers 23,000 square miles. It contains 850 cubic miles of water, reaching a maximum depth of 750 feet. The coast is dotted with lighthouses, many of which can be toured by appointment during the summer months.

Contact: Huron County Visitors Bureau (517) 269-6431

Lake Michigan Circle Tour

Imagine a riviera that stretches nearly 575 miles. Better yet, drive along its hundreds of miles of sand beaches, charming villages, sweeping panoramas, orchards, vineyards, towering dunes, harbors, inlets, and marinas—and always the sparkling blue of Lake Michigan stretching to the western horizon.

Lake Michigan is the third largest of the Great Lakes. It is 307 miles long, 118 miles wide, and 925 feet deep. It contains 1,180 cubic miles of water and covers 22,278 square miles.

The Lake Michigan Circle Tour often splits off into well-marked parallel scenic routes that follow the shoreline closer than the main route.

Contact: West Michigan Tourist Association (616) 456-8557

Lake Superior Circle Tour

A Michigan scene never feels quite right without a vast lake stretching to the horizon. Using Michigan as a starting point, motorists can circle the world's largest freshwater lake—Lake Superior—in all its splendor.

As travelers cruise the Lake Superior shoreline, they can contemplate these staggering facts: This wild and sometimes raging freshwater sea is 350 miles long and 160 miles wide, covering 31,699 square miles, reaching a maximum depth of 1,335 feet, and containing 2,934 cubic miles of water.

The Michigan segment of this three-state, two-nation circuit is just under 500 miles long. It follows the north shore of Michigan's Upper Peninsula—an area larger than Massachusetts, Rhode Island, Connecticut, and Delaware combined—where wilderness abounds but visitors are never more than 30 miles from restaurants, motels, and campgrounds. The Upper Peninsula is filled with wildlife refuges and punctuated with more than 150 waterfalls.

Contact: Upper Peninsula Travel and Recreation Association (906) 774-5480

MICHIGAN WELCOME CENTERS

Michigan Welcome Centers are open year around to provide travel information and rest stops for travelers.

All information at these Welcome Centers is available at no cost including a free phone reservation service.

Travelers can use the available phones to call anywhere in Michigan for reservations or more information.

1. IRONWOOD - US-2 at state line
2. IRON MOUNTAIN - US-2 two miles north of state line
3. MENOMINEE - US-41 at state line
4. MARQUETTE - 2201 South US-41
5. SAULT STE. MARIE -.I-75 south of International Bridge
6. ST. IGNACE - I-75 north of Mackinac Bridge
7. MACKINAW CITY - M-108 in Mackinaw City
8. CLARE - US-27 north of Clare
9. PORT HURON - I-94, 2260 Water Street
10. MONROE - I-75 ten miles north of state line
11. DUNDEE - US-23 six miles north of state line
12. COLDWATER - I-69 six miles north of state line
13. NEW BUFFALO - I-94 at state line

Zoos

Source: Michigan Travel Bureau

Belle Isle Aquarium
Belle Isle Park
East Jefferson at Grand Boulevard
Detroit, MI 48207
(313) 267-7159
The oldest freshwater aquarium in the United States.

Belle Isle Zoo
Belle Isle Park
East Jefferson at Grand Boulevard
Detroit, MI 48207
(313) 267-7160
A 13-acre zoo housing exotic and native animals.

Detroit Zoo
Woodward Avenue at Ten Mile Road
Royal Oak, MI 48068
(313) 398-0903
More than 300 species of animals, from polar bears to chimpanzees, are exhibited in barless and natural habitats, in Michigan's largest zoo.

Potter Park Zoo
1301 S. Pennsylvania
Lansing, MI 48910
(517) 483-4222
Nestled along the Grand River, this facility features 125 species of animals and offers pony rides, canoe rentals, and a playground.

Saginaw Children's Zoo
1435 S. Washington
Saginaw, MI 48601
(517) 759-1657
The facility offers animal and bird exhibits and an opportunity to stroll across the covered bridge, feed and pet the animals, or ride on the minitrain.

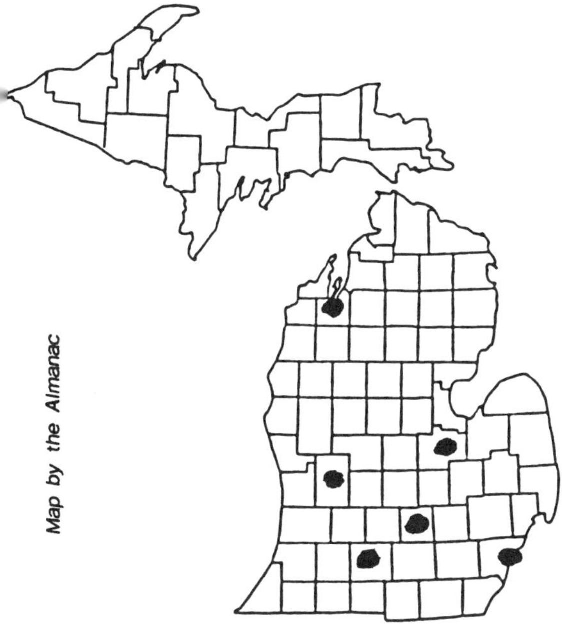

Binder Park Zoo
7400 Division Drive
Battle Creek, MI 49017
(616) 979-1351
This attraction features a separate children's zoo with educational hands-on displays and train rides on the Z.O. & O. Railroad.

Map by the Almanac

John Ball Zoological Garden
1300 W. Fulton Street
Grand Rapids, MI 49504
(616) 776-2591
Michigan's second largest, this facility is home to 185 species of animals in attractive terraced gardens.

Accessible Lighthouses

Of Michigan's 116 lighthouses and navigational lights, only those listed below are accessible or open to the public. We suggest calling ahead for dates and hours of operation.

Source: Michigan Travel Bureau

Lake Superior

Copper Harbor Lighthouse Museum
Fort Wilkins State Park
East US-41
Copper Harbor, MI 49918
(906) 289-4215

Eagle Harbor Light Station Museum Complex
Star Route 1
Eagle Harbor, MI 49951
(906) 337-2303

Au Sable Point Lighthouse Museum
Pictured Rocks National Lakeshore
Munising, MI 49862
(906) 387-3700

Whitefish Point—Great Lakes Shipwreck Museum
111 Ashmun
Sault Ste. Marie, MI 49783
(906) 635-1742
(summer & winter)
(906) 492-3392 (summer only)

Point Iroquois Lighthouse Museum
Bay Mills Township
Hiawatha National Forest
Sault Ste. Marie Ranger Office
4000 I-75 Business Spur
Sault Ste. Marie, MI 49783
(906) 635-5311

Lake Huron

New Presque Isle Lighthouse Museum
4500 E. Grand Lake Road
Presque Isle, MI 49777
(517) 595-2059

Old Presque Isle Lighthouse
5295 Grand Lake Road
Presque Isle, MI 49777
(517) 595-2787

Sturgeon Point Lighthouse Museum
Sturgeon Point Road
Harrisville, MI 48740
(517) 471-2088

Tawas Point Lighthouse
US Coast Guard Station
600 Lighthouse Road
East Tawas, MI 48730
(517) 362-4428
(517) 362-4429

Point Aux Barques Lighthouse Museum
7320 Lighthouse Road
Port Hope, MI 48468
(517) 428-4749

Fort Gratiot Lighthouse
Garfield Street at Omar
Port Huron, MI 48060
(313) 984-2424
(313) 982-3691

Lightship *Huron* Museum
Pine Grove Park at the St. Clair River
Port Huron, MI 48060
(313) 982-0891

Lake Michigan

Delta County Historical Society Lighthouse
18 Water Plant Road
Escanaba, MI 49829
(906) 786-3763
(906) 786-3428

Peninsula Point Lighthouse
Hiawatha National Forest
8181 US-2
Rapid River, MI 49878
(906) 474-6442

Seul Choix Lighthouse
Seul Choix Point
Gulliver, MI 49840
(906) 283-3169

Beaver Island Harbor Lighthouse
St. James, MI 49782
Open for tours once a year.
Call for schedule.
(616) 448-2254
(616) 448-2486

Beaver (Head) Island Lighthouse
St. James, MI 49782
(616) 547-3200

Grand Traverse Lighthouse Museum
Leelanau Point
Northport, MI 49670
(616) 386-7553

South Manitou Island Lighthouse
South Manitou Island, MI
(616) 326-5134

Big Sable Point Lighthouse
M-116
Ludington, MI 49431
(616) 845-1335

White River Light Station
6199 Murray Road
Whitehall, MI 49461
(616) 894-8265

Accessible Lighthouses

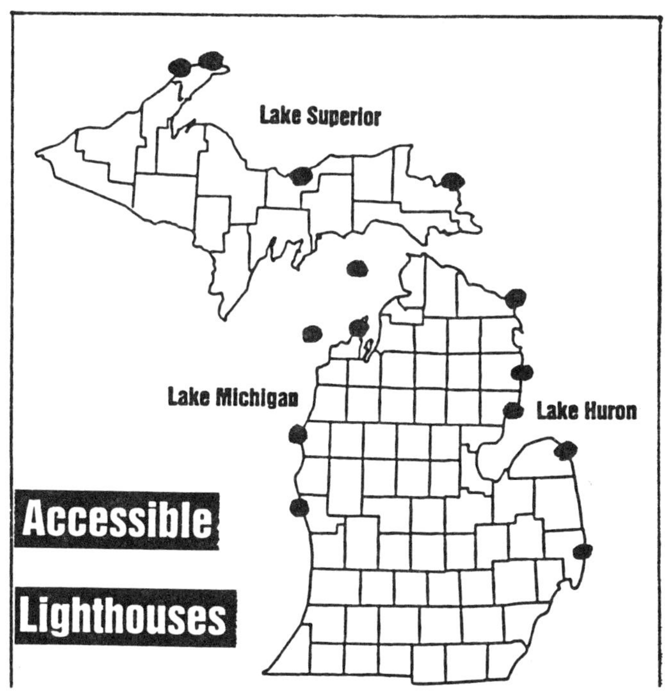

Peak Fall Color

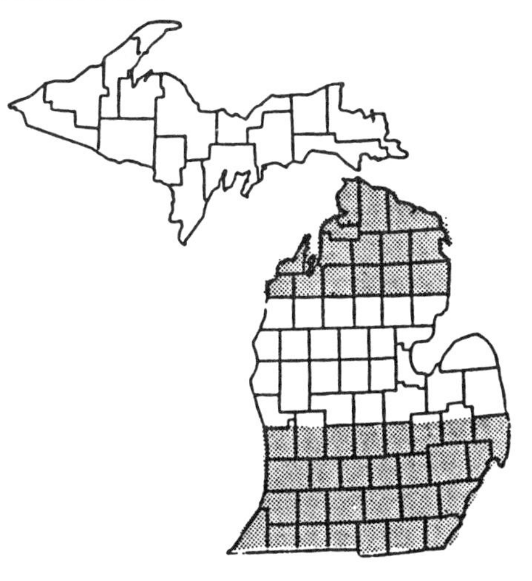

Map by the Almanac

Upper Peninsula
Mid-September to early October

Northern Lower Peninsula
Late September to mid-October

Central Lower Peninsula
Early to mid-October

Southern Lower Peninsula
Mid- to late October

INDIAN GAMING CASINOS IN MICHIGAN

Eleven gaming casinos are legally operated by native Indians, under tribal sovereignty, on federally controlled American Indian reservations in Michigan.

Gambling "has been a real economic boost. It's brought all kinds of new jobs. It's been great," the superintendent of the Michigan agency of the U.S. Bureau of Indian Affairs said in a Detroit Free Press report (4-1-88), and the Michigan Travel Bureau credited it with "creating 2,000 jobs, boosting local economies and Michigan tourism, and raising capital for tribal community development in the areas where casinos exist," according to an article in AAA's Michigan magazine (Jan., 1995).

CASINO, CITY, (COUNTY), TRIBE, CASINO TELEPHONE

1 SOARING EAGLE CASINO, Mt. Pleasant (Isabella County). Saginaw Chippewa Tribe. Tel. (800) 992-2306.

2 LEELANAU SANDS CASINO, Suttons Bay (Leelanau County0. Grand Traverse Band of Ottawa & Chippewa Indians. Tel. (800) 962-4646.

3 KEWADIN SHORES, St. Ignace, (Mackinac County). See 5.

4 KEWADIN SLOTS, Hessel, (Mackinac County). See 5

5 KEWADIN CASINOS (VEGAS KEWADIN), Saulte Ste. Marie, (Chippewa County). Sault Tribe of Chippewa Indians. Tel. (800) KEWADIN.

6 KING CLUB CASINO, Brimley, (Chippewa County). Bay Mill Indian Community. Tel.(906) 248-3241.

7 KEWADIN SLOTS, Manistique, (Schoolcraft County). See 5.

8 KEWADIN SLOTS, Christmas, (Alger County). See 5.

9 CHIP-IN CASINO, Harris, (Menominee County). Potawatomi Tribe. Tel. (800) 682-6040.

10 OJIBWA CASINO, Baraga, (Baraga County). Keweenwa Bay Indian Community. Tel. (906) 353-6333.

11 LAC VIEUX DESERT, Watersmeet, (Gogebic County). Lac Vieux (Ojibwa) Desert Band. Tel, (906) 358-4227.B

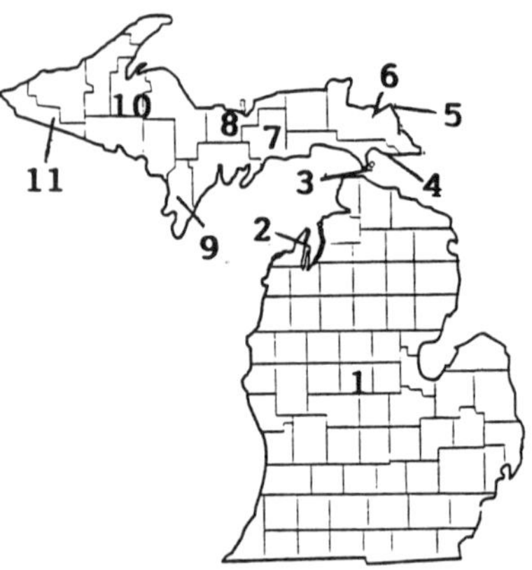

MAJOR VISITOR ATTRACTIONS IN MICHIGAN

	ATTRACTION	LOCATION	APROX. 1989 ATTENDANCE
1.	Frankemuth	Frankemuth	3,000,000
2.	Henry Ford Museum and Greenfield Village	Dearborn	1,300,000
3.	Sleeping Bear Dunes Nat'l Lakeshore	Empire	1,250,000
4.	Mackinac Island	Mackinac Island	950,000
5.	Detroit Institute of Arts	Detroit	948,000
6.	Detroit Zoo	Detroit	878,000
7.	Soo Locks	Sault Ste. Marie	738,000
8.	Pictured Rocks Nat'l Lakeshore	Munsing	565,000
9.	Tahquamenon Falls State Park	Newberry	499,000
10.	Porcupine Mountains Wilderness State Prk.	Silver City	462,000
11.	Interlochen Center for the Arts	Interlochen	250,000
12.	Michigan Historical Museum	Lansing	236,000
13.	Hartwick Pines State Park	Grayling	226,000
14.	Fort Mackinac	Mackinac Island	205,000
15.	Fort Wilkins State Park	Copper Harbor	168,000
16.	Crossroads Village	Flint	143,000
17.	Fort Michilimackinac State Historic Park	Mackinaw City	135,000
18.	Fayette State Park	Fayette	115,000
19.	Meadowbrook Hall	Rochester	99,000
20.	Gerald R. Ford Presidential Museum	Grand Rapids	78,000
21.	Cook Energy Information Center	Bridgman	68,000
22.	Palms Book State Park	Manistique	64,000
22.	Mill Creek State Historic Park	Mackinaw City	61,000
23.	State Capitol Tours	Lansing	58,000
24.	Seney National Wildlife Refuge	Seney	55,000
25.	Hidden Lake Gardens	Tipton	51,000
26.	The Sloop Welcome	Mackinaw City	40,000
27.	Edsel and Eleanor Ford House	Grosse Pte. Shores	40,000
28.	Kellogg Bird Sanctuary	Augusta	35,000
29.	Henry Ford Estate	Dearborn	28,000
30.	White Pine Village	Ludington	19,000
31.	Isle Royale National Park	In Lake Superior	16,000
32.	Father Marquette Nat'l Memorial and Museum	St. Ignace	16,000
33.	Michigan Iron Industry Museum	Negaunee	13,000
34.	Walker Tavern Historic Complex	Cambridge Junction	9,000
35.	Civilian Conservation Corps Museum	Roscommon	7,000
36.	Coppertown USA Mining Museum	Calumet	4,000
37.	Sanilac Petroglyps	New Greenleaf	4,000
38.	Mann House	Concord	1,000

ANNUAL FESTIVALS AND EVENTS

INTERNATIONAL FREEDOM FESTIVAL, early June to early July, Detroit (and Windsor). Includes giantic fire works display, attracts 1 million people, riverfront Jazz Festival, etc. Tel. (313) 259-5400.

BAY CITY FIREWORKS FESTIVAL, early July. Rates one of the top 5 displays in U.S. Tel. (517) 893-1222.

BATTLE CREEK INTERNATIONAL BALLOON CHAMPIONSHIP, July , Battle Creek. Tel (616) 962-0592.

NORTH AMERICAN INTERNATIONAL AUTO SHOW, Jan., Cobo C/E Center, Detroit. Tel. (313) 567-1170

DETROIT BOAT SHOW, Feb., Cobo C/E Center, Tel. (313) 427-5770

PLYMOUTH ICE SCULPTURE SPECTACULAR, Jan., Plymouth. Tel. (313) 453-1540

DETROIT GRAND PRIX, June, Detroit. Tel. (313) 259-5400.

NATIONAL CHERRY FESTIVAL, early July Traverse City. Tel. (616) 947-4230.

ANN ARBOR STREET ART 3-FAIRS, mid-July. Tel. (313) 995-7281

MILLER LITE MONTREAUX DETROIT JAZZ FESTIVAL, early Sept., Detroit. (Tel. (313) 259-5400.

MICHIGAN THANKSGIVING DAY PARADE, Detroit. Tel. (313) 923-7400

TULIP TIME FESTIVAL, May, Holland. Tel. 800-822-2977

PORT HURON TO MACKINAW SAILBOAT RACE, late July. (313)987-6000

STRAITS AREA ANTIQUE AUTO SHOW, late June, St Ignace. Tel (906) 643-8087.

SLOAN SUMMER ARTS FAIR (+ 1,000 classic & antique cars), late June, Flint. (313)760-1169.

MICHIGAN CHALLENGE BALLOONFEST, late June, Howell. (313)546-3920

CHRISTMAS AT CROSSROADS, Dec., Flint. (Tel (313) 736-7100

WINTER CARNIVALS, late Jan, Petoskey (616)347-4105), Houghton (906) 487-2818, Gun Lake (616) 672-7822, Alpena, early Feb, Tel 800-582-1906.

NORTH AMERICA SNOW MOBILE FESTIVAL, early Feb, Cadillac, Tel 800-22-LAKES.

EAST LANSING MICHIGAN FESTIVAL, mid to late Aug. Tel. (517) 351-6620.

ALPENFEST, mid-July, Gaylord (Mich's Alpine Village). Tel (517) 732-4000.

BAVARIAN FESTIVAL, mid-June, Frankenmuth. Tel (517) 652-8155.

SPIRIT OF DETROIT - BUDWEISER THUNDERBIRD CHAMPIONSHIP, June. Tel (313) 771-7333.

OLD CAR FESTIVAL, Sept., Henry Ford Museum & Greenfield Village, Dearborn. Tel (313) 271-1620.

SPIRIT OF DETROIT CAR SHOW & SWAP MEET at Historic Fort Wayne. Tel (313) 297-9360.

MICHIGAN RENAISSANCE FESTIVAL, mid-Aug. to late Sept, Holly. Tel (313) 645-9640.

MATRIX: MIDLAND FESTIVAL, early June, Midland. Tel. 1-800-678-1961.

DETROIT RIVERFRONT ETHNIC FESTIVALS, May through Sept. (313) 224-1184.

CONCOURS D'ELEGANCE, Aug., Rochester. Tel (313) 370-3140.

MICHIGAN WINE & HARVEST FESTIVAL, early Sept, Kalamazoo and Paw Paw. Tel (616) 381-4003.

BLUE WATER FESTIVAL, mid-July, Port Huron. Tel (313), Tel (313) 982-9281

GREAT LUMBERTOWN MUSIC FESTIVAL, late June-early July, Muskegon. Tel. (616) 722-6520.

NORTH AMERICA SKI JUMPING TOURNAMENT, early Feb, Ishpeming, Tel. (906) 486-9281

BLOSSOMTIME FESTIVAL (state's oldest and largest festival), late Apr-early May, Benton Harbor (Tel (616) 926-7397

ANN ARBOR SUMMER FESTIVAL, mid June-July, Ann Arbor (313)747-2278.

NATIONAL TROUT FESTIVAL, late Apr, Kalkaska. (616) 258-9103

MICHIGAN WILDLIFE ART FESTIVAL, early Apr, Southfield. Tel (517) 882-3630.

UP 200 SLED DOG CHAMPIONSHIP, mid Feb, Marquette. (909) 226-9094.

INTERNATIONAL STRAWBERRY FESTIVAL, early May, Hamtramck. Tel (313) 871-2778.

ANNUAL COUNTY FAIRS

MICHIGAN STATE FAIR - Oldest in the U.S.(since 1848). Detroit, late August. More than 500,000 attend. Tel. (313) 368-1000.

Also see: Delta County (Upper Peninsula State Fair).

* Harness racing

Source - Mich Dept of Agriculture

COUNTY	CITY, DATE, ATTENDANCE
Alcona*	- Lincoln, late Aug, 5,000, (517) 736-6556
Alger	- Chatham, late July
Allegan*	- Allegan, mid Sept, 251,000 (616) 673-6501
Alpena*	- Alpena, late Aug, 35,000, (517) 379-3206
Arenac*	- Standish, late July, 11,000, (517) 846-4461
Baraga	- Pelkie, mid Aug, 4,500, (906) 524-6300
Barry*	- Hastings, mid July, 50,000, (616) 945-2224
Bay	- Bay City, mid Aug, 19,000, (517) 872-7994
Berrien	- Berrien Springs, mid Aug, 135,000, (616) 473-4251
Branch	- Coldwater, mid Aug, 80,000, (517) 278-5367
Calhoun*	- Marshall, mid Aug, 102,000, (616) 781-8161
Cass*	- Cassopolis, late July, 58,000, (616) 445-8265
Cheboygan	- (Northern Mich), Cheboygan, mid Aug, 14,000, (616) 627-9611
Chippewa*	- Kinross, early Sept, 25,000, (906) 495-5132
Clare*	- Harrison, early Aug, 50,000, (517) 539-9011
Clinton	- St. Johns, early Aug, 10,000, (517) 224-3288
Delta	- (Upper Peninsula State Fair), Escanaba, 110,000 (906) 786-4011
Dickinson*	- Norway, early Sept, 58,000, (906) 774-0363
Eaton*	- Charlotte, late July, 75,000, (517) 543-4510
Emmet*	- Petoskey, mid Aug, 15,500, (616) 347-1010
Genesee	- Flint, mid Aug, 157,000, 810 640-1701
Gladwin*	- Gladwin, late July, 14,000 (517) 426-2311
Gogebic*	- Ironwood, mid Aug, 25,000, (906) 932-1420
Grand Traverse*	- (Northwestern Mich), Traverse City, late Aug, 50,000, (616) 943-4150
Gratiot	- Alma, late July, 40,000 (517) 875-4125 (+Ithaca)
Hillsdale*	- Hillsdale, late Sept, 180,000, (517) 437-3622
Houghton	- Hancock, mid Aug, 15,000, (906) 482-5830
Huron*	- Bad Axe, early Aug, 35,000, (517) 269-7542
Ingham*	- Mason, early Aug, 190,000, (517) 676-2428
Ionia	- Ionia, late July, 580,000, (616) 527-1310
Iosco*	- Hale, late July, 13,000, (517) 728-3841
Iron	- Iron River, mid Aug, 11,000, (906) 265-9403
Isabella	- Mt. Pleasant, mid Aug, 34,000, (517) 773-9070
Jackson	- Jackson, mid Aug, 225,000, (517) 788-4405
Kalamazoo*	- Kalamazoo, late Aug, 126,000, (616) 672-5541
Kalkaska	- Kalkaska, late Aug, 10,000, (616) 258-2105
Kent	- (4H Youth), Lowell, mid Aug, (616) 698-8540
Lapeer*	- Imlay City, mid Aug, 22,000, 810 724-4145
Lenawee*	- Adrian, mid Aug, 81,000, (517) 263-3007
Livingston*	- (Fowlerville Fair), Fowlerville, mid July, 85,000, (313) 223-8186
Luce	- Newberry, mid Sept, 8,200, (906) 293-8785
Mackinac	- Moran, early Sept, 3,500, (906) 643-9469
Macomb	- (Armada Agric), Armada, mid Aug, 122,000, 810 784-5488

Manistee* - Onekama, early Sept, 28,500, (616) 889-5566
Marquette - Marquette, mid Sept, 16,000, (906) 942-7670
Mason* - (Western Mich), Ludington, late Aug, 15,000, (616) 843-8563
Mecosta* - Big Rapids, mid July, 40,000, (616) 796-2347
Menominee - Stephenson, late July, 10,000, (906) 753-2209
Midland* - Midland, mid Aug, 199,000, (517) 835-7901
Missaukee - (Agric Youth), Falmouth, early Aug, 750, (616) 825-2626
Monroe - Monroe, early Aug, 157,000, (313) 241-5775
Montcalm - (4-H) - Greenville, early July, 30,000
Montmorency - Atlanta, mid Aug, 14,500, (517) 785-3316
Muskegon * - Fruitport, early Aug, 8,000, (616) 788-4568
Newaygo - Fremont, mid Aug, 22,000, (616) 652-1513
Oakland - (4-H), Davisburg, late July, 45,000, 810 887-6388
Oceana* - Hart, late Aug, 35,000, (616) 873-2955
Ogemaw - West Branch, mid Aug, 12,500, (517) 345-5393
Ontonagon - Greenland, early Aug, 3,000 (906) 884-4386
Osceola - (4-H & FFA), Evart, 10,000, (616) 734-5481
Oscoda - Mio, mid Aug, 6,750, (517) 848-5626
Otsego* - Gaylord, mid Aug, 8,500, (517) 983-2341
Ottawa* - Holland, late July, 85,000, (616) 396-6671
Roscommon - Roscommon, early Aug, 6,500, (517) 275-4181
Saginaw - Saginaw, mid Sept, 298,000, (517) 753-4408
St. Clair - (4-H & Youth) Goodells, early Aug, 50,000 810 985-7169
St. Joseph* - Centreville, late Sept, 148,000, (616) 467-8935
Sanilac - Sandusky, early Aug, 30,000, 810 648-2515
Schoolcraft - Manistique, late Aug, 8,500, (906) 341-5663
Shiawassee - Corunna, mid Aug, 79,000, (517) 743-2274
Tuscola* - Caro, late July, 40,000, (517) 673-2161
Van Buren - (Youth Fair), Hartford, mid July, 55,000 (616) 621-2038
Wayne - Belleville, late July, 45,000, (313) 697-7002
Wexford - (Northern Dist. Fair), Cadillac, mid Aug, 20,000, (616) 77

ALSO:

Lake - Baldwin, mid August
Gratiot* - (Agri), Ithaca, late July
Barlin Fair - Marne, mid July
Chelsea - Chelsea, late August
Chippewa - (Agri), Stalwart, mid-Sept
Croswell - (Agri), Croswell, mid July
Hudsonville - Hudsonville, late August
Lake Odesa* - Lake Odessa, early July
Manchester - Manchester, early July
Marion* - (Agri), Marion, late June
Saline - Saline, mid Sept
Sparta - Sparta, late July
Vassar* - Vassar, mid July
Washtesnaw - Ann Arbor, late July
Western Mich* - Ludington, late Aug

Theaters and Symphonies

Adrian

Croswell Opera House
(517) 263-5674

Adrian Symphony
(517) 264-3121

Alpena

Thunder Bay Theatre
(517) 354-2267

Ann Arbor

Ann Arbor Civic Theatre
(313) 662-7282

Hill Auditorium, U of M
(313) 764-2538

Lydia Mendelssohn Theatre
(313) 763-TKTS

Michigan Theater
(313) 668-8480

Power Center, U of M
(313) 764-2538

Ann Arbor Symphony
(313) 994-4801

Augusta

Barn Theatre
(616) 731-4121

Battle Creek

Battle Creek Symphony
(616) 962-2518

Bay City

Bay City Players
(517) 893-5555

Calumet

Calumet Theatre
(906) 337-2610

Cheboygan

The Opera House
(616) 627-5841

Clio

Clio Cast and Crew
(313) 687-2588

Coldwater

Tibbits Opera House
(517) 278-6029

Dearborn

Dearborn Symphony
(313) 565-2424

Detroit

Attic Theatre
(313) 875-8285

Bonstelle Theatre
(313) 577-2960

Community Arts Auditorium, WSU
(313) 577-1795

Detroit Repertory Theatre
(313) 868-1347

Fisher Theatre
(313) 872-1000

Fox Theatre
(313) 567-6000

Hilberry Theatre
(313) 577-2972

Masonic Temple Theatre
(313) 832-2232

Michigan Opera Theatre
(313) 874-7850

Music Hall Center for the Performing Arts
(313) 963-7680

Detroit Symphony
(313) 833-3700

Dowagiac

Lyons Theatre
(616) 782-5113

East Lansing

MSU Dinner Theatre
(517) 355-3354

University Auditorium MSU
(517) 336-2000

Wharton Center, MSU
(517) 336-2000
(800) WHARTON

Flint

Bower Theatre
(313) 235-6963

Buckham Alley Theatre
(313) 239-4477

New Vic Supper Theatre
(313) 235-8866

Flint Symphony
(313) 238-9651

Gladwin

Dinner Theatre
(517) 426-9231

Grand Rapids

Broadway Theatre Guild
(616) 235-6285

Grand Rapids Civic Theater
(616) 456-9301

Opera Grand Rapids
(616) 451-2741

Grand Rapids Symphony
(616) 454-9451

Holland

Hope College Repertory Theatre
(616) 394-7890

Houghton

Keweenaw Symphony MTU
(906) 487-2207

Interlochen

Interlochen Center for the Arts
(616) 276-6230

Ironwood

Historic Ironwood Theatre
(906) 932-0618

Jackson

Potter Center Music Hall
(517) 789-1600

Jackson Symphony
(517) 782-3221

Jonesville

Sauk Theatre
(517) 849-9100

Kalamazoo

Chenery Auditorium
(616) 381-4346

Dalton Center, WMU
(616) 387-4667

Dance Centre
(616) 343-3027

Fontana Concert Society
(616) 382-0826

Kalamazoo Civic Theatre
(616) 343-1313

Miller Auditorium, WMU
(616) 387-2300
(800) 228-9858

New Vic Supper Theatre
(616) 381-3328

Laura V. Shaw Theatre, WMU
(616) 387-6222

Kalamazoo Symphony
(616) 349-7759

Lansing

BoarsHead Theater
(517) 484-7805

Dart Auditorium, LCC
(517) 483-1623

Lansing Civic Players
(517) 484-9115

Lansing Symphony
(517) 487-5001

Livonia

Livonia Symphony
(313) 458-6575

Manistee

Ramsdell Theatre
(616) 723-9948

Marshall

Cornwell's Dinner Theatre
(616) 781-4315
(800) 888-7933

Midland

Midland Center for the Arts
(517) 631-8250

Midland Music Society
(517) 631-5930

Midland Theater Guild
(517) 631-7557

Midland Symphony
(517) 631-4234

Mount Clemens

Macomb Center for the Performing Arts
(313) 286-2045

Mount Pleasant

Warriner Auditorium CMU
(517) 774-3000

Muskegon

Cherry County Playhouse
(616) 722-0229

Frauenthal Theater
(616) 722-4538

Muskegon Civic Theater
(616) 722-3852

Overbrook Theater, MCC
(616) 777-0324

Muskegon West Shore Symphony
(616) 726-3231

Plymouth

Plymouth Symphony
(313) 451-2112

Pontiac

Pontiac-Oakland Symphony
(313) 334-6024

Richmond

Community Theatre
(313) 727-9518

Rochester

Rochester Symphony
(313) 651-4181

Varner Theatre, OU
(313) 370-3013

Saginaw

Pit & Balcony Theatre
(517) 754-6588

Saginaw Symphony
(517) 755-6471

St. Joseph

Twin City Players
(616) 429-0400

Southwest Michigan Symphony
(616) 983-4334

Traverse City

City Opera House
(616) 922-2050

Michigan Ensemble Theatre
(616) 922-1552

Old Town Playhouse
(616) 947-2210

Traverse Symphony
(616) 947-7120

Twin Lake

Blue Lake Fine Arts Camp
(616) 894-1966

Ypsilanti

Theater Productions, EMU
(313) 487-1221

Chambers of Commerce

Lower Peninsula

Albion	(517) 629-5533
Algonac	(810) 794-5511
Allegan	(616) 673-2479
Allen	(517) 439-4341
Alma	(517) 463-5525
Alpena	(517) 354-4181
	(800) 582-1906
Arcadia	(616) 723-2575
Atlanta	(517) 785-3400
Baldwin	(616) 745-4331
Bear Lake	(616) 723-2575
Bellaire	(616) 533-6023
Belleville	(313) 697-7151
Benzonia	(616) 882-5802
Beulah	(616) 882-5802
Big Rapids	(616) 796-7649
Blissfield	(517) 486-3642
Boyne City	(616) 582-6222
Brethren	(616) 723-2575
Brooklyn-Irish Hills	(517) 592-8907
Caro	(517) 673-5211
Caseville	(517) 856-3818
Cass City	(517) 872-3434
Cedar Springs	(616) 696-3260
Central Lake	(616) 544-3322
Charlevoix	(616) 547-2101
Charlotte	(517) 543-0400
Cheboygan	(616) 627-7183
Chelsea	(313) 475-1145
Chesaning	(517) 845-3055
Clare	(517) 386-2442
Coldwater	(517) 278-5985
Coloma	(616) 468-3377
Colon	(517) 278-5985
Davison	(810) 653-6266
Dearborn	(313) 584-6100
Dowagiac	(616) 782-8212
Durand	(517) 288-3715
East Jordan	(616) 536-7351
Elk Rapids	(616) 264-8202
Evart	(616) 734-5554
Farmington	(810) 474-3440
Fennville	(616) 561-5013
Fenton	(810) 629-5447
Frankfort	(616) 352-7251
Fremont	(616) 924-0770
Gladwin	(517) 426-5451
Grand Beach	(616) 469-5409
Grand Haven-Spring Lake	(616) 842-4910
Grand Ledge	(517) 627-2383
Grandville	(616) 531-8890
Greenville	(616) 754-5697
Grosse Pointe Shores	(810) 777-2741
Harbert	(616) 469-5409
Harbor Country	(800) 362-7251
Harbor Springs	(616) 347-0200
Harrison	(517) 539-6011
Harrisville	(517) 724-5107
Hastings	(616) 945-2454
Hillman	(517) 742-3739
Hillsdale	(517) 439-4341
Holland	(616) 392-2389
Honor	(616) 882-5802
Houghton Lake	(517) 366-5644
	(800) 292-9071
Howell	(517) 546-3920
Idlewild	(616) 745-4331
Indian River	(616) 238-9325
Ionia	(616) 527-2560
Ithaca	(517) 875-3640
Jackson	(517) 782-8221
Jonesville	(517) 439-4341
Kaleva	(616) 723-2575
Kalkaska	(616) 258-9103
Lakeside	(616) 469-5409
Lansing	(517) 487-6340
Lewiston	(517) 786-2293
Lexington	(810) 359-2262
Mackinaw City	(616) 436-5574
Madison Heights	(810) 542-5010
Manchester	(313) 428-7722
Manistee	(616) 723-2575
Marine City	(810) 765-4501
Marshall	(616) 781-5163
Marysville	(810) 364-6180
McBain	(616) 825-2416
Mesick	(616) 885-1280
Michiana	(616) 469-5409
Milford	(810) 685-7129
Mio	(517) 826-3331
Monroe	(313) 242-3366
Montague	(616) 893-4585
Mount Clemens	(810) 463-1528
New Buffalo	(616) 469-5409
Northville	(810) 349-7640
Novi	(810) 349-3743
Onaway	(517) 733-2874
Onekama	(616) 723-2575
Oscoda	(517) 739-7322
Otsego	(616) 694-6880
Owosso	(517) 723-5149
Oxford	(810) 628-0410
Paw Paw	(616) 657-5395
Pentwater	(616) 869-4150
Petoskey	(616) 347-4150
Pigeon	(517) 453-2506
Pinconning	(800) 44-PINNY
Plainwell	(616) 685-8877
Plymouth	(313) 453-1540
Pontiac	(810) 335-9600
Port Huron	(810) 985-7101
Rochester	(810) 651-6700
Rockford	(616) 866-2000
Rogers City	(517) 734-2535
	(800) 622-4148
Romeo	(810) 752-4436
Royal Oak	(810) 547-4000
St. Clair Shores	(810) 777-2741
St. Helen	(517) 389-3725
St. James	(616) 448-2505
St. Johns	(517) 224-7248
Saline	(313) 429-4494
Sandusky	(810) 648-4445
Sawyer	(616) 469-5409
Scottville	(616) 757-4729
Sebewaing	(517) 883-2150
South Haven	(616) 637-5171
Sparta	(616) 887-2454
Standish	(517) 846-7867
Stevensville	(616) 429-1170
Sturgis	(616) 651-5758
Swartz Creek	(810) 635-9643
Tawas City	(517) 362-8643
	(800) 55-TAWAS
Tecumseh	(517) 423-3740
Thompsonville	(616) 882-5802
Three Oaks	(616) 469-5409
Three Rivers	(616) 278-8193
Tipton	(517) 592-8907
Traverse City	(616) 947-5075
Trufant	(616) 984-2555
Union City	(517) 278-5985
Union Pier	)616) 469-5409
Utica	(810) 731-5400
Waterford	(810) 683-4747
Wayland	(616) 792-2265
Wayne	(313) 721-0100
Wellston	(616) 723-2575
West Bloomfield	(810) 626-3636
West Branch	(517) 345-2821
White Cloud	(616) 689-6607
Whitehall	(616) 893-4585
Williamston	(517) 655-1549
Wyoming	(616) 531-5990
Ypsilanti	(313) 482-5920
Zeeland	(616) 772-2494

Upper Peninsula

Bergland	(906) 575-3265
Bessemer	(906) 663-4542
Caspian	(906) 265-3822
Cedarville	(906) 484-3935
Crystal Falls	(906) 265-3822
De Tour Village	(906) 297-5987
Drummond Island	(906) 493-5245
Escanaba	(906) 786-2192
Garden	(906) 786-2192
Gladstone	(906) 786-2192
Grand Marais	(906) 494-2766
Houghton	(906) 482-5240
Iron Mountain	(906) 774-2002
Iron River	(906) 265-3822
Ironwood	(906) 932-1122
Ishpeming-Negaunee	(906) 486-4841
Mackinac Island	(906) 847-6418
	(800) 225-6225
Manistique	(906) 341-5010
Marquette	(906) 226-6591
Menominee	(906) 863-2679
Munising	(906) 387-2138
Ontonagon	(906) 884-4735
Rapid River	(906) 786-2192
St. Ignace	(906) 643-8717
Sault Ste. Marie	(906) 632-3301
Wakefield	(906) 224-2222

Michigan Travel Bureau
1-800-5432-YES

ROAD MILEAGE BETWEEN SELECT CITIES

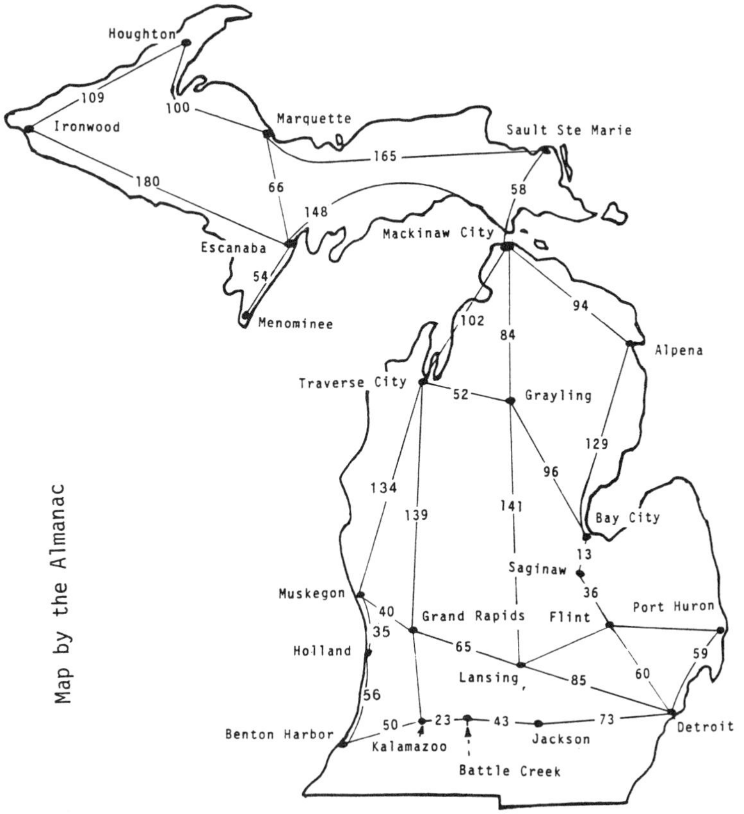

Houghton
109
100
Ironwood
Marquette
Sault Ste Marie
165
180
66
58
148
Mackinaw City
Escanaba
54
Menominee
94
102
84
Alpena
Traverse City
52
Grayling
129
96
134
139
141
Bay City
13
Saginaw
36
Muskegon
40
Grand Rapids
Flint
Port Huron
35
Holland
65
59
Lansing
85
60
56
50
23
43
73
Benton Harbor
Kalamazoo
Jackson
Detroit
Battle Creek

Map by the Almanac

The Mackinac Bridge

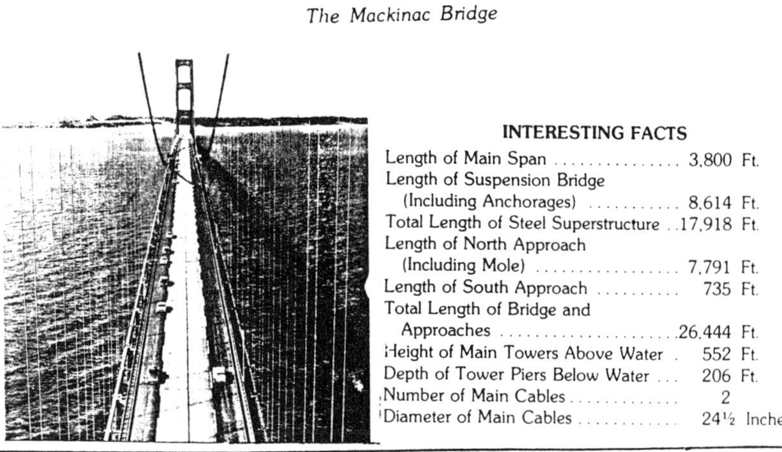

INTERESTING FACTS

Length of Main Span	3,800 Ft.
Length of Suspension Bridge (Including Anchorages)	8,614 Ft.
Total Length of Steel Superstructure	17,918 Ft.
Length of North Approach (Including Mole)	7,791 Ft.
Length of South Approach	735 Ft.
Total Length of Bridge and Approaches	26,444 Ft.
Height of Main Towers Above Water	552 Ft.
Depth of Tower Piers Below Water	206 Ft.
Number of Main Cables	2
Diameter of Main Cables	24½ Inches

Tips for International Visitors

Climate:
Michigan's location in the heart of the Great Lakes region gives it a moderate climate that is unique to the Midwest—a coastal climate in the heart of a continent. The average temperatures are (degrees Fahrenheit): January to February—high 34, low 16; March to April—high 58, low 27; May to June—high 82, low 61; September to October—high 63, low 52; November to December—high 48, low 22.

Proof of Citizenship:
You may be asked to prove citizenship at the port of entry with a passport or a birth, baptismal, or naturalization certificate.

Currency Exchange:
Currency exchange facilities are available at the headquarters of all major banks.

Customs Information:
U.S. Customs Service
477 Michigan Avenue
Detroit, MI 48226
(313) 226-3166

Time Zone:
Eastern Standard Time, except the Upper Peninsula counties of Gogebic, Iron, Dickinson, and Menominee, which are in the Central Standard Time zone—also affected by Daylight Savings Time.

Sales Tax:
Michigan sales tax is 6 percent. Food items purchased in stores are tax free.

Postage:
Letters in the U.S. need 32 cents postage, postcards 20 cents.

Traffic Laws:
Right turn on red permitted after full stop, unless otherwise indicated. Safety-belt use by front-seat passengers is required. Children ages 1 to 4 must be in a safety seat if in the front seat, and a safety seat or safety belt if in the back. Children ages 4 to 16 must wear a safety belt wherever they are seated.

By the Way...
Distances in the United States are in miles. If you are accustomed to using kilometers, this might be a little confusing. However, the following formula should help. To convert miles to kilometers, simply multiply the miles by 1.6 (1 mile = 1.6 km), e.g., 50 miles x 1.6 = 80 km. To convert kilometers to miles, divide the kilometers by 1.6, e.g., 80 km ÷ 1.6 = 50.

Liquor Laws:
Licensed premises serve beer, wine, and mixed drinks until 2 a.m. Off-premises establishments, such as convenience stores, sell wine and beer until 12 midnight. Persons must be 21 years old to buy beer, wine, and distilled spirits.

AIRLINE TELEPHONE NUMBERS FOR MICHIGAN AIR CARRIER AIRPORTS REVISED FEBRUARY 1, 1995

Source - MI Dept of Transportation

	AIR CARRIER	LOCAL NUMBER	TOLL-FREE NUMBER
Alpena	United Express	517/354-8543	800/241-6522
Detroit Metropolitan Wayne County	American Airlines		800/433-7300
	American Trans Air		800/225-9919
	British Airways		800/247-9297
	Business Express/		800/221-1212
	Delta Connection		
	Comair/Delta Connection		800/247-9297
	Continental Airlines		800/221-1212
	Continental Express		800/525-0280
	Delta Airlines		800/525-0280
	KLM Royal Dutch Airlines		800/221-1212
	Mesaba Airlines/		800/374-7747
	NWA Airlink		800/225-2525
	Northwest Airlines		800/225-2525
	Skyway Airlines/Midwest		800/452-2022
	Express Connection		
	Southwest Airlines		800/531-5601
	Spirit Airlines		800/772-7117
	Trans World Airlines		800/221-2000
	United Airlines		800/241-6522
	USAir		800/428-4322
	USAir Express/Jetstream Intl		800/428-4322
Escanaba	Mesaba/NW Airlink		800/225-2525
	United Express	906/786-8179	800/241-6522
Flint	Mesaba/NW Airlink	810/767-6011	800/225-2525
	Skyway Airlines	810/767-2933	800/452-2022
	USAir	810/234-6155	800/428-4322
Grand Rapids	America West Express		800/235-9292
	American Airlines		800/433-7300
	Chicago Express		800/264-3929
	Comair/Delta Connection		800/354-9822
	Northwest		800/225-2525
	Skyway Airlines/Midwest		800/452-2022
	Express Connection		
	TWA		800/221-2000
	United		800/241-6522
	USAir		800/428-4322
Houghton-Hancock	Mesaba/NW Airlink	906/482-3660	800/225-2525
Iron Mountain	United Express	906/774-3980	800/241-6522
Ironwood	United Express	906/932-5808	800/241-6522
Kalamazoo	American Eagle	—	800/433-7300
	Comair/Delta Connection	616/342-0675	800/354-9822
	Northwest	616/381-7593	800/225-2525
	USAir	616/345-7353	800/428-4322

CITY	AIR CARRIER	LOCAL NUMBER	TOLL-FREE NUMBER
Lansing	American Eagle Chicago Express Comair/Delta Connection Northwest Skyway Airlines/Midwest Express Connection United Express USAir		800/433-7300 800/264-3929 800/354-9822 800/225-2525 800/452-2022 800/241-6522 800/428-4322
Manistee	United Express	616/723-8661	800/241-6522
Marquette	American Eagle Mesaba/NW Airlink United Express	906/475-7821 906/475-7897 906/475-7853	800/433-7300 800/225-2525 800/241-6522
Menominee	United Express	906/863-1236	800/241-6522
Muskegon	American Eagle Mesaba/NW Airlink Skyway/Midwest Express Connection	— — —	800/433-7300 800/225-2525 800/452-2022
Pellston	Mesaba/NW Airlink United Express	616/539-8423 616/539-8502	800/531-5601 800/241-6522
Saginaw	Comair/Delta Connection Northwest Skyway/Midwest Express Connection United USAir		800/354-9822 800/225-2525 800/452-2022 800/241-6522 800/428-4322
Sault Ste. Marie	United Express	906/495-5044	800/241-6522
Traverse City	American Eagle Comair/Delta Connection (Seasonal) Mesaba/NW Airlink Northwest Skyway/Midwest Express Connection (Seasonal) United Express	616/941-5304 — 616/929-4300 616/929-4300 616/946-8575 616/946-8575	800/433-7300 800/354-9822 800/225-2525 800/225-2525 800/452-2022 800/241-6522

/maf

Meadow Brook Hall (Dodge-Wilson Home)

Location: Take I-75 to University Dr. exit (Rochester). Follow University Dr. east to Adams Road. Turn right (south) on Adams to entrance.

Oakland University • Rochester, MI 48063 • (313) 370-3140

Meadow Brook Hall photos by H. K. Barnett

Edsel & Eleanor Ford House

Location: On Lake Shore Road between Vernier and 9 Mile Roads. Take I-94 to the 9 Mile Road exit and follow 9 Mile east to Jefferson Ave. Turn right on Jefferson and follow until Jefferson becomes Lake Shore Road. Entrance is on the left just past the Grosse Pointe border.

1100 Lake Shore Road • Grosse Pointe Shores, MI 48236 •
(313) 884-4222 Tours: (313) 884-3400

Fisher Mansion (Lawrence Fisher)

Location: Off East Jefferson Ave. between Conner and Alter Roads. Take I-94 to the Conner Ave. exit and take Conner south to Jefferson. Turn left (east) on Jefferson, go two stop lights to Dickerson, turn right on Dickerson and follow until Dickerson becomes Lenox.

383 Lenox, Dept. PR-2 • Detroit, MI 48215 • (313) 331-6740

Fairlane (Henry & Clara Ford House)

Location: On the University of Michigan-Dearborn campus. Entrance on Evergreen Rd. between Michigan Ave. and Hubbard Dr.

University of Michigan • Dearborn, MI 48128-1491 • (313) 593-5590

TRAVEL INFORMATION AND
CONFERENCE AND VISITORS BUREAUS

Source; Michigan Travel Bureau

Travel Information

Michigan Travel Bureau
P.O. Box 3393
Livonia, MI 48151-3393
(800) 5432-YES
(U.S. and Canada)

For the hearing impaired:
TDD (800) 722-8191
(U.S. and Canada)

For specific trip-planning information, contact the following travel associations and convention and visitors bureaus (listed alphabetically by city):

Lenawee County Conference & Visitors Bureau
1629 W. Maumee
Adrian, MI 49221
(800) 536-2933
(U.S. only)
(800) 682-6580
(U.S. and Canada)

Allegan County Tourist & Recreation Council
300 Water Street
P.O. Box 338
Allegan, MI 49010
(616) 673-2479

CVB of Thunder Bay Region
133 Johnson Street
P.O. Box 65
Alpena, MI 49707-0065
(517) 354-4181
(800) 4-ALPENA
(U.S. and Canada)

Ann Arbor CVB
120 W. Huron Street
Ann Arbor, MI 48104
(313) 995-7281

Huron County Visitors Bureau
250 E. Huron Avenue
Bad Axe, MI 48413
(517) 269-6431
(800) 35-THUMB
(U.S. and Canada)

Battle Creek Area Visitor & Convention Bureau
34 W. Jackson Street
Suite 4-B
Battle Creek, MI 49017
(616) 962-2240
(800) 397-2240
(U.S. only)

Bay Area CVB
901 Saginaw Street
Bay City, MI 48708
(517) 893-1222
(800) 424-5114
(U.S. and Canada)

Lake Michigan CVB
185 E. Main Street
P.O. Box 428
Benton Harbor, MI 49023
(616) 925-6100

Southwestern Michigan Tourist Council
2300 Pipestone Road
Benton Harbor, MI 49022
(616) 925-6301

Mecosta County CVB
246 N. State Street
Big Rapids, MI 49307
(616) 796-7640
(800) 833-6697
(U.S. and Canada)

Cadillac Area Visitors Bureau
222 Lake Street
Cadillac, MI 49601
(616) 775-9776
(800) 22-LAKES

Keweenaw Tourism Council
1197 Calumet Avenue
Calumet, MI 49913
(906) 337-4579

River Country Tourism Council
150 N. Main Street
P.O. Box 70
Centreville, MI 49032
(616) 467-4505

Charlevoix Area CVB
408 Bridge Street
Charlevoix, MI 49720
(800) 367-8557
(MI only)

Cheboygan Area Tourist Bureau
124 N. Main Street
P.O. Box 69
Cheboygan, MI 49721
(616) 627-7183
(800) 968-3302
(U.S. and Canada)

Metropolitan Detroit CVB
100 Renaissance Center
Suite 1950
Detroit, MI 48243
(313) 259-4333
(800) DETROIT
(U.S. and Canada)

Delta County Tourism & Convention Bureau
230 Ludington Street
Escanaba, MI 49829
(800) 437-7496
(U.S. and Canada)

Flint Area CVB
400 N. Saginaw Street
Suite 101-A
Flint, MI 48502
(810) 232-8900
(800) 288-8040
(U.S. and Canada)

Frankenmuth CVB
635 S. Main Street
Frankenmuth, MI 48734
(517) 652-6106
(800) FUN-TOWN
(U.S. and Canada)

Gaylord Area Convention & Tourism Bureau
101 W. Main Street
P.O. Box 3069
Gaylord, MI 49735
(517) 732-6333
(800) 345-8621
(U.S. and Canada)

Grand Haven-Spring Lake CVB
One S. Harbor Drive
Grand Haven, MI 49417
(616) 842-4499
(800) 303-4094
(U.S. and Canada)

Grand Rapids Area CVB
140 Monroe Center, NW
Suite 300
Grand Rapids, MI 49503-2832
(616) 459-8287
(800) 678-9859
(U.S. and Canada)

Grayling Area Visitors Council
213 N. James Street
P.O. Box 217
Grayling, MI 49738
(517) 348-2921
(800) 937-8837
(U.S. and Canada)

Oceana County Tourism Bureau
P.O. Box 168
Hart, MI 49420-0168
(616) 873-7141

Elk Country Visitors Bureau
P.O. Box 507
Hillman, MI 49746
(517) 742-3739

Holland Area CVB
171 Lincoln Avenue
Holland, MI 49423
(616) 396-4221
(800) 822-2770
(U.S. and Canada)

Keweenaw Tourism Council
326 Shelden Avenue
P.O. Box 336
Houghton, MI 49931
(906) 482-2388
(800) 338-7982
(U.S. and Canada)

Livingston County Visitors Bureau
207 N. Michigan Avenue
P.O. Box 138
Howell, MI 48844
(517) 548-1795
(800) 686-8474
(U.S. and Canada)

Indian River Tourist Bureau
P.O. Box 414
Indian River, MI 49749
(616) 238-9325

Tourism Association of Dickinson County
P.O. Box 672
Iron Mountain, MI 49801
(906) 774-2002
(800) 236-2447
(U.S. only)

Iron County Tourism Council
50 E. Genesee Street
Iron River, MI 49935
(906) 265-3822
(800) 255-3620
(U.S. only)

Ironwood Tourism Council
100 E. Aurora Street
Ironwood, MI 49938
(906) 932-1000

Western Upper Peninsula CVB
137 E. Cloverland Drive
P.O. Box 706
Ironwood, MI 49938
(906) 932-4850
(800) 272-7000
(out of MI)

Jackson Convention & Tourist Bureau
6007 Ann Arbor Road
Jackson, MI 49201
(517) 764-4440
(800) 245-5282
(U.S. and Canada)

Kalamazoo County CVB
128 N. Kalamazoo Mall
P.O. Box 1169
Kalamazoo, MI 49007
(616) 381-4003

Baraga County Tourist & Recreation Association
755 E. Broad Street
L'Anse, MI 49946
(906) 524-7444

Greater Lansing CVB
119 Pere Marquette Drive
P.O. Box 15066
Lansing, MI 48901
5066
(517) 487-6800
(800) 648-6630
(U.S. and Canada)

Ludington Area CVB
5827 W. US-10
P.O. Box 160
Ludington, MI 49431
(616) 845-0324
(800) 542-4600
(U.S. only)

Mackinac Island Chamber of Commerce
P.O. Box 451
Mackinac Island, MI 49757
(906) 847-6418
(800) 4-LILACS
(U.S. only)

Mackinaw Area Tourist Bureau
708 S. Huron
P.O. Box 160
Mackinaw City, MI 49701
(616) 436-5664
(800) 666-0160
(U.S. and Canada)

Manistique Area Tourist Council
P.O. Box 37
Manistique, MI 49854
(906) 341-5838
(800) 342-4282
(U.S. and Canada)

Marquette Country CVB
2552 W. US-41
Suite 300
Marquette, MI 49855
(906) 228-7749
(800) 544-4321
(U.S. and Canada)

Midland County CVB
300 Rodd Street
Midland, MI 48640
(517) 839-9901
(800) 678-1961
(U.S. and Canada)

Monroe County Convention & Tourism Bureau
22 W. Second Street
P.O. Box 1094
Monroe, MI 48161
(313) 457-1030
(800) 252-3011
(U.S. and Canada)

Macomb County CVB
58 North Avenue
Mount Clemens, MI 48043
(313) 463-1528

Mount Pleasant Area CVB
144 E. Broadway
Mount Pleasant, MI 48858
(517) 772-4433
(800) 77-CHIEF
(MI only)

Munising Visitors Bureau
422 E. Munising Avenue
P.O. Box 405
Munising, MI 49862
(906) 387-2138

Muskegon County CVB
349 W. Webster
P.O. Box 1087
Muskegon, MI 49443-1087
(616) 722-3751
(800) 235-FUNN
(U.S. and Canada)

Harbor Country Lodging Association
P.O. Box 497
New Buffalo, MI 49117
(616) 469-5409
(800) 362-7251

Newberry Area Tourism Association
P.O. Box 308
Newberry, MI 49868
(906) 293-5562
(800) 831-7292
(U.S. and Canada)

Four Flags Area Council on Tourism
321 E. Main Street
P.O. Box 1300
Niles, MI 49120
(616) 683-3720

Ontonagon Tourism Council
600 River Road
P.O. Box 266
Ontonagon, MI 49953
(906) 884-4735

Greenbush-Oscoda-Au Sable Lodging Association
P.O. Box 397
Oscoda, MI 48750
(800) 235-GOAL
(U.S. and Canada)

Paradise Area Tourism Council
P.O. Box 64
Paradise, MI 49768
(906) 492-3927

Boyne Country CVB
401 E. Mitchell Street
P.O. Box 694
Petoskey, MI 49770
(616) 348-2755
(800) 845-2828
(U.S. and Canada)

Blue Water Convention & Tourist Bureau
520 Thomas Edison Parkway
Port Huron, MI 48060
(810) 987-8687
(800) 852-4242
(U.S. and Canada)

Rogers City Travelers & Visitors Bureau
540 W. Third Street
Rogers City, MI 49779
(800) 622-4148
(MI only)

Saginaw County CVB
901 S. Washington
Saginaw, MI 48601
(517) 752-7164
(800) 444-9979
(U.S. and Canada)

St. Ignace Area Tourist Association
11 S. State Street
St. Ignace, MI 49781
(906) 643-8717
(800) 338-6660
(U.S. and Canada)

Saugatuck-Douglas CVB
P.O. Box 28
Saugatuck, MI 49453
(616) 857-1701

Sault Ste. Marie Tourist Bureau
2581 I-75 Business Spur
Sault Ste. Marie, MI 49783
(906) 632-3301
(800) MI-SAULT
(U.S. and Canada)

Lakeshore CVB
415 Phoenix Street
P.O. Box 890
South Haven, MI 49090
(616) 637-5252

Tawas Bay Tourist & Convention Bureau
402 E. Lake Street
P.O. Box 10
Tawas City, MI 48764-0010
(517) 362-8643
(800) 55-TAWAS
(U.S. and Canada)

Traverse City CVB
415 Munson Avenue
Suite 200
Traverse City, MI 49684
(616) 947-1120
(800) 872-8377
(U.S. and Canada)

West Branch-Ogemaw County Travel & Visitors Bureau
422 W. Houghton Avenue
West Branch, MI 48661
(517) 345-2821
(800) 755-9091
(MI only)

Ypsilanti CVB
301 W. Michigan Avenue
Suite 101
Ypsilanti, MI 48197
(313) 483-4444

Additional Sources of Information

Camping

For a *Michigan Campground Directory*, send $3 for postage and handling to:
Michigan Association of Private Campground Owners
P.O. Box 68
Williamsburg, MI 49690

Fishing & Hunting

For fishing and hunting license information, contact:
Michigan Department of Natural Resources
License Control Division
P.O. Box 30028
Lansing, MI 48909
(517) 373-1204

Remember, when transporting firearms, they must be fully unloaded and carried disassembled in a case. They cannot be accessible in the passenger compartment.

Historic Resources

For information on historic resources, contact:
Michigan Historic Preservation Network
P.O. Box 398
Clarkston, MI 48347
(810) 625-8181

Lodging

For a *Michigan Lodging & Tourism Directory*, send a self-addressed #10 envelope with 52 cents postage to:
Michigan Hotel Motel & Resort Association
6105 W. St. Joseph
Suite 204
Lansing, MI 48917
(517) 323-1818

For a *Michigan Bed & Breakfast* directory, send $3 (MasterCard and VISA accepted) for postage and handling to:
B&B Directory
P.O. Box 428
Saugatuck, MI 49453
(800) 832-6657

Regional Information

For travel information on the Upper Peninsula, contact:
Upper Peninsula Travel & Recreation Association
618 Stephenson Avenue
P.O. Box 400
Iron Mountain, MI 49801
(906) 774-5480
(800) 562-7134
(U.S. and Canada)

For travel information on the western Lower Peninsula, contact:
West Michigan Tourist Association
136 E. Fulton Street
Grand Rapids, MI 49503
(616) 456-8557

For travel information on the northeastern Lower Peninsula, contact:
Michigan's Sunrise Side, Inc.
1361 Fletcher Street
National City, MI 48748
(517) 469-4544
(800) 424-3022
(U.S. and Canada)

State Parks

For information on state parks and recreation areas, contact:
Michigan Department of Natural Resources
Parks & Recreation Division
P.O. Box 30257
Lansing, MI 48909
(517) 373-9900

TRAVEL AND TOURIST INFORMATION

MICHIGAN TRAVEL BUREAU
333 S. Capitol Ave.
Lansing, MI 48933
Ph: 1-800-5432-YES
(Anywhere in Continental U.S.)

DEPARTMENT OF NATURAL RESOURCES
Lansing: (517)373-1220
Grand Rapids: (616)456-5071

1
2
NE
SE

MICHIGAN'S REGIONAL TOURIST ASSOCIATIONS

1. Upper Peninsula Travel & Recreation Association
PO Box 400
Iron Mountain, MI 49801
Ph:(906)774-5480 or 1-800-562-7134

2. West Michigan Tourist Association
136 E. Fulton St.
Grand Rapids, MI 49503
Ph:(616)456-8557

NE Michigan's Sunrise Side, Inc.
1361 Fletcher St.
National City, MI 48748-9666
Ph: 1-800-424-3022

SE Metro Detroit CVB, Renaissance Center, Detroit 48243, Ph (313) 259-4333, (800) DETROIT

VOTE FOR GOVERNOR, BY COUNTY

November 8, 1994, Term: 1995-1998

Source; Secretary of State
Official

COUNTY	Wolpe Stabenow DEM	Engler Binsfeld REP
01 ALCONA	1,239	3,060
02 ALGER	1,301	2,060
03 ALLEGAN	7,152	22,242
04 ALPENA	3,741	7,044
05 ANTRIM	1,978	5,814
06 ARENAC	1,812	3,326
07 BARAGA	1,120	1,568
08 BARRY	5,170	12,933
09 BAY	15,982	24,244
10 BENZIE	1,658	3,558
11 BERRIEN	12,144	30,906
12 BRANCH	3,438	8,629
13 CALHOUN	15,432	26,383
14 CASS	3,670	9,109
15 CHARLEVOIX	2,512	6,366
16 CHEBOYGAN	2,401	5,824
17 CHIPPEWA	3,669	6,615
18 CLARE	3,022	5,895
19 CLINTON	7,371	16,323
20 CRAWFORD	1,184	3,235
21 DELTA	5,595	7,788
22 DICKINSON	3,637	5,783
23 EATON	13,177	24,130
24 EMMET	2,695	7,972
25 GENESEE	73,873	73,759
26 GLADWIN	2,538	5,522
27 GOGEBIC	3,001	3,231
28 GD. TRAVERSE	6,774	20,003
29 GRATIOT	3,462	7,931
30 HILLSDALE	2,994	9,335
31 HOUGHTON	4,065	6,939
32 HURON	3,294	9,268
33 INGHAM	43,790	53,088
34 IONIA	5,080	11,911
35 IOSCO	3,090	7,163
36 IRON	2,142	3,103
37 ISABELLA	5,467	10,030
38 JACKSON	13,829	32,282
39 KALAMAZOO	29,072	44,158
40 KALKASKA	1,298	3,338
41 KENT	42,027	121,988
42 KEWEENAW	366	607
43 LAKE	1,252	2,068
44 LAPEER	7,468	18,825
45 LEELANAU	2,255	6,063
46 LENAWEE	9,912	17,029
47 LIVINGSTON	10,951	35,583
48 LUCE	811	1,124
49 MACKINAC	1,678	2,947
50 MACOMB	74,473	173,003
51 MANISTEE	2,758	5,465
52 MARQUETTE	9,938	11,331
53 MASON	3,048	7,312
54 MECOSTA	3,157	6,600
55 MENOMINEE	2,665	4,721
56 MIDLAND	8,687	20,579
57 MISSAUKEE	1,099	3,714
58 MONROE	14,126	24,218
59 MONTCALM	4,607	11,149
60 MONTMORENCY	1,003	2,621
61 MUSKEGON	19,430	28,911
62 NEWAYGO	3,755	9,307
63 OAKLAND	35,004	269,511
64 OCEANA	2,320	5,158
65 OGEMAW	2,182	4,661
66 ONTONAGON	1,418	2,032
67 OSCEOLA	2,030	5,087
68 OSCODA	747	2,266
69 OTSEGO	1,749	5,215
70 OTTAWA	12,001	58,321
71 PRESQUE ISLE	1,607	3,979
72 ROSCOMMON	2,945	6,461
73 SAGINAW	29,169	43,545
74 ST. CLAIR	14,233	34,078
75 ST. JOSEPH	4,104	11,073
76 SANILAC	3,513	10,425
77 SCHOOLCRAFT	1,246	1,689
78 SHIAWASSEE	7,971	16,447
79 TUSCOLA	5,862	12,188
80 VAN BUREN	6,612	13,894
81 WASHTENAW	43,066	49,779
82 WAYNE	357,798	269,501
83 WEXFORD	2,526	6,758
TOTALS	1,188,438	1,899,101

VOTE FOR GOVERNOR

November 6, 1990

BY COUNTY

County	Blanchard (Dem.)	Engler (Rep.)	Roundtree (Worw.)
Alcona	1,313	2,031	14
Alger	1,821	1,700	10
Allegan	7,934	16,342	205
Alpena	4,319	4,333	58
Antrim	2,711	3,572	48
Arenac	2,305	1,937	25
Baraga	1,181	1,298	12
Barry	5,567	8,785	166
Bay	19,646	14,886	214
Benzie	1,917	2,305	27
Berrien	13,480	24,019	344
Branch	3,778	5,946	62
Calhoun	16,823	18,819	539
Cass	4,308	6,149	48
Charlevoix	3,109	3,863	141
Cheboygan	2,895	3,461	36
Chippewa	4,493	4,442	39
Clare	3,765	3,741	130
Clinton	8,412	11,023	216
Crawford	1,197	1,961	60
Delta	6,675	5,155	41
Dickinson	4,803	4,190	14
Eaton	13,818	16,264	516
Emmet	3,343	4,338	128
Genesee	67,057	45,456	1,676
Gladwin	3,170	3,097	109
Gogebic	3,989	2,089	20
Gd. Traverse	8,519	12,344	142
Gratiot	4,799	5,283	87
Hillsdale	3,823	6,779	72
Houghton	4,686	5,696	57
Huron	4,769	6,365	39
Ingham	46,143	34,878	2,068
Ionia	6,658	8,721	122
Iosco	3,904	4,258	130
Iron	2,512	2,397	20
Isabella	6,541	6,913	202
Jackson	16,702	22,051	430
Kalamazoo	29,086	30,431	812
Kalkaska	1,450	2,289	26
Kent	50,060	95,254	2,237
Keweenaw	442	449	1
Lake	1,423	1,385	66
Lapeer	7,639	11,792	422
Leelanau	2,620	3,757	29
Lenawee	11,239	13,753	103
Livingston	12,162	21,102	535
Luce	994	1,053	6
Mackinac	1,901	2,206	25
Macomb	96,088	110,387	2,668
Manistee	3,386	4,289	46
Marquette	10,676	7,305	122
Mason	3,964	5,138	99
Mecosta	4,019	5,170	61
Menominee	3,559	2,979	18
Midland	12,783	13,087	317
Missaukee	1,306	2,585	69
Monroe	14,811	16,865	199
Montcalm	5,863	8,036	114
Montmorency	997	1,556	11
Muskegon	21,948	21,519	288
Newaygo	4,120	6,902	89
Oakland	153,429	172,462	2,848
Oceana	2,794	3,933	60
Ogemaw	2,981	2,824	86
Ontonagon	1,687	1,699	19
Osceola	2,299	3,436	39
Oscoda	839	1,361	37
Otsego	2,400	3,241	62
Ottawa	15,888	43,993	338
Presque Isle	2,168	2,328	50
Roscommon	3,478	3,891	53
Saginaw	36,036	29,130	681
St. Clair	15,757	22,858	558
St. Joseph	5,404	8,661	87
Sanilac	4,732	7,778	55
Schoolcraft	1,786	1,332	10
Shiawassee	10,751	10,473	174
Tuscola	7,046	8,118	104
Van Buren	7,230	9,827	143
Washtenaw	43,934	32,942	913
Wayne	308,902	175,344	5,098
Wexford	3,577	4,327	46
Totals	1,258,539	1,276,134	28,091

COUNTY VOTE FOR GOVERNOR - 1990

BLANHARD - DEM

ENGLER - REP

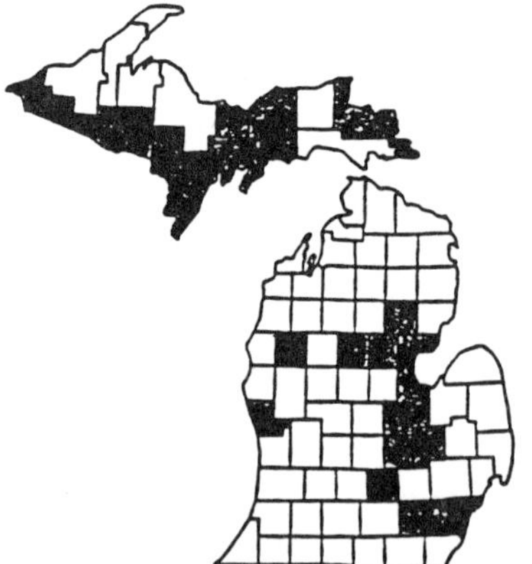

COUNTY VOTE FOR GOVERNOR - 1994

Wolpe - Dem

O Engler - Rep

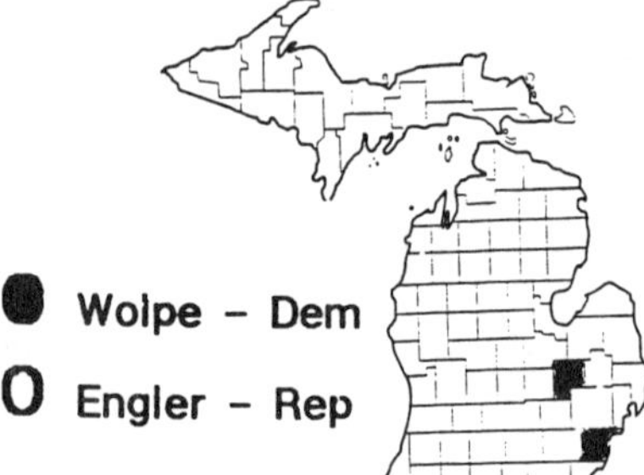

VOTE FOR SECRETARY OF STATE, BY COUNTY

November 8, 1994, Term: 1995-1998

Source: Secretary of State
Official

COUNTY	Richard Austin DEM	Candice Miller REP
ALCONA	1,713	2,492
ALGER	1,762	1,537
ALLEGAN	9,295	19,712
ALPENA	4,906	5,594
ANTRIM	3,282	4,493
ARENAC	2,578	2,448
BARAGA	1,332	1,367
BARRY	6,272	11,324
BAY	21,521	16,991
BENZIE	2,315	2,822
BERRIEN	14,357	28,375
BRANCH	4,170	7,458
CALHOUN	17,963	23,324
CASS	4,600	7,729
CHARLEVOIX	3,904	4,962
CHEBOYGAN	3,673	4,400
CHIPPEWA	5,596	4,699
CLARE	4,262	4,451
CLINTON	9,437	14,021
CRAWFORD	1,918	2,467
DELTA	7,656	5,685
DICKINSON	4,792	4,568
EATON	15,862	21,419
EMMET	4,497	6,162
GENESEE	84,350	62,531
GLADWIN	3,904	3,928
GOGEBIC	3,892	2,281
GD. TRAVERSE	10,586	16,068
GRATIOT	4,553	6,630
HILLSDALE	4,137	7,852
HOUGHTON	5,010	5,926
HURON	4,359	7,710
INGHAM	49,693	45,913
IONIA	6,452	9,900
IOSCO	4,986	5,097
IRON	2,793	2,332
ISABELLA	7,045	8,198
JACKSON	18,181	27,545
KALAMAZOO	30,681	41,523
KALKASKA	2,045	2,528
KENT	56,651	105,368
KEWEENAW	450	526
LAKE	1,734	1,544
LAPEER	10,337	15,540
LEELANAU	3,239	4,983
LENAWEE	10,822	16,034
LIVINGSTON	15,688	30,616
LUCE	953	939
MACKINAC	2,323	2,360
MACOMB	95,254	148,553
MANISTEE	3,670	4,422
MARQUETTE	11,639	9,169
MASON	4,392	5,805
MECOSTA	4,529	5,533
MENOMINEE	3,548	3,741
MIDLAND	11,864	16,841
MISSAUKEE	1,758	3,041
MONROE	16,279	21,348
MONTCALM	5,949	9,246
MONTMORENCY	1,514	2,044
MUSKEGON	22,268	25,055
NEWAYGO	5,105	7,767
OAKLAND	159,016	243,195
OCEANA	3,023	4,251
OGEMAW	3,377	3,259
ONTONAGON	1,758	1,613
OSCEOLA	2,904	4,084
OSCODA	1,330	1,604
OTSEGO	2,970	3,933
OTTAWA	17,384	52,789
PRESQUE ISLE	2,508	2,944
ROSCOMMON	4,399	4,971
SAGINAW	36,793	35,687
ST. CLAIR	18,545	29,588
ST. JOSEPH	5,135	9,545
SANILAC	4,510	9,240
SCHOOLCRAFT	1,545	1,289
SHIAWASSEE	11,853	12,433
TUSCOLA	7,314	10,063
VAN BUREN	7,437	12,357
WASHTENAW	49,467	42,574
WAYNE	381,357	238,711
WEXFORD	3,944	5,331
TOTALS	1,416,865	1,634,398

VOTE FOR ATTORNEY GENERAL, BY COUNTY

November 8, 1994, Term: 1995-1998

Source: Secretary of State
Official

COUNTY	Frank Kelley DEM	John Smietanka REP
01 ALCONA	2,312	1,870
02 ALGER	2,006	1,272
03 ALLEGAN	11,182	17,417
04 ALPENA	6,539	4,045
05 ANTRIM	3,602	4,059
06 ARENAC	3,074	1,868
07 BARAGA	1,483	1,195
08 BARRY	7,445	9,910
09 BAY	24,951	12,942
10 BENZIE	2,547	2,514
11 BERRIEN	13,863	28,685
12 BRANCH	4,907	6,400
13 CALHOUN	21,729	18,565
14 CASS	4,940	7,169
15 CHARLEVOIX	4,442	4,345
16 CHEBOYGAN	4,098	3,901
17 CHIPPEWA	5,918	4,234
18 CLARE	4,682	3,975
19 CLINTON	11,507	11,760
20 CRAWFORD	2,072	2,291
21 DELTA	8,824	4,366
22 DICKINSON	5,536	3,501
23 EATON	18,750	17,909
24 EMMET	5,483	5,116
25 GENESEE	100,437	45,753
26 GLADWIN	4,540	3,224
27 GOGEBIC	4,180	1,953
28 GD. TRAVERSE	12,395	13,876
29 GRATIOT	5,253	5,741
30 HILLSDALE	4,941	6,837
31 HOUGHTON	5,812	5,042
32 HURON	6,161	5,646
33 INGHAM	55,710	36,854
34 IONIA	7,484	8,612
35 IOSCO	6,145	3,828
36 IRON	3,327	1,768
37 ISABELLA	7,613	6,943
38 JACKSON	22,578	22,638
39 KALAMAZOO	35,855	35,465
40 KALKASKA	2,248	2,248
41 KENT	93,827	64,664
42 KEWEENAW	415	556
43 LAKE	1,441	1,685
44 LAPEER	13,294	11,579
45 LEELANAU	3,872	4,259
46 LENAWEE	14,412	11,775
47 LIVINGSTON	22,862	22,988
48 LUCE	1,046	806
49 MACKINAC	2,528	2,052
50 MACOMB	134,125	101,122
51 MANISTEE	3,870	4,106
52 MARQUETTE	13,400	7,307
53 MASON	4,561	5,229
54 MECOSTA	4,833	5,158
55 MENOMINEE	4,045	3,062
56 MIDLAND	13,056	14,554
57 MISSAUKEE	2,031	2,737
58 MONROE	20,855	16,218
59 MONTCALM	6,698	8,257
60 MONTMORENCY	1,788	1,718
61 MUSKEGON	27,205	19,271
62 NEWAYGO	5,550	7,145
63 OAKLAND	216,173	180,145
64 OCEANA	3,374	3,754
65 OGEMAW	4,090	2,484
66 ONTONAGON	1,960	1,364
67 OSCEOLA	2,961	3,897
68 OSCODA	1,515	1,403
69 OTSEGO	3,228	3,586
70 OTTAWA	22,725	47,047
71 PRESQUE ISLE	3,059	2,414
72 ROSCOMMON	4,939	4,327
73 SAGINAW	45,952	25,744
74 ST. CLAIR	18,152	19,404
75 ST. JOSEPH	5,862	8,550
76 SANILAC	6,147	7,375
77 SCHOOLCRAFT	1,767	1,039
78 SHIAWASSEE	13,866	10,167
79 TUSCOLA	9,098	8,035
80 VAN BUREN	8,064	10,961
81 WASHTENAW	59,455	31,280
82 WAYNE	447,590	164,516
83 WEXFORD	4,497	4,685
TOTALS	1,717,591	1,273,330

VOTE FOR U. S. SENATOR, BY COUNTY

November 8, 1994, Term: 1995-1998

Source: Secretary of State
Official

COUNTY NAME	Bob Carr DEM	Spencer Abraham REP
ALCONA	1,394	2,706
ALGER	1,471	1,676
ALLEGAN	7,789	20,117
ALPENA	4,233	6,047
ANTRIM	2,421	4,797
ARENAC	2,214	2,587
BARAGA	1,155	1,371
BARRY	5,456	11,538
BAY	19,647	17,696
BENZIE	1,856	2,974
BERRIEN	12,822	28,815
BRANCH	3,661	7,513
CALHOUN	16,417	22,639
CASS	4,019	7,945
CHARLEVOIX	3,149	5,156
CHEBOYGAN	2,990	4,619
CHIPPEWA	4,373	5,368
CLARE	3,706	4,552
CLINTON	7,860	13,926
CRAWFORD	1,577	2,432
DELTA	6,424	5,992
DICKINSON	3,935	4,940
EATON	13,186	21,390
EMMET	3,358	6,632
GENESEE	83,847	57,474
GLADWIN	3,283	4,273
GOGEBIC	3,530	2,388
GD. TRAVERSE	8,131	16,612
GRATIOT	3,888	6,795
HILLSDALE	3,220	8,304
HOUGHTON	4,382	5,905
HURON	4,106	7,455
INGHAM	46,378	43,905
IONIA	5,385	10,213
IOSCO	4,014	5,639
IRON	2,427	2,416
ISABELLA	6,300	8,191
JACKSON	16,348	26,650
KALAMAZOO	28,456	40,564
KALKASKA	1,582	2,667
KENT	46,941	107,802
KEWEENAW	431	489
LAKE	1,508	1,549
LAPEER	8,670	15,299
LEELANAU	2,670	5,122
LENAWEE	10,116	15,489
LIVINGSTON	13,510	29,360
LUCE	720	1,068
MACKINAC	1,775	2,571
MACOMB	86,760	136,728
MANISTEE	3,220	4,443
MARQUETTE	10,594	9,376
MASON	3,643	6,023
MECOSTA	3,665	5,854
MENOMINEE	3,049	3,903
MIDLAND	10,345	17,305
MISSAUKEE	1,287	3,177
MONROE	15,293	20,857
MONTCALM	5,044	9,624
MONTMORENCY	1,207	2,180
MUSKEGON	21,273	24,658
NEWAYGO	4,039	8,332
OAKLAND	151,144	223,129
OCEANA	2,485	4,523
OGEMAW	2,914	3,484
ONTONAGON	1,520	1,653
OSCEOLA	2,292	4,294
OSCODA	991	1,802
OTSEGO	2,286	4,202
OTTAWA	13,931	53,857
PRESQUE ISLE	2,172	3,061
ROSCOMMON	3,848	5,086
SAGINAW	34,432	34,373
ST. CLAIR	16,889	27,303
ST. JOSEPH	4,265	9,982
SANILAC	4,193	8,914
SCHOOLCRAFT	1,273	1,321
SHIAWASSEE	9,495	13,118
TUSCOLA	6,552	10,145
VAN BUREN	6,758	12,193
WASHTENAW	44,605	42,659
WAYNE	369,543	214,117
WEXFORD	3,222	5,466
TOTALS	1,300,960	1,578,770

STATE ELECTION RESULTS

Nov. 8, 1994 Official

Source: Secretary of State

Winners in **bold.** Third party candidates are included when their vote exceeded the winner's plurality.

GOVERNOR	RESIDENCE	VOTE
Howard Wolpe (0)	East Lansing	1,188,438
John Engler (R)	**Mt Pleasant**	**1,899,101**

SECRETARY of STATE		
Richard Austin (D)	Detroit	1,416,865
Candice Miller (R)	**Harrison Twp.**	**1,634,398**

ATTORNEY GENERAL		
Frank Kelley (D)	**Okemos**	**1,727,992**
John Smietanka (R)	Ada	1,273,330

U.S. SENATOR		
Bob Carr (D)	E. Lansing	1,300,960
Spencer Abraham (R)	**Auburn Hills**	**1,578,770**

STATE BOARD OF EDUCATION		
Gumenecindo Sales (D)	E. Lansing	1,068,662
Carol Thomas (D)	Southfield	1,281,265
Clark Durant (R)	**Grosse Pointe**	**1,336,385**
Sharon Wise (R)	**Owosso**	**1,401,738**
Erwin Has (LIB)	Grand Rapids	87,860
David Raaflaub (LIB)	Ann Arbor	57,049
Selina Babcock (NLP)	Farmington Hills	56,338

STATE ELECTION RETURNS

Nov 8, 1994 Pre Official

SUPREME COURT

Conrad L. Mallett Jr., Detroit* 1,088,382
Elizabeth A. Weaver, Glen Arbor .. 982,558
Richard Griffin, Traverse City 957,853
Donald E. Shelton, Saline 593,974
George F. Killeen, Flint 450,009

BALLOT PROPOSALS

PROPOSAL A

General revision of the state constitution

Yes 775,587
No 1,998,663

PROPOSAL B

Limit appeals by criminal defendants who pleads guilty or no contest

Yes 2,104,038
No 771,883

PROPOSAL C

Amendment to auto insurance laws

Yes 1,161,035
No 1,805,629

PROPOSAL P

Establish a state parks endowment fund

Yes 1,986,732
No 804,935

CONGRESS

1ST DISTRICT

Bart Stupak, D-Menominee* 120,838
Gil Ziegler, R-Williamsburg 89,295
Michael McPeak,N-DeWitt 2,401

2ND DISTRICT

Peter Hoekstra, R-Holland* 145,368
Marcus Hoover, D-Copemish 46,069
Lu Wiggins, N-Grand Rapids 1,880

3RD DISTRICT

Vernon J. Ehlers, R-Gr. Rapids* .. 135,819
Betsy J. Flory, D-Grand Rapids 43,485
Barrie Leslie Konicov, L-Alto 2,958
Susan H. Normandin, N-Grand Rapids 1,814

4TH DISTRICT

Dave Camp, R-Midland* 142,623
Damion Frasier, D-Owosso 49,407
Michael Lee, N-Trufant 2,705

5TH DISTRICT

James A. Barcia, D-Bay City* 126,519
William T. Anderson, R-Auburn 61,385
Larry Fairchild, I-Frankenmuth 3,017
Susan Arnold, N-Ann Arbor 2,321

6TH DISTRICT

Fred Upton, R-St. Joseph* 121,925
David Taylor, D-Edwardsburg 42,373
E.A. Berker, N-Portage 1,694

7TH DISTRICT

Nick Smith, R-Addison* 113,721
Kim McCaughtry, D-Tecumseh 57,393
Kenneth L. Proctor, L-Charlotte 3,313
Scott K. Williamson, N-Battle Creek .. 1,221

8TH DISTRICT

Dick Chrysler, R-Brighton 109,663
Bob Mitchell, D-Okemos 95,383
Gerald Ralph Turcotte Jr., L-Holly 4,348
Susan Ilene McPeak, N-DeWitt 3,076

9TH DISTRICT

Dale Kildee, D-Flint* 97,024
Megan O'Neill, R-Clarkston 89,091
Karen Blasdell, N-Grand Rapids 3,236

10TH DISTRICT

David Bonior, D-Mt. Clemens* 121,516
Donald Lobsinger, R-St. Clair Shores 73,671

11TH DISTRICT

Joe Knollenberg, R-Bloom. Hills* 155,158
Mike Breshgold, D-Farmington Hills . 69,337
John R. Hocking, N-West Bloomfield Twp. .. 2,940

12TH DISTRICT

Sander Levin, D-Royal Oak* 103,420
John Pappageorge, R-Troy 92,625
Eric R. Anderson, N-Fairfield 1,476
Jerome White, I-Southfield 1,384

13TH DISTRICT

Lynn Rivers, D-Ann Arbor 87,445
John Schall, R-Ann Arbor 75,889
Craig L. Seymour, L-Wayne 3,137
Helen Halyard, I-Detroit 1,329
Gail Anne Petrosoff, N-Battle Creek 591

14TH DISTRICT

John Conyers Jr., D-Detroit* 129,850
Richard Charles Fournier, R-Detroit 26,417
Richard R. Miller, N-Utica 2,967

15TH DISTRICT

Barbara-Rose Collins, D-Detroit* 119,328
John W. Savage II, R-Detroit 20,039
Cynthia M. Jaquith, I-Detroit 986
Henry Ogden Clark, N-Traverse City 849
Larry Roberts, I-Southfield 651

16TH DISTRICT

John Dingell, D-Dearborn* 105,301
Ken Larkin, R-Lincoln Park 70,429
Noha F. Hamze, N-Utica 1,962

MICHIGAN SENATE

1ST DISTRICT

Joe Young Jr., D-Detroit 39,179
Peter Ecklund Jr., R-Gros. Pte. Park 26,566

2ND DISTRICT

Virgil C. Smith Jr., D-Detroit* 47,442
Carolyn Smith, R-Detroit 6,247

3RD DISTRICT

Henry Edward Stallings II, D-Detroit 45,747
Carole Cromwell, R-Detroit 3,884
Stephen O. McCoy, I-Detroit 943

4TH DISTRICT

Jackie Vaughn III D-Detroit* 62,910
Eunice M. Myles, R-Detroit 2,880

5TH DISTRICT

Michael O'Brien, D-Detroit* 52,007
Tondria M. Canty, R-Detroit 5,190

6TH DISTRICT

George Z. Hart, D-Dearborn* 43,947
Nancy Hubbard, R-Dearborn 39,576

7TH DISTRICT

Christopher D. Dingell, D-Ecorse* .. 40,458
Bob Keller, R-Trenton 24,918

8TH DISTRICT

Loren N. Bennett, R-Canton 30,799
Charles Griffin, D-Westland 28,953

9TH DISTRICT

Robert Geake, R-Northville* 59,463
Patrick O'Neil, D-Livonia 30,376

10TH DISTRICT

Arthur J. Miller Jr. D-Warren* 42,421
Mary R. Giordano, R-Warren 28,861

11TH DISTRICT

Kenneth DeBeaussaert, D-New Balt. 42,275
Gilbert DiNello, R-Clinton Twp.* 37,075

12TH DISTRICT

Douglas Carl, R-Mt Clemens* 56,492
Morton Kripke, D-Washington 23,977

13TH DISTRICT

Michael Bouchard, R-Birmingham* 59,451
Robert Boyd, D-Huntington Woods . 28,779
Henry Freriks, L-Royal Oak 2,137

14TH DISTRICT

Gary Peters, D-Pontiac 48,283
Michael David Warren Jr., R-Southfield 33,721
Richard Gach, L-Bloomfield Hills 1,883
Stuart J. Goldberg, N-Southfield 1,423

15TH DISTRICT

Dave Honigman, R-W. Bloomfield* 65,800
Vicki Barnett, D-Farmington Hills 32,553
David S. Thompson, L-Farm. Hills 3,747

16TH DISTRICT

Mat Dunaskiss, R-Lake Orion* 63,812
Kevin F. Kelly, D-Lake Orion 25,427
Leslie C. Balian, L-Leonard 4,680

17TH DISTRICT

Jim Berryman, D-Adrian* 37,681
Sharon Miller, R-Newport 34,032

18TH DISTRICT

Alma Wheeler Smith, D-South Lyon 46,715
Joseph Mikulec, R-Ypsilanti 35,586

19TH DISTRICT

Philip E. Hoffman, R-Horton* 46,699
Bob Clark, D-Hanover 18,245
Nicholas G. Bennett, L-Horton II 1,620

20TH DISTRICT

Harry Gast, R-St. Joseph* 46,674
John M. Brademas, D-Niles 19,815

21ST DISTRICT

Dale Shugars, R-Portage 42,171
Kristin Carambula, D-Portage 30,383
Nancy Brancheau, N-Portage 833

22ND DISTRICT

William VanRegenmorter, R-Hudson* 61,718
Jose R. Blanco, D-Shelbyville 18,173

23RD DISTRICT

Joanne Emmons, R-Big Rapids* ... 49,119
Scott Manning, D-Six Lakes 22,521

24TH DISTRICT

John Schwarz, R-Battle Creek* 54,194
Violet Hinton, D-Battle Creek 28,743

25TH DISTRICT

Dianne Byrum, D-Lansing 54,646
Marie Elena Martell, R-East Lansing 32,012

26TH DISTRICT

Mike Rogers, R-Howell 58,055
Mike Hatty, D-Brighton 32,251

27TH DISTRICT

Dan DeGrow, R-Port Huron* 56,815
Ron Stablein, D-St. Clair 28,813

28TH DISTRICT

John D. Cherry Jr., D-Clio* 46,741
Dominick Vincentini, R-Oxford 29,071

29TH DISTRICT

Joe Conroy, D-Flint* 57,263
Jeff Goodrich, R-Swartz Creek 23,933

30TH DISTRICT

Glen Steil, R-Grand Rapids 43,760
David Doyle, D-Grand Rapids 30,613
Steve Butler, L-Grand Rapids 1,165
Constantine Katsoris, N-Grand Rapids 852

31ST DISTRICT

Dick Posthumus, R-Alto* 65,719
Donald T. Reid, D-Wyoming 17,604

32ND DISTRICT

Leon Stille, R-Spring Lake 48,065
Julia Dennis, D-Spring Lake 32,341

33RD DISTRICT

Jon Cisky, R-Saginaw* 48,646
Rose Aquilina, D-Saginaw 34,764

34TH DISTRICT

Joel D. Gougeon, R-Bay City* 48,743
W. Dennis Hayes, D-Bay City 30,585

35TH DISTRICT

96% of precincts reporting

Bill Schuette, R-Midland 58,220
Rosemary Ax, D-Midland 22,605

36TH DISTRICT

George A. McManus, R-Trav. City* 65,241
Joel Caster, D-Traverse City 26,793

37TH DISTRICT

Walter North, R-St. Ignace 53,940
Mike McElroy, D-Cross Village 31,547

38TH DISTRICT

Don Koivisto, D-Ironwood* 55,830
Charles E. Best, R-Ironwood 22,710

MICHIGAN HOUSE

1ST DISTRICT

William Bryant, R-G.P. Farms* 24,003
Kerry Baltinger, D-Detroit 10,471

2ND DISTRICT

Curtis Hertel, D-Detroit* 15,202
Robert L. Ridley, R-Detroit 2,082

3RD DISTRICT

Mary Lou Parks, D-Detroit* 17,890
Donald D. Campbell, R-Detroit 1,061
William G. Tinsley, I-Detroit 382
Joann M. Karpinski, L-Detroit 185
Jasper Young, I-Detroit 113

4TH DISTRICT

Ed Vaughn, D-Detroit *..................... 18,048
Dovie Pickett, R-Detroit 721
Durk L. Barton, W-Detroit 183

5TH DISTRICT

Ted Wallace, D-Detroit* 17,399
Gladys L. Smith, R-Detroit 1,855

6TH DISTRICT

Martha G. Scott, D-Highland Park . 15,891
Raymond F. Prus, R-Hamtramck 1,961

7TH DISTRICT

Raymond Murphy, D-Detroit* 19,086
John Scarberry, R-Detroit 812
Joyce A. Erickson, W-Detroit 310
Scott Avery Boman, L-Detroit 233

8TH DISTRICT

Ilona Varga, D-Detroit* 11,827
Sandra K. Wallace, R-Detroit 1,559

9TH DISTRICT

Carolyn Cheeks Kilpatrick, D-Detroit* 18,989
Christopher Flournoy, R-Detroit 793
Gertrude Cook, W-Detroit 214

10TH DISTRICT

Nelson W. Saunders, D-Detroit* 26,243
Alice Graves, R-Detroit 1,148

11TH DISTRICT

Morris Hood Jr., D-Detroit* 20,612
Conley S. Worsham, R-Detroit 1,945

12TH DISTRICT

Alma Stallworth, D-Detroit* 26,024
Bill Ashe, R-Detroit 1,334

13TH DISTRICT

Burton Leland, D-Detroit* 17,124
Tony Spearman-Leach, R-Detroit 1,613

14TH DISTRICT

Michael J. Bennane, D-Detroit* 16,574
Joyce James, R-Detroit 1,861

15TH DISTRICT

Agnes Dobronski, D-Dearborn* 17,807
Douglas B. Thomas, R-Dearborn 14,657
Ted Tifrea, L-Dearborn 1,263

16TH DISTRICT

James R. Ryan, R-Redford 18,416
Kevin Kelley, D-Redford 16,073

17TH DISTRICT

Thomas Kelly, D-Wayne* 14,264
Edward F. Juarez, R-Garden City 6,821
Alex Stevenson, L-Inkster 449
William K. Lowry, I-Garden City 188

18TH DISTRICT

Eileen DeHart, D-Westland 9,365
Michael Novak, R-Westland 8,865

19TH DISTRICT

Lyn Bankes, R-Redford* 18,617
Elaine Miller, D-Livonia 12,172
John J. Tatar, L-Livonia 1,123

20TH DISTRICT

Gerald Law, R-Plymouth 25,320
Carolyn A. Blanchard, D-Northville .. 12,402

21ST DISTRICT

Deborah Whyman, R-Canton 15,909
Donna F. Clark, D-Belleville 10,016

22ND DISTRICT

Gregory E. Pitoniak, D-Taylor* 12,371
Joseph D. Slaven, R-Taylor 7,078

23RD DISTRICT

Vincent Joe Porreca, D-Trenton* .. 17,772
Walter Barron, R-Flat Rock 11,656

24TH DISTRICT

Joseph Palamara, D-Wyandotte* 18,269
Raymond Krutsch, R-Southgate 7,853

25TH DISTRICT

Robert A. DeMars, D-Lincoln Park* 15,333
Gary R. Fisher, R-Lincoln Park 10,132

26TH DISTRICT

Tracey A. Yokich, D-St. Cl. Shores* 17,100
Tom Ulrich, R-St. Clair Shores 14,743
Keith P. Edwards, L-St. Clair Shores 626
Beverley K. Bloedel, W-St. Cl. Shores .. 248

27TH DISTRICT

Nick Ciaramitaro, D-Roseville* 17,658
Hugh Hodges, R-Eastpointe 7,946
Mathew Robert Ignash, L-Roseville 1,033

28TH DISTRICT

Lloyd Weeks, D-Warren* 15,061
Dan Nixon, R-Warren 8,164

29TH DISTRICT

Dennis Olshove, D-Warren* 19,656
Michael Wiecek, R-Warren 14,565
Paul Soyk, L-Sterling Hts. 443

30TH DISTRICT

Sue Rocca, R-Sterling Hts. 16,947
Cynthia Wowk, D-Sterling Hts........... 11,504

31ST DISTRICT

Sharon L. Gire, D-Clinton Twp.*..... 14,663
James Tignanelli, R-Fraser 11,820
John W. Fagan, L-Fraser 749

32ND DISTRICT

Dave Jaye, R-Washington Twp.* ... 17,613
Dick Kennedy, D-Shelby Twp............ 12,848
Bob Van Oast, L-Richmond 1,239

33RD DISTRICT

Alvin Kukuk, R-Macomb Twp.* 17,379
Gina L. Bertolini, D-Macomb Twp. ... 11,830
Jim Boyle, L-Mt. Clemens 1,079

34TH DISTRICT

John F. Freeman, D-Madison Hts.* 14,756
Kathryn R. Kling, R-Madison Hts. 8,096
Mary Wayfield, L-Madison Hts. 797

35TH DISTRICT

David Gubow, D-Hunt. Woods* 19,569
John T. Fillicaro, R-Hunt. Woods 8,253

36TH DISTRICT

Maxine Berman, D-Southfield* 22,244
Calvin X. Williams Jr., R-Southfield 6,053

37TH DISTRICT

Jan Dolan, R-Farmington Hills* 23,350
Richard M. Dailey, D-Farmington 9,390
Yepram DerVahanian, L-Farm. Hills 978

38TH DISTRICT

Willis J. Bullard Jr., R-Milford* 20,782
Bob Havey, D-Wixom 7,573

39TH DISTRICT

Barbara Dobb, R-Commerce Twp.* 22,737
Daniel J. Cherrin, D-W. Bloom. Twp. 12,152

40TH DISTRICT

John Jamian, R-Bloomfield Hills* .. 28,585
Joe Patt, D-Bloomfield Twp. 11,692

41ST DISTRICT

Shirley Johnson, R-Royal Oak* 22,226
Edward T. Hamilton, D-Troy 7,921

42ND DISTRICT

Greg Kaza, R-Rochester* 21,006
Jon Buller, D-Rochester Hills 7,642

43RD DISTRICT

Hubert Price Jr., D-Pontiac* 11,906
John J. Demers, R-Auburn Hills 5,682

44TH DISTRICT

David N. Galloway, R-White Lake* 20,141
George Montgomery, D-Waterford Twp....... 9,932

45TH DISTRICT

Penny M. Crissman, R-Rochester* 24,106
Paul D. Sweda, D-Rochester Hills 6,281
Kay Barr Suri, L-Oakland 794

46TH DISTRICT

Tom Middleton, R-Ortonville* 21,749
Steve Allen, D-Ortonville 8,385

47TH DISTRICT

Sandra J. Hill, R-Montrose* 16,207
Rose Bogardus, D-Davison 16,137

48TH DISTRICT

86% of precincts reporting

Floyd Clack, D-Flint* 20,765
John C. Callahan, R-Flushing 2,810

49TH DISTRICT

Robert L. Emerson, D-Flint* 17,908
Lawrence Romanowski, R-Flint 5,492

50TH DISTRICT

Deborah Cherry, D-Burton 16,082
Bruce Rider, R-Grand Blanc 14,331

51ST DISTRICT

Candace A. Curtis, D-Swartz Creek* 17,546
David B. Robertson, R-Swartz Creek 15,967

52ND DISTRICT

Mary Schroer, D-Ann Arbor* 17,519
Martin Straub, R-Chelsea 14,001
James Lewis Hudler, L-Chelsea 620

53RD DISTRICT

Elizabeth Brater, D-Ann Arbor 13,941
Renee Birnbaum, R-Ann Arbor 10,627

54TH DISTRICT

Kirk A. Profit, D-Ypsilanti 14,781

55TH DISTRICT

Beverly S. Hammerstrom, R-Temperance 18,048
Herbert S. Moyer, D-Temperance 8,069

56TH DISTRICT

Lynn Owen, D-Newport* 12,208
Dan Maletich, R-Monroe 11,071

57TH DISTRICT

Tim Walberg, R-Tipton* 16,942
Cindy Helinski, D-Adrian 9,238

58TH DISTRICT

Michael E. Nye, R-Litchfield* 18,302
Iva Heim, D-Coldwater 4,722

59TH DISTRICT
District 59

District 59
Glenn Oxender, R-Sturgis* 16,881
Burke H. Webb, D-Marcellus 5,304

60TH DISTRICT

Edward LaForge, D-Kalamazoo 11,149
Jacqueline Morrison, R-Kalamazoo ... 9,520

61ST DISTRICT

Charles Perricone, R-Kalamazoo ... 20,141
Betsy Rice, D-Mattawan 12,909

62ND DISTRICT

Eric Bush, R-Battle Creek 14,397
Ron Amy, D-Battle Creek 11,113

63RD DISTRICT

Donald Gilmer, R-Augusta* 18,750
Jerry Johnson, D-Tekonsha 9,332

64TH DISTRICT

Michael J. Griffin, D-Jackson* 12,192
Kathy Schmaltz, R-Jackson 9,365
Tom Slaughter, L-Jackson 312

65TH DISTRICT

Clyde LeTarte, R-Horton 16,220
John J. Riggs, D-Clark Lake 9,090

66TH DISTRICT

Susan Grimes Munsell, R-Howell* . 23,755
Donald C. Coveny, D-Howell 8,371

67TH DISTRICT

Dan Gustafson, R-Williamston* 21,235
Winifred Motherwell, D-Haslett 8,479

68TH DISTRICT

Lingg Brewer, D-Holt 15,114
Linda Ploeg, R-Holt 12,364

69TH DISTRICT

Lynne Martinez, D-Lansing 14,740
Jeff Brenner, R-Lansing 7,716

70TH DISTRICT

Laura Baird, D-Okemos 14,019
David Rizor, R-East Lansing 10,688

71ST DISTRICT

Frank M. Fitzgerald, R-Grand Ledge* 21,525
Art Luna, D-Charlotte 12,085

72ND DISTRICT

Walter J. DeLange, R-Gr. Rapids* . 25,311
Al Rice, D-Caledonia 7,315

73RD DISTRICT

Jack Horton, R-Belmont* 25,302
Cliff Worden, D-Grand Rapids 9,317

74TH DISTRICT

Ken Sikkema, R-Grandville* 22,913
John Sobotta, D-Grand Rapids 6,422

75TH DISTRICT

William Byl, R-Grand Rapids 17,457
Linda Pugh Steimel, D-Gnd. Rapids .. 8,651
Jim Lundy, L-Grand Rapids 680

76TH DISTRICT

Thomas Mathieu, D-Grand Rapids* 14,103
Steve Johnson, R-Grand Rapids 7,599
Dan Marsh, L-Grand Rapids 839

77TH DISTRICT

Harold Voorhes, R-Grandville* 10,215
Douglas G. Hyman, D-Wyoming 4,533

78TH DISTRICT

Carl F. Gnodtke, R-Sawyer* 13,338
Marti Wegner, D-Niles 8,033

79TH DISTRICT

Bob Brackenridge, R-St. Joseph* . 14,482
Helen McKenzie, D-Benton Harbor 6,674
Scott Beavers, L-Benton Harbor 364

80TH DISTRICT

James M. Middaugh, R-Paw Paw* . 17,000
MaDonna Childs Martin, D-Hartford .. 7,107

81ST DISTRICT

Terry London, R-Marysville* 18,539
Howard T. Heidemann, D-North Street 11,074

82ND DISTRICT

Karen Willard, D-Algonac* 14,864
Jud Gilbert II, R-Algonac 14,435

83RD DISTRICT

Kim A. Rhead, R-Sandusky* 19,165
Bob Dillon, D-Fostoria 7,923

84TH DISTRICT

Mike Green, R-Mayville 17,260
Russell Davis, D-Vassar 11,654

85TH DISTRICT

Clark A. Harder, D-Owosso* 14,008
Mike Dvorak, R-Owosso 13,207

86TH DISTRICT

Alan L. Cropsey, R-DeWitt* 18,552
Martin Lankford, D-Portland 10,482

87TH DISTRICT

Terry Geiger, R-Lake Odessa 15,848
Bob Edwards, D-Hastings 7,909

88TH DISTRICT

Paul C. Hillegonds, D-Holland* 21,472
W.T. Delp, D-Wayland 5,315
Thomas Houseman, I-Holland 1,648

89TH DISTRICT

Jon Jellema, R-Grand Haven 15,518
Albert Dallas, D-Nunica 4,237

90TH DISTRICT

Jessie Dalman, R-Holland* 26,916
Cynthia Sloan, D-Hudsonville 5,087

91ST DISTRICT

Paul Baade, D-Muskegon* 16,313
Richard Bray, R-Muskegon 10,388

92ND DISTRICT

James G. Agee, D-Muskegon* 13,391
Eric J. Strattan, R-Muskegon 6,905

93RD DISTRICT

Gary L. Randall, R-Elwell* 17,349
John L. Willard, D-Edmore 7,163

94TH DISTRICT

Michael J. Goschka, R-Brant* 19,423
Jerrold Humpula, D-Chesaning 9,980

95TH DISTRICT

Michael Hanley, D-Saginaw 14,328
Richard Haines, R-Saginaw 4,034

96TH DISTRICT

Roland J. Jersevic, R-Saginaw* 17,284
Sue Kaltenbach, D-Saginaw 15,550

97TH DISTRICT

Howard Wetters, D-Kawkawlin 17,893
Carl Smith Jr., R-Bay City 7,909

98TH DISTRICT

James McNutt, R-Midland* 19,364
Karen Sherwood, D-Midland 9,063

99TH DISTRICT

James McBryde, R-Mt. Pleasant* ... 11,940
Kathleen Ling, D-Mt. Pleasant 7,953

100TH DISTRICT

John Llewellyn, R-Fremont* 17,964
Thomas Rundquist, D-Big Rapids 7,561

101ST DISTRICT

Bill Bobier, R-Hesperia* 21,910
Ronald Wandrych, D-Manistee 7,790

102ND DISTRICT

John Gernaat, R-McBain* 21,509
Rodney Parker Sr., D-Lake City 7,786

103RD DISTRICT

Tom Alley, D-West Branch* 19,897
Mary Ellen Good, R-Prescott 10,278

104TH DISTRICT

Michelle McManus, R-Lake Leelanau* 21,181
Geraldine D. Greene, D-Trav. City ... 13,990

105TH DISTRICT

Allen Lowe, R-Grayling* 22,952
Kathy Tripp, D-Gaylord 10,773

106TH DISTRICT

Beverly Bodem, R-Alpena* 19,411
G.T. Long, D-Boyne City 13,914

107TH DISTRICT

Patrick M. Gagliardi, D-Drum. Island* 17,478
Shannon Brower, R-Petoskey 12,892

108TH DISTRICT

David Anthony, D-Escanaba* 16,377
Laurie Bink, R-Iron Mountain 15,178

109TH DISTRICT

Dominic Jacobetti, D-Negaunee* .. 17,081
Terry Tato, Negaunee 7,436

110TH DISTRICT

Paul Tesanovich, R-L'Anse* 16,354
Stephen Dresch, D-Hancock 13,888

UNIVERSITY OF MICHIGAN REGENTS

Andrea Fischer, R-Birmingham ..1,395,740
Dan Horning, R-Grand Haven 1,242,962
Paul Brown, D-Mack. Island* 1,170,224
James L. Waters, D-Muskegon* ...1,104,236
Emily H. Salvette, L-Ann Arbor 103,736
Gary R. Bradley, L-St. Johns 85,975
Kevin Carey, W-Detroit 40,797
William B. Quarton, N-Ann Arbor 31,130

MICHIGAN STATE UNIVERSITY TRUSTEES

Donald Nugent, R-Frankfort 1,302,293
Colleen McNamara, D-Lansing ...1,281,772
Paul Wartner, R-Portage 1,218,413
Joel Ferguson, D-Lansing* 1,150,222
Mary J. Ruwart, L-Kalamazoo 96,687
Benjamin Bachrach, L-Dearborn 82,688
Kristen Hamel, W-Detroit 64,282

WAYNE STATE UNIVERSITY GOVERNORS

Diane Dunaskiss, R-Lake Orion ..1,385,164
Leon H. Atchison, D-Detroit* 1,168,497
Edward L. Haroutunian, R-Detroit .1,157,120
Alan Amen, D-Dearborn Hts. 1,130,135
Thomas W. Jones, L-Detroit 104,955
Brian Richard Wright, L-Farm. Hills ..102,169

VOTE FOR PRESIDENT BY COUNTY, 1992 AND 1988

County	1992 Clinton (D)	1992 Bush (R)	1992 Perot (I)	1988 Dukakis (D)	1988 Bush (R)
Alcona	2,390	2,247	1,117	1,918	2,966
Alger	2,144	1,471	941	2,210	1,830
Allegan	13,005	19,255	8,838	10,785	22,163
Alpena	6,894	4,878	3,236	6,341	6,664
Antrim	3,431	3,984	2,525	3,159	5,231
Arenac	3,278	2,330	1,608	3,211	3,064
Baraga	1,695	1,160	720	1,753	1,630
Barry	8,444	9,153	6,303	7,983	12,546
Bay	26,496	16,367	11,236	28,225	20,710
Benzie	2,715	2,438	1,619	2,437	3,240
Berrien	22,180	27,399	13,133	21,948	37,999
Branch	5,849	5,954	4,668	5,231	9,225
Calhoun	25,538	19,791	13,058	22,717	26,771
Cass	8,147	7,393	4,728	7,444	10,229
Charlevoix	4,063	4,017	3,360	3,875	5,802
Cheboygan	4,459	3,867	2,495	3,943	5,395
Chippewa	5,434	5,462	2,706	5,222	6,786
Clare	5,345	3,915	2,808	4,710	5,661
Clinton	10,116	12,216	7,877	9,225	15,497
Crawford	2,252	2,193	1,441	1,825	3,097
Delta	8,387	6,027	3,485	8,891	7,114
Dickinson	5,689	4,273	3,012	6,129	6,158
Eaton	16,524	18,385	12,136	15,322	24,193
Emmet	4,245	5,312	3,575	4,170	7,105
Genesee	104,794	47,524	46,043	104,880	70,922
Gladwin	4,457	3,616	2,649	4,164	4,746
Gogebic	4,792	2,838	1,543	5,151	3,509
Gr Traverse	11,148	13,629	9,495	10,098	17,191
Gratiot	5,681	6,279	3,866	5,719	8,447
Hillsdale	5,244	7,579	4,968	4,763	10,571
Houghton	6,558	5,575	2,906	6,510	7,098
Huron	6,023	6,491	4,064	5,714	9,419
Ingham	61,596	43,926	27,683	55,984	58,363
Ionia	8,430	9,136	6,211	8,160	12,028
Iosco	5,369	4,912	3,131	4,929	7,234
Iron	3,647	1,999	1,341	3,774	2,866
Isabella	8,773	7,706	5,434	7,960	10,362
Jackson	23,693	25,421	15,214	21,865	33,885
Kalamazoo	43,568	38,035	21,666	39,457	50,205
Kalkaska	2,196	2,068	1,853	2,092	3,369
Kent	83,219	125,628	44,028	73,467	131,910
Keweenaw	582	378	212	631	536
Lake	2,351	1,194	981	1,958	1,713
Lapeer	11,982	12,326	10,541	10,736	16,670
Leelanau	3,449	3,996	2,634	3,331	5,215
Lenawee	15,400	14,288	9,515	13,690	19,115
Livingston	27,851	27,539	15,971	13,749	31,331
Luce	972	958	660	864	1,528
Mackinac	2,384	2,368	1,251	2,093	3,127
Macomb	127,788	144,199	66,358	112,856	175,632

County	Clinton	Bush	Perot	Dukakis	Bush
Manistee	3,549	2,472	2,200	4,765	5,368
Marquette	16,038	9,665	5,768	15,418	11,704
Mason	4,829	5,102	3,096	4,531	6,800
Mecosta	6,096	6,047	3,607	4,736	8,181
Menominee	4,559	3,995	2,479	4,918	5,440
Midland	13,382	16,149	8,945	13,452	19,994
Missaukee	1,893	2,829	1,306	1,621	3,566
Monroe	24,957	20,450	13,551	21,847	26,189
Montcalm	8,721	8,420	5,499	7,664	10,963
Montmorency	1,903	1,794	1,077	1,563	2,514
Muskegon	32,156	23,666	15,242	28,977	33,567
Newaygo	6,455	7,332	4,056	5,389	9,896
Oakland	241,062	241.438	94,861	174,745	283,359
Oceana	3,846	3,944	2,712	3,356	5,693
Ogemaw	4,016	2,936	2,121	4,012	4,091
Ontonagon	2,449	1,464	805	2,517	2,023
Osceola	3,529	3,606	2,199	2,860	5,218
Oscoda	1,471	1,583	754	1,170	1,972
Otsego	3,129	3,393	2,635	2,635	4,620
Ottawa	22,192	56,872	16,864	18,769	61,515
Presque Isle	3,303	2,397	1,612	3,025	3,614
Roscommon	5,243	4,170	2,551	4,394	5,866
Saginaw	43,812	32,103	30,522	45,616	42,401
St. Clair	23,590	24,119	18,490	20,909	32,336
St. Joseph	7,818	9,836	6,208	7,017	13,084
Sanilac	5,876	7,891	4,837	5,445	10,653
Schoolcraft	2,139	1,253	721	2,071	1,802
Shiawassee	12,629	10,930	8,632	13,056	15,506
Tuscola	9,138	8,639	6,745	9,060	12,093
Van Buren	12,540	10,356	7,235	10,668	14,522
Washtenaw	73,201	41,303	21,747	61,799	55,029
Wayne	500,521	255,304	101,111	450,222	291,996
Wexford	4,894	4,696	2,900	4,287	6,043
Totals	**1,854,603**	**1,585,251**	**819,931**	**1,675,783**	**1,965,486**

VOTE FOR PRESIDENT, BY COUNTY, 1988 and 1992

1992		1988
Clinton	Democratic	Dukakis
Bush	Republican	Bush

Map by the Almanac

VOTE FOR GOVERNOR
1835 -1994

Candidates listed in the order of their vote. Included are "third party" candidates whose vote exceeded the winner's plurality.

Woodbridge resigned in 1841 to become U.S. Senator. Lt. Gov. James Wright Gordon became Acting Governor.

Filch resigned in 1847 to become U.S. Senator. Lt. Gov. William L. Greenley became Acting Governor.

McClelland resigned in 1853 to become U.S. Secretary of Interior. Lt. Gov. Andrew Parsons became Acting Governor.

Fitzgerald died 1939, and was succeeded by Lt. Gov. Luren Dickinson.

Romney resigned 1969 to become U.S. Secretary of Housing & Urban Devel, and was succeeded by Lt. Gov. William Milliken.

YEAR	NAME,POLITICS	VOTE
1835	Mason,Democrat	7,558
	Biddle,Whig	814
1837	Mason,Democrat	15,314
	Trowbridge,Whig	14,546
1839	Woodbridge,Whig	18,195
	Farnsworth,Democrat	17,037
1841	Barry, Democrat	20,993
	Fuller,Whig	15,449
1843	Barry,Democrat	21,392
	Pitcher,Whig	14,899
1845	Felch, Democrat	20,123
	Vickery,Whig	16,316
1847	Ransom,Democrat	24,639
	Edmunds, Whig	18,990
1849	Barry,Democrat	27,847
	Littlejohn,Whig & Free Soil	23,540
1851	McClelland,Democrat	23,827
	Gridley,Whig	16,901
1852	McClelland, Democrat	42,798
	Chandler,Whig	34,660
1854	Bingham,Republican	43,652
	Barry,Democrat	38,675
1856	Bingham,Republican	71,402
	Felch,Democrat	54,085
1858	Wisner,Republican	65,202
	Stuart,Democrat	56,067
1860	Blair,Republican	87,806
	Barry,Democrat	67,221
1862	Blair,Republican	68,716
	Stout, Union	62,102
1864	Crapo, Republican	81,744
	Fenton, Democrat	71,301
1866	Crapo,Republican	96,746
	Williams,Democrat	67,708
1868	Baldwin,Republican	128,051
	Moore,Democrat	97,290
1870	Baldwin,Republican	100,176
	Comstock,Democrat	83,391
1872	Bagley,Republican	137,602
	Flair,Liberal	80,958
1874	Bagley,Republican	111,519
	Chamberlain,Democrat	105,550
1876	Croswell,Republican	165,926
	Webber,Democrat	142,585
1878	Croswell,Republican	126,280
	Barnes,Democrat	78,503
	Smith,Greenback	73,313
1880	Jerome,Republican	178,944
	Holloway,Democrat	137,671
1882	Begole,Fusionist	154,269
	Jerome,Republican	149,697
	Sagendorph,Prohibition	5,854
1884	Alger,Republican	190,840
	Begole,Fusionist	186,887
	Preston,Prohibition	22,207
1886	Luce,Republican	181,474
	Yaple,Fusionist	174,042
	Dickie,Prohibition	25,179
1888	Luce,Republican	233,580
	Burt,Fusionist	216,450
	Cheney,Prohibition	20,342
1890	Winans,Democrat	183,725
	Turner,Republican	172,205
	Partridge,Prohibition	28,681
	Belden,Industrial	13,198
1892	Rich,Republican	221,228
	Morse,Democrat	205,138
	Ewing,People's Party	21,417
	Russell,Prohibition	20,777
1894	Rich,Republican	237,215
	Fisher,Democrat	130,823
1896	Pingree,Republican	304,431
	Sligh,DPUS	221,022
1989	Pingree,Republican	243,239
	Whiting,DPUS	168,142
1900	Bliss,Republican	305,612
	Maybury,Democrat	226,228
1902	Bliss,Republican	211,261
	Durand,Democrat	174,077
1904	Warner,Republican	283,799
	Ferns,Democrat	223,571
1906	Warner,Republican	227,567
	Kimmerle,Democrat	130,018
1908	Warner,Republican	262,141
	Hemans,Democrat	252,611
	Gray,Prohibition	16,092
	Stirton,Socialist	9,447
1910	Osborn,Republican	202,803
	Hemans,Democrat	159,770
1912	Ferris,Democrat	194,017
	Musselman,Republican	169,963
	Watkins,Natl Progressive	152,909
1914	Ferris,Democrat	212,063
	Osborn,Republican	176,254
	Pattengill,Progressive	36,747
1916	Sleeper,Republican	363,724
	Sweet,Democrat	264,440
1918	Sleeper,Republican	266,738
	Bailey,Democrat	158,142
1920	Groesbeck,Republican	703,180
	Ferris,Democrat	310,566
1922	Groesbeck,Republican	356,933
	Cummings,Democrat	218,252
1924	Groesbeck,Republican	799,225
	Frensdorf,Democrat	343,577

Year	Candidate	Votes
1926	Green,Republican	399,564
	Comstock,Democrat	227,155
1928	Green,Republican	961,179
	Comstock,Democrat	404,546
1930	Brucker,Republican	483,990
	Comstock,Democrat	357,664
1932	Comstock, Democrat	887,672
	Brucker,Republican	696,935
1934	Fitzgerald,Republican	659,743
	Lacy,Democrat	577,044
1936	Murphy,Democrat	892,774
	Fitzgerald,Republican	843,855
1938	Fitzgerald,Republican	847,245
	Murphy,Democrat	753,752
1940	VanWagoner,Democrat	1,077,065
	Dickinson,Republican	945,784
1942	Kelly,Republican	645,335
	VanWagoner,Democrat	573,314
1944	Kelly,Republican	1,208,859
	Fry,Democrat	989,307
1946	Sigler,Republican	1,003,878
	VanWagoner,Democrat	644,540
1948	Williams,Democrat	1,128,664
	Sigler,Republican	964,810
1950	Williams,Democrat	935,152
	Kelly,Republican	933,998
	Hayden,Prohibition	8,511
1952	Williams,Democrat	1,431,893
	Alger,Republican	1,423,275
	Munn,Prohibition	8,990
1954	Williams,Democrat	1,216,308
	Leonard,Republican	963,300
1956	Williams,Democrat	1,666,689
	Cobo,Republican	1,376,376
1958	Williams,Democrat	1,225,533
	Bagwell,Republican	1,078,089
1960	Swainson,Democrat	1,643,634
	Bagwell,Republican	1,602,022
1962	Romney,Republican	1,420,086
	Swainson,Democrat	1,339.513
1964	Romney,Republican	1,764,355
	Staebler,Democrat	1,381,442
1966	Romney,Republican	1,490,430
	Ferency,Democrat	963,383
1970	Milliken,Republican	1,339,047
	Levin,Democrat	1,294,638
1974	Milliken,Republican	1,356,865
	Levin,Democrat	1,242.247
1978	Milliken,Republican	1,623,485
	Fitzgerald,Democrat	1,237,256
1982	Blanchard,Democrat	1,561.291
	Headlee,Republican	1,369,582
1986	Blanchard,Democrat	1,632,138
	Lucas,Republican	753,647
1990	Engler, Republican	1,276,134
	Blanchard, Democrat	1,258,537
	Roundtree, WorldWorkers	28,091
1994	Engler, Republican	1,899,101
	Wolpe, Democrat	1,188,438

MICH VOTE FOR PRESIDENT 1928-1992

Candidates listed in the order of their vote in Michigan. Candidate in **bold** was elected in U.S. total. Included are third party when vote exceeded the winner's pluarality.

YEAR	CANDIDATES	POLITICS	VOTE
1992	Bill Clinton	Dem	1,854,803
	George Bush	Rep	1,585,251
	Ross Perot	Ind	819,931
1988	**George Bush**	REP	1,819,718
	Michael S. Dukakis	DEM	1,581,559
1984	**Ronald Reagan**	REP	2,251,571
	Walter F. Mondale	DEM	1,529,638
1980	**Ronald Reagan**	REP	1,915,225
	Jimmy Carter	DEM	1,661,532
	John Anderson	IND	275,223
1976	Gerald R. Ford	REP	1,893,742
	Jimmy Carter	DEM	1,696,714
1972	**Richard M. Nixon**	REP	1,961,721
	George S. McGovern	DEM	1,459,435
1968	Hubert H. Humphrey	DEM	1,593,082
	Richard M. Nixon	REP	1,370,665
	George C. Wallace	AM.IND	331,968
1964	**Lyndon B. Johnson**	DEM	2,136,615
	Barry Goldwater	REP	1,060,152
1960	**John F. Kennedy**	DEM	1,687,269
	Richard M. Nixon	REP	1,620,428
1956	**Dwight D. Eisenhower**	REP	1,713,647
	Adlai E. Stevenson	DEM	1,359,898
1952	**Dwight D. Eisenhower**	REP	1,551,529
	Adlai E. Stevenson	DEM	1,230,657
1948	Thomas E. Dewey	REP	1,038,595
	Harry S. Truman	DEM	1,003,448
	Henry A. Wallace	PROG	46,515
1944	**Franklin D. Roosevelt**	DEM	1,106,899
	Thomas E. Dewey	REP	1,084,423
1940	Wendell L. Willkie	REP	1,039,947
	Franklin D. Roosevelt	DEM	1,032,991
	Norman Thomas	SOC	7,593
1936	**Franklin D. Roosevelt**	DEM	1,016,794
	Alfred M. Landon	REP	699,733
1932	**Franklin D. Roosevelt**	DEM	871,700
	Herbert Hoover	REP	739,894
1928	**Herbert Hoover**	REP	965,396
	Alfred E. Smith	DEM	396,762

GUIDE TO WRITING - LOBBYING YOUR REPRESENTATIVES

Source - MI Senate staff

LETTER WRITING

A personal letter is usually the most effective way of contacting your legislator, whether in Lansing or Washington. If you're new at this type of letter writing, here are some suggestions on how your letters can be most effective:

1. **Address it properly:** Know your legislator's full name and correct spelling. For specific addresses, see individual lists. Here are some examples:

U.S. SENATOR
The Honorable (full name)
United States Senator
Address
Dear Senator (last name):

U.S. REPRESENTATIVE
The Honorable (full name)
United States Representative
Dear Congressman/woman (last name):

STATE SENATOR
The Honorable (full name)
State Senator
State Capitol
Lansing, MI 48913
Dear Senator (last name):

STATE REPRESENTATIVE
The Honorable (full name)
State Representative
State Capitol
Lansing, MI 48913
Dear Representative (last name):

2. **Always include your last name and address on the letter itself.** (printed or typed). A letter cannot be answered if there is no return address or the signature is not legible.

3. **Use your own words.** Avoid form letters and petitions. They tend to be identified as organized pressure campaigns, and are often answered with form replies. However, a petition does let the legislator know that the issue is of concern to a large number of people (addresses with zip codes should be given for each signature). One thoughtful, factual, well-reasoned letter carries more weight than 100 form letters or printed postcards.

4. **Time the arrival of your letter.** Try to write to your legislator, and the chairperson of the committee dealing with a bill, while a bill is still in committee and there is still time to take effective action. Sometimes a bill is out of committee, or has been passed, before a helpful, informative letter arrives which could have made a difference in the way the bill was written or in the final decision.

5. **Know what you are writing about.** Identify the bill or issue of concern to you. Thousands of bills and resolutions are introduced in each session. If you write about a bill, try to give the bill number or describe it by popular title, such as "Land Use Bill," or "Mechanics Licensing."

6. **Be reasonably brief.** Many issues are complex, but a single page, presenting your opinions, facts, arguments or proposals as clearly as possible, is preferred and welcomed by most legislators.

7. **Give reasons for your position.** Explain how the issue would affect you, your family, your business or profession, or the effect on your community or our state. If you have specialized knowledge, share it with your legislator. Concrete, expert arguments for or against the bill can be used by the legislator in determining the final outcome of a bill.

8. **Be constructive.** If a bill deals with a problem you admit exists, but you believe the bill is the wrong approach, explain what you believe to be the right approach.

9. **Groups and individuals should determine their priority concerns** and contact the legislator on those specific issues rather than on every issue. The "pen pal" who writes every few days on every conceivable subject tends to become a nuisance, rather than an effective voice of concern.

10. **You may not always receive a long, detailed response to your letter.** Legislators are very busy and usually cannot respond with long, personal replies to each correspondent.

11. **Write a letter of appreciation** when you feel a legislator has done a good job. Legislators are human too and seldom receive "thank you" letters of encouragement.

Remember, on any particular issue, even a few letters to one legislator can have an important impact. Sometimes just one letter, from a new perspective or with clear-cut, persuasive arguments can be the decisive factor in a legislator's action.

OFFICE TELEPHONES OF MICHIGAN LEGISLATORS

Area 517

■ Address mail to a representative at P.O. Box 30014, Lansing, Mich. 48909

HOUSE

James Agee, D-Muskegon,	373-2646
Tom Alley, D-West Branch	373-3817
David Anthony D-Escanaba	373-0156
Paul Baade, D-Muskegon	373-3436
Laura Baird, D-Okemos	373-1786
Lyn Bankes, R-Livonia	**373-3920**
Michael Bennane, D-Detroit	373-1705
Maxine Berman, D-Southfield	373-1788
William Bobier, R-Hesperia	373-0825
Beverly Bodem, R-Alpena	373-0833
Robert Brackenridge, R-St. Joseph	**373-1403**
Liz Brater, D-Ann Arbor	373-2577
Lingg Brewer, D-Holt	373-1770
William Bryant, Jr., R-Grs. Pte. Farms	373-0154
Willis Bullard, Jr., R-Milford	373-0827
Eric Bush, R-Battle Creek	**373-0555**
William Byl, R-Grand Rapids	373-2668
Deborah Cherry, D-Burton	373-3906
Nick Ciaramitaro, D-Roseville	373-0854
Floyd Clack, D-Flint	373-7557
Penny Crissman, R-Rochester	**373-1773**
Alan Cropsey, R-DeWitt	373-1778
Candace Curtis, D-Swartz Creek	373-1780
Jessie Dalman, R-Holland	373-0830
Eileen DeHart, D-Westland	373-2576
Walter DeLange, R-Grand Rapids	**373-0840**
Robert DeMars, D-Lincoln Park	373-0855
Barbara Dobb, R-Commerce Twp.	373-1799
Agnes Dobronski, D-Dearborn	373-0847
Jan Dolan, R-Farmington Hills	373-1793
Bob Emerson, D-Flint	**373-7515**
Frank Fitzgerald, R-Grand Ledge	373-0853
John Freeman, D-Madison Heights	373-3818
Pat Gagliardi, D-Drummond Island	373-2629
David Galloway, R-White Lake	373-2616
Terry Geiger, R-Lake Odessa	**373-0842**
John Gernaat R-McBain	373-1747
Donald Gilmer, R-Augusta	373-1787
Sharon Gire, D-Clinton Twp.	373-0159
Carl Gnodtke, R-Sawyer	373-1796
Michael Goschka, R-Brant	**373-0837**
Mike Green, R-Mayville	373-0476
Michael Griffin, D-Jackson	373-1795
David Gubow, D-Huntington Woods	373-0478
Dan Gustafson, R-Haslett	**373-0587**
Beverly Hammerstrom, R-Temperance	373-0828
Michael Hanley, D-Saginaw	373-0152
Clark Harder, D-Owosso	373-0841
Curtis Hertel, D-Detroit	373-1983
Sandra Hill, R-Montrose	**373-3944**
Paul Hillegonds, R-Holland	373-0836
Morris Hood, Jr., D-Detroit	373-3815
Jack Horton, R-Belmont	373-0218
John Jamian, R-Bloomfield Hills	373-0824
David Jaye, R-Washington Twp.	**373-0843**
John Jellema, R-Grand Haven	373-0838
Roland Jersevic, R-Saginaw	373-1797
Shirley Johnson, R-Royal Oak	373-1783
Greg Kaza, R-Rochester Hills	373-0615
Thomas Kelly, D-Wayne	**373-0849**
Carolyn Cheeks Kilpatrick, D-Detroit	373-0844
Alvin Kukuk, R-Macomb	373-0820
Edward LaForge, D-Kalamazoo	373-1785
Burton Leland, D-Detroit	373-6990
Clyde LeTarte, R-Horton	**373-1775**
Gerald Law, R-Plymouth	373-3816
John Llewellyn, R-Fremont	373-7317
Terry London, R-Marysville	373-1790
Allen Lowe, R-Grayling	373-0829
Lynne Martinez, D-Lansing	**373-0826**
Thomas Mathieu, D-Grand Rapids	373-0822
Jim McBryde, R-Mt. Pleasant	373-1789
Michelle McManus, R-Traverse City	**373-1766**
James McNutt, R-Midland	373-1791
James Middaugh, R-Paw Paw	373-0839
Thomas Middleton, R-Ortonvill	373-1798
Susan Grimes Munsell, R-Howell	373-1784
Raymond Murphy, D-Detroit	**373-0589**
Michael Nye, R-Litchfield	373-1794
Dennis Olshove, D-Warren	373-1772
Lynn Owen, D-Monroe	373-2617
Glenn Oxender, R-Sturgis	373-0832
Joseph Palamara, D-Wyandotte	**373-0140**
Mary Lou Parks, D-Detroit	373-1776
Charles Perricone, R-Kalamazoo	373-1774
Gregory Pitoniak, D-Taylor	373-0852
Vincent Porreca, D-Trenton	373-0845
Hubert Price Jr., D-Pontiac	**373-0475**
Kirk Profit, D-Ypsilanti	373-1771
Gary Randall, R-Elwell	373-0834
Kim Rhead, R-Sandusky	373-0835
Sue Rocca, R-Sterling Heights	373-7768
James Ryan, R-Redford	**373-0857**
Nelson Saunders, D-Detroit	373-1782
Mary Schroer, D-Ann Arbor	373-1792
Martha Scott, D-Highland Park	373-0144
Ken Sikkema, R-Grandville	373-0846
Alma Stallworth, D-Detroit	**373-2276**
Paul Tesanovich, D-L'Anse	373-0850

Ilona Varga, D-Detroit	373-0832
Ed Vaughn, D-Detroit	**373-1008**
Harold Vorhees, R-Wyoming	373-2277
Timothy Walberg, R-Tipton	373-1706
Ted Wallace, D-Detroit	373-0106
Lloyd Weeks, D-Warren	373-2275
Howard Wetters, D-Kawkawlin	**373-0158**
Deborah Whyman, R-Canton	373-2575
Karen Willard, D-Fair Haven	373-1800
Tracey Yokich, D-St. Clair Shores	373-0113

■ **Address mail to a senator at P.O. Box 30036, Lansing, Mich. 48909.**

SENATE

Loren Bennett, R-Canton	**373-7350**
Jim Berryman, D-Adrian	373-3543
Michael Bouchard, R-Birmingham	373-2523
Dianne Byrum, D-Holt	373-1734
Doug Carl, R-Mt. Clemens	373-7670
John Cherry, Jr., D-Clio	**373-1636**
Jon Cisky, R-Saginaw	373-1760
Joe Conroy, D-Flint	373-0142
Kenneth DeBeaussaert, D-New Balt.	373-7315
Dan DeGrow, R-Port Huron	373-7708
Christopher Dingell, D-Trenton	**373-7800**
Mat Dunaskiss, R-Lake Orion	373-2417
Joanne Emmons, R-Big Rapids	373-3760
Harry Gast, R-St. Joseph	373-6960
Robert Geake, R-Northville	373-1707
Joel Gougeon, R-Bay City	**373-1777**
George Hart, D-Dearborn	373-6820
Philip Hoffman, R-Horton	373-2426
Dave Honigman, R-West Bloomfield	373-1758
Don Kovisto, D-Ironwood	373-7840
George McManus, Jr., R-Traverse City	**373-1725**
Arthur Miller, Jr., D-Warren	373-8360
Walter North, R-St. Ignace	373-2413
Michael O'Brien, D-Detroit	373-0994
Gary Peters, D-Pontiac	373-7888
Dick Posthumus, R-Alto	**373-0797**
Mike Rogers, R-Howell	373-2420
Bill Schuette, R-Midland	373-7946
John Schwarz, R-Battle Creek	373-3447
Dale Shugars, R-Portage	373-0793
Alma Wheeler Smith, D-South Lyon	**373-2406**
Virgil Smith, Jr., D-Detroit	373-7748
Henry Stallings II, D-Detroit	373-0990
Glenn Steil, R-Grand Rapids	373-1801
Leon Stille, R-Spring Lake	373-1635
William VanRegenmorter, R-Hudsonville	**373-6920**
Jackie Vaughn III, D-Detroit	373-7918
Joe Young Jr., D-Detroit	373-7346

CONGRESSIONAL DISTRICTS

APPORTIONMENT AND DISTRICTING PLAN OF 1992

SENATORIAL DISTRICTS

APPORTIONMENT AND DISTRICTING PLAN OF 1992

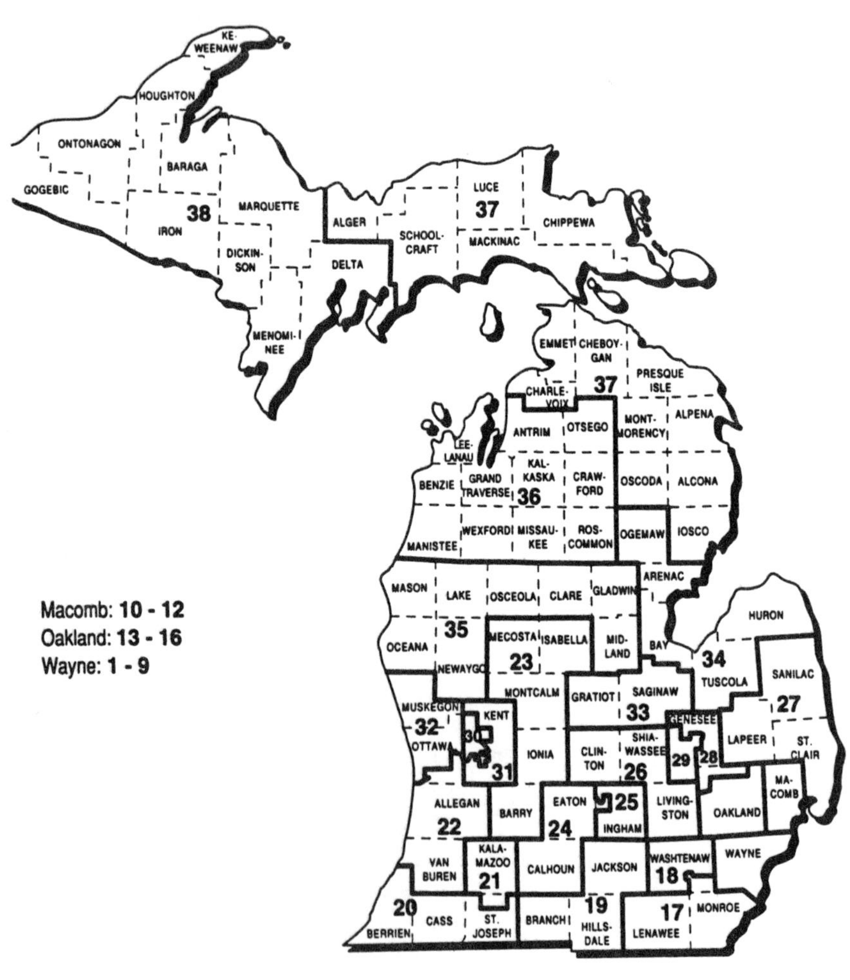

REPRESENTATIVE DISTRICTS

APPORTIONMENT AND DISTRICTING
PLAN OF 1992

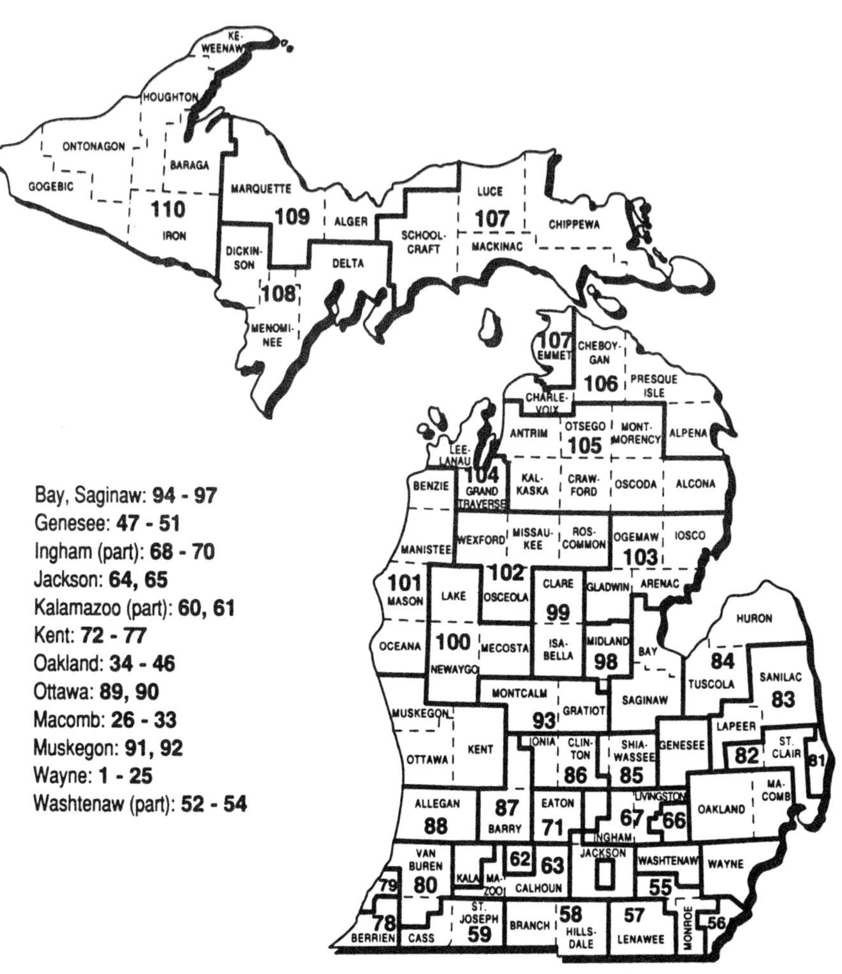

REPRESENTATIVE DISTRICTS CITY OF DETROIT

APPORTIONMENT AND DISTRICTING PLAN OF 1992

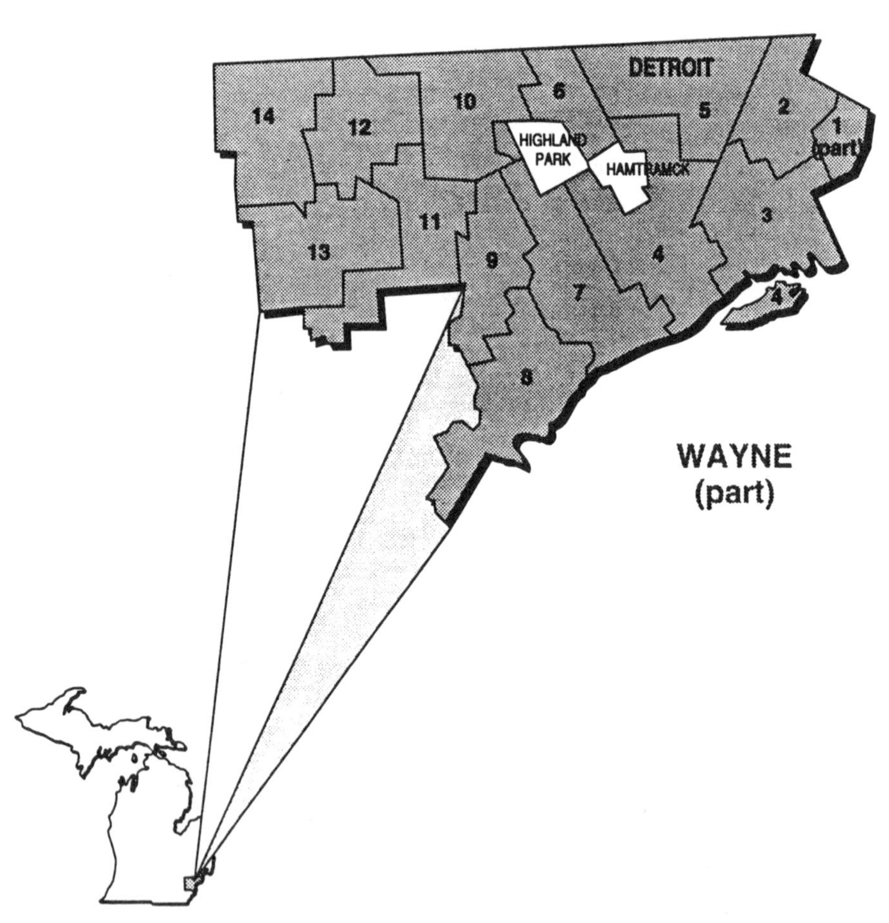

1995 SENATE STANDING COMMITTEES

SOURCE: Secretary of the Senate
Revised 1-18-95
C = Chairman

AGRICULTURE AND FORESTRY
Senator North (C), Gougeon McManus, Byrum, Berryman

APPROPIATIONS
Senator Gast (C), Geake, Cisky, DeGrow, Hoffman, McManus, Schwarz, Steil, Conroy, Koivisto, Alma Smith, Virgil Smith, Vaughn

ECONOMIC DEVELOPMENT, INTERNATIONAL TRADE AND REGULATORY AFFAIRS
Senator Schuette (C), Shugars, Gougeon, Stallings, O'Brien

EDUCATION
Senator Stille (C), Carl, North, DeBeaussaert, Peters

FAMILIES, MENTAL HEALTH AND HUMAN SERVICES
Senator Gougeon (C), Bouchard, Geake, Hart, Young, Jr.

FINANCE
Senator Emmons (C), Carl, Shugars, Peters, Stallings

FINANCIAL SERVICES
Senator Bouchard (C), Bennett, Rogers, Berryman, DeBeaussaert

GOVERMENT OPERATIONS
Senator Emmons (C), Steil, Hoffman, Hart, Cherry

HEALTH POLICY AND SENIOR CITIZENS
Senator Shugars (C), Schwarz, Honigman, O'Brien, Byrum

JUDICIARY
Senator VanRegenmorter (C), Rogers, Cisky, Geake, Dingell, Peters, Young, Jr.

HUMAN RESOURCES, LABOR AND VETERANS AFFAIRS
Senator Rogers (C), Honigman, Stille, Cherry, Stallings

LOCAL, URBAN, AND STATE AFFAIRS
Senator Honigman (C), Dunaskiss, Bennett, Young, Jr. O'Brien

NATURAL RESOURCES AND ENVIROMENTAL AFFAIRS
Senator Bennett (C), Dunaskiss, Gast, Dingell, DeBeaussaert

TECHNOLOGY AND ENERGY
Senator Dunaskiss (C), Schuette, Bouchard, Berryman, Byrum

TRANSPORTATION AND TOURISM
Senator Carl (C), Stille, North, O'Brien, Hart

1995 STATUTORY STANDING COMMITTEES

LEGISLATIVE RETIREMENT
Senator McManus, Emmons, Schwarz, Conroy

JOINT COMMITTEE ON ADMINSTRATIVES RULES
Senator Honigman, North, VanRegenmorter, Dingell, Cherry

LEGISLATIVE COUNCIL

Senator Posthumus, DeGrow, Schwarz, Steil, Miller, Cherry

CAPITOL COMMITTEE

Senator Schwartz, DeGrow, Dunaskiss, Byrum

SENATE FISCAL AGENCY GOVERNING BOARD

Senator Gast (C), Geake, Posthumus, Miller, Conroy

APPROPRIATIONS SUBCOMMITTEES 1995

AGRICULTIRE : Senator McManus (C), Gast, Koivisto

CAPITAL OUTLAY : Senator Gast (C), Geake, DeGrow, Schwarz, McManus, Virgil Smith, Koivisto, Conroy

COMMUNITY COLLEGES : Senator Gast (C) DeGrow, Vaughn

CORRECTIONS : Senator Cisky (C), Hoffman, Vaughn

GENERAL GOVERMENT : Senator DeGrow (C), Steil, Alma Smith

HIGHER EDUCATION : Senator Schwarz (C), Cisky, Koivisto

MENTAL HEALTH : Senator Geake (C), Hoffman, Alma Smith

NATURAL RESOURCES : Senator McManus (C), Gast, Koivisto

PUBLIC HEALTH : Senator Schwarz (C), McManus, Conroy

REGULATORY : Senator Steil (C), Geake, Virgil Smith

RETIREMENT : Senator Steil (C), Cisky, Alma Smith

SCHOOL AID (K-12) & DEPT. OF ED. : Senator DeGrow (C), Schwarz, Conroy

STATE POLICE AND MILITARY AFFAIRS : Senator Cisky (C), Hoffman, Vaughn

SOCIAL SERVICES : Senator Geake (C), Schwarz, Conroy

TRANSPORTATION : Senator Hoffman (C), DeGrow, Virgil Smith

SENATE MAJORITY LEADERSHIP

Majority Leader	Dick Posthumus
Assistant Majority Leader	Michael J. Bouchard
Majority Floor Leader	Dan L. DeGrow
Assistant Majority Floor Leader	William Van Regenmorter
Majority Caucus Chairman	Mat Dunaskiss

SENATE DEMOCRATIC LEADERSHIP

Democratic Leader	Arthur J. Miller, Jr.
Assistant Democratic Leader	Michael J. O'Brien
Democratic Floor Leader	John D. Cherry, Jr.
Assistant Democratic Floor Leader	Jim Berryman
Democratic Caucus Chairman	Dianne Byrum

1995 MICHIGAN HOUSE STANDING COMMITTEES

Source: Clerk of the House (Jan 1995)

COMMITTEE MEMBERSHIP

AGRICULTURE & FORESTRY: Gnodtke (chair), Green (majority vice-chair), Randall, Hill, London, Horton, Goschka, Gernaat, *Anthony (minority vice-chair), Baade, Curtis, Harder, Vaughn, Wetters, Willard*

APPROPRIATIONS: Gilmer (chair), Johnson (majority vice-chair), Bankes, Bobier, Dolan, Geiger, Gustafson, Jellema, LeTarte, McBryde, McNutt, Middleton, Oxender, Rhead, Walberg, *Hood (minority vice-chair), Berman, Ciaramitaro, Emerson, Kilpatrick, Mathieu, Owen, Price, Tesanovich, Yokich*

COMMERCE: Randall (chair), Gernaat (majority vice-chair), Middaugh, Jaye, Kaza, Kukuk, Lowe, Perricone, *Palamara (minority vice-chair), Alley, Griffin, Porreca, Profit, Weeks, Baird*

CONSERVATION, ENVIRONMENT & GREAT LAKES: Middaugh (chair), Hill (majority vice-chair), Gnodtke, Munsell, Sikkema, McManus, Bodem, Byl, *Alley (minority vice-chair), Freeman,Murphy, Brater, DeHart, LeForge, Wetters*

EDUCATION: Bryant (chair), Crissman (majority vice-chair), Dalman, Cropsey, Horton, Kukuk, Randall, Voorhees, *Agee (minority vice-chair), Brewer, Cherry, Gire, Kelly, Schroer, Scott*

HEALTH POLICY: Jamian (chair), Rocca (majority vice-chair), Hammerstrom, Sikkema, Crissman, Bodem, Jaye, Law, McManus, *Bennane (minority vice-chair), Griffin, Palamara, Porreca, Gire, Martinez, Stallworth*

HIGHER EDUCATION: Dalman (chair), Voorhees (majority vice-chair), Llewellyn, Perricone, *Harder (minority vice-chair), Brater, Brewer*

HOUSE OVERSIGHT & ETHICS: Fitzgerald (chair), Sikkema (majority vice-chair), Hill, Nye, Llewellyn, *Gagliardi (minority vice-chair), Kelly, Parks, Cherry*

HUMAN RESOURCES & LABOR: DeLange (chair), Llewellyn (majority vice-chair), Munsell, Nye, Perricone, *Murphy (minority vice-chair),Freeman, Cherry, LaForge*

HUMAN SERVICES: Horton (chair), Whyman (majority vice-chair), Green, McManus, *Gire (minority vice-chair), Hanley, Martinez*

INSURANCE: Llewellyn (chair), Law (majority vice-chair), Bullard, Fitzgerald, London, Jamian, Voorhees, Hill, Bush, *Saunders (minority vice-chair), Varga, Weeks, DeHart, Pitoniak, Schroer, Scott*

JUDICIARY & CIVIL RIGHTS: Nye (chair), Dalman (majority vice-chair), Fitzgerald, Galloway, Cropsey, Bush, Jersevic, Law, Lowe, Ryan, *Wallace (minority vice-chair), Clack, Curtis, Baird, Saunders, Schroer, Willard*

LOCAL GOVERNMENT: Brackenridge (chair), Voorhees (majority vice-chair), Bullard, Crissman, Hammerstrom, *Dobronski (minority vice-chair), Brewer, Martinez, Parks*

MENTAL HEALTH: Hammerstrom (chair), Galloway (majority vice-chair), Horton, Jamian, *Gubow (minority vice-chair), Baird, Brater*

PUBLIC UTILITIES: Dobb (chair), Ryan (majority vice-chair), Galloway, Middaugh, Whyman, *Stallworth (minority vice-chair), DeMars, Dobronski, Olshove*

REGULATORY AFFAIRS: Munsell (chair), Jaye (majority vice-chair), DeLange, Rocca, *Varga (minority vice-chair), Vaughn, Weeks*

SENIOR CITIZENS & VETERANS AFFAIRS: Lowe (chair), Bush (majority vice-chair), Kaza, Ryan, *DeMars (minority vice-chair), Anthony, DeHart*

TAX POLICY: Bullard (chair), Perricone (majority vice-chair), Brackenridge, Bryant, Dobb, Munsell, Gernaat, Goschka, Jaye, Whyman, *Profit (minority vice-chair), Freeman, Agee, Bennane, Gubow, Wallace, Wetters*

TOURISM & RECREATION: Bodem (chair), Goschka (majority vice-chair), Brackenridge, Jamian, Lowe, *Baade (minority vice-chair), Clack, Vaughn, Willard*

TRANSPORTATION: London (chair), Kukuk (majority vice-chair), DeLange, Byl, Galloway, Gernaat, Gnodtke, Green, *Pitoniak (minority vice-chair), Baade, Curtis, Harder, Kelly, Leland, Parks*

URBAN POLICY: Kaza (chair), Byl (majority vice-chair), Bryant, Jersevic, *Hanley (minority vice-chair), Clack, LeForge*

JOINT COMMITTEE ON ADMINISTRATIVE RULES: Cropsey (chair), Jersevic (majority vice-chair), Rocca, *Leland (minority vice-chair), Olshove*

REPUBLICAN LEADERSHIP

Speaker of the House:	Paul Hillegonds
Speaker Pro Tempore:	Frank Fitzgerald
Associate Speakers Pro Tempore:	Jessie Dalman Penny Crissman
Floor Leader:	Ken Sikkema

DEMOCRATIC LEADERSHIP

Minority Leader:	Curtis Hertel
Minority Leader Pro Tempore:	Raymond Murphy
Associate Minority Leader Pro Tempore:	Sharon Gire
Minority Floor Leader:	Patrick Gagliardi

STATE GOVERNMENT DEPARTMENTS

Source: Michigan Manual and Dept of Mgt. & Budget

ALL PHONES AREA CODE (517)

DEPARTMENT OF AGRICULTURE
611 WEST OTTAWA STREET
4TH FLOOR, OTTAWA BUILDING
NORTH TOWER
P.O. BOX 30017
LANSING 48909
Gordon Guyer Director
Information 373-1104
Food Division 373-1060
Press and Public Affairs Division 373-1104
Office of Racing Commissioner .... (313) 462-2400

DEPARTMENT OF ATTORNEY GENERAL
525 WEST OTTAWA
P.O. BOX 30210
LANSING 48909
Frank J. Kelley, Attorney General
Information 373-1110
Consumer Complaints 373-1140
Charitable Trusts 373-1152

DEPARTMENT OF CIVIL RIGHTS

LANSING 48913
Nanette Reynolds, Director
Lansing Office 335-3165
Detroit Office .... (313) 256-2579

DEPARTMENT OF CIVIL SERVICE
CAPITAL COMMONS
400 S. PINE ST.
P.O. BOX 30002
LANSING 48909
Martha Bibbs, State Personnel Director
Information 373-3030

DEPARTMENT OF COMMERCE
LAW BUILDING, 4TH FLOOR
P.O. BOX 30004
LANSING 48909
Arthur Ellis, Director
Information 373-1820
Bureau of Occupational and Professional Regulation 373-9879
Corporation and Securities Bureau 334-6212
Financial Institutions Bureau 373-3460
Insurance Bureau 373-0240
Liquor Control Commission 322-1345
Michigan Business Ombudsman 373-6241
Michigan State Housing Development Authority 373-6022
Office of Health Services 373-7902
Public Service Commission 334-6445
Travel Bureau 373-0670

DEPARTMENT OF CORRECTIONS
GRAND VIEW PLAZA BUILDING
P.O. BOX 30003
LANSING 48909
Kenneth L. McGinnis, Director
Information 335-1426

DEPARTMENT OF EDUCATION
P.O. BOX 30008
LANSING 48909
Robert E. Schiller, Superintendent of Public Instruction
Information 373-4333
State Board of Education 373-3900
Student Financial Assistance Services 373-3399

EXECUTIVE OFFICE
STATE CAPITOL
P.O. BOX 30013
LANSING 48909
John Engler, Governor
Information 373-3400
Lieutenant Governor's Office 373-6800
Washington, D.C. Office .... (202) 624-5840
Northern Michigan Office .... (906) 228-2850
Southeast Michigan Office .... (313) 256-1003

DEPARTMENT OF LABOR
VICTOR OFFICE CENTER

P.O. BOX 30015
LANSING 48909
Lowell Perry, Director
Information 322-1287
Commission for the Blind 373-2062
Bureau of Construction Codes 322-1701
Bureau of Employment Standards 322-1825
Commission on Handicapper Concerns 373-8397
Bureau of Safety and Regulation 322-1814
Bureau of Worker's Disability Compensation 373-3480
Michigan Employment Security Commission .... *

* *Check your telephone directory for the office nearest you.*

DEPARTMENT OF MANAGEMENT AND BUDGET
LEWIS CASS BUILDING
320 SOUTH WALNUT STREET
P.O. BOX 30026
LANSING 48909
Mark Murray, Acting Director
Information 373-1004
Council for the Arts .... (313) 256-3735

Crime Victims Compensation Board 373-7373
Indian Affairs Commission 373-0654
Office of Purchasing..373-0330
Bureau of Retirement Systems 322-6215
Commission on Spanish Speaking
Affairs 373-8339
Michigan Women's Commission 373-2884

DEPARTMENT OF MENTAL HEALTH
LEWIS CASS BUILDING, FIFTH FLOOR
320 SOUTH WALNUT STREET
LANSING 48913
James Haveman, Director
Information 373-3740

DEPARTMENT OF MILITARY AFFAIRS
2500 SOUTH WASHINGTON AVENUE
LANSING 48913
General Errol Gordon Stump, Director
Information 483-5507

DEPARTMENT OF NATURAL RESOURCES
STEVENS T. MASON BUILDING
P.O. BOX 30028
LANSING 48909
Roland Harmes, Director
Information ....~~373-3229~~
Region I, Marquette.............................(906) 228-6561
Region II, Roscommon..................................275-5151
Region III, Dimondale....................................322-1300
Air Quality Division 373-7023
Office of Litigation and
Program Services.......................................373-3503

DEPARTMENT OF NATURAL RESOURCES
(Continued)
Fisheries Division...373-1280
Forest Management Division 373-1275
Geological Survey Division 334-6907
Land and Water Management
Division...373-1170
Recreation Division 373-9900
Surface Water Quality Division 373-1949
Waste Management Division 373-2730
Wildlife Division 373-1263

DEPARTMENT OF PUBLIC HEALTH
3423 NORTH LOGAN STREET
P.O. BOX 30195
LANSING 48909
Vernice Davis-Anthony, Director
Information 335-8024
Bureau of Environmental and
Occupational Health.................................335-9218
Bureau of Health Facilities 335-8500
Center for Health Promotion 335-8368
Vital Statistics...335-8655

DEPARTMENT OF SOCIAL SERVICES
GRAND TOWER
P.O. BOX 30037
LANSING 48909
Gerald Miller, Director
Information 373-2000
Office of Child Support...................................373-7570
Office of Children and Youth Services 335-6158
Medical Services Administration 335-5000
Bureau of Regulatory Services
(Adult Foster and Child Day
Care Licensing)..373-6614

DEPARTMENT OF STATE
TREASURY BUILDING, FIRST FLOOR
P.O. BOX 30045
LANSING 48918
Candice Miller Secretary of State
Information 373-2510
Bureau of Elections..373-2540
Bureau of Driver and Vehicle Records..........322-1528
Bureau of Driver Improvement.......................322-1000
Office of Hearings and Legislation 373-8141
Bureau of Automotive Regulation 373-7858
Bureau of History 373-0510

DEPARTMENT OF STATE POLICE
714 SOUTH HARRISON ROAD
EAST LANSING 48823
Colonel Michael Robinson, Director
Information 332-6157
Fire Marshal Division......................................322-5847
Highway Safety Planning Division.................373-6287
Motor Carrier Division 336-6195
Traffic Services Division.................................332-2521

DEPARTMENT OF TRANSPORTATION
TRANSPORTATION BUILDING
425 WEST OTTAWA STREET
P.O. BOX 30050
LANSING 48909
Patrick Nowak, Director
Information 373-2090
Bureau of Aeronautics.....................................373-1834
Bureau of Highways..373-1884
Bureau of Transportation Planning 373-0343
Bureau of Urban and Public
Transportation..373-2282

DEPARTMENT OF TREASURY
P.O. BOX 15128
LANSING 48922
Douglas Roberts, State Treasurer
Information 373-3223
Income Tax Division 1-800-487-7000
Michigan Education Trust..............................335-4767
Sales, Use, and Withholding
Taxes Division..373-2746
Tax Tribunal 334-6521

ORGANIZATION OF THE EXECUTIVE BRANCH

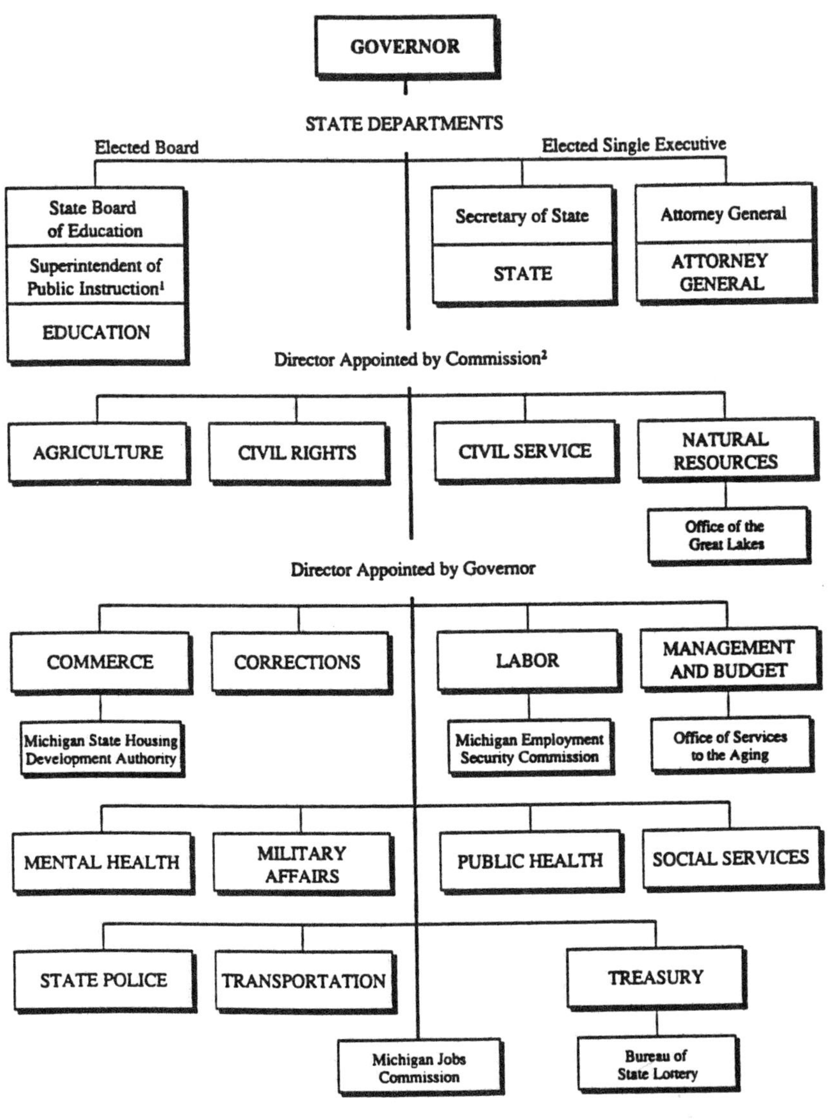

PROFILE OF THE EXECUTIVE BRANCH

The executive power is vested in the governor, who is responsible for the faithful execution of the laws of the state. Elected by the people to a 4-year term, the governor:

- Supervises the principal departments of the executive branch and appoints members to state boards and commissions;
- May direct an investigation of any department of state government and may require written information from executive and administrative state officers on any subject relating to the performance of their duties;
- May remove elective and appointive officers of the executive branch for cause, as well as elective county, city, township, and village officers;
- Submits messages to the legislature and recommends measures considered necessary or desirable;
- Submits an annual state budget to the legislature, recommending sufficient revenues to meet proposed expenditures;
- May convene the legislature in extraordinary session;
- May call a special election to fill a vacancy in the legislature or the U.S. House of Representatives, and may fill a vacancy in the U.S. Senate by appointment;
- May grant reprieves, commutations of sentences, and pardons;
- May seek extradition of fugitives from justice who have left the state and may issue warrants at the request of other governors for fugitives who may be found within this state;
- Signs all commissions, patents for state lands, and appoints notaries public and commissioners in other states to take acknowledgements of deeds for this state;
- Serves as chairperson of the State Administrative Board, which supervises and approves certain state expenditures, and has veto power over its actions; and
- Serves as commander-in-chief of the state's armed forces.

The lieutenant governor is nominated at party convention and elected with the governor. The term of office, beginning in 1966, changed from 2 years to 4 years. The lieutenant governor serves as President of the Michigan Senate, but may vote only in case of a tie. The lieutenant governor may perform duties requested by the governor, but no power vested in the governor by the Constitution of 1963 may be delegated to the lieutenant governor. The lieutenant governor is a member of the State Administrative Board and would succeed the governor in case of death, impeachment, removal from office, or resignation.

PROFILE OF THE MICHIGAN LEGISLATURE

The legislative power of the State of Michigan is vested in a bicameral (2-chamber) body comprised of a senate and a house of representatives. The senate consists of 38 members who are elected by the qualified electors of districts having approximately 212,400 to 263,500 residents (under the 1992 apportionment plan, Senate districts range in population from approximately 225,000 to 265,000 residents). Senators are elected at the same time as the governor and serve 4-year terms concurrent with the governor's term of office. The house of representatives consists of 110 members who are elected by the qualified electors of districts having approximately 77,000 to 91,000 residents. Representatives are elected in even-numbered years to 2-year terms. Legislative districts are drawn on the basis of population figures obtained through the federal decennial census. Terms for senators and representatives begin on January 1, following the November general election.

The state legislature enacts the laws of Michigan; levies taxes and appropriates funds from money collected for the support of public institutions and the administration of the affairs of state government; proposes amendments to the state constitution, which must be approved by a majority vote of the electors; and considers legislation proposed by initiatory petitions. The legislature also provides oversight of the executive branch of government through the administrative rules and audit processes, committees, and the budget process; advises and consents, through the senate, on gubernatorial appointments; and considers proposed amendments to the Constitution of the United States. The majority of the legislature's work, however, entails lawmaking. Through a process defined by the state constitution, statute, and legislative rules, the legislature considers thousands of bills (proposed laws) during each 2-year session.

LEGISLATIVE BRANCH

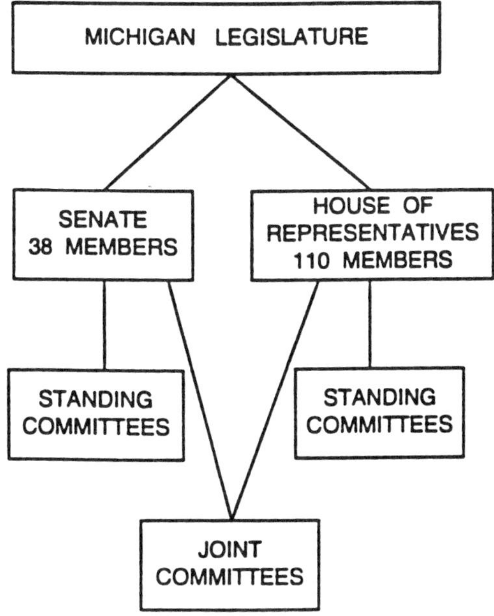

PROFILE OF THE JUDICIAL BRANCH

The *Constitution of the State of Michigan of 1963* provides that "the judicial power of the state is vested exclusively in one court of justice which shall be divided into one supreme court, one court of appeals, one trial court of general jurisdiction known as the circuit court, one probate court, and courts of limited jurisdiction that the legislature may establish by two-thirds vote of the members elected to and serving in each house."

JUDICIAL SYSTEM OF MICHIGAN

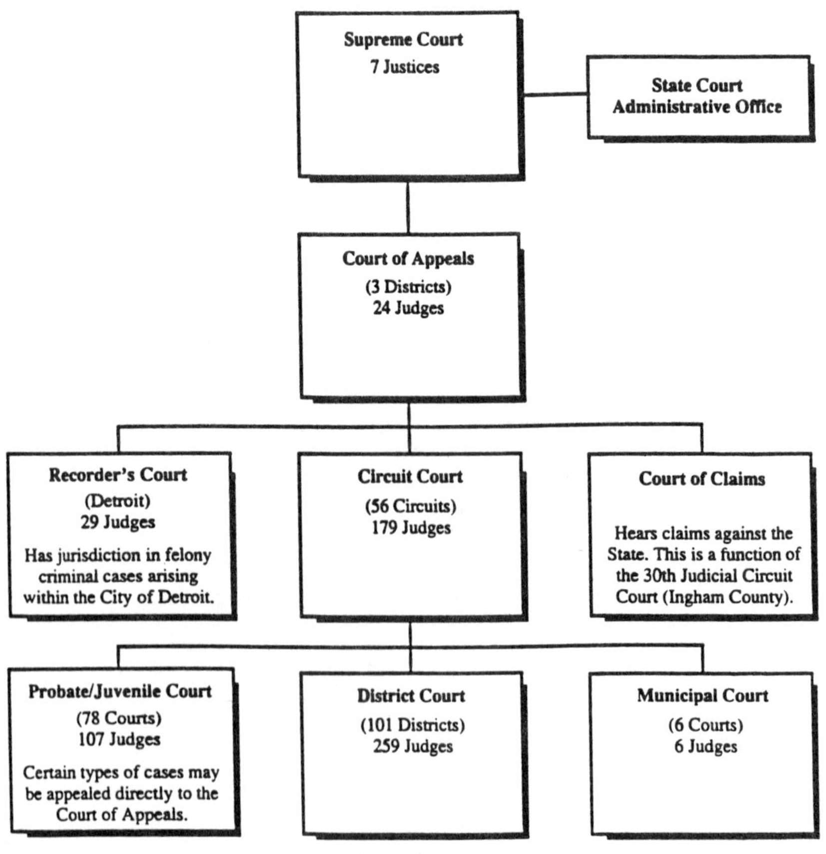

Financial Information for Fiscal Year 1993

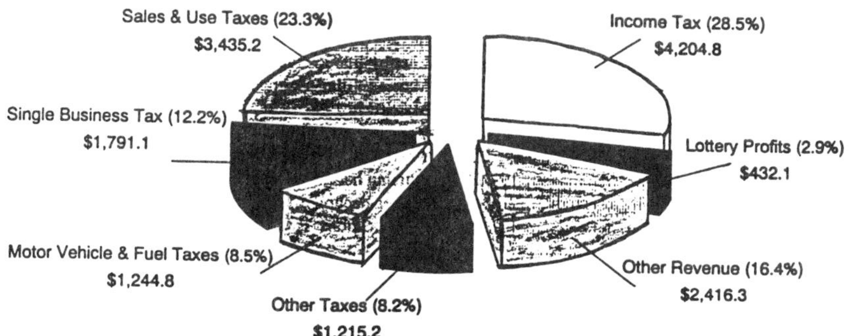

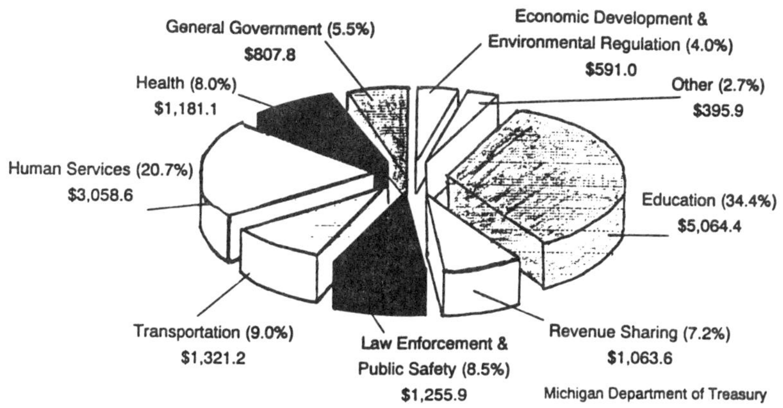

Michigan Department of Treasury

CONSTITUTION OF THE STATE OF MICHIGAN OF 1963

PREAMBLE

We, the people of the State of Michigan, grateful to Almighty God for the blessings of freedom, and earnestly desiring to secure these blessings undiminished to ourselves and our posterity, do ordain and establish this constitution.

ARTICLE I
DECLARATION OF RIGHTS

Political power.
Sec. 1. All political power is inherent in the people. Government is instituted for their equal benefit, security and protection.

Equal protection; discrimination.
Sec. 2. No person shall be denied the equal protection of the laws; nor shall any person be denied the enjoyment of his civil or political rights or be discriminated against in the exercise thereof because of religion, race, color or national origin. The legislature shall implement this section by appropriate legislation.

Assembly, consultation, instruction, petition.
Sec. 3. The people have the right peaceably to assemble, to consult for the common good, to instruct their representatives and to petition the government for redress of grievances.

Freedom of worship and religious belief; appropriations.
Sec. 4. Every person shall be at liberty to worship God according to the dictates of his own conscience. No person shall be compelled to attend, or, against his consent, to contribute to the erection or support of any place of religious worship, or to pay tithes, taxes or other rates for the support of any minister of the gospel or teacher of religion. No money shall be appropriated or drawn from the treasury for the benefit of any religious sect or society, theological or religious seminary; nor shall property belonging to the state be appropriated for any such purpose. The civil and political rights, privileges and capacities of no person shall be diminished or enlarged on account of his religious belief.

Freedom of speech and of press.
Sec. 5. Every person may freely speak, write, express and publish his views on all subjects, being responsible for the abuse of such right; and no law shall be enacted to restrain or abridge the liberty of speech or of the press.

Bearing of arms.
Sec. 6. Every person has a right to keep and bear arms for the defense of himself and the state.

Military power subordinate to civil power.
Sec. 7. The military shall in all cases and at all times be in strict subordination to the civil power.

Quartering of soldiers.
Sec. 8. No soldier shall, in time of peace, be quartered in any house without the consent of the owner or occupant, nor in time of war, except in a manner prescribed by law.

Slavery and involuntary servitude.
Sec. 9. Neither slavery, nor involuntary servitude unless for the punishment of crime, shall ever be tolerated in this state.

Attainder; ex post facto laws; impairment of contracts.
Sec. 10. No bill of attainder, ex post facto law or law impairing the obligation of contract shall be enacted.

Searches and seizures.

Sec. 11. The person, houses, papers and possessions of every person shall be secure from unreasonable searches and seizures. No warrant to search any place or to seize any person or things shall issue without describing them, nor without probable cause, supported by oath or affirmation. The provisions of this section shall not be construed to bar from evidence in any criminal proceeding any narcotic drug, firearm, bomb, explosive or any other dangerous weapon, seized by a peace officer outside the curtilage of any dwelling house in this state.

Constitutionality: The last sentence of this section was held invalid as in conflict with U.S. Const., Amend. IV. Lucas v. People, 420 F.2d 259 (C.A. Mich. 1970); Caver v. Kropp, 306 F.Supp. 1329 (D.C. Mich. 1969); People v. Pennington, 383 Mich. 611, 178 N.W. 2d 460 (1970); People v. Andrews, 21 Mich. App. 731, 176 N.W. 2d 460 (1970).

Habeas corpus.

Sec. 12. The privilege of the writ of habeas corpus shall not be suspended unless in case of rebellion or invasion the public safety may require it.

Conduct of suits in person or by counsel.

Sec. 13. A suitor in any court of this state has the right to prosecute or defend his suit, either in his own proper person or by an attorney.

Jury trials.

Sec. 14. The right of trial by jury shall remain, but shall be waived in all civil cases unless demanded by one of the parties in the manner prescribed by law. In all civil cases tried by 12 jurors a verdict shall be received when 10 jurors agree.

Double jeopardy; bailable offenses; commencement of trial if bail denied; bail hearing; effective date.

Sec. 15. No person shall be subject for the same offense to be twice put in jeopardy. All persons shall, before conviction, be bailable by sufficient sureties, except that bail may be denied for the following persons when the proof is evident or the presumption great:

(a) A person who, within the 15 years immediately preceding a motion for bail pending the disposition of an indictment for a violent felony or of an arraignment on a warrant charging a violent felony, has been convicted of 2 or more violent felonies under the laws of this state or under substantially similar laws of the United States or another state, or a combination thereof, only if the prior felony convictions arose out of at least 2 separate incidents, events, or transactions.

(b) A person who is indicted for, or arraigned on a warrant charging, murder or treason.

(c) A person who is indicted for, or arraigned on a warrant charging, criminal sexual conduct in the first degree, armed robbery, or kidnapping with intent to extort money or other valuable thing thereby, unless the court finds by clear and convincing evidence that the defendant is not likely to flee or present a danger to any other person.

(d) A person who is indicted for, or arraigned on a warrant charging, a violent felony which is alleged to have been committed while the person was on bail, pending the disposition of a prior violent felony charge or while the person was on probation or parole as a result of a prior conviction for a violent felony.

If a person is denied admission to bail under this section, the trial of the person shall be commenced not more than 90 days after the date on which admission to bail is denied. If the trial is not commenced within 90 days after the date on which admission to bail is denied and the delay is not attributable to the defense, the court shall immediately schedule a bail hearing and shall set the amount of bail for the person.

As used in this section, "violent felony" means a felony, an element of which involves a violent act or threat of a violent act against any other person.

This section, as amended, shall not take effect until May 1, 1979.

Bail; fines; punishments; detention of witnesses.

Sec. 16. Excessive bail shall not be required; excessive fines shall not be imposed; cruel or unusual punishment shall not be inflicted; nor shall witnesses be unreasonably detained.

Self-incrimination; due process of law; fair treatment at investigations.

Sec. 17. No person shall be compelled in any criminal case to be a witness against himself, nor be deprived of life, liberty or property, without due process of law. The right of all individuals, firms, corporations and voluntary associations to fair and just treatment in the course of legislative and executive investigations and hearings shall not be infringed.

Witnesses; competency, religious beliefs.

Sec. 18. No person shall be rendered incompetent to be a witness on account of his opinions on matters of religious belief.

Libels, truth as defense.

Sec. 19. In all prosecutions for libels the truth may be given in evidence to the jury; and, if it appears to the jury that the matter charged as libelous is true and was published with good motives and for justifiable ends, the accused shall be acquitted.

Rights of accused in criminal prosecutions.

Sec. 20. In every criminal prosecution, the accused shall have the right to a speedy and public trial by an impartial jury, which may consist of less than 12 jurors in prosecutions for misdemeanors punishable by imprisonment for not more than 1 year; to be informed of the nature of the accusation; to be confronted with the witnesses against him; to have compulsory process for obtaining witnesses in his favor; to have the assistance of counsel for his defense; to have an appeal as a matter of right; and as provided by law, when the trial court so orders, to have such reasonable assistance as may be necessary to perfect and prosecute an appeal.

Imprisonment for debt.

Sec. 21. No person shall be imprisoned for debt arising out of or founded on contract, express or implied, except in cases of fraud or breach of trust.

Treason; definition, evidence.

Sec. 22. Treason against the state shall consist only in levying war against it or in adhering to its enemies, giving them aid and comfort. No person shall be convicted of treason unless upon the testimony of two witnesses to the same overt act or on confession in open court.

Enumeration of rights not to deny others.

Sec. 23. The enumeration in this constitution of certain rights shall not be construed to deny or disparage others retained by the people.

Rights of crime victims; enforcement; assessment against convicted defendants.

Sec. 24. (1) Crime victims, as defined by law, shall have the following rights, as provided by law:

The right to be treated with fairness and respect for their dignity and privacy throughout the criminal justice process.

The right to timely disposition of the case following arrest of the accused.

The right to be reasonably protected from the accused throughout the criminal justice process.

The right to notification of court proceedings.

The right to attend trial and all other court proceedings the accused has the right to attend.

The right to confer with the prosecution.

The right to make a statement to the court at sentencing.

The right to restitution.

The right to information about the conviction, sentence, imprisonment, and release of the accused.

(2) The legislature may provide by law for the enforcement of this section.

(3) The legislature may provide for an assessment against convicted defendants to pay for crime victims' rights.

History: Add. H.J.R. P, approved Nov. 8, 1988, Eff. Dec. 24, 1988.

How to Successfully Appeal Your Property Tax Assessment

Source - House of Representatives staff

STEP 1 Go to your local assessor's office and obtain a copy of your worksheet or appraisal card for your property. This should list the number of rooms in your house, the type of construction, special features, etc. The worksheet contains other information such as style of your home, utilities, construction date, number of baths, fireplaces, and kitchen range hoods. Ask the assessing department to explain the document until you completely understand the abbreviations and numbers. You can also obtain worksheets of similar properties which recently sold in the area which the assessor is using to determine the value of your property.

STEP 2 Carefully check the worksheet for errors. The assessor may agree to change some of the information or figures at that time, or you may have to make your case with the local Board of Review. There should be a "percent good" calculation on your worksheet which shows you how much your house has depreciated. The Michigan Assessor's Manual requires that every property have a "percent good" calculation. If your house is 10 years old, it will be about 90 percent good. Percent good is another factor to use when comparing your home with other homes.

STEP 3 The assessor uses recently sold comparable properties to estimate the value of yours. However, these homes are often painted and repaired to a better condition and therefore may have a greater value than other homes which are not currently on the market. For example, some homes have all wiring, plumbing, and other features brought up to building code standards to satisfy a buyer or lender.

Sometimes we simply cannot afford necessary repairs or procrastinate and live with defects today which will be improved before a future home sale. Therefore it is necessary to perform a complete inside inspection of your home. Written repair estimates and photographs are very good evidence of defects which could affect the property value.

STEP 4 Realtors say that location is the single most important feature which determines the value of your home. If you live near an airport, major road, landfill, business or industry, your home is less desirable than the same home located in a purely residential neighborhood. You may live in a mixed zoning area which includes commercial, industrial and residential property. You may have a well, septic system or dirt road. Get copies of citizen complaints about area drug houses, rowdy party homes, and neighborhood eyesores. Take pictures of traffic jams, debris and eyesores. Tape record factory, truck or party noise.

If undesirable conditions are present, they may contribute to a deteriorating value of your home and you should be able to show this to the Board.

STEP 5 One of the most common mistakes home buyers can make is that they fail to inform the assessor of personal property and other valuable items which were included in the sale. Personal property items often included in a home's sale price such as furniture, curtains, washer, dryer, etc. are exempt from assessment. If you do not inform your assessor in writing about these items, your assessment may erroneously include this value.

STEP 6 Comparable property assessments are one of the most important tools for a property tax assessment appeal. If comparable properties are assessed lower than yours, you may argue that your property is overassessed. Make your comparable study by asking for the worksheets of similar homes which have recently sold in your area. Check the assessed value, the state equalized value, type of house and zoning.

STEP 7 If you do not have the time or patience to collect comparables, many local realtors will help you determine the value of your property. Call several and ask for comparable sales in your area. The realtors may even do an appraisal for free hoping you might send them business when you sell your home in the future. Or you may wish to have your home professionally appraised. A professional appraisal is the best evidence against an improper assessment and the best proof of value. It may cost you as much as you would save from lower property taxes, however.

STEP 8 The last step in the process is to put all your information into letter form. An example is on this page.

STEP 9 If you are not satisfied with the decision of your local Board of Review, you may want to continue your appeal. In order to do this, you must send a letter to the State Tax Tribunal, P. O. Box 30232, Lansing, MI 48909 before June 30 and ask them to mail you the necessary forms for appeal.

You can get three years' back taxes on the difference if you were wrongly assessed for the same reason for three years if you win an appeal from the Michigan Tax Tribunal. **You must appear before the local Board of Review before you can appeal to the State Tax Tribunal.**

GENERAL STRATEGY Bring a presentation copy for yourself and each of the three Board of Review members. Read your presentation to the Board. You may have about five minutes, so make your points, show photographs and stay professional.

Sample Appeal Letter

Date
Name, Address, Telephone

To the Board of Review/Tax Tribunal:

I wish to appeal my property tax assessment for the following reasons:

1. According to my Worksheet/Property Record, I have noted the following discrepancies:

   A. I do not have a fireplace as indicated.
   Estimated value $1,800

   B. I do not have a tile bath as indicated.
   Estimated value $1,200

   C. According to my worksheet, I have 1500 square feet of living space. I have 1000 square feet.
   Reduced value $6,920

This amount should be deducted from true cash value $9,920

2. I have noted the following defects on my property. They reduce the value of the property by the following amounts:

   A. Cracked foundation $3,800

   B. Cracked exterior wall $2,200

This amount should be deducted from true cash value $6,000

3. I live in an area that has mixed zoning and next door there is a new junkyard which emits loud noises and noxious odors. This affects the value of my property. I feel my true cash value has been reduced by.....$3,000

3a. Grand Total, add #1, 2 and 3 above........$18,920

4. I wish to make the following comparables:

   231 Main Street, assessed value ____________

   (list all comparables and ask for an average reduction. Note: add all items you noted as discrepancies, comparable amounts, etc.)

   Example:

   True cash value $60,000

   Minus Discrepancy/Grand Total$18,920

   New True Cash Value..................$41,080

   One half = Assessed value (SEV)$20,540

NOTE: This sample letter indicates many of the grounds for a reduced assessment. It is very unlikely than an assessment could be reduced by nearly one-third, as illustrated here, but every reduction is important.

Tele-Court

A Michigan Public Information System

Call 1-800-968-5669 or 1-800-YOU-KNOW

COURTS
1122 Which Court Do I Need?
1123 Circuit Court
1131 District Court
1132 Probate Court
1133 Small Claims Court
1211 Court of Claims
1212 Friend of the Court
1213 Supreme Court
1221 Court of Appeals
1222 Bankruptcy Court
1223 Recorder's Court

TYPES OF COURT CASES
1111 Types of Court Cases
1112 What is a Civil Case?
1113 What is a Criminal Case?
1121 What is a Juvenile Case?
1222 Bankruptcy Cases

CIVIL ISSUES
1112 What is a Civil Case?
1133 Small Claims Court
1313 Landlord & Tenant Disputes
1311 How to Collect Garnishments
1312 How to Respond to a Garnishment
1231 Traffic - Civil Infractions
2231 Divorce
3122 How to Find an Attorney
3322 Community Dispute Resolution

CRIMINAL ISSUES
1113 What is a Criminal Case?
1321 What Happens if You're Arrested?
1333 Types of Crimes
1322 Types of Bonds
1323 Probation vs Parole
1332 Court Appointed Attorneys
3213 How to Get a Restraining Order
2112 Juvenile Delinquents and the Court
1131 District Court
3132 Victim's Rights
3122 How to Find an Attorney

TRAFFIC
3323 Traffic Violations - General
1231 Traffic - Civil Infractions
1232 Adult Traffic Misdemeanors
1233 Minors and Traffic Misdemeanors
3311 Drunk Driving Violations
3312 Restricted Driver's License
3321 Points and your Driving Record
1131 District Court
3122 How to Find an Attorney

FAMILY
2231 Divorce
1212 Friend of the Court
2313 Child Custody
2321 Visitation
2322 How to Get Child Support
2331 Child Support Guidelines
2312 Marriage by the Court
2311 Adoptions
2333 Paternity - General
3111 Paternity - Information for Men
3112 Paternity - Information for Women
1123 Circuit Court
1132 Probate Court
3122 How to Find an Attorney

JUVENILE
1121 What is a Juvenile Case?
2112 Juvenile Delinquents and the Court
1233 Minors and Traffic Misdemeanors
1333 Types of Crimes
3212 Status Offenses
2113 Emancipation
2132 Parental Consent Waiver
2123 Conservators for Minors
2122 Guardians for Minors
2133 Child Abuse and Neglect
2211 Name Changes -Adults and Minors Age 14 and Older
2212 Name Changes for Minors Under the Age of 14
3132 Victim's Rights
3122 How to Find an Attorney

PROBATE

2221 What is a Will?
2222 Decedent's Estates
2121 Guardian/Conservator - General
2122 Guardians for Minors
2123 Conservators for Minors
3233 Power of Attorney
2133 Child Abuse and Neglect
2223 Mental Health Commitments
2213 How to get Birth or Death Certificates
2211 Name Changes - Adults and Minors Age 14 and Older
2212 Name Changes for Minors Under the Age of 14
2311 Adoptions
2333 Paternity - General
3132 Victim's Rights
1132 Probate Court

GENERAL ISSUES

3121 Jury Duty
3131 What is a Witness?
3132 Victim's Rights
3221 Complaints about the Court
3232 Where to get Court Forms
1332 Court Appointed Attorneys
3122 How to Find an Attorney
2133 Child Abuse and Neglect
3322 Community Dispute Resolution
3233 Power of Attorney

Call toll-free
1-800-YOU-KNOW

Tele-Court was developed under a grant from the State Justice Institute. Points of view expressed herein are those of the Michigan State Court Administrative Office and do not necessarily represent the official position or policies of the State Justice Institute.

MICHIGAN STATE POLICE

Department Headquarters
S. Harrison Road, East Lansing, MI 48823
Telephone: 517/ 332-2521

Emergencies Only,
Call the nearest post or dial toll-free: 1-800-525-5555
(on cellular phones, dial 911) VOICE/TDD 517/322-1911

Location	Telephone
DETROIT AREA	
Brighton	810/227-1051
Detroit	313/256-9636
Flat Rock	313/782-2434
New Baltimore	810/725-7503
Northville	810/348-1505
Pontiac	810/332-9132
Romeo	313/752-5222
St. Clair	313/329-2233
Ypsilanti	313/482-1211
E. MICHIGAN	
Bad Axe	517/269-6441
Bay City	517/684-2234
Bridgeport	517/777-3700
Caro	517/673-2156
East Tawas	517/362-3434
Flint	810/732-1111
Gladwin	517/426-4811
Lapeer	810/684-2905
Owosso	517/723-6761
Sandusky	810/648-2233
West Branch	517/345-0955
S. MICHIGAN	
Adrian	517/263-0033

Location	Telephone
Battle Creek	616/968-6115
Coldwater	517/278-2373
Erie	313/848-2015
Jackson	517/782-9443
Jonesville (Hillsdale)	517/849-9922
Lansing	517/322-1911
New Buffalo	616/469-1111
Niles	616/683-4411
Paw Paw	616/657-5551
White Pigeon	616/483-7611
W. MICHIGAN	
Grand Haven	616/842-2100
Hart	616/873-2171
Hastings	616/948-8283
Ionia	616/527-3600
Lakeview	517/352-8444
Newaygo	616/652-1661
Rockford	616/866-4411
St. Joseph	616/429-1111
Saugatuck	616/857-2800
South Haven	616/637-2125
Wayland	616/792-2213
N. MICHIGAN	
Alpena	517/354-4101
Cadillac	616/775-2433

Location	Telephone
Cheboygan	616/627-9973
Gaylord	517/732-5141
Houghton Lake	517/422-5101
Ithaca	517/875-4111
Kalkaska	616/258-2831
Manistee	616/723-3535
Mt. Pleasant	517/773-5951
Petoskey	616/347-8101
Reed City	616/832-2221
Traverse City	616/946-4646
UPPER PENINSULA	
Calumet	906/337-2211
Gladstone	906/428-4411
Iron Mountain	906/774-2121
Iron River	906/265-9916
L'Anse	906/524-6161
Manistique	906/341-2101
Munising	906/387-4550
Negaunee	906/475-9922
Newberry	906/293-5151
St. Ignace	906/643-8383
Sault Ste. Marie	906/632-2216
Stephenson	906/753-2275
Wakefield	906/224-9691

Visit Michigan's Capitol, Library & Historical Center

HOW TO REACH . . .

Lansing—Michigan's capital city—is accessible by all forms of transportation. If traveling by motor vehicle, take I-69, I-496 or I-96 to the "Downtown Lansing" exit and follow signs to the "Capitol Loop." The Logan/M. L. King Street (M-99) exit is just one block west of the Michigan Library and Historical Center.

The Capitol is located at the intersection of Michigan and Capitol avenues, five blocks north of I-496. Scheduled tours begin on the main floor, east wing.

The Michigan Library and Historical Center is between Allegan and Washtenaw streets, and west of the Capitol. Library tours begin at the first floor of the west wing off the central lobby, while Museum tours start at the Information Desk on the first floor of the east wing. Entrances to the Center are clearly marked.

Limited automobile and bus parking is available directly south of the Center between Butler and Sycamore streets. The main entrance to parking and the building is from Washtenaw Street near the main entrance circle. For a parking map and information about parking lots, please phone (517) 373-2353.

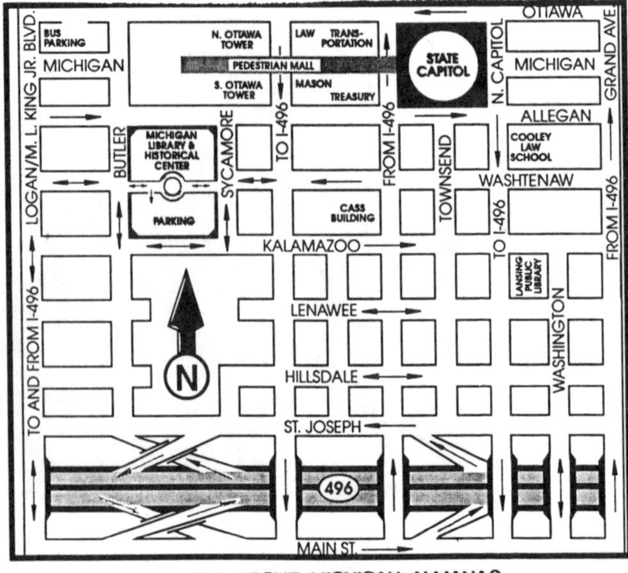

MICHIGAN'S CAPITOL COMPLEX

Lansing has been the home of Michigan government for 130 years. In 1879 the state built its present Capitol, still the most distinctive attraction downtown.

The Capitol has been joined by the Michigan Library and Historical Center as a destination for tours. Located two blocks southwest of the Capitol, the 312,000-square-foot building with its copper-lined courtyard and five-story atriums is a recent, spectacular addition to the Capitol Complex. Included in the Center are the Michigan Historical Museum, the Library of Michigan and the State Archives.

There is no charge for tours of the Capitol or the Michigan Library and Historical Center. To arrange visits or tours for groups of 10 or more, please call the Capitol Tour Guide and Information Service: (517) 373-2353 weekdays, or (517) 373-2348 weekends and holidays.

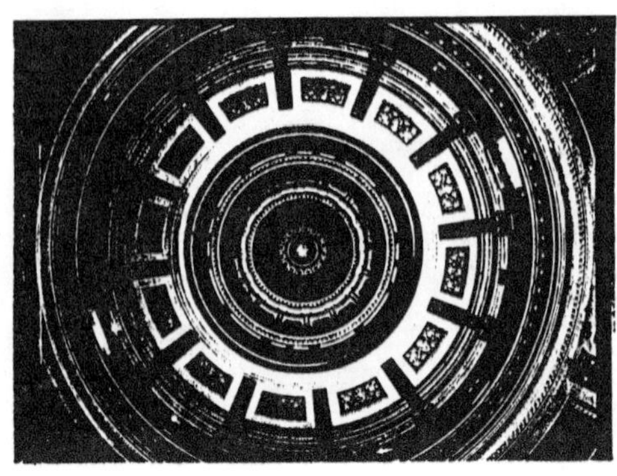

STATE CAPITOL

Scheduled tours are offered seven days a week by the Capitol Tour Guide and Information Service, a ready reference for questions about the Capitol and state government. Tours encompass the public areas of the Capitol and include visits to the House and Senate galleries. Architectural restoration is underway. Guides provide historical and contemporary information on the Capitol and the legislative process.

Visits may be made from **9 am to 4 pm Mondays-Fridays; 10 am to 4 pm Saturdays and Holidays; and Noon to 4 pm Sundays**.

45-minute tours for groups of 10 or more must be scheduled in advance with the Capitol Tour Guide and Information Service, Capitol Building, Lansing, MI 48909. Call (517) 373-2353 for more information.

LIBRARY OF MICHIGAN

With 5.6 million items, 27 miles of shelving and the second largest state library building in the nation, the Library of Michigan is our state's version of the Library of Congress. This research and documents library has aided state government and the people of Michigan since 1828. Visitors will find the 10th largest collection of genealogy information in the U.S. and

the state's Service for the Blind and Physically Handicapped. Library hours are **8 am to 6 pm weekdays, 9 am to 5 pm Saturdays and 1 pm to 5 pm Sundays**. Closed on official holidays. Phone (517) 373-5400 for current schedule or (517) 373-1580 for additional information.

MICHIGAN HISTORICAL MUSEUM

Permanent exhibits featuring life-like facades of a lumber baron's mansion and Michigan's Territorial Capitol are offered by the Michigan Historical Museum. A walk-through replica copper mine, woodland diorama, audio-visual presentations and a temporary exhibit gallery are also included. Open **weekdays 9 am to 4:30 pm, 10 am to 4 pm Saturdays, and 1 pm to 5 pm Sundays**. For general information, call the Museum office at (517) 373-3559.

STATE ARCHIVES OF MICHIGAN

The State Archives offer researchers access to 80 million documents, some 330,000 photographs and 500,000 maps and drawings in a state-of-the-art facility. The Archives is open **weekdays from 9 am to 5 pm**.

For general information or to schedule research, please call (517) 373-1408.

MICHIGAN LIBRARY AND HISTORICAL CENTER

Michigan's Library of Congress

Since territorial days in 1828, the Library of Michigan has served state government and the people of Michigan much as the Library of Congress works at a federal level. The Library's early task was to collect, compile and store Michigan territorial laws and other important documents which formed the basis for how Michigan government exists today.

Over time the Library's responsibility has expanded to include the collection of all Michigan state government publications as well as important journals, books and other materials. A large newspaper collection is both current and in microform back to the 1700's. The Library's genealogy collection is the 10th largest in the U.S., with historical census data, ship crossing logs and related family information from the northeastern United States and eastern Canada found on its shelves.

Hundreds of Michigan periodicals are available, ranging from general interest magazines to journals published by trade associations and special interest groups. Also collected are economic and census data about Michigan and its business and industrial organizations. Historical and biographical works in the Michigan Collection include the only fictional materials found at the Library.

Mission of the Library

The Library of Michigan exists to:

I. Meet the information needs of the Legislature and State Government,

II. Meet the administrative, developmental and technical assistance needs of Michigan libraries, and

III. Meet library service needs of individuals and agencies as a statewide resource.

Responsibilities

The Library of Michigan is the official state library agency for Michigan and has been administratively responsible to the state legislature since 1983. Library collections housed at the Michigan Library and Historical Center, at the State Law Library Division in downtown Lansing and at the Upper Peninsula Branch in Escanaba total more than three million hard cover books, bound periodical volumes and government documents. Extensive newspaper files in microform raise the collection total to more than 5.6 million items, stored on over 27 miles of shelving.

The Lewis Cass state office building housed the Library until this devastating 1951 fire. The collection was then stored at various locations before moving to its new home at the Michigan Library and Historical Center in late 1988.

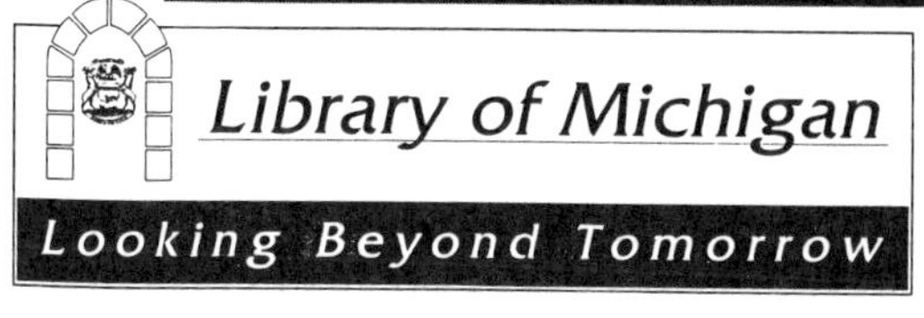

A Computerized Catalog

The Library's computerized NOTIS "ANSWER" system replaces traditional card catalogs and locates holdings by **A**uthor, **K**eyword, **S**ubject or **T**itle. Over 90 terminals are conveniently located to enable searches from any area of the Library. **K**eyword searching enables a combination of terms to be examined at the same time, such as "Indians" and "Chippewa". Michigan residents can also dial into the "ANSWER" system toll-free by modem from any home/office computer if they call 1-800-669-8779 or 373-6788 if in the Lansing area.

Reference Services

Amidst a broad variety of materials, the Library's reference service provides answers to questions about most subjects. A special highlight is in-depth data about and for state government, such as directories of human service agencies and of businesses. Walk-in patrons have access to numerous CD-ROM (compact disc) materials collections. In addition, the Library provides dial-up access to the catalogs of a half dozen other major Michigan libraries. Over 400 commercial online databases are also available on a fee basis. Telephone inquiries are received by the Reference Research Center (RRC) at 517-373-1300.

Federal & State Documents

All materials published by the U.S. Government Printing Office are received and stored at the Library of Michigan, with more than one million volumes ranging from agriculture to zoology. This Library and the Detroit Public Library are Michigan's only regional federal document depository libraries. The Library of Michigan also distributes state government publications to about 60 depository libraries across the state. The Michigan Documents Collection includes all state executive and legislative publications issued since 1805, with more than 100,000 items.

Genealogy

Over 100,000 books and microforms provide an array of resources for those with Michigan ancestry. Census records beginning in 1790 are kept for states east of Iowa and north of Tennessee, as well as eastern Canada. Soundex indices begin with 1880 data. Also in the collection are city directories for U.S. cities, county histories, over 20,000 individual and collective family histories, land records, maps and atlases, the Michigan Vertical File, military records up to World War I, 70,000 reels of Michigan newspapers on microfilm, 250 genealogical and historical periodicals and Michigan vital record indices to 1914. Another 10,000 titles are found in the extensive genealogy and local history microfiche collection.

The Michigan Collection

Materials about Michigan from all time periods and subjects are available at the Library. This includes books, periodicals, popular trade publications, as well as scholarly and literary works.

Law Library Services

The Law Library Division is located at 525 W. Ottawa Street in the Law Building, approximately one block northeast of the main Library of Michigan. It collects federal and state law plus related materials and subscribes to online databases such as HERMES, LEXIS and WESTLAW. QUESTOR contains the current compiled laws of Michigan. Online access to the status of pending Michigan legislation is offered via BILL STATUS. The Law Library also receives numerous legal periodicals and law reviews and can be phoned at 517-373-0630.

SPECIAL SERVICES

Service for the Blind & Physically Handicapped (SBPH)

The Library's SBPH is one of two regional libraries in Michigan and is part of a nationwide network administered by the National Library Service at the Library of Congress, Washington D.C. The regional library at the Library of Michigan circulates materials to individuals and institutions in 24 counties and braille materials to all Michigan residents. Ten subregional libraries in Alpena, Ann Arbor, Farmington Hills, Flint, Grand Rapids, Marquette, Mt. Clemens, Muskegon, Port Huron and Traverse City also provide NLS disc and cassette books and the equipment to play them. For information, call 517-373-1590 or 1-800-992-9012 or TDD to 517-373-1592.

MICHIGAN HALL OF FAME

Henry Ford and Steven Mason are the first two people inducted into the new Michigan Hall of Fame which has began its existence as a feature in the 1993 *ALL ABOUT MICHIGAN ALMANAC.*

Two more outstanding people have been added by the 1995 Almanac. One was named for achievement since 1900 and the other for the pre-1900 period. They are:

William C. Durrant, automotive pioneer and Flint resident- visionary who founded the General Motors Corp, which became the world's largest manufacturing company.

Antoine de la Moth Cadillac, French pioneer administrator who founded Detroit (Fort Pontchartrain) in 1701. It became the nations's fourth largest city in the mid-1900's , the world auto center and the Arsenal of Democracy in World War II.

Gerald Ford and Lee Iacocca have been listed on the Hall's Michigan Roll of Honor in recognition of their more contemporary achievements.

Additional people will be added annually to both lists. They will be selected by a panel of objective Michigan journalists, educators, historians and other authorities.

Henry Ford was named for outstanding achievement since 1900, and Steven Mason for the pre-1900 period.

Ford founded the Ford Motor Company in 1903, where he inaugurated automotive mass production. Before the end of the 1920's he had produced more than half the cars of the world, and his 15 million Model T's "put the world on wheels."

Ford introduced the 8 hour day (it had been 10), and the $5 a day minimum wage (almost doubling the prevailing 1914 standard). This inspired mass immigration to Michigan from other states and Europe, and created a whole new class of car buyers, the prosperous workers themselves. Born in 1863, in Dearborn, Michigan, he died in 1947, and is buried in St. Martha's Episcopal Church cemetery, Grand River and Greenfield, Detroit.

Mason was the "Father" of the State of Michigan, although he was not much more than a "boy" himself. He became Acting Governor of the Michigan Territory at age 19, and was elected Michigan's first Governor at age 23. Mason was re-elected at age 25, and died at age 31.

During his brief, but dynamic, life, he led the territory into statehood, and reluctantly accepted for the state a large portion of the Upper Peninsula, to relinquish Michigan's original claim to Toledo, Ohio. Prior to the settlement, he mobilized the Michigan militia for the "Toledo War." When the dispute was settled, under pressure from President Andrew Jackson, Michigan was admitted to the Union as the 26th state.

Mason was born in Virginia, in 1812, and is buried in Capitol Park, in downtown Detroit. A statue marks his grave, on the site of the first State Capitol (before it was relocated to Lansing). The Park is located on State, at the corner of Griswold.

Gerald Ford was listed on the Roll of Honor for his healing service as the 38th President of the U.S. Born in Nebraska, in 1913, his mother moved to Michigan where he became the 13-term Congressman from Grand Rapids (1948-1973), where the Gerald Ford Presidential Museum is now located.

Lee Iacocca, Chairman and CEO of Chrysler Corporation, until December 31, 1992, was listed on the Roll of Honor for his leadership in saving and restoring the giant auto firm to eminence (vital to the state's economic health). He was born in Pennsylvania, October 15, 1924, and was the president of Ford Motor Company prior to joining Chrysler.

It can be noted that Michigan has a large number of very notable achievers to be considered for the Michigan Hall of Fame and the Roll of Honor in future years. Antoine Cadillac, French founder of Detroit (1701); William Beaumont, who conducted a revolutionary and world famous medical study on Mackinac Island (1815); William Durant, founder of General Motors Corporation (1908), who preserved the names of such automotive pioneers as Olds, Buick and Chevrolet, while he himself is almost forgotten (although the company he founded is still the world's largest industrial firm); Walter Reuther, innovative President of the UAW (United Auto Workers) during the expansive years of 1946-1970); William Kellogg, progenitor of the world's breakfast food industry; Ralph Bunch, a black Detroiter who became U.N. Undersecretary General and won the Nobel Peace Prize (1950); Martha Griffiths, first Congresswoman elected from Michigan (10-terms), and first woman elected to a Michigan executive office (Lt. Governor, 1982-90); and Sojurner Truth, a freed slave who became a renowned leader for black emancipation and women's rights.

Readers of the *ALL ABOUT MICHIGAN ALMANAC* are invited to submit nominations (P.O. Box 202, Hartland, MI 48353).

Stevens Mason, Michigan's boy Governor

Henry Ford, the auto pioneer who put the "world on wheels"

STATE OF MICHIGAN
SPORTS HALL OF FAME

MICHIGAN'S GREATEST ATHLETES

Five of the states's greatest athletes were elected to the State of Michigan Sports Hall of Fame in 1995, six in 1994 and five in 1993. They join more than 100 others who preceded them, plus half that number of outstanding coaches, executives and personalities, whose plaques are exhibited in Cobo Hall, Detroit.

1995

BARNEY Mc COSKEY, baseball

TERRY BARR, football

RUDY TOMJANOVICH, MSU basketball and coach of the Houston Rockets.

JIM NORTHRUP, baseball

DICK ENBERG, TV network broadcaster (NFL, baseball, tennis)

1994

REGGIE McKENZIE, football, U of M and NFL

MICKEY STANLEY, baseball

CARL ANGELO, amateur baseball (still pitching at age 60).

RON MASON, MSU hockey coach.

MIKE HALL, pro golf

BUDD LYNCH, sports broadcaster (Red Wings).

1993

SPENCER HAYWOOD, U of D basketball star, and Olympic, NBA and ABA player.

DAVE HILL, 13-time winner in the PGA tour and now a top player on Senior PGA tour.

MICKI KING HOGUE, U of M diver and 1972 Olympic gold metal winner.

HARVEY KEUNN, Detroit Tiger all star (he later managed the Milwaukee Brewers in the 1982 World Series).

BUBBA SMITH, Michigan State football star, who later played for the Baltimore Colts and Oakland Raiders.

All people named to the Hall prior to 1993 were reported in the last edition of this Almanac. A conplete, up to date report, is scheduled for the Almanac next year.

Note; Tickets for the 1995 induction dinner to be held May 17 at Cobo Hall are available by phoning (810) 362-5870.

NCAA BASKETBALL CHAMPIONSHIP GAMES

1993 NC over Michigan, 77-71
1992 Duke over Michigan, 71-51
1989 Michigan over Seton Hall, 80-79
1979 Michigan State over Indiana State, 75-64
1976 Indiana over Michigan, 86-68
1965 UCLA over Michigan, 91-80

NCAA HOCKEY CHAMPIONS

YEAR	COLLEGE
1992	Lake Superior
1991	Northern Michigan
1988	Lake Superior St.
1986	Michigan State
1975	Michigan Tech
1966	Michigan State
1965	Michigan Tech
1964	Michigan
1962	Michigan Tech
1956	Michigan
1955	Michigan
1953	Michigan
1952	Michigan
1951	Michigan
1948	Michigan

NATIONAL FOOTBALL CHAMPIONS

Several sources have picked the mythical national champion of college football annually since 1883. The NCAA does not yet hold an actual championship tournament in football as it does in other sports. Michigan colleges which were selected as champion, or co-champion when polls differed between two schools (*), are listed below.

YEAR		RECORD
1966*	Michigan State	9-0-1
1965*	Michigan State	10-1-0
1952*	Michigan State	9-0-0
1948	Michigan	9-0-0
1947*	Michigan	10-0-0
1933	Michigan	7-0-1
1932*	Michigan	8-0-0
1902	Michigan	11-0-0
1901	Michigan	11-0-0

FOOTBALL BOWLS

ROSE BOWL

YEAR	
1993	MICHIGAN over Washington, 38-31
1992	Washington over Michigan, 34-14
1990	USC over Michigan 17-10
1989	MICHIGAN over USC 22-14
1988	MICHIGAN STATE over USC 20-17
1987	Arizona State over Michigan 22-15
1983	UCLA over Michigan 24-14
1981	MICHIGAN over Washington 23-6
1979	USC over Michigan 17-10
1978	MICHIGAN over Washington
1977	USC over Michigan 14-6
1972	Stanford over Michigan 13-12
1970	USC over Michigan 10-3
1966	UCLA over Michigan State 14-12
1965	MICHIGAN over Oregon State 34-7
1956	MICHIGAN STATE over UCLA 17-14
1954	MICHIGAN STATE over UCLA 28-20
1951	MICHIGAN over California 14-6
1948	MICHIGAN over USC 49-0
1902	MICHIGAN over Stanford 49-0

ORANGE BOWL

1976 Oklahoma over Michigan

SUGAR BOWL

1984 Auburn over Michigan

JOHN HANCOCK BOWL

1990 MICHIGAN over USC

GATOR BOWL

1991 MICHIGAN over Miss
1989 Georgia over Mich St
1979 NC over Michigan

FIESTA BOWL

1986 MICHIGAN over Nebraska

HOLIDAY BOWL

1995 MICHIGAN over Colorado St
1984 BYU over Michigan

CALIFORNIA BOWL

1990 San Jose St over C.M.
1987 E.M. over San Jose St

ALOHA BOWL

1989 MICH ST over Hawaii

HALL OF FAME BOWL

1988 MICHIGAN over Alabama

MICHIGAN WOMEN'S HALL OF FAME

Michigan Women's Historical Center
and Hall of Fame
213 W. Main St., Lansing, MI 48933

The following women have been added to the distinquished group which were reported in full in the last edition of the All About Michigan Almanac.

CATHERINE CARTER BLACKWELL, pioneer in African-American Studies.

JEAN W. CAMPBELL, a major force in the creation of what is now the CENTER FOR EDUCATION OF WOMEN.

JEANNE OMELENCHUK, U.S. Olympic speed skater and premier National Champion.

MILDRED CLARK WOODMAN, Colonel in Army Nurse Corps who won changes in regulation that discriminated against women.

EDITH VOSBURGH ALVORD (1876-1962), Detroit Community Leader and Suffragest.

KATHERINE HILL CAMPBELL (1868-1942), first Superintendent of the Detroit House of Corrections.

LEANNA FRANCES COOPER (1875-1961), pioneer in the development of dietetics.

ROBERTA GRIFFITH (1870-1941), Champion for the Blind.

BINA WEST MILLER (1867-1954), pioneer to provide insurance for women.

SIPPIE WALLACE (1899-1986), "Queen of the Blues."

EDNA NOBLE WHITE (1879-1954), founding director of the Merrill-Palmer Institute.

RUTH CARLTON, pioneer of adoption in mass media.

FLOSSIE COHEN M.D., research and clinical pediatrician.

BERTHA A. DAUBENDICK, pioneer in the establishment of 142 new nature sanctuaries in 51 Michigan Counties.

GENORA JOHNSON DOLLINGER, a leader in women's activities in the UAW-CIO since 1937 (Historic GM-Flint sit-down strike).

FLORA HOMMEL, founder of the Childbirth Without Pain Education Association, which has had over 18,000 students.

MARIE-THERESE GUNYON-CADILLAC (1671-1746), first white woman to cross 750 miles of uncharted and hostile wilderness from Quebec and settle in Detroit (Fort Pontchartrain).

SARAH VAN HOOSEN JONES (1892-1972), first woman in the U.S. to earn a Doctorate in Animal Genetics.

ALEDA E. LUTZ (1915-1944), flew 196 air missions evacuating 3,500 wounded men, before being killed in World War II, she was the most highly decorated servicewoman of this century.

HELEN WALTEER McANDREW (1826-1906), pioneer M.D., specialized in diseases of women and children, and a leader in bringing about the admission of women into U of M's Medical Dept. (1870).

Trivia

Q In which year did Michigan copper miners strike for 9-months in support of the 8-hour day ?

A 1919

Q How many people survived the airline crash in 1987 at Metro Detroit which claimed 156 lives ?

A One

Q Where was the first world's major shopping mall opened ?

A Southfield (Northland", in 1954)

The Historic Top Ten Automotive Men

SELECTED BY HENRY FORD II (1986)

Source: Detroit Section, Society of Automotive Engineers

- **Henry Ford** I, of course, whose achievements are too numerous to mention.
- **Ransom Olds**, who saw the need for a low-priced car produced in large volume which resulted in the curved-dash runabout — "The Merry Oldsmobile" made famous in song.
- **Henry M. Leland**, who nurtured the two surviving luxury nameplates, Cadillac and Lincoln. He achieved fame for his precision tooling and manufacturing, and setting standards for automotive parts interchangeability.
- **William C. Durant**, founder of General Motors. At an early time he envisioned roads swarming with cars and realized that a large multidivision company was one of the best ways to build them.
- **John** and **Horace Dodge**, built a car with a reputation for dependability and showed "true grit" by taking on Henry Ford I in a famous intra-company lawsuit, and won.
- **Walter P. Chrysler**, whose 1924 Chrysler set a first year sales record and was the founder of the last major American company to enter the business and stay in it.
- **Charlie (Charles F.) Kettering**, gave the industry Ethyl gasoline, fast drying paints, high compression engines, improved diesels, and the electric starter.
- **Alfred P. Sloan, Jr.**, GM Chairman, for being a superb administrator. He pioneered the annual model change, developed the industry's finest research organization and first proving ground, and introduced the 10-day sales report which to this day helps coordinate demand and supply.
- **Charlie Nash**, an executive for Durant-Dort Carriage Company, then president of Buick and General Motors, and the head of Nash Motors. His time span in the industry surpassed even Henry Ford I.

The automotive industry owes a great deal to these men; they are all pioneers in the business. And there are certainly more than ten people who have made significant contributions to the U.S. auto industry. However, if forced to pick ten, these names seem to represent a very good choice.

MICHIGAN BLUE RIBBON SCHOOLS OF THE YEAR

1994–95 Source - Mich Dept Of Education

Selected for strong leadership and effective working relationships among schools, parents and community, an orderly and conductive learning atmosphere, and effective resolution of problems, with virtually all students developing academic skills.

SCHOOL	CITY	COUNTY	PRINCIPAL
Rockford High School	Rockford	Kent	James Haskins
Van Hoosen Middle Sch	Rochester	Oakland	Marv Rubin
East Grand Rapids H.S.	E. Gd Rapids	Kent	Patrick Cwayna
Smith Middle School	Troy	Oakland	Stuart Redpath
Caledonia High School	Caledonia	Kent	Tonya Porter
Everett High School	Lansing	Ingham	Gary Bredahl
McPherson Middle Sch.	Howell	Livingston	G. Douglas Paige
Holt Jr High School	Holt	Ingham	Susan York
Byron Cntr High Sch.	Byron	Kent	William Skilling
L'Anse Creuse H.S. N.	Harrison	Macomb	Tom Denewith

MICHIGAN TEACHER OF THE YEAR *1980–1995*

Source - Mich Dept of Education

YEAR	NAME	CITY	COUNTY	GRADE LEVEL	SUBJECT
1994/95	**Sharon Green**	**Marquette**	**Marquette**	**High School**	**Music/Computers**
1993/94	**Robt. L. VanCamp**	**Utica Schools**	**Macomb**	**High School**	**E. Asian Studies**
1992/93	Nancy Flanagan	Hartland	Livingston	Middle School	Instrumental/Vocal
1991/92	Thomas Fleming	W.I.S.D.	Washtenaw	Secondary	Special Education
1990/91	Katherine Afendoulis	Grand Rapids	Kent	3rd Grade	All subjects
1989/90	Cynthia Ann Broad	Mt. Clemens	Macomb	K-6	Special Education
1988/89	Andrea R. Willis	Warren	Macomb		
1987/88	Edward Manning	Ypsilanti	Washtenaw	High School	Art Teacher
1986/87	Nancy Bray	Jenison	Ottawa	Middle School	Vocal/ Music
1985/86	Jacquelyn Caffey	Detroit	Wayne	Elementary	All subjects
1984/85	Judyth Dobbert	Albion	Calhoun	Elementary	All subjects
1983/84	Marvelle J. Vannest	Kalkaska	Kalkaska		
1982/83	Hugh P. Spagnuolo	Lansing	Ingham	High School	English
1981/82	Melvin A. Miller	Mt. Clemens	Macomb	Middle School	Social Studies
1980/81	Joan Hammersmith	Grand Rapids	Kent	1st Grade	All subjects

WORLD FAMOUS ENTERTAINERS BORN IN MICHIGAN

Mentioning some of Michigan's most famous entertainers by their original names would produce the following:

Edna Gilhooley, Vincent Furnier, Janet Cole, Betty Thornberg, Louise Ciccone, Harvey Yeary, Patricia Early, Amos Jacobs, Wayne McMeekan and Stevland Morris.

Not impressed?

Let's list them again, using their stage names:

Ellen Burstyn, Alice Cooper, Julie Harris, Betty Hutton, Madonna, Lee Majors, Della Reese, Danny Thomas, David Wayne and Stevie Wonder.

They, together with these others, make up an impressive list of 53 Michigan natives who are among the world's most famous entertainers:

Harry Blackstone, Jr.	Three Rivers	6-30-34
Sonny Bono	Detroit	2-16-35
Ellen Burstyn	Detroit	12-7-32
Timothy Busfield	Lansing	6-12-57
Alice Cooper	Detroit	2-4-48
Francis Coppola	Detroit	4-7-39
Pam Dawber	Farmington Hls	10-18-51
Sherilyn Fenn	Detroit	
Max Gail	Detroit	4-5-43
David Alan Grier	Detroit	6-30-55
Julie Harris	Grosse Pte Pk	12-2-25
Kim Hunter	Detroit	11-12-22
Betty Hutton	Battle Creek	2-26-21
Arte Johnson	Benton Harbor	1-20-29
Casey Kasem	Detroit	
Christine Lahti	Detroit	4-5-50
Ruth Laredo	Detroit	11-20-37
Piper Laurie	Detroit	1-22-32
Joan Leslie	Detroit	1-28-26
Madonna (Ciccone)	Bay City	8-16-58
Dick Martin	Detroit	1-30-23
Donna McKechnie	Pontiac	11-16-42
Lonette McKee	Detroit	
Ed McMahon	Detroit	3-6-23
Martin Milner	Detroit	12-28-27
Lee Majors	Wyandotte	4-23-40
Harry Morgan	Detroit	4-10-15
Michael Moriarty	Detroit	4-5-41
Denise Nickolas	Detroit	

Joyce Randolph	Detroit	10-21-25
Della Reese	Detroit	7-6-31
Smokey Robinson	Detroit	2-19-40
Diana Ross	Detroit	3-26-44
Mitch Ryder	Hamtramck	
Roz Ryan	Detroit	7-7-51
Steven Seagal	Lansing	4-10-51
Tom Selleck	Detroit	1-29-45
Burt Reynolds	Lansing	2-11-36
Tom Skerritt	Detroit	8-25-33
Richard Stahl	Detroit	1-4-32
Elaine Stritch	Detroit	2-2-26
Sinbad	Benton Harbor	
Marlo Thomas	Detroit	11-21-43
Lily Tomlin	Detroit	9-1-39
Robert Wagner	Detroit	2-10-30
David Wayne	Traverse City	1-30-14
Margaret Whiting	Detroit	7-22-24
Elizabeth Wilson	Gd. Rapids	4-4-25
Stevie Wonder	Saginaw	5-13-50
Max Wright	Detroit	

Trivia

Q Who was the first female inducted into the Rock & Roll Hall of Fame?

A Aretha Franklin (Motown Star).

Q Which was the first city in the U.S. to add flouride to it's drinking water?

A Grand Rapids (1945).

Q Where was the pneumatic hammer invented ?

A Detroit (by C.B. King).

Q One lump of pure copper discovered in the U.P. weighed how much ?

A 14,000 lbs

Q Where is the world's oldest freshwater acquarium ?

A Belle Isle, Detroit.

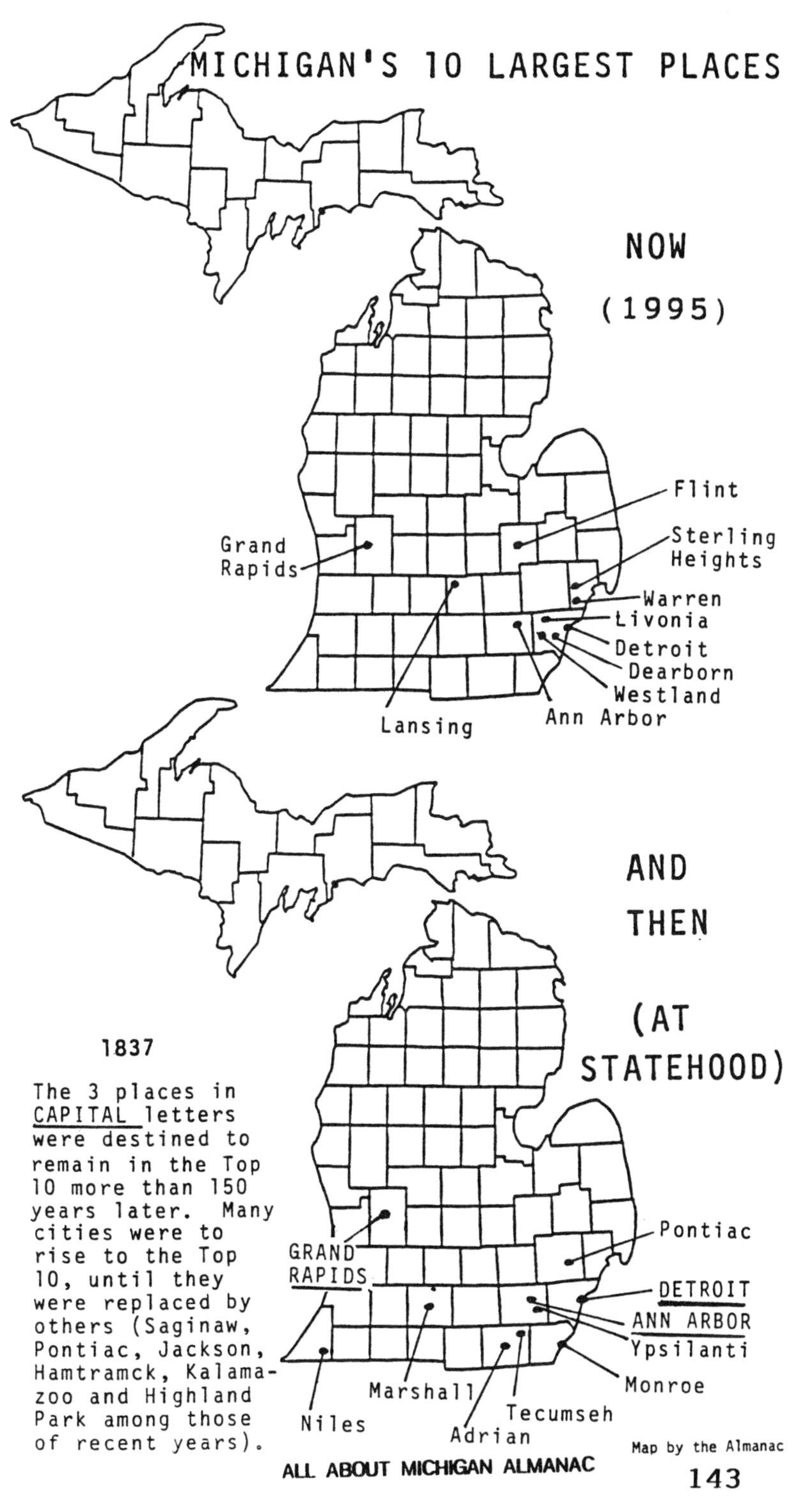
MICHIGAN'S 10 LARGEST PLACES
NOW
(1995)
Flint
Sterling Heights
Grand Rapids
Warren
Livonia
Detroit
Dearborn
Westland
Lansing
Ann Arbor
AND THEN
(AT STATEHOOD)
1837
The 3 places in CAPITAL letters were destined to remain in the Top 10 more than 150 years later. Many cities were to rise to the Top 10, until they were replaced by others (Saginaw, Pontiac, Jackson, Hamtramck, Kalamazoo and Highland Park among those of recent years).
Pontiac
GRAND RAPIDS
DETROIT
ANN ARBOR
Ypsilanti
Monroe
Marshall
Tecumseh
Niles
Adrian
Map by the Almanac

CITIES and PLACES IN MICHIGAN

Zip
Population
County location
Unit of government

NOTE Population 1990 U.S. Census. Partial zip codes, such as 487xx, are for large cities served by more than one zip. The last two digits for a specific address in such city is available from your local post office or library. Compiled by the Almanac. Sources - U.S. Bureau of the Census, U.S. Postal Service, Michigan Manual, MI Dept of Transportation.

PLACE, COUNTY, ZIP / C - CITY, V - VILLAGE - T - TOWNSHIP, POPULATION

A

Acme, Grand Traverse, 49610/ T 3,447
Ada, Kent, 49301/ T 7,758
Addison, Lenawee, 49220/ V 632
Adrian, Lenawee, 49221/ C 22,097
Afton, Cheboygan, 49705
Ahmeek, Keeweenaw, 49901/ V 148
Akron, Tuscola, 49701/ V 421
Alanson, Emmet, 49706/ V 677
Alba, Antrin, 49611
Albion, Calhoun, 49224/ C 10,066
Alden,Antrim, 49612
Alger, Arenac, 48610/
Algonac, St Clair, 48001/ C 4,551
Allegan, Allegan, 49010/ C 4,547
Allen, Hillsdale, 49227/ V 201
Allendale, Ottawa, 49401/ T 8,022
Allen Park, Wayne, 48101/ C 31,092
Allenton, St Clair, 48002
Allouez, Keweenaw, 49805/ T 1,422
Alma, Gratiot, 48003/ C 9,034
Almont, Lapeer, 48003/ V 2,354
Alpena, Alpena, 49707/ C 11,354
Alpha, Iron, 49902/ V 219
Alto, Kent, 49302
Amasa, Iron, 49903
Anchorville, St Clair, 48004
Andrews, Berrien, 49104
Ann Arbor, Washtenaw, 481XX/ C 109,592
Applegate, Sanilac, 48401/ V 297
Arcadia, Manistee, 49613/ T 553
Argyle, Sanilac, 48410/ T 820
Armada, Macomb, 48005/ V 1,548
Arnold, Marguette, 49819
Ashley, Gratiot, 48806/ V 518
Athens, Calhoun, 49011/ V 990
Atlanta, Montmorency, 49709
Atlantic Mine, Houghton, 49905

Atlas, Genesee, 49411/ T 5,551
Attica, Lapeer, 48412/ T 3,873
Auburn, Bay, 48611/ C 1,855
Auburn Hills, Oakland,48326/ C 17,076
Au Gres, Arenac, 48703/ V 838
Augusta, Kalamazoo, 49012/ V 927
Au Train, Alger, 49806/ T 1,047
Avoca, St Clair, 48006
Azalia, Monroe, 48110

B

Bad Axe, Huron, 48413/ C 3,484
Bailey, Muskegon, 49303
Baldwin, Lake, 49304/ V 821
Bancroft, Shiawassee, 48414/ V 599
Bangor, Van Buren, 49013/ C 1,922
Bannister, Gratiot, 48807
Baraga, Baraga, 49908/ V 1,231
Barbeau, Chippewa, 49710
Bark River, Delta, 49807/ T 1,548
Baroda, Berrien, 49101/ V 657
Barryton, Mecosta, 49305/ V 393
Barton City, Alcona, 49705
Bath, Clinton, 48808/ T 6,387
Battle Creek, Calhoun, 490XX/ C 53,540
Bay City, Bay, 487XX/ C 38,936
Bay Port, Huron, 48720
Bayshore, Charlevoix, 49711
Bay View, Emmet, 49770
Bear Lake, Manistee, 49614/ V 339
Beaverton, Gladwin, 48612/ C 1,150
Bedford, Calhoun, 49020/ T 9,810
Beechwood, Iron, 49909
Belding, Ionia, 48809/ C 5,769
Bellaire, Antrim, 49615/ V 1,104
Belleville, Wayne, 48111/ C 3,270
Bellevue, Eaton, 49021/ V 1,401
Belmont, Kent, 49306
Bentley, Bay, 48613
Benton Harbor, Berrien, 49022/C 12,818
Benzonia, Benzie, 49616/ V 449
Bergland, Ontonagon, 49910/ T 618
Berkley, Oakland, 48072/ C 16,960
Berrien Springs, Berrien, 49102
Berrian Springs, Berrien,49103/V 1,927
Bessemer, Gogebic, 49911/ C 2,272
Beulah, Benzie, 49617/ V 421
Beverly Hills, Oakland, 48809/ V 10,610
Big Bay, Marquette, 49808
Big Rapids, Mecosta, 49307/ C 12,603
Bingham Farms, Oakland, 48010/ V 1,001
Birch Run, Saginaw, 48415/ V 992
Birmingham, Oakland, 480XX/ C 19,997
Bitely, Newaygo, 49309
Black River, Alcona, 49712
Blanhard, Isabella, 49310
Blissfield, Lenawee, 49228/ V 3,172
Bloomfield Hills, Oakland,48013/C 4,288
Bloomingdale, VanBuren, 49026/ V 503

Boon, Wexford, 49618/ T 562
Boyne City, Charlevoix, 49712/ C 3,478
Boyne Falls, Charlevoix, 49713/ V 369
Bradley, Allegan, 49311
Brampton, Delta, 49837
Branch, Lake, 49402
Brant, Saginaw, 48614/ T 1,942
Breckinridge, Gratiot, 48615/ V 1,301
Breedsville, VanBuren, 49027/ V 213
Brethran, Manistee, 49619
Bridgeport, Saginaw, 49722/ T 12,747
Bridgewater, Washtenaw, 48115/ T 1,304
Bridgman, Berrien, 49106/ C 2,140
Brighton, Livingston, 48116/ C 5,686
Brimley, Chippewa, 49715
Britton, Lenawee, 49229/ V 694
Brohman, Newaygo, 49312
Bronson, Branch, 49028/ C 2,342
Brooklyn, Jackson, 49230/ V 1,027
Brown City, Sanilac, 48416/ C 1,244
Bruce Crossing, Ontonagon, 49912
Brunswick, Newaygo, 49313
Brutus, Emmet, 49716
Buchanan, Berrien, 49107/ C 4,992
Buckley, Wexford, 49620/ V 402
Burlington, Calhoun, 49029/ V 294
Burnips, Allegan, 48314
Burr Oak, St Joseph, 49030/ V 882
Burt, Saginaw, 48417
Burt Lake, Cheboygan, 49717/ T 533
Burton, Genesee, 485XX/ C 27,617
Byron, Shiawassee, 48418/ V 573
Byron Center, Kent, 49315/ T 13,235

C

Cadillac, Wexford, 49601/ C 10,104
Cadmus, Lenawee, 49231
Caledonia, Kent, 49316/ V 885
Calumet, Houghton, 49913/ V 818
Camden, Hillsdale, 49232/ V 482
Camp Grayling, Crawford, 49739
Canal, Chippewa, 49783
Cannonsburg, Kent, 49317
Canton, Wayne, 481XX/ T 57,040
Capac, St Clair, 48014/ V 1,583
Carland, Clinton, 48831
Carleton, Monroe, 48117/ V 2,770
Carney, Menominee, 49812/ V 197
Caro, Tuscola, 48723/ V 4,054
Carp Lake, Emmet, 49718/ T 597
Carrollton, Saginaw, 48724/ T 6,521
Caron City, Montcalm, 48811/ C 1,158
Carsonville, Sanilac, 48419/ V 583
Casco, St Clair, 48064/ T 552
Caseville, Huron, 48725/ V 857
Casnovia, Muskegon, 49318/ V 376
Caspian, Iron, 49915/ C 1,031
Cass City, Tuscola, 48726/ V 2,276

Cassopolis, Cass, 49031/ V 1,822
Cadar, Leelanau, 49621
Cedar Lake, Montcalm, 48812
Cedar River, Menominee, 49813
Cedar Springs, Kent, 49319/ C 2,600
Cedarville, Mckinac, 49719
Cement City, Lenawee, 49233/ V 493
Center Line, Macomb, 48015/ C 9,026
Central Lake, Antrim, 49622/ V 934
Central Mich Un, Mt Pleasant, 48859
Centerville, St Joseph, 49023/ V 1,516
Ceresco, Calhoun, 49033
Campion, Marquette, 49814/ T 346
Channing, Dickinson, 49815
Charlevoix, Charlevoix, 49720/ C 3,116
Charlotte, Eaton, 48813/ C 8,083
Chase, Lake, 49623/ T 999
Chassell, Houghton, 49916
Chatham, Alger, 49816 V 268
Cheboygan, Cheboygan, 49721/ C 4,999
Chelsea, Washtenaw, 48118? V 3,772
Chesaning, Saginaw, 48616/ V 2,567
Chesterfield, Macomb, 48051/ T 25,905
Chippewa Lake, Mecosta, 49320
Christmas, Alger, 49862
Clare, Clare, 48617/ C 3,021
Clarklake, Jackson, 49234
Clarkston, Oakland, 480XX/ V 1,005
Clarksville, Ionia, 48815/ V 360
Clawson, Oakland, 48017/ C 13,874
Clayton, Lenawee, 49235/ V 384
Clifford, Lapeer, 48727/ V 354
Climax, Kalamazoo, 49034/ V 677
Clinton, Lenawee, 49236/ V 2.475
Clinton Twp, Macomb, 480XX/ T 85,866
Cohoctah, Livingston, 48816/ T 2,693
Coldwater, Branch, 49036/ C 9,607
Coleman, Midland, 48618/ C 1,237
Coloma, Berrien, 49038/ C 1,679
Colon, St Joseph, 49040/ V 1,224
Columbiaville, Lapeer, 48421 V 934
Columbus, St Clair, 48063/ T 3,235
Comins, Oscoda, 48619/ T 1,785
Commerce, Oakland, 48382/ T 26,955
Comstock, Kalamazoo, 49041
Comstock Park, Kent, 49321
Concord, Jackson, 49237/ V 944
Conklin, Ottawa, 49403
Constantine, St Joseph, 49042/ V 2,032
Conway, Emmet, 49722
Cooks, Schoolcraft, 49817
Coppersville, Ottawae, 49404/ C 3,421
Copemish, Manistee, 49625/ V 222
Copper City, Houghton, 49917/ V 198
Copper Harbor, Keweenaw, 49918
Coral, Montcalm, 49322
Cornell, Delta, 49818/ T 529

Corunna, Shiawassee, 48817/ C 3,091
Corvert, Van Buren, 49043/ T 2,855
Covington, Baraga, 49919/ T 651
Cross Village, Emmet, 49723/ T 201
Croswell, Sanilac, 48422/ C 2,174
Crystel, Montcalm, 48818/ T 2,541
Crystal Falls, Iron, 49920/ C 1,922
Curran, Alcona, 48728
Curtis, Mackinac, 49820
Custer, Mason, 49405? V 312

D

Dafter, Chippewa, 49724/ T 1,083
Daggert, Menominee, 49821/ V 260
Dalton, Muskegon, 49445/ T 6,276
Dansville, Ingham, 48819/ V 437
Davisburg, Oakland, 48350
Davison, Genessee, 48423/ C 5,693
Dearborn, Wayne, 481XX/ C 89,286
Dearborn Htgs, Wayne, 481XX/ C 60,838
Decatur, Van Buren, 49045/ V 1,760
Decker, Sanilac, 48426
Deckerville, Sanilac, 48427/ V 1,015
Deerfield, Lenawee, 49238/ V 922
Deerton, Alger, 49822
Deford, Tuscola, 48729
Delton, Barry, 49046
De Tour Village. Chippewa, 49725/V 407
Detroit, Wayne, 482XX/ C 1,027,974
DeWitt, Clinton, 48820/ C 3,964
Dexter, Washtenaw, 48130/ V 1,497
Dimondale, Eaton, 48821/ V 1,247
Dodgeville, Houghton, 49921
Dollar Bay, Houghton, 49922
Dorr, Alegan, 49323/ T 5,453
Douglas, Allegan, 49406/ V 1,040
Dowagiac, Cass, 49047/ C 6,409
Dowling, Barry, 49050
Drayton Plains, Oakland, 48330
Drummond Island, Chippewa, 49726
Dryden, Lapeer, 48428/ V 628
Dundee, Monroe, 48131/ V 2,664
Durand, Shiawassee, 48429/ C 4,283
Dutton, Kent, 49316

E

Eagle, Clinton, 48822/ V 120
Eagle Harbor, Keweenaw, 49950/ T 82
Eagle River, Keweenaw, 49924
E. China, St Clair, 48054
Eastpointe, Macomb,48021/C 35,283
E. Grand Rapids, Kent, 495XX/C 10,807
E. Jordan, Charlevoix, 49727/ C 2,240
Eastlake, Manistee, 49626/ V 473
E. Lansing, Ingham, 48823/ C 50,677
E. Leroy, Calhoun, 49051
Eastport, Antrim, 49627
E. tawas, Iosco, 48730/ C 2,287
Eaton Rapids, Eaton, 48827/ C 4,695
Eau Claire, Berrien, 49111/ V 494
Eben Junction, Alger, 49825

Eckerman,
Ecorse, Wayne, 48229/ C 12,180
Edenville, Midland, 48620/ T 2,367
Edmore, Montcalm, 48829/ V 1,126
Edwardsburg, Cass, 49112/ V 1,142
Elberta, Benzie, 49628/ V 478
Elk Rapids, Antrim, 49629/ V 1,626
Elkton, Huron, 48731/ V 958
Ellsworth, Antrim, 49729/ V 418
Elm Hall, Gratiot, 48830
Elmira, Otsego, 49730/ T 1,038
Eloise, Wayne, 48185
Elsie, Clinton, 48831/ V 957
Elwell, Gratiot, 48832
Emmett, St Clair, 48022/ V 297
Empire, Leelanau, 69630/ V 355
Engadine, Mackinac, 49827
Erie, Monroe, 48133/ T 4,492
Escanaba, Delta, 49829/ C 13,659
Essexville, Bay, 49732/ C 4,088
Estral Beach, Monroe, 481XX/ V 430
Eureka, Clinton, 48833
Evart, Osceola, 49631/ C 1,744
Ewen, Ontonagon, 49925

F

Fairgrove, Tuscola, 48733/ V 592
Fair Haven, St Clair, 48023
Fairview, Oscoda, 48621
Falmouth, Missaukee, 49632
Fargo, St Clair, 48006
Farmington, Oakland, 480XX/ C 10,132
Farmington Hls,Oakland,480XX/C 74,652
Farwell, Clare, 48622/ V 851
Felch, Dickinson, 49831
Fennville, Allegan, 49408/ C 1,023
Fenton, Genesee, 48430/ C 8,444
Fenwick, Montcalm, 48834
Ferndale, Oakland, 48220/ C 25,084
Ferrysburg, Ottawa, 49409/ C 2,919
Fibre, Chippewa, 49780
Fife Lake, Gd Traverse,49633/ V 394
Filer City, Manistee, 49634/ T 1,966
Filion, Huron, 48432
Flat Rock, Wayne, 48134/ C 7,290
Flint, Genesee, 485XX/ C 140,761
Flushing, Genesee, 48433/ C 8,542
Forestville, Sanilac, 48434/ V 153
Fort Gratiot, St Clair,48059/T 8,968
Foster City, Dickinson, 49834
Fostoria, Tuscola, 48435
Fountain, Mason, 49410/ V 165
Fowler, Clinton, 48835/ V 912
Fowlerville,Livingston,48836/V 2,648
Frankenmuth, Saginaw,48734/ C 4,408
Frankfort, Benzie, 49635/ C 1,546
Franklin, Oakland, 48025/ V 2,626
Fraser, Macomb, 48026/ C 13,899
Frederic, Crawford, 49733/ T 1.287

Freeland, Saginaw, 48623
Freeport, Barry, 48325/ V 458
Free Soil, Mason, 49411/ V 148
Fremont, Newaygo, 49412/ C 3,875
Frontier, Hillsdale, 49239
Fruitport, Muskegon, 49415/ V 1,090
Fulton, Kalamazoo, 49052

G

Gaastra, Iron, 49927/ C 376
Gagetown, Tuscola, 49735/ V 337
Gaines, Genesee, 48436/ V 427
Galesburg, Kalamazoo,49053/ C 1,863
Galien, Berrien, 49113/ V 596
Garden, Delta. 49835/ V 268
Garden City, Wayne, 48135/C 31,846
Gay, Houghton, 49945
Gaylord, Otsego, 49735/ C 3,256
Genesee, Genesee, 48437/ T 24,093
Germfask, Schoolcraft,49836/ T 542
Gibraltar,Wayne, 48173/ C 4,297
Gilford, Tuscola, 48736/ T 824
Gladstone, Delta, 49837/ C 4,565
Gladwin, Gladwin, 48624/ C 2,682
Glen Arbor, Leelanau,49636/ T 644
Glenn, Allegan, 49416
Glennie, Alcona, 48737
Gobles, Van Buren, 49055/ C 769
Goetzville, Chippewa, 49736
Goodells, St Clair, 48027
Good Hart, Emmet, 49737
Goodison, Oakland, 483XX
Goodrich, Genesee, 48438/ V 916
Gould City, Mackinac, 49838
Gowen, Montcalm, 49326
Grand Beach, Berrien/ V 146
Grand Blnac, Genesee, 48439/C 7,760
Grand Haven,Ottawa, 49417/ C 11,951
Grand Junction, VanBuren, 49056
Grand Ledge, Eaton, 48837/ C 7,579
Grand Marias, Alger, 49839
Grand Rapids,Kent,495XX/ C 189,126
Grandville, Kent, 49418/ C 15,624
Grant, Newaygo, 9327/ C 764
Grass Lake, Jackson, 49240/ V 903
Grawn, Grand Traverse, 49637
Grayling, Crawford, 49738/ C 1,944
Greenbush, Alcona, 48738/ T 1,373
Greenland, Ontonagon,49929/ T 1,001
Greenville, Montcalm, 48838/ C 8,101
Gregory, Livimgston, 48137
Grindstone City, Huron, 48467
Grosse Ile, Wayne, 48138/ T 9,781
Grosse Pte, Wayne, 48230/ C 5,681
Grosse Pte. Farms, Wayne,48236/C 12,092
Grosse Pte. Park, Wayne,48230/ C 12,857
Grosse Pte Shores,Wayne,48236/V 2,955
Grosse Pte Woods, Wayne,48236/C 17,715

Gulliver, Schoolcraft, 49840
Gwinn, Marquette, 49841

H

Hadley, Lapeer, 48440/ T 3,830
Hagar Shores, Berrien, 49039
Hale, Iosco, 48739
Hamburg, Livingston, 48139/ T 13,083
Hamilton, Allegan, 49419
Hamtramck, Wayne, 48212/ C 18,372
Hancock, Houghton, 49930/ C 4,547
Hanover, Jackson, 49241/ V 481
Harbert, Berrien, 49115
Harbor Beach, Huron, 48441/ V 2,089
Harbor Point, Emmet, 49740
Harbor Springs, Emmet, 49740/ V 1,540
Hardwood, Delta, 49807
Harper Woods, Wayne, 48225/ C 14,903
Harrietta, Wexford, 49638/ V 157
Harris, Menominee, 49845/ T 1,542
Harrison, Clare, 48625/ C 1,835
Harrison Twp., Macomb,48045/T 24,685
Harrisville, Alcona, 48740/ V 470
Harsens Island, St Clair, 48028
Hart, Oceana, 49420/ C 1,942
Hartford, Van Buren, 49057/ C 2,341
Hartland, Livingston, 49353/ T 6,860
Harvey, Marquette, 49855
Haslett, Ingham, 48840
Hastings,, Barry, 49058/ C 6,549
Hawks, Presque Isle, 49743
Hazel Park, Oakland, 48030/ C 20,851
Hemlock, Saginaw, 48626
Henderson, Shiawassee, 48841
Hermansville, Menominee, 49847
Herron, Alpena, 49744
Hersey, Osceola, 49639/ V 354
Hesperia, Oceana, 49421/ V 848
Hessel, Mackinac, 49745
Hickory Corners, Barry, 49060
Higgins Lake, Roscommon, 48627
Highland, Oakland, 483XX/ T 17,941
Highland Park, Wayne, 482XX/ C 20,121
Hillman, Montmorency, 49746/ V 643
Hillsdale, Hillsdale, 49242/ C 8,170
Holland, Ottawa, 494XX/ C 30,745
Holly, Oakland, 48422/ V 5,595
Holt, Ingham, 48842
Holton, Muskegon, 49445/ T 2,318
Homer, Calhoun, 49245/ V 1,758
Honor, Benzie, 49640/ V 292
Hope, Midland, 48628/ T 1,220
Hopkins, Allegan, 49328/ V 546
Horton, Jakcson, 49246
Houghton, Houghton, 49931/ C 7,498
Houghton Lake, Roscommon, 48629
Houghton Heights, Roscommon, 48630
Howard City, Montcalm, 49329/V 1,351
Howell, Livingston, 48843/ C 8,148

Hubbard Lake, Alpena, 49747
Hubbardston, Ionia, 48845/ V 404
Hubbel, Houghton, 49934
Hudson, Lenewee, 49247/ C 2,580
Hudsonville, Ottawa, 49426/ C 6,170
Hubert, Chippewa, 49748/ T 208
Huntington Wds, Oakland, 48070/C 6,149

I

Ida, Monroe, 48140/ T 4,554
Idlewood, Lake, 49642
Imlay City, Lapeer, 48444/ C 2,921
Indian River, Cheboygan, 49749
Ingalls, Monominee, 49848
Inkster, Wayne, 48141/ C 30,772
Interlochen, Grand Traverse, 49643
Ionia, Ionia, 48846/ C 5,935
Iron Mt., Dickinson, 49801/ C 8,525
Iron River, Iron, 49935/ C 2,095
Irons, Lake, 49644
Iron wood, Gogebic, 49938/ C 6,849
Ishpeming, Marquette, 49849/ C 7,200
Ithaca, Gratiot, 48847/ C 3,009

J

Jackson, Jackson, 492XX/ C 37,446
Jamestown, Ottawa, 49427/ T 4,059
Jasper, Lenawee, 49248
Jeddo, St Clair, 49032
Jenison, Ottawa, 49428
Jerome, Hillsdale, 49249
Johannesburg, Otsego, 49751
Jones, Cass, 49061
Jonesville, Hillsdale, 49250/V 2,283

K

Kalamazoo, Kalamazoo, 490XX/C 80,277
Keleva, Manistee, 49645/ V 484
Kalkaska, Kalkaska, 49646/ V 1,952
Karlin, Grand Traveruse, 49647
Kawkawlin, Bay, 48631/ T 4,852
Kearsarge, Houghton, 49942
Keego Harbor, Oakland, 48320/C 2,932
Kendall, Van Buren, 49062
Kent City, Kent, 49330/ V 877
Kenton, Houghton, 49943
Kentwood, Kent, 49518/ C 37826
Kewadin, Antrim, 49648
Keweenaw, Bay, 49908
Kincheloe, Chippewa, 49788
Kinde, Huron, 48445/ V 473
Kingsford, Dickinson, 49801/ C 5,428
Kingsley, Gd Traverse, 49649/ V 738
Kingston, Tuscola, 48741/ V 439
Kinross, Chippewa, 49752/ T 6,566

L

L'Anse, Baraga, 49946/ V 2,151
Lachine, Alpena, 49753
Lacota- Van Buren, 49063
Lainsburg, Shiawassee,48848/C 1,148
Lake, Clare, 48632
Lake Angelus, Oakland,48326/ C 328
Lake Ann, Benzie, 49650/ V 217
Lake City, Missaukee, 49651/C 858

Lake George, Clare, 48633
Lake Leelanau, Leelanau, 49653
Lake Linden, Houghton, 49945/ V 1,203
Lake Odessa, Ionia, 48849/ V 2,256
Lake Orion, Oakland,483XX/ V 3,057
Lakeland, Livingston, 48143
Lakeside, Berrien, 49116
Lakeview, Montcalm, 48850/ V 1,108
Lakeville, Oakland, 48336
Lamont, Ottawa, 49430
Lansing, Ingham, 489XX/ C 127,321
Lapeer, Lapeer, 48446/ C 7,759
LaSalle, Monroe, 48145/ T 4,985
LanthrupVillage,Oakland,48076/C 4,329
Laurium, Houghton, 49913/ V 2,268
Lawrence, Van Buren, 49064/ V 915
Lawton, Van Buren, 49065/ V 1,685
Leland, Leelanau, 49654
Lennon, Shiawassee, 48449/ V 534
Leonard, Oakland, 48369/ V 357
Leonidas, St Joseph, 49006/ T 1,171
LeRoy, Osceola, 49655/ V 251
Leslie, Ingham, 49251/ C 1,872
Levering, Emmet, 49755
Lewiston, Montmorency, 49756
Lexington, Sanilac, 48450/ V 779
Limestone, Alger, 49816/ T 334
Lincoln, Alcona, 48742/ V 337
Lincoln Parke, Wayne, 48146/C 41,832
Linden, Genesee, 48451/ C 2,415
Linwood, Bay, 48634
Litchfield,Hillsdale,49252/ C 1,317
Liitle Lake, Marquette, 49833
Livonia, Wayne, 481XX/ C 100,850
Long Lake, Iosco, 48743
Loretto, Dickinson, 49852
Lowell, Kent, 49331/ C 3,983
Ludington, Mason, 49431/ C 8,507
Lum, Lapeer, 48452
Luna Pier, Monroe, 48157/ C 1,507
Lupton, Ogemaw, 48635
Luther, Lake, 49656/ V 343
Luzerne, Oscoda, 48636
Lyons, Ionia, 48851/ V 824

M

Macatawa, Ottawa, 49434
Mackinac Is, Mackinac,49757/C 469
Mackinac City,Cheboygan,49701/V 876
Madison Hgts, Oakland,48071/C 32,196
Mancelona, Antrim, 49659/ V 1,370
Manchester, Washtenaw,48158/ V 1,753
Manistee, Manistee, 49660/ C 6,734
Manistique,Schoolcraft,49854/C 3,456
Manitou Beach, Lenawee, 49253
Manton, Wexford, 49663/ C 1,161
Maple City, Leelanau, 49664
Maple Rapids, Clinton, 48853/ V 680
Marcellus, Cass, 49067/ V 1,193

Marenisco, Gogebic, 49947/ T 959
Marine City, St Clair, 48039/ C 4,556
Marion, Oceola, 49665/ V 807
Marlette, Sanilac, 48453/ C 1,924
Marne, Ottawa, 49435
Marquette, Marquette, 49855/C 21,977
Marshall, Calhoun, 49068/ C 6,891
Martin, Allegan, 49070/ V 462
Marysville, St Clair, 48040/ C 8,515
Mason, Ingham, 48854/ C 6,768
Mass City, Ontonagon, 49948
Mattawan, Van Buren, 49071/ V 2,456
Maybee, Monroe, 48159/ V 500
Maufield, Gd. Traverse, 49666/T 967
Mayville, Tuscola, 49744/ V 1,010
McBain, Missaukee, 49657/ C 692
McBrides, Montcalm, 48852/ V 236
McMillan, Luce, 49853/ T 2,961
Means, Oceana, 49436
Mecosta, Mecosta, 49332/ V 393
Melvin, Sanilac, 48454/ V 148
Melvindale, Wayne, 48122/ C 11,216
Memphis, St Clair, 48041/ C 1,221
Mendon, St Joseph, 49072/ V 920
Menominee, Menominee,49858/C 9,398
Merrill, Saginaw, 48637/ V 755
Merritt, Missaukee, 49667
Mesick, Wexford, 49668/ V 406
Metamora, Lapeer, 48455/ V 447
Michigamme, Marquette, 49861/ V 164
Michigan Ctr, Jackson, 49254
Middleton, Gratiot, 48856
Middleville, Barry, 49333/ V 1,966
Midland, Midland, 486XX/ C 35,053
Mikado, Alcona, 48745/ T 852
Milan, Washtenaw, 48160/ C 4,040
Milford, Oakland, 480XX/ V 5,511
Millbrook, Mecosta, 49332
Millersburg,PresqueIsle,49759/V 250
Millington, Tuscola,48746/ V 1,114
Minden City, Sanilac, 48456/ V 233
Mio, Oscoda, 48647
Mohawlk, Keweenaw, 49950
Moline, Allegan, 49335
Monroe, Monroe, 48161/ C 22,902
Montague, Muskegon,49437/ C 2,276
Montgomery, Branch, 49255/ V 388
Montrose, Genesee, 48457/ C 1,811
Moorestown, Missaukee, 49651
Moran, Mackinac, 49760/ T 836
Morenci, Lenawee, 49256/ C 2,342
Morley, Mecosta, 49336/ V 528
Morrice, Shiawassee, 48857/ V 630
Moscow, Hillsdale, 49257/ T 1,353
Mosherville, Hillsdale, 49258
Mt Clemens, Macomc,480XX/ C 18,405
Mt Morris, Genesee, 48458/ C 3,292

Mt Pleasant, Isabella,48804/ C 23,285
Muir, Ionia, 48860/ V 667
Mullett Lake, Cheboygan, 49761
Mulliken, Eaton, 48861/ V 590
Munger, Bay, 48747
Munising, Alger, 49862/ C 2,783
Munith, Jackson, 49259
Muskegon, Muskegon, 494XX/ C 40,283
Muskegon Hgts,Muskegon,49444/C 13,176

N

Nadeau, Menominee, 49863/ T 1,161
Nahma, Delta, 49864/ T 491
Napoleon, Jackson, 49261/ T 6,273
Nashville, Barry, 49073/ V 1,654
National City, Iosco, 48748
National Mine, Marquette, 49865
Naubinway, Mackinac, 49762
Nazareth, Kalamazoo, 49074
Negaunee, Marquette, 49866/C 4,741
Newyaygo, Newaygo, 49337/ C 1,336
New Baltimore,Macomb,480XX/C 5,798
Newberry, Luce, 49868/ V 1,873
New Boston, Wayne, 48164
New Buffalo, Berrien, 49117/C 2,217
New Era, Oceana, 49446/ V 520
New Haven, Mcomb, 480XX/ V 2,331
New Hudson, Oakland, 48165
New Lothrop, Shiawassee48460/V 596
Newport, Monroe, 48166
New Richmond, Allegan, 49447
New Sanzy, Marquette, 49841
New Troy, Berrien, 49119
Niles, Berrien, 49120/ C 12,458
Nisula, Houghton, 49952
N. Adams, Hillsdale, 49262/ V 512
N. Bradley, Midland, 48618
N. Branch, Lapeer, 48461/ v 1,023
N. Muskegon, Muskegon,49445/C 3,919
Northport, Leelanau, 49670/ V 605
North Star, Gratiot, 48862/T 1,055
Northville, Wayne, 48161/ C 6,226
Norton Shores,Muskegon,494XX/C 21,755
Norvell, Jackson, 49263/ T 2,657
Norway, Dickinson, 49870/ C 2,910
Nottawa, St Joseph, 49075/ T 3,637
Novi, Oakland, 480XX/ C 32,998
Nuncia, Ottawa, 49448

O

Oak Grove, Livingston, 48863
Oakland,Oakland,48363/ T 8,227
Oakley, Saginaw, 48649/ V 362
Oak Park, Wayne, 48237/ C 30,462
Oden, Emmet, 49764
Okemos, Ingham, 48864
Old Mission, Grand Traverse, 49673
Olivet, Eaton, 49076/ C 1,604
Omena, Leelanau, 49674
Omer, Arenac, 48749/ C 385
Onaway,Presque Isle,49765/ C 1,039

Onekama, Manistee, 49675/ V 515
Onondaga, Ingham, 49264
Onsted, Lenawee, 49265/ V 801
Ontonagon, Ontonagon, 49953/V 2,040
Orchard Lake,Oakland.483XX/ C 2,286
Orleans, Ionia, 48865/ T 2,548
Ortonville, Oakland, 48462/ V 1,252
Oscoda, Iosco, 48750/ T 11,958
Oshtemo, Kalamazoo, 49077/ T 13,401
Osseo, Hillsdlae, 49266
Ossineke, Alpena, 49766.
Otisville, Genesee, 48463/ V 724
Otsego, Allegan, 49078/ C 3,937
Ottawa lake, Monroe, 49267
Otter Lake, Lapeer, 48464/ V 474
Ovid, Clinton, 49966/ V 1,442
Owendale, Huron, 48754/ V 285
Owosso, Shiawassee, 48867/C 16,322
Oxford, Oakland, 483XX/ V 2,929

P

Painedale, Houghton, 49955
Palmer, Marquette, 49871
Palms, Sanilac, 48465
Palmyra, Lenawee, 49268/ T 2,602
Palo, Ionia, 48870
Paradise, Chippewa, 49768
Parchment, Kalamazoo, 49004/C 1,968
Paris, Mecosta, 49338
Parma, Jackson, 49269/ V 809
Paw Paw, Van Buren, 49079/ V 3,169
Pearl Beach, St Clair, 48001
Peck, Sanilac, 48466/ V 558
Pelkie, Baraga, 49958
Pellston, Emmet, 49769? V 583
Pentwater, Oceana, 49449/ V 1,050
Perkins, Delta, 49872
Perrinton, Gratiot, 48871/ V 393
Perronville, Menominee, 49873
Perry, Shiawassee, 48872/ C 2,163
Petersburg, Monroe, 49270/ C 1,201
Petsokey, Emmet, 49770/ C 6,056
Pewamo, Ionia, 48873/ V 520
Pickford, Chippwa, 49774/ T 1,360
Pierson, Montcalm, 49339/ V 207
Pigeon, Huron, 48755/ V 1,207
Pinckney, Livingston, 48169/ V 1,603
Pinconning, Bay, 48650/ C 1,291
Pittsford, Hillsdale, 49271/ T 1,595
Plainwell, Allegan, 49080/ C 4,057
Pleasant Lake, Jackson, 49272
Plymouth, Wayne, 48170/ C 9,560
Pointe Aux Pins, Mackinac, 49775
Pompeii, Gratiot, 48874
Pontiac, Oakland, 480XX/ C 71,166
Portage, Kalamazoo, 49081/ C 41,042
Port Austin, Huron, 48467/ V 815

Port Hope, Huron, 48468/ V 313
Port Huron, St Clair, 48060/ C 33,694
Portland, Ionia, 48875/ C 3,889
Port Sanilac, Sanilac, 48469/ V 656
Posen, Presque Isle, 49776/ V 263
Potterville, Eaton, 48876/ C 1,523
Powers, Menominee, 49874/ V 271
Prattville, Hillsdale, 49273
Prescott, Ogemaw, 48756/ V 314
Presque Isle,PresqueIsle,49777/T 1,312
Princeton, Marquette, 49871
Prudenville, Roscommon, 48651
Pullman, Allegan, 49450

Q

Quincy, Branch, 49082/ V 1,680
Quinnesee, Dickinson, 49876

R

Raco, Chippwa, 49715
Raiseville, Monroe, 48161/ T 4,634
Ralph, Dickinson, 49877
Ramsay, Gogebic, 49959
Rapid City, Kalkaska, 49676
Rapid River, Delta, 49878
Ravenna, Muskegon, 49451/ V 919
Ray, Macomb, 48096/ T 3,230
Reading, Hillsdale, 49274/ C 1,127
Redford, Wayne, 482XX/ T 54,387
Reed City, Osceola, 49677/ C 2,379
Reese, Tuscola, 48757/ V 1,414
Remus, Mecosta, 49340
Republic, Marquette, 49879/ T 1,170
Rhodes, Gladwin, 48652
Richland, Kalamazoo, 49083/ V 465
Richmond, Macomb, 48062/ C 4.141
Richville, Tuscola, 48758
Ridgeway, Lenawee, 49275/ T 1,572
Riga, Lenawee, 49276/ T 1,471
Riley, St Clair, 48041/ T 2,154
Riverdale, Gratiot, 48877
River Rouge, Wayne, 48218/ C 11,314
Riverside, Berrien, 49084
Riverview, Wayne, 48192/ C 13,894
Rives Junction, Jackson, 49277
Rochester, Oakland, 483XX/ C 7,130
Rochester Hills,Oakland,483XX/C 61,766
Rock, Delta, 49880
Rockford, Kent, 49341/ C 3,750
Rockland, Ontonagon, 49960/ T 371
Rockwood, Wayne, 48173/ C 3,141
Rodney, Mecosta, 49342
RogersCity,PresqueIsle,49779/C 3,642
Rollin, Lenawee, 49278/ T 3,323
Romeo, Macomb, 48065/ V 3,520
Romulus, Wayne, 48174/ C 22,897
RooseveltPark,Muskegon,49441/C 3,885
Roscommon, Roscommon, 48653/ V 858
Rosebush, Isabella, 48878/ V 333
Rose City, Ogemaw, 48654/ C 686
Roseville, Macomb, 48066/ C 51,412

Rothbury, Oceana, 49452/ V 407
Royal Oak, Oakland, 480XX/ C 65,410
Ruby, St Clair, 48049
Rudyard, Chippewa, 49780/ T 1,270
Rumley, Alger, 49826
Ruth, Huron, 48470

S

Saginaw, Saginaw, 486XX/ C 69,512
Sagola, Dickinson, 49881/ T 1,166
St Charles, Saginaw, 48655/ V 2,144
St Clair, St Clair, 48079/ C 5,116
St Clair Shores, Macomb,480XX/C 68,107
St Helen, Roscommon, 46656
St Ignace, Mackinac,49781/ C 2,568
St James, Charlevoix, 49782/ T 276
St Johns, Clinton, 48879/ C 7,284
St Joseph, Berrien, 49085/ C 9,214
St Louis, Gratiot, 48880/ C 3,828
Salem, Washtenaw, 48175/ T 3,734
Saline, Washtenaw, 48176/ C 6,660
Samaria, Monroe, 48177
Sand Creek, Lenawee, 49279
Sand Lake, Kent, 39343/ V 456
Sandusky, Sanilac, 48471/ C 2,403
Sanford, Midland, 48657/ V 889
Saranac, Ionia, 48881/ V 1,461
Saugatuck, Allegan, 49453/ C 954
SaultSteMarie,Chippewa,49783/C 14,689
Sawyer, Berrien, 49125
Schaeffer, Delta, 49807
Schoolcraft,Kalamazooo,49087/V 1,517
Scotts, Kalamazoo, 49088
Scottsville, Mason, 49454/ C 1,287
Sears, Osceola, 49679
Sebewaing, Huron, 48759/ V 1,923
Selfridge ANGB, Macomb, 48045
Seneca, Lenawee, 49280/ T 1,289
Seney, Schoolcraft, 49883/ T 185
Shaftsburg, Shiawassee, 48882
Shelby, Oceana, 49455/ V 1,871
Shelby Twp, Macomb, 483XX/ T 48,655
Shelbyville, Allegan, 49344
Shepard, Isabella, 48883/ V 1,413
Sheridan, Montcalm, 48884/ V 930
Sherwood, Branch, 49089/ V 320
Shingleton, Alger, 49884
Sidnaw, Houghton, 49961
Sidney, Montcalm, 48885/ T 2,375
Silverwood, Lapeer, 48760
Six Lakes, Montcalm, 48886
Skandia, Marquette, 49885/ T 933
Skanee, Baraga, 49962
Skidway lake, ogemaw, 48756
Smiths Creek, St Clair, 48074
Smyrna, Ionia, 48887
Snover, Sanilac, 48472
Sodus, Berrien, 49126/ T 2,065
Somerset, Hillsdale, 49281/ T 3,416

Somerset Center, Hillsdale, 49282
S. Boardman, Kalkaska, 49680
S. Branch, Ogemaw, 48761
Southfield, Oakland,480XX/ C 75,728
Southfield Twp, Oakland,48025/T 14,255
Southgate, Wayne, 48195/ C 30,771
SouthHaven, Van Buren,49090/ C 5,563
S. Lyon, Oakland, 48178/ C 5,857
South Range, Houghton,49963/ V 745
Rockwood, Monroe, 48179/ V 1,121
Spalding, Monominee, 49886/ T 1,536
Sparta, Kent, 49345/ V 3,968
Spring Arbor, Jackson, 49283/ T 6,939
Spring Lake,Ottawa, 49456/ V 2,537
Springfield, Calhoun,490XX/ C 5,582
Springport, Jackson, 49284/ V 707
Spruce, Alcona, 48762
Stalwart, Chippewa, 49789
Stambaugh, Iron, 49964/ C 1,281
Standish, Arenac, 48658/ C 1,377
Stanton, Montcalm, 48888/ C 1,504
Stanwood, Mecosta, 49346/ V 174
Stephenson,Menominee, 49887/ C 904
Sterling, Arenac, 48659/ V 520
Sterling Hgts, Macomb,480XX/ C 117,810
Stevensville,Berrien, 49127/ V 1,230
Stockbridge, Ingham, 49285/ V 1,202
Stronach, Manistee, 49660/ T 688
Strongs, Chippewa, 49790
Sturgis, St Joseph, 49091/ C 10,130
Sumner, Gratiot, 48889/ T 1,799
Sunfield, Eaton, 48890/ V 610
Suttons Bay, Leelenau,49682/ V 561
Swartz Creek,Genesee,48473/ C 4,851
Sylvan Lake, Oakland, 48320/ C 1,884

T

Tawas City, Iosco, 48763/ C 2,007
Taylot, Wayne, 48180/ C 70,811
Tecumseh, Lenawee, 49286/ C 7,462
Tekonsha, Calhoun, 49092/ V 722
Temperance, Monroe, 48182
Thompson, Schoolcraft, 49854
Thompsonville,Benzie,49683/ V 416
Three Oaks, Berrien, 49128/ V 1,786
Three Rivers,St Joseph,49093/ C 7,413
Tipton, Lenawee. 49287
Toivola, Houghton, 49965.
Topinabee, Cheboygan, 49791
Tower, Cheboygan, 49792
Traunik, Alger, 49890
Traverse City, Gd Trvrse,49684/C 15,155
Trenary, Alger, 49891
Trenton, Wayne, 48183/ C 20,586
Trout Creek, Ontonagon, 49967
Trout Lake, Chippewa, 49793/ T 429
Troy, Oakland, 480XX/ C 72,884
Trufant, Montcalm, 49347

Turner, Arenac, 48765/ V 158
Tuscola, Tuscola, 48769/ T 2,144
Tustin, Osceola, 49688/ V 836
Twining, Arenac, 48766/ V 169
Twin Lake, Muskegon, 49457

U

Ubly, Huron, 48475/ V 821
Union, Cass, 49130
Union City,Branch,49094/ V 17,67
Union Lake, Oakland, 48387
Union Pier, Berrien, 49129
Unionville, Tuscola, 48767/ V 590
Utica, Macomb, 483XX/ C 5,081

V

Vandalia, Cass, 49095/ V 357
Vanderbilt, Otsego, 49795/ V 605
Vassar, Tuscola, 48768/ C 2,559
Vermontville, Eaton, 49096/ V 776
Vernon, Shiawassee, 48476/ V 913
Vestaburg, Montcalm, 48891
Vicksburg, Kalamazoo, 49097/ V 2,316
Vulcan, Dickinson, 49892

W

Wabaningo, Muskegon, 49463
Wakefield, Gogebic, 49968/ C 2,318
Waldron, Hillsdale, 49288/ V 581
Walhalla, Mason, 49458
Walker, Kent, 495XX/ C 17,279
Walkerville, Oceana, 49459/ V 262
Wallace, Menominee, 49893
Wallaed Lake, Oakland, 48390/ C 6,278
Walloon Lake, Charlevoix, 49796
Warren, Macomb, 480XX/ C 144,864
Washington, Macomb, 480XX/ T 13,087
Waterford, Oaklanu, 483XX/ T 66,692
Waters, Otsego, 49797
Watersmeet, Gogebic, 49969/ T 1,048
Waterviet, Berrien, 49098/ C 1,867
Watton, Baraga, 49970
Wayland, Allegan, 49348/ C 2,751
Wayne, Wayne, 48184/ C 19,899
Webberville, Ingham, 48892/ V 1,698
Weidman, Isabella, 48893
Wells, Delta, 49894/ T 5,159
Wellston, Manistee, 49689
Wequetonsing, Emmet, 49740
W. Bloomfield,Oakland,483XX/ T 54,516
WestBranch, Ogemaw, 48661/ C 1,914
Westland, Wayne, 48185/ C 84,724
West Olive, Ottawa, 49460
Weston, Lenawee, 49289
Westphalia, Clinton, 48894/ V 780
Wetmore, Alger, 49895
Wheeler, Gratiot, 48662/ T 2,926
White Cloud, Newaygo, 49349/ C 1,147
Whitehall, Muskegon, 49461/ C 3,027
White Lake, Oakland, 483XX/ T 22,608
White Pigeon, St Joseph,49099/V 1,458

White Pine, Ontonagon, 49971
Whitmore Lake, Washtenaw, 48189
Whittaker, Washtenaw, 48190
Whittmore, Iosco, 48770/ C 463
Williamsburg, Gd Traverse, 49690
Williamston, Ingham, 48895/ C 2,922
Willis, Washtenaw, 48191
Wilson, Menominee, 49896
Winn, Isabella, 48896
Wixon, Oakland, 48393/ C 8,550
Wolverine, Cheboygan, 49799/ V 283
WolverineLake,Oakland,48393/ V 4,727
Woodhaven, Wayne, 48183/ C 11,631
Woodland, Barry, 48897/ V 466
Wurtsmith AFB, Iosco, 48753
Wyandotte, Wayne, 48192/ C 30,938
Wyoming, Kent, 495XX/ C 63,891

Y

Yale, Sy Clair, 48097/ C 1,977
Ypsilanti, Washtenaw,481XX/ C 24,846
Ypsilanti Twp,Washtenaw,481XX/T 45,307

Z

Zeeland, Ottawa, 49464/ C 5,417
Zilwaukee, Saginaw, 486XX/ C 1,850

MICHIGAN URBAN & RURAL POPULATION, 1810-1990

YEAR	URBAN MICH.	RURAL MICH.	TOTAL MICHIGAN	TOTAL U.S.
1810	0	4,762	4,762	7,239,881
1820	0	8,896	8,896	9,638,453
1830	0	31,639	31,639	12,866,020
1840	9,102	203,165	212,267	17,069,453
1850	29,025	368,629	397,654	23,191,876
1860	99,701	649,412	749,113	31,443,321
1870	237,985	946,074	1,184,059	38,558,371
1880	405,412	1,231,525	1,636,937	50,189,209
1890	730,294	1,363,596	2,093,890	62,979,766
1900	952,323	1,468,659	2,420,982	76,212,168
1910	1,327,044	1,483,129	2,810,173	92,228,496
1920	2,241,560	1,426,852	3,668,412	106,021,537
1930	3,302,075	1,540,250	4,842,325	123,202,624
1940	3,454,867	1,801,239	5,256,106	132,164,569
1950	4,166,165	2,205,601	6,371,766	151,325,798
1960	5,085,882	2,737,312	7,823,194	179,323,175
	current definition			
1950	4,503,084	1,868,682	6,371,766	151,325,798
1960	5,739,132	2,084,062	7,823,194	179,323,175
1970	6,553,773	2,321,310	8,875,083	203,211,926
1980	6,551,551	2,710,527	9,262,078	226,545,805
1990	6,556,000	2,739,000	9,295,297	248,709,873

Source - U.S. Bureau of the Census

TOWNSHIPS WITH 10,000 PEOPLE OR MORE

Asterisk (*) indicates one of 10 largest. Clinton Twp (Macomb County) is the state's largest, 85,866.

Source - U.S. Bureau of the Census

County	TOWNSHIP	1990
Bay	Bangor	16,028
Berrien	Benton	17,163
	Lincoln	13,604
	Niles	12,828
Calhoun	Emmet	10,764
Clinton	DeWitt	10,448
Eaton	Delta	26,129
Genesee	Davison	14,671
	Fenton	10,055
	Flint	34,081
	Genesee	24,093
	Grand Blanc	25,392
	Mt Morris	25,198
	Mundy	11,511
	Vienna	13,210
Gd Traverse	Garfield	10,516
Ingham	Delhi	19,190
	Meridian *	35,644
Iosco	Oscoda	11,958
Jackson	Blackman	20,492
	Leoni	13,435
	Summit	21,130
Kalamazoo	Comstock	11,834
	Kalamazoo	20,976
	Oshtemo	13,401
Kent	Byron	13,235
	Cascade	12,869
	Gaines	14,533
	Gd Rapids	10,760
	Plainfield	24,946
Livingston	Brighton	14,815
	Geneo	10,820
	Green Oak	11,604
	Hamburg	13,083
Macomb	Chesterfield	25,905
	Clinton *	85,866
	Harrison	24,685
	Macomb	22,714
	Shelby *	48,655
	Washington	13,087
Monroe	Bedford	23,748
	Frenchtown	18,010
	Monroe	11,909
Muskegon	Fruitport	11,485
	Muskegon	15,302
Oakland	Bloomfield *	42,473
	Brandon	12,051
	Commerce	26,955
	Highland	17,941
	Independance	24,722
	Milford	12,121
	Orion	24,076
	Oxford	11,933
	Southfield	14,255
	Waterford *	66,692
	W Bloomfield*	54,516
	White Lake	22,608
Ottawa	Georgetown	32,672
	Holland	17,523
	Park	13,541
	Spring Lake	10,721
Saginaw	Bridgeport	12,749
	Buena Vista	10,900
	Saginaw *	37,684
	Thomas	10,971
Washtenaw	Pittsfield	17,668
	Scio	11,077
	Ypsilanti *	45,307
Wayne	Brownstown	18,811
	Canton *	57,040
	Huron	10,447
	Northville	17,313
	Plymouth	23,648
	Redford *	54,387
	Sumpter	10,891
	Van Buren	21,010

and 5 smallest

Pointe Aux Barques(Huron)	15
Grand Island (Alger)	21
Sherman (Keweenaw)	39
Houghton (Keweenaw)	54
Bois Blanc (Mackinac)	59

VILLAGES - 10 LARGEST and 5 smallest

VILLAGE (COUNTY)	1990
Beverly Hills (Oakland)	10,600
Holly (Oakland)	5,500
Milford (Oakland)	5,500
Wolverine Lk (Oakland)	4,700
Caro (Tuscola)	4,000
Sparta (Kent)	3,900
Chelsea (Washtenaw)	3,700
Romeo (Macomb)	3,500
Paw Paw (Van Buren)	3,100
Lake Orion (Oakland)	3,000

THE 5 SMALLEST VILLAGES

Eagle (Clinton)	120
Grand Beach (Berrien)	146
Free Soil (Mason)	148
Melvin (Sanilac)	148
Forestville (Sanilac)	153

Source - U.S. Bureau of the Census

INDIAN POPULATION % OF MAJOR CITIES

55,000 American Indians live in Michigan (1990 census). They are 0.6% of the state population. Listed below are the 10 major cities with the largest % of American Indian people.

RANK	CITY	PERCENT
1	Lansing	1%
2	Burton	1
3	Muskegon	0.9
4	Ferndale	0.8
5	Port Huron	0.8
6	Grand Rapids	0.8
7	Pontiac	0.8
8	Bay City	0.8
9	Flint	0.7
10	Battle Creek	0.6

HISPANIC POPULATION % OF MAJOR CITIES

201,000 Hispanic people live in Michigan (1990 census). They are 2.1% of the state population. Listed below are the 20 major cities with the largest % of Hispanic people (Note: Hispanics may be of any race).

RANK	CITY	PERCENT
1	Holland	14%
2	Saginaw	10
3	Pontiac	8
4	Lansing	7
5	Bay City	5
6	Grand Rapids	4
7	Lincoln Park	3
8	Muskegon	3
9	Wyoming	3
10	Port Huron	3
11	Allen Park	3
12	Flint	2
13	Dearborn	2
14	Detroit	2
15	Kalamazoo	2
16	Ann Arbor	2
17	Jackson	2
18	East Lansing	2
19	Dearborn Hts	2
20	Burton	2

Source - U.S. Bureau of the Census

BLACK POPULATION % OF MAJOR CITIES

1,292,000 black people live in Michigan (1990 census). They are 13.9% of the state population. Listed below are the 25 major cities with the largest % of black people.

RANK	CITY	PERCENT
1	Highland Pk.	92%
2	Detroit	75
3	Inkster	62
4	Flint	47
5	Pontiac	42
6	Saginaw	40
7	Oak Park	34
8	Southfield	29
9	Muskegon	27
10	Kalamazoo	18
11	Lansing	18
12	Grand Rapids	18
13	Jackson	17
14	Battle Creek	16
15	Ann Arbor	9
16	East Lansing	6
17	Port Huron	6
18	Kentwood	5
19	Taylor	4
20	Westland	3
21	Portage	2
22	Wyoming	2
23	Burton	2
24	Bay City	2
25	Farmington Hls	1

ASIAN POPULATION % OF MAJOR CITIES

105,000 Asian people live in Michigan (1990 census). They are 1.1% of the state population. Listed below are the 10 major cities with the largest % of Asian people.

RANK	CITY	PERCENT
1	Ann Arbor	7%
2	East Lansing	6
3	Farmington Hls	3
4	Holland	3
5	Bay City	2
6	Madison Hts	2
7	Southfield	2
8	Oak Park	2
9	Portage	2
10	Kentwood	1

ETHNIC GROUPS IN MICHIGAN

Ethnic groups in Michigan, with 100,000 or more persons in the U.S. (1980 U.S. Census). Please see Index for population by race and Spanish-speaking origin.

RANK IN MICH.	ANCESTRY GROUP	MICHIGAN POPULATION	MICH RANK AMONG STATES	PERCENT OF U.S. TOTAL
1	German	2,487,871	6	5.1
2	English	2,036,021	6	4.1
3	Irish	1,521,796	9	3.8
4	French[1]	871,912	3	6.8
5	Polish	824,721	4	10.0
6	Dutch	546,678	2	8.7
7	Scottish	432,606	7	4.3
8	Italian	344.402	10	2.8
9	Swedish	194,973	5	4.5
10	Hungarian	126,819	6	7.1
11	Finnish	111,702	1	18.1
12	Russian[2]	79,597	10	2.9
13	Czech	75,005	10	4.0
14	Norwegian	72,084	12	2.1
15	French Canadian	71,328	2	9.1
16	Belgian	60,001	1	16.7
17	Danish	51,590	9	3.4
18	Welsh	51,265	9	3.1
19	Ukranian	47,189	5	6.5
20	Canadian	40,314	4	8.8
21	Greek	39,386	9	4.1
22	Lithuanian	37,375	8	5.0
23	Slovak	31,209	6	4.0
24	Austrian	30,669	8	3.2
25	Lebanese	30,456	2	10.3
26	Swiss	28,097	12	2.9
27	Yugoslavian[3]	23,413	5	6.5
28	Rumanian	22,213	4	7.0
29	Croatian	17,755	4	7.0
30	Armenian	14,289	5	6.7
31	Scandinavian[3]	12,285	9	2.6
32	Slavic[3]	10,154	7	5.9
33	Serbian	7,816	5	7.7
34	Syrian	7,450	6	7.0
35	Portuguese	4,416	20	0.4
36	Iranian	3,613	7	2.8
37	Slovene	3,487	7	2.8
38	Jamaican	2,911	11	1.1
39	Columbian	1,125	13	0.7
40	Dominican	236	17	0.1

[1] Excludes French Basque.

[2] Includes Russians, Georgian, and other related European and Asian groups.

[3] A general response which may encompass several specific groups.

STATISTICS FOR MICHIGAN SCHOOLS

Michigan State
Board of Education

NATIONAL EDUCATION GOALS

By the year 2000, all children in America will start school ready to learn.

By the year 2000, the high school graduation rate will increase to at least 90 percent.

By the year 2000, American students will leave grades four, eight, and twelve having demonstrated competency in challenging subject matter including English, mathematics, science, foreign languages, civics and government, economics, arts, history, and geography; and every school in America will ensure that all students learn to use their minds well, so they may be prepared for responsible citizenship, further learning, and productive employment in our nation's modern economy.

By the year 2000, the nation's teaching force will have access to programs for the continued improvement of their professional skills and the opportunity to acquire the knowledge and skills needed to instruct and prepare all American students for the next century.

By the year 2000, U.S. students will be first in the world in science and mathematics achievement.

By the year 2000, every adult American will be literate and will possess the knowledge and skills necessary to compete in a global economy and exercise the rights and responsibilities of citizenship.

By the year 2000, every school in America will be free of drugs and violence and the unauthorized presence of firearms and alcohol and will offer a disciplined environment conducive to learning.

1992-93
LOCAL PUBLIC SCHOOL STUDENTS FULL TIME ENROLLMENT

Grade	Enrollment
Kindergarten	135,703
First	131,025
Second	127,283
Third	121,612
Fourth	119,063
Fifth	119,034
Sixth	118,360
Seventh	118,916
Eighth	114,454
Ninth	125,005
Tenth	107,998
Eleventh	96,171
Twelfth	89,282
Special Education	57,152
Total	1,581,058

ADULT EDUCATION

Adult High School Completion	52,559
Adult Basic Education	27,491
Postgraduate	0
Total	80,050
Grand Total	1,661,108

LOCAL PUBLIC SCHOOL STAFF

CLASSROOM TEACHERS	Number
Kindergarten	3,142
Elementary	29,422
Middle/junior high	14,517
High School	18,865
Special Education	8,853
Compensatory Education	2,405
Vocational Education	2,387
Adult Education	5,757
Total	85,348

Nonprofessional instructional staff	12,964
Professional instructional support staff (counselors, media specialists, etc.)	10,405
Professional noninstructional staff	8,204
Nonprofessional instructional support staff	5,614
Nonprofessional noninstructional support staff	45,820
Total	83,007
Grand Total	168,355

PUBLIC SCHOOLS ('93-'94)	Number
Local K-12 districts	556
Intermediate school districts	57

PUBLIC SCHOOL BUILDINGS ('93-'94)	Number
Elementary (Pre-K-8)	2,065
Middle School	411
Junior High School (7-8 or 7-9)	151
Junior-Senior High School (7-12)	159
High School (9-12 or 10-12)	484
K-12 School	318

PUBLIC SCHOOL FINANCIAL FACTS

Total K-12 state school aid	$3,394,298,280
Total public school operating expenditures	$9,741,178,756
SEV per state aid member	$91,343
Pupil membership	1,675,465
Number of teachers	66,247
Average teacher salary	$43,870
Pupil/teacher ratio	22:1

* Includes FICA and retirement paid on school districts' behalf.

PUBLIC SCHOOL DROPOUT RATE (GRADES 9-12)

	%
1991-92	4.8

Dropout rate refers to the percentage of students who have left a school district over a 12-month period. In calculating the dropout rate, adjustment is made for those students who transfer in, transfer out, and graduate.

GENDER DISTRIBUTION OF MICHIGAN PUBLIC SCHOOL TEACHERS AND ADMINISTRATORS

	MALE %	FEMALE %
Teachers	30.8	69.2
Administrators	65.6	34.4

STATE FUNDED PRE-SCHOOL PROGRAM

State Funded Pre-School Program $32,917,000

RACIAL-ETHNIC DISTRIBUTION OF MICHIGAN PUBLIC SCHOOL TEACHERS, ADMINISTRATORS, AND STUDENTS

TEACHERS

American Indian	0.4
Asian American	0.3
Black	9.4
Hispanic	0.6
White	89.4

ADMINISTRATORS

American Indian	0.3
Asian American	0.2
Black	17.8
Hispanic	0.7
White	80.8

STUDENTS

American Indian	1.0
Asian American	1.4
Black	17.0
Hispanic	2.4
White	78.2

CAREER AND TECHNICAL EDUCATION

One in every three Michigan high school students (36.5%) in the 11th or 12th grade was enrolled in a vocational-technical education program leading to a paid job. Ninety percent of the vocational education completers are either working or in school, with an unemployment rate of only 6%.

Wage Earning	67,692
Non-wage Earning	46,969
Total enrollments	114,661

--Wage earning indicates those programs that prepare a student for gainful employment.

--Non-wage earning indicates those programs that prepare a student for life management.

HIGHER EDUCATION

Colleges and Universities	Number
Public four-year	15
Public two-year	29
Independent two-year, four-year, and professional	52
Proprietary schools	231
Total	327

Colleges and Universities	Enrollment
Public four-year	260,366
Public two-year	228,211
Independent two-year, four-year, and professional	86,701
Proprietary schools	36,727
Total	612,005

State Funding (Estimate)	Amount
Community colleges	$ 240,000,000
Public universities	1,306,604,900
Total	1,546,604,900

STATE-FUNDED STUDENT FINANCIAL AID

Michigan Competitive Scholarships	$28,648,500
Michigan Tuition Grants	50,467,266
Adult Part-Time Grants	2,197,982
Michigan Educational Opportunity Grants	1,738,176
Michigan Work-Study Program	5,868,666
Indian Tuition Waivers	2,239,287
Degree Reimbursements	9,156,949

LOANS GUARANTED BY THE MICHIGAN GUARANTY AGENCY

Unsubsidized Stafford Loans	$ 32,951,296
Stafford Loans (GSLs)	338,951,296
PLUS Loans	23,521,374
SLS Loans	45,556,349
Consolidation Loans	8,274,432

LOANS ACQUIRED BY THE STATE SECONDARY MARKET

Unsubsidized Stafford Loans	$ 21,282
Stafford Loans (GSLs)	86,060,900
PLUS Loans	6,253,336
SLS Loans	5,067,410

LOANS DISBURSED OR ACQUIRED BY MICHIGAN HIGHER EDUCATION STUDENT LOAN PROGRAM

Unsubsidized Stafford Loans	$ 613,294
Stafford Loans (GSLs)	24,191,316
PLUS Loans	1,769,820
SLS Loans	4,278,865
Consolidation Loans	5,461,721
MI-LOAN Program	6,314,415

NON-PUBLIC SCHOOLS

NONPUBLIC SCHOOL BUILDINGS ('93-'94)	Number
Elementary (K-8)	738
Middle School (5-8)	14
Junior High School (7-9)	1
Senior High School (7-12)	21
Senior High School (9-12)	66
K-12	166
Special Education	1
Grade level not indicated	63
Total	1,070

NONPUBLIC SCHOOLS ('93-'94)

Grade	Enrollment
Kindergarten	15,970
First	16,601
Second	15,824
Third	15,517
Fourth	14,767
Fifth	14,321
Sixth	14,194
Seventh	13,326
Eighth	12,295
Ninth	10,245
Tenth	9,200
Eleventh	8,623
Twelfth	8,230
Total	169,113
Special Education	2,170
Part-Time	394
PUBLIC SCHOOLS ('93-'94)	Number

Michigan Educational Assessment Program

meap

Michigan State Board of Education

The Michigan Educational Assessment Program (MEAP) is a statewide testing program initiated by the State Board of Education, supported by the Governor and funded by the Legislature.

The MEAP tests in reading and mathematics are administered in the fall to all fourth, seventh, and tenth graders. The MEAP Science test is given in the fall to fifth, eighth and eleventh graders.

The 1994–1995 MEAP test results for your school district, and all other school districts in your county or ISD, is available

FREE !

to you as a reader of the 1995 All About Michigan Almanac. For your free copy of the MEAP (while supply lasts), simply send a stamped, self-addressed return envelope to:

Dept. Info–MEAP
All About Michigan Almanac
P.O. Box 202
Hartland, MI 48353

Please include a note with the name of your school district and county, so we can send you the correct results. It will also be helpful to us if you mention in your note where you acquired this book (library, school, bookstore, other -- name of place not necessary).

MICHIGAN COLLEGES

NOTE: 2-YEAR COLLEGES ARE IDENIFIED BY AN ASTERICK (*) AFTER THE NAME

NAME	CITY	ZIP	TELEPHONE	FOUND
ADRIAN COLL.	ADRIAN	49221	(517) 265-5161	1859
			(800) 877-2246	
ALBION COLLEGE	ALBION	49224	(517) 629-0321	1835
			(800) 858-6770	
ALMA COLLEGE	ALMA	48801	(517) 463-7139	1886
			(800) 321-2562	
ALPENA COMM. C *	ALPENA	49707	(517) 356-9021	1952
ANDREWS COLLEGE	BERRIEN SPRINGS	49104	(616) 471-3353	1874
			(800) 253-2874	
AQUINAS COLLEGE	GRAND RAPIDS	49506	(616) 732-4460	1922
BAKER COLLEGE *	AUBURN HILLS	49601	(616) 775-8458	1888
BAKER COLLEGE	CADILLAC	49601	(616) 775-8458	1888
BAKER COLLEGE	FLINT	48507	(810) 766-4000	1911
			(800) 822-2537	
BAKER COLLEGE *	JACKSON	49201	(517) 789-6123	1887
BAKER COLLEGE *	CLINTON	48033	(810) 791-6610	1990
BAKER COLLEGE	MUSKEGON	49442	(616) 726-4904	1888
			(800) 937-0337	
BAKER COLLEGE	OWOSSO	48867	(517) 723-5251	
			(800) 879-3797	
BAKER COLLEGE	PORT HURON	48060	(810) 985-7000	1990
BAY DE NOC COMM C *	ESCANABA	49829	(906) 786-5802	1962
CALVIN COLLEGE	GRAND RAPIDS	49546	(616) 957-6106	1876
			(800) 748-0122	
COLL OF ART & DESIGN	DETROIT	48202	(313) 872-3118	1926
			(800) 952-2787	
CENTRAL MICHIGAN U	MT. PLEASANT	48859	(517) 744-3076	1892
CHARLES STEWART MOTT *	FLINT	48503	(313) 762-0241	1923
CLEARY COLLEGE	YPSILANTI	48197	(313) 483-4400	1883
			(800) 686-1883	

ENROLLMENT-TOTAL	% GRADUATE	ENROLLMENT-FACULTY RATIO	TUTIONS & FEES-ANNUAL	ROOM & BOARD-ANNUAL	BOOKS & SUPPLIES-ANNUAL	OTHER EXPENCES-ANNUAL	TOTAL ANNUAL EXP	AFFLIATION
1.1	55%	8	$11.3	$3.8	$0.4	$0.7	$16.2	METHODIST
[illegible].7	69%	12	$14.0	$4.6	$0.5	$0.5	$19.6	PRIVATE
1.3	70%	11	$12.6	$5.0	$0.7	$0.6	$14.4	PRIVATE
2.1	NA	16	$1.4	NA	$0.3	$0.6	$2.3	PUBLIC
3.0	NA	9	$10.1	$3.1	$1.0	NA	$14.2	PRIVATE
2.5	53%	12	$11.2	$4.1	$0.4	$0.7	$16.4	PRIVATE
435	NA	NA	$5.4	NA	$0.6	NA	$6.0	PRIVATE
472	NA	9	$5.4	NA	$0.8	NA	$6.2	PRIVATE
4.1	NA	32	$5.4	$1.7	$0.7	$2.5	$10.3	PRIVATE
275	NA	NA	$5.5	NA	$0.5	$2.0	$8.0	PRIVATE
470	NA	18	$5.4	NA	$0.7	$2.5	$8.6	PRIVATE
1.9	NA	31	$5.5	$1.6	$0.8	$2.0	$10.0	PRIVATE
1.4	NA	17	$5.7	$1.7	$0.8	$2.0	$10.2	PRIVATE
623	NA	14	$5.4	NA	$0.5	$2.0	$7.9	PRIVATE
2.2	NA	15	$1.6	$1.6	$0.4	$0.6	$4.2	PUBLIC
3.7	65%	13	$10.2	$3.7	$0.4	$0.7	$15.0	PRIVATE
850	NA	52	$11.2	$4.1	$2.4	$0.9	$18.6	PRIVATE
16.3	31%	18	$2.9	$3.9	$0.6	$1.0	$8.4	PUBLIC
11.2	NA	24	$1.7	NA	$0.6	$0.6	$2.9	PUBLIC
1.1	NA	16	$6.7	NA	$0.8	$1.0	$8.5	PRIVATE

NAME	CITY	ZIP	TELEPHONE	FOUNDE
CONCORDIA COLLEGE	ANN ARBOR	48105	(313) 995-7322	1962
			(800) 253-0680	
CORNER STONE COLL	GRAND RAPIDS	49505	(616) 285-9426	1941
			(800) 968-4722	
DAVEN PORT COLLEGE *	GRAND RAPIDS	49503	(616) 451-3511	1866
OF BUSINESS			(800) 632-9569	
DELTA COLLEGE *	UNIVERSITY CNTR	48710	(517) 686-9092	1957
DETROIT COLL OF BUS.	DEARBORN	48126	(313) 581-4400	1962
EASTERN MICH UNIV.	YPSILANTI	48197	(313) 487-3060	1849
			(800) 468-6368	
FERRIS ST. UNIVERSITY	BIG RAPIDS	49307	(616) 592-2100	1884
GLEN OAKS COMM C *	CENTREVILLE	49032	(616) 467-9945	1965
GMI ENGINEERING &	FLINT	48504	(313) 762-7865	1919
MANAGEMENT			(800) 955-4464	
GOGEBIC COMM C *	IRONWOOD	49938	(906) 932-4231	1932
GRACE BIBLE C	GRAND RAPIDS	49509	(616) 538-2330	1945
			(800) 968-1887	
GRAND RAPIDS COMM C *	GRAND RAPIDS	49503	(616) 771-4101	1914
GRAND VALLEY STATE U	ALLENDALE	49401	(616) 895-2025	1960
GREAT LAKES CHRISTIAN C	LANSING	48917	(517) 321-0242	1949
GREAT LAKES JR BUS C *	SAGINAW	48607	(517) 755-3444	1907
HENRY FORD COMM C *	DEARBORN	48128	(313) 845-9766	1938
HIGHLAND PARK COMM C *	HIGHLAND PARK	48203	(313) 252-0475	1918
HILLSDALE COLLEGE	HILLSDALE	49242	(517) 437-7341	1844
HOPE COLLEGE	HOLLAND	49422	(616) 394-7850	1862
			(800) 968-7850	
JACKSON COMM C *	JACKSON	49201	(517) 787-0800	1928
JORDON COLLEGE	CEDAR SPRINGS	49319	(616) 696-1180	1967
			(800) 968-0330	
KALAMAZOO COLLEGE	KALAMAZOO	49006	(616) 337-7166	1833
			(800) 253-3602	

AND UNIVERSITIES

ENROLLMENT-TOTAL	% GRADUATE	ENROLLMENT-FACULTY RATIO	TUTIONS & FEES-ANNUAL	ROOM & BOARD-ANNUAL	BOOKS & SUPPLIES-ANNUAL	OTHER EXPENCES-ANNUAL	TOTAL ANNUAL EXP	AFFLIATION
00	50%	8	$10.5	$5.0	$0.6	$1.1	$17.2	PRIVATE
00	34%	58	$7.0	$4.0	$0.5	$1.1	$12.6	PRIVATE
9.8	NA	12	$7.4	$2.50	$0.7	$0.8	$11.4	PRIVATE
1.2	NA	22	$1.5	NA	$0.5	$0.6	$2.6	PUBLIC
.8	NA	19	$6.4	NA	$0.6	$0.9	$7.9	PRIVATE
5.6	36%	23	$2.9	$4.1	$0.5	$0.6	$8.1	PUBLIC
2.4	5%	16	$3.2	$4.0	$0.54	$0.7	$8.0	PUBLIC
.3	NA	14	$1.3	NA	$0.5	$0.8	$2.6	PUBLIC
.1	NA	23	$11.7	$3.5	$0.6	$2.3	$18.1	PRIVATE
.3	NA	14	$1.0	$1.1	$0.4	$0.8	$3.5	PUBLIC
33	20%	4	$5.0	$3.2	$0.3	$0.7	$9.2	BIBLE
3.6	NA	23	$1.4	NA	$1.0	$0.5	$2.9	PUBLIC
.0	35%	21	$3.0	$4.0	$0.6	$0.5	$8.1	PUBLIC
29	NA	13	$4.3	$2.8	$0.5	$1.5	$9.1	BIBLE
1	NA	14	$5.0	NA	$0.5	$0.5	$6.0	PRIVATE
.0	NA	15	$1.5	NA	$0.5	$0.5	$2.5	PUBLIC
0	NA	NA	$1.7	NA	$0.3	$1.3	$3.3	PUBLIC
1	75%	10	$11.3	$4.7	$0.6	$0.9	$17.5	PRIVATE
7	65%	11	$12.3	$4.3	$0.5	$0.9	$18.0	PRIVATE
1	NA	18	$1.3	NA	$0.4	$0.7	$2.4	PUBLIC
1	NA	11	$5.7	NA	$1.05	NA	$6.75	PRIVATE
2	73%	11	$16.1	$5.1	$0.5	$0.6	$22.3	BAPTIST

NAME	CITY	ZIP	TELEPHONE	FOUND
KALAMAZOO VLY COMM *	KALAMAZOO	49009	(616) 372-5346	1966
KELLOGG COMM C *	BATTLE CREEK	49017	(616) 965-3931	1956
			(800) 955-4522	
KENDALL COLLEGE	GRAND RAPID	40503	(616) 451-2787	1928
OF ART & DESIGN			(800) 676-2787	
KIRTLAND COMM C *	ROSCOMMON	48653	(517) 275-5121	1966
LAKE MICHIGAN C *	BENTON HARBOR	49022	(616) 927-3571	1946
LK SUPERIOR ST U	S. STE MARIE	49783	(906) 635-2231	1946
LANSING COMM C *	LANSING	48901	(517) 483-1200	1957
LAWRENCE TECT UNIV	SOUTHFIELD	48075	(313) 356-0200	1932
LEWIS COLL OF BUS *	DETROIT	48235	(313) 862-6300	1874
MACOMB COMM C *	WARREN	48093	(313) 445-7999	1954
MaDONNA UNIVERSITY	LIVONIA	48150	(313) 591-5052	1947
MARYGROVE COLLEGE	DETROIT	48221	(313) 862-5200	1910
MICHIGAN ST U	E LANSING	48824	(517) 355-8332	1855
MICH CHRISTIAN C	ROCHESTER HILLS	48307	(810) 651-5800	1959
			(800) 521-6010	
MICHIGAN TECT U	HOUGHTON	49931	(906) 487-2335	1885
MID MICH COMM C *	HARRISON	48625	(517) 386-3635	1965
MONROE CO COMM C *	MONROE	48161	(313) 242-7300	1964
MONTCALM COMM C *	SIDNEY	48885	(517) 328-2111	1965
MUSKEGON COMM *	MUSKEGON	49442	(616) 777-0363	1926
N CENTRAL MICH C *	PETOSKEY	49770	(616) 348-6600	1958
NORTHERN MI UNIV	MARQUETT	49855	(906) 227-2650	1899
NORTHWESTERN MI C *	TRAVERSE CTY	49684	(616) 922-1054	1951
			(800) 748-0566	
NORTHWOOD UNIV	MIDLAND	48640	(517) 837-4200	1959
			(800) 457-7878	
OAKLAND COMM C *	BLOOMFIELD HILLS	48304	(810) 540-1549	1964
OAKLND UNIVERSITY	ROCHESTER	48309	(810) 370-3360	1957

ENROLLMENT-TOTAL	% GRADUATE	ENROLLMENT-FACULITY RATIO	TUTIONS & FEES-ANNUAL	ROOM & BOARD-ANNUAL	BOOKS & SUPPLIES-ANNUAL	OTHER EXPENCES-ANNUAL	TOTAL ANNUAL EXP'	AFFLIATION
9.6	NA	23	$1.0	$1.8	$0.5	$1.2	$4.5	PUBLIC
7.6	NA	28	$1.2	$0.9	$0.5	$0.6	$3.2	PUBLIC
0.6	40%	10	$10.0	NA	$1.6	$1.0	$12.6	PRIVATE
1.3	NA	13	$1.4	NA	$0.5	NA	$1.9	PUBLIC
3.8	NA	15	$1.3	$0.6	$0.5	$1.0	$3.4	PUBLIC
3.3	60%	18	$3.2	$4.0	$0.5	$0.6	$8.3	PUBLIC
21.8	NA	17	$1.2	$1.6	$0.7	$1.0	$4.5	PUBLIC
4.8	NA	15	$7.0	$2.5	$1.3	$0.8	$11.6	PRIVATE
0.4	NA	NA	$5.0	NA	$0.5	NA	$5.5	PRIVATE
28.1	NA	33	$1.5	NA	$0.5	$0.7	$2.7	PUBLIC
4.4	NA	18	$5.1	$4.0	$0.4	$0.7	$10.2	PRIVATE
1.3	NA	21	$7.5	$4.0	$0.5	$1.3	$13.3	PRIVATE
40.0	64%	10	$4.5	$3.7	$0.5	$1.2	$10.0	PUBLIC
0.4	NA	11	$5.0	$3.0	$0.3	$0.7	$9.0	PRIVATE
7.0	49%	19	$3.4	$4.0	$0.6	$0.6	$8.6	PUBLIC
2.1	NA	10	$1.3	NA	$0.4	$1.0	$2.7	PUBLIC
4.0	NA	22	$1.1	NA	$0.7	$1.0	$2.8	PUBLIC
1.7	NA	15	$1.3	NA	$0.5	$0.9	$2.7	PUBLIC
5.2	NA	34	$1.2	NA	$0.4	$0.8	$2.4	PUBLIC
2.2	NA	21	$1.3	$3.0	$0.6	$0.4	$5.3	PUBLIC
9.0	NA	25	$2.6	$4.0	$0.4	$0.8	$7.8	PUBLIC
4.3	NA	18	$1.7	$4.0	$0.5	$0.8	$7.0	PUBLIC
1.7	35%	27	$10.0	$5.0	$0.6	NA	$15.6	PRIVATE
29.3	NA	37	$1.5	NA	$0.7	$0.4	$2.6	PUBLIC
13.0	60%	21	$2.7	$4.0	$0.4	$0.7	$7.8	PUBLIC

NAME	CITY	ZIP	TELEPHONE	FOUNDE
OLIVET COLLEGE	OLIVET	49076	(616) 749-7635	1844
			(800) 456-7189	
REFORMED BIBLE C	GRAND RAPIDS	49505	(616) 363-2050	1939
SACRED HEART MAJOR SEM	DETROIT	48206	(313) 883-8500	1919
SAGINAW VALLEY ST U	UNIVERSITY CNTR	48710	(517) 790-4200	1963
ST CLAIR CO COMM C *	PORT HURON	48061	(810) 989-5500	1923
ST MARY'S COLLEGE	ORCHARD LAKE	48324	(810) 683-0523	1885
SCHOOLCRAFT C *	LIVONIA	48152	(313) 462-4426	1961
SIENA HEIGHTS C	ADRIAN	49221	(517) 263-0731	1919
SOUTHWESTERN MI C *	DOWAGIAC	49047	(616) 782-5113	1964
			(800) 456-8675	
SPRING ARBOR C *	SPRING ARBOR	49283	(517) 750-1200	1873
			(800) 968-0011	
SUOMI COLLEGE *	HANCOCK	49930	(906) 487-7274	1896
			(800) 682-7604	
UNIV OF DET MERCY	DETROIT	48221	(313) 993-1245	1991
UNIV OF MICHIGAN	ANN ARBOR	48109	(313) 764-7433	1817
U OF M DEARBORN	DEARBORN	48128	(313) 593-5100	1959
U OF M FLINT	FLINT	48502	(810) 762-3300	1956
WALSH C ACCT & BUS *	TROY	48007	(810) 689-8282	1922
WASHTENAW COMM C *	ANN ARBOR	48106	(313) 973-3543	1965
WAYNE CO COMM C *	DETROIT	48226	(313) 496-2651	1967
WAYNE ST UNIVERSITY	DETROIT	48202	(313) 577-3577	1868
WEST SHORE COMM C *	SCOTTVILLE	49454	(616) 845-6211	1967
WESTERN MICH U	KALAMAZOO	49008	(616) 387-2000	1903
WILLIAM TYNDALE C	FARMINGTON HILLS	48331	(313) 533-7200	1945
YESHIVA-BETH YEHUDA	OAK PARK	48237	(313) 968-8613	
YESHIVA GEDOLAH OF DET				

ENROLLMENT-TOTAL	% GRADUATE	ENROLLMENT-FACULITY RATIO	TUTIONS & FEES-ANNUAL	ROOM & BOARD-ANNUAL	BOOKS & SUPPLIES-ANNUAL	OTHER EXPENCES-ANNUAL	TOTAL ANNUAL EXP'	AFFLIATION
0.8	NA	10	$11.0	$4.0	$0.6	$0.5	$16.1	PRIVATE
0.2	NA	10	$6.3	$3.2	$0.4	$0.7	$10.6	CHRISTIAN
0.1	NA	16	$4.2	$4.1	$0.5	$1.5	$10.3	CATHOLIC
7.0	NA	18	$3.1	$3.8	$0.6	$0.9	$8.4	PUBLIC
5.0	NA	20	$1.6	NA	$0.5	$0.5	$2.6	PUBLIC
256	NA	6	$5.5	$3.3	$0.5	NA	$9.3	CATHOLIC
10.1	NA	22	$1.3	NA	$0.4	$0.8	$2.5	PUBLIC
1.2	NA	10	$10.0	$4.0	$0.5	$0.6	$15.1	CATHOLIC
3.0	NA	16	$1.4	NA	$0.5	$0.6	$2.S	PUBLIC
1.0	37%	NA	$9.6	$3.8	$0.4	$0.7	$14.5	METHODIST
0.6	NA	NA	$10.0	$4.0	$0.5	$0.8	$15.3	PRIVATE
16.0	60%	12	$12.0	$4.2	$0.5	$1.4	$18.1	PRIVATE
14.0	83%	22	$5.0	$5.0	$0.5	$1.2	$11.7	PUBLIC
7.0	NA	NA	$3.4	NA	$0.5	$1.0	$4.9	PUBLIC
6.6	27%	31	$3.0	$05	NA	$0.9	$4.4	PUBLIC
3.5	NA	34	$5.6	NA	NA	$0.9	$6.5	PRIVATE
11.0	NA	14	$1.5	NA	$0.5	$0.6	$2.6	PUBLIC
9.5	NA	19	$1.7	NA	$0.4	$1.0	$3.1	PUBLIC
35.1	37%	13	$3.0	$6.0	$0.5	$0.9	$10.4	PUBLIC
1.5	NA	21	$1.2	NA	$0.6	$1.0	$2.8	PUBLIC
27.3	45%	24	$3.0	$4.0	$0.5	$1.2	$8.7	PUBLIC
0.6	NA	NA	$5.5	$2.5	$0.5	$0.6	$9.1	BIBLE
0.24	NA	NA	NA	NA	NA	NA	NA	PRIVATE

MAP OF STADIUMS & ARENAS IN METRO DETROIT

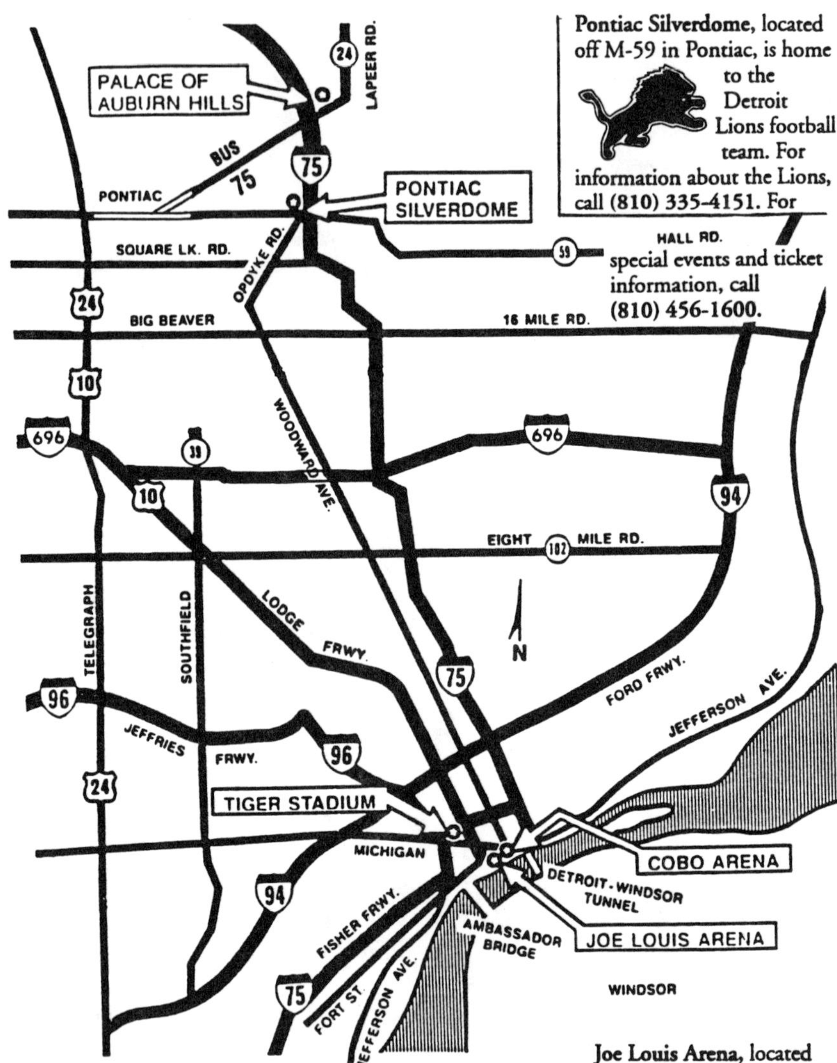

Pontiac Silverdome, located off M-59 in Pontiac, is home to the Detroit Lions football team. For information about the Lions, call (810) 335-4151. For special events and ticket information, call **(810) 456-1600.**

The Palace of Auburn Hills, located off the I-75/M-24 interchange, is home to the Detroit Pistons basketball team. For a schedule of events and for ticket information, call (810) 377-0100.

Tiger Stadium, located in downtown Detroit, is the home of the Detroit Tigers baseball team. For ticket and events information, call (313) 963-9944, or (313) 962-4000.

Joe Louis Arena, located on Civic Center Drive, off Jefferson Avenue in downtown Detroit, is home to the Detroit Red Wings hockey team. For a schedule of events and ticket information for the Red Wings, call (313) 396-7600, or (313) 396-7444.

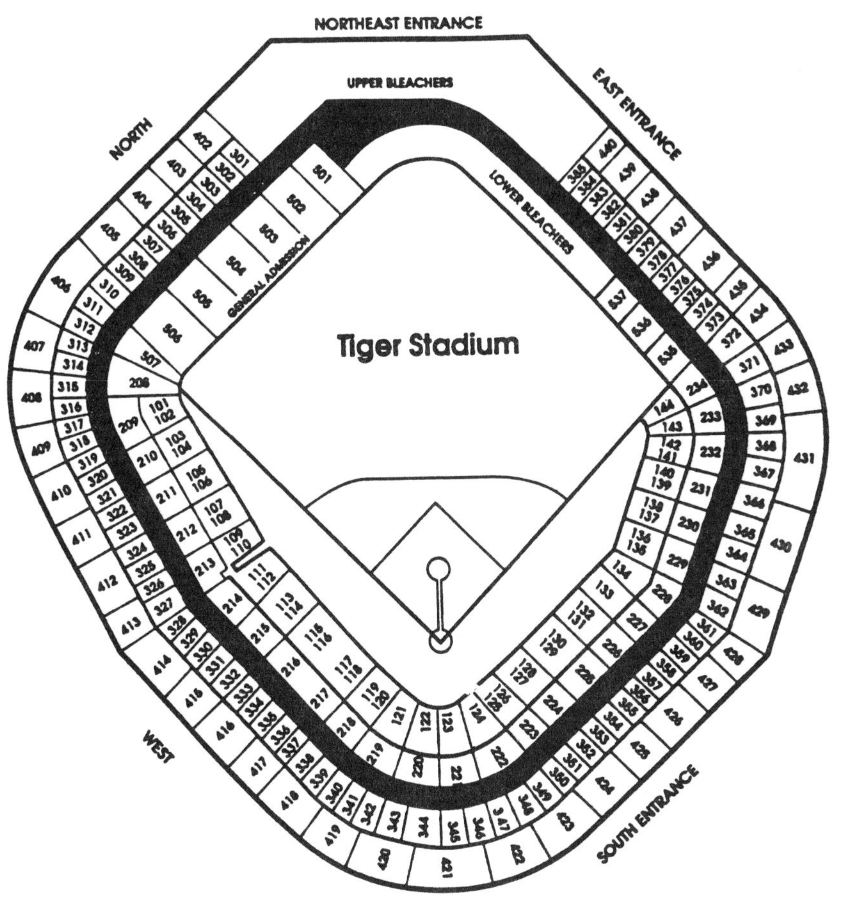
NORTHEAST ENTRANCE
UPPER BLEACHERS
EAST ENTRANCE
NORTH
LOWER BLEACHERS
GENERAL ADMISSION
Tiger Stadium
WEST
SOUTH ENTRANCE

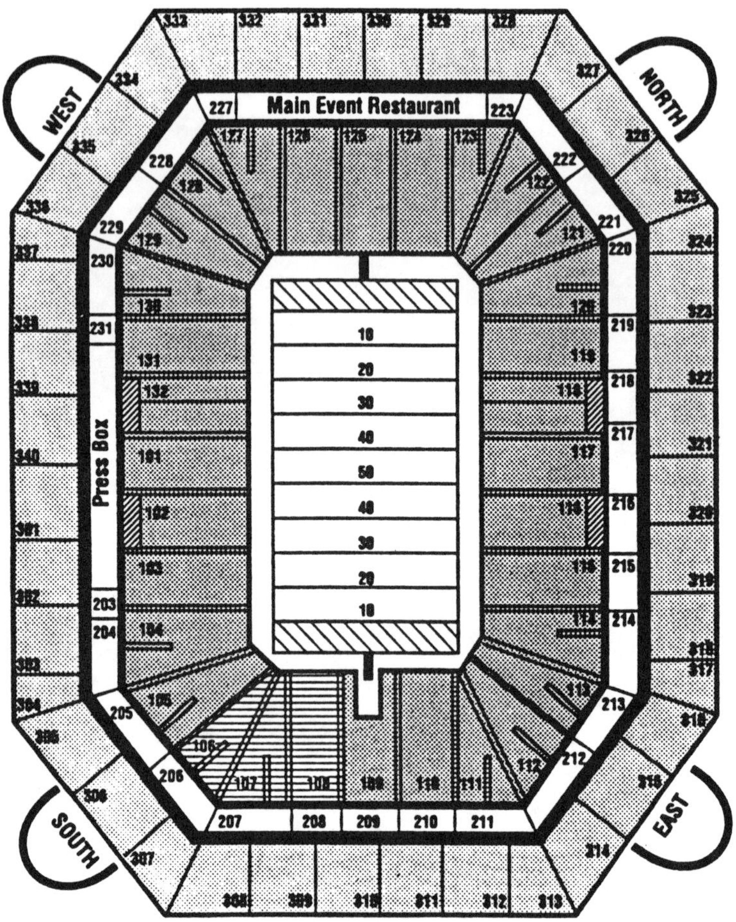

Pontiac Silverdome

Upper Level

Club Level

Lower Level

Bleacher Section

Wheelchair Section

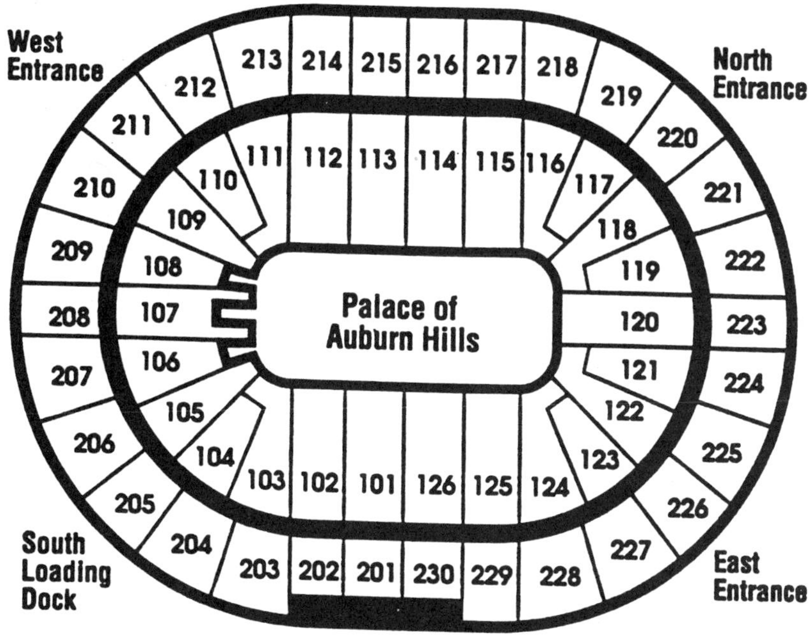
West Entrance
North Entrance
South Loading Dock
East Entrance
Palace of Auburn Hills
213 214 215 216 217 218
212 211 210 209 208 207 206 205 204
203 202 201 230 229 228
219 220 221 222 223 224 225 226 227
111 112 113 114 115 116
110 109 108 107 106 105 104
103 102 101 126 125 124
117 118 119 120 121 122 123

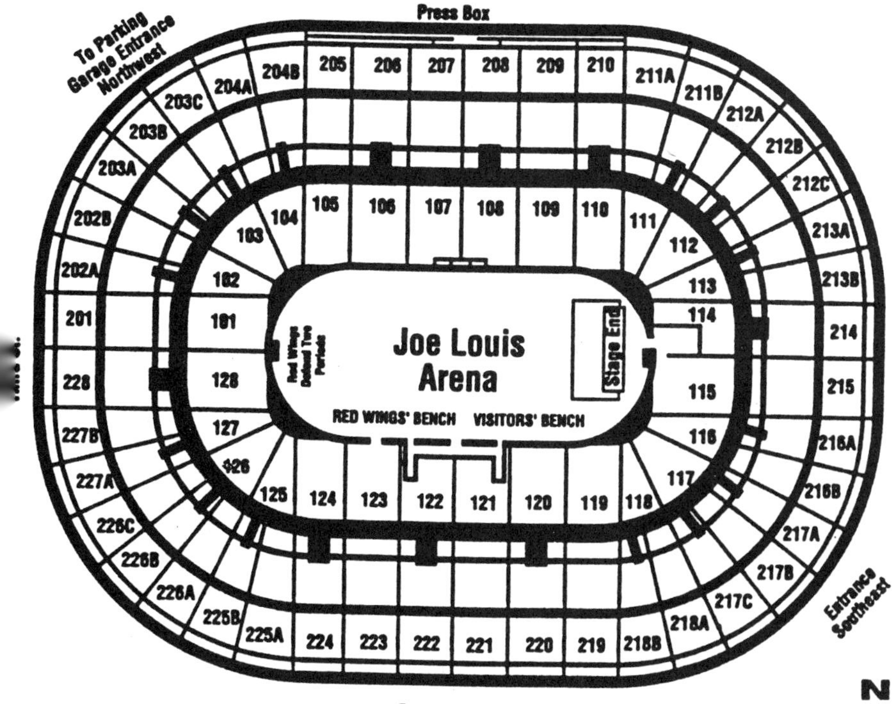
Press Box
To Parking Garage Entrance Northwest
Joe Louis Arena
Red Wings Defend Two Periods
Stage End
RED WINGS' BENCH
VISITORS' BENCH
Entrance Southeast
204B 205 206 207 208 209 210 211A
204A 203C 203B 203A 202B 202A 201 228 227B 227A 226C 226B 226A 225B 225A
224 223 222 221 220 219 218B
211B 212A 212B 212C 213A 213B 214 215 216A 216B 217A 217B 217C 218A
105 106 107 108 109 110
104 103 102 101 128 127 126 125
124 123 122 121 120 119 118
111 112 113 114 115 116 117
Detroit River
N

DETROIT TIGERS WORLD SERIES CHAMPIONS

YEAR	
1984	Won 4 games to 1 over San Diego
1968	Won 4 - 3 over St. Louis
1945	Won 4 - 3 over Chicago
1935	Won 4 - 2 over Chicago

YEAR	LOST IN WORLD SERIES:
1940	to Cincinnati, 3 - 4
1934	to St. Louis, 3 - 4
1909	to Pittsburgh, 3 - 4
1908	to Chicago, 0 - 4
1907	to Chicago, 0 - 4

AMERICAN LEAGUE CHAMPIONS

YEAR	SEASON	PCT.
1984	Won 3 games to 0 over Kansas City	
1968	Won 103 - 59	.636
1945	Won 88 - 65	.574
1940	Won 90 - 64	.584
1935	Won 93 - 58	.616
1934	Won 101 - 53	.656
1909	Won 98 - 54	.645
1908	Won 90 - 63	.588
1907	Won 92 - 58	.613

AMERICAN LEAGUE - EAST CHAMPS

YEAR	SEASON	PCT.
1987	Won 98 - 64	.605
1984	Won 104 - 58	.642
1972	Won 86 - 70	.551

DETROIT PISTONS NBA WORLD BASKETBALL CHAMPIONS

1990	Won 4 games to 1 over Portland Trail Blazers.
1989	Won 4 games to 0 over L.A. Lakers.
1988	Lost 4 games to 3 against L.A. Lakers.

DETROIT LIONS NFL FOOTBALL CHAMPIONSHIPS

YEAR	
1935	26-7 over N.Y. Giants
1952	17-7 over Cleveland Browns
1953	17-16 over Cleveland Browns
1957	59-14 over Cleveland Browns
1954	10-56 loss to Cleveland

WEST DIVISION CHAMPIONS

1935	7 wins, 3 losses, 2 ties
1952	9 - 3 - 0
1953	10 - 2 - 0
1954	9 - 2 - 1
1957	8 - 4 - 0

CENTRAL CHAMPIONS

1983	9 - 7 - 0 Lost 23-24 to San Francisco Raiders in NFC final.
1992	12 - 4 - 0 Lost 10-41 to Washington Red Skins in NFC final.

DETROIT RED WINGS IN STANLEY CUP HOCKEY PLAYOFFS

YEAR	WINNER	DEFEATED
1966	Montreal	Detroit
1964	Toronto	Detroit
1963	Toronto	Detroit
1961	Toronto	Detroit
1956	Montreal	Detroit
1955	Detroit	Montreal
1954	Detroit	Montreal
1952	Detroit	Montreal
1950	Detroit	N.Y.Rangers
1949	Toronto	Detroit
1948	Toronto	Detroit
1945	Toronto	Detroit
1943	Detroit	Boston
1942	Toronto	Detroit
1941	Boston	Detroit
1937	Detroit	N.Y.Rangers
1936	Detroit	Toronto
1934	Chicago	Detroit

MICHIGAN HIGH SCHOOL ATHLETIC

RECORD OF CHAMPIONS

(Points of Interest)

Some All-Time Michigan Sports Records

Source; MI High Achool Athletic Association

Below you will find some all-time scoring and performance records in various Michigan high school sports obtained from Michigan High School Athletic Association data and also as a service from Ron Pesch, 1447 Henry St., Muskegon, Michigan 49441. Suggestions for additions to these records are welcomed.

BASEBALL

Individual Records:

Season:

Most Wins — 43 — Harper Woods - Bishop Gallagher (1985)
Most Strikeouts (7-innings) — 20 — Ken Beardslee, Vermontville vs Saranac (1949)
Most Strikeouts (9-innings) — 26 — Ken Beardslee, Vermontville vs Holt (1949)
Most Strikeouts (10-innings) — 25 — Ken Beardslee, Vermontville vs Middleville (1949)
Most Strikeouts (13-innings) — 29 — George Mills, Fremont vs Ludington (1915)

Career:

Strikeouts — 452 — Ken Beardslee, Vermontville (1947-49)
No-Hitters — 8 — Ken Beardslee, Vermontville (1947-49)
Wins — 49 — Steve Nowak, Gaylord - St. Mary Cathedral (1986-89)

Team Records:

Longest Win Streak (no ties) — 56 — Grand Haven (1960-62)
Most Innings (one game) — 19 — Farwell 5 vs Clare 4 (1980)

Most Coaching Victories:

545 — James Bresciami (Harper Woods - Bishop Gallagher) (1965-85)

BASKETBALL (Boys)

Individual Records – Points:

Season Scoring — 969 — Mark Brown, Hastings (1984-85)
Career Scoring — 2,841 — Jay Smith, Mio - AuSable (1976-79)
Individual Scoring (single game) — 97 — Ed Burling, Crystal Falls - Forest Park vs Iron River (1911)
Consecutive Free Throws — 70 — Mark Wittbrodt, Auburn - Bay City Western (2-11-92/3-3-92)

Team Records:

Longest Win Streak — 65 — Chassell (1956-59)
Longest Game — 8 overtimes — Mattawan defeated Parchment 10-8 (1971)
Most Team Points, Game — 171 — Glen Arbor - Leelanau 171 vs Freesoil 94 (1988-89)
Most Team Points, Two Teams — 265 — Glen Arbor - Leelanau 171 vs Freesoil 94 (1988-89)
Most Team Points, Losing Team — 112 — Kinde - North Huron 112 vs Caseville 128 (1973)
Season Scoring Average Per Game — 97.8 — Ewen – Ewen - Trout Creek (1966-67)

Most Coaching Victories:

739 — Lofton Greene (primarily at River Rouge) (1941-84)
635 — Paul Cook (primarily at Lansing - Eastern) (1949-91)

BASKETBALL (Girls)

Individual Records – Points:

Season Scoring — 812 — Julie Polakowski, Leland (1981)
Career Scoring — 2,307 — Tonya Edwards, Flint - Northwestern (1982-85)
Individual Scoring (single game) — 63 — Debra Walker, Detroit - Mumford vs Detroit - Central (1979)

Team Records:

Longest Win Streak — 78 — Carney – Carney - Nadeau (1989-91)
Most Team Points, Game — 137 — Detroit Northeastern (1979)

Most Coaching Victories:

423-44 — Art Pelzer (Frankenmuth) (1975-93)
392-175 — Diane Laffey (Harper Woods - Regina) (1962-93)
350-108 — Larry Baker (Farmington Hills - Mercy) (1975-93)

FOOTBALL

Individual Records – Points:

Season Scoring (12 games) — 268 — Tony Ceccacci, Rudyard (1982)
Career Scoring — 553 — Rick Granata, Imlay City (1991-93)
Individual Scoring (single game) — 66 — Duke Christie, Escanaba vs Ishpeming (1920)
100 Yard Games (20 consecutive) — Steve Ampey, Gobles (1981-82)

Team Records:

All-Time Wins — 613 — Muskegon (1895-1993) 613-222-42
Longest Win Streak (no ties) — 72 — Hudson (1968-75)
Most Consecutive Shutout Victories — 15 — North Muskegon (1940-42)
Most Team Points, Game — 216 — Muskegon 216 vs Hastings 0 (1912)
Most Team Points, Season — 607 — Battle Creek - Pennfield – 12 games (1992)
Most Team Points, Season — 590 — Dowagiac - Dowagiac - Union – 13 games (1990)

Overtimes:

Consecutive Overtime Games — 4 — Detroit - Central (1983)
Longest Game — 9 OT — Detroit - Southeastern 42 vs Detroit - Northeastern 36 (1977)
Most Overtime Periods, Season — 11 — Waldron – 4-OT games – 5,3,2,1 (1979)
Most Overtime Games, Season — 5 — Lake Linden – One 2-OT games, Four each 1-OT games (1976)

Most Coaching Victories:

273 — Bill Maskill (primarily at Galesburg – Galesburg - Augusta) (1951-91) 273-84-2
268 — Leo Boyd (Saginaw - Nouvel Catholic Central) (1953-93) 268-94-4
265 — Walt Braun (primarily at Marysville) (1956-93) 265-85-3
239 — Dick Mettlach (Crystal Falls - Forest Park) (1956-1990) 239-73-6

Longest Field Goal:

58 Yards — John Langeloh, Utica (1985)

ICE HOCKEY

Most Goals Scored in One Season:

94 — Ron Rolston, Flint - Luke M. Powers Catholic (1983-84)

Most Assists in One Season:

63 — Ron Rolston, Flint - Luke M. Powers Catholic (1983-84)

SOFTBALL

Individual Records:

Season:

Consecutive No-Hit Games Pitched — 4 — Christy Bacha, Taylor - Baptist Park Christian (1986)
Hits — 92 — Kelly Kennedy, Taylor - Light & Life Christian (1993)
Highest Batting Average — .672 — Kelly Kennedy, Taylor - Light & Life Christian (1993)
Most Doubles — 59 — Lapeer - Lapeer West (1991)
Most Triples — 29 — Taylor - Light & Life Christian (1993)
Pitching Victories — 41 — Connie Rolison, Mt. Morris - E.A. Johnson (1985)
RBI's — 105 — Kelly Kennedy, Taylor - Light & Life Christian (1993)
Runs Scored — 77 — Kelly Kennedy, Taylor - Light & Life Christian (1993)
Strikeouts — 384 — Donna Russell, Flint - Kearsley (1987)
Stolen Bases — 78 — Lynn Hockett, Frankfort (1991)

Career:

Hits — 218 — Tracy Carr, Lapeer - Lapeer West (1989-92)
Pitching Victories — 136 — Tracy Carr, Lapeer - Lapeer West (1989-92)
RBI's — 231 — Kelly Kennedy, Taylor - Light & Life Christian (1991-93)
Runs Scored — 251 — Lynn Hockett, Frankfort (1988-91)
Shutouts — 65 — Jill Klein, Waterford - Our Lady of the Lakes (1986-89)
Stolen Bases — 215 — Lynn Hockett, Frankfort (1988-91)
Strikeouts — 1,142 — Tracy Carr, Lapeer - Lapeer West (1989-92)

Team Records:

Most Consecutive Coaching Championships — 3 — Dave Lazar, Fenton (1978-80)
Runs Scored — 543 — Taylor - Light & Life Christian (1993)
Season Hits — 508 — Taylor - Light & Life Christian (1993)
Season Stolen Bases — 233 — New Lothrop (1980)

SWIMMING (Boys)

Event	School – Competitors	Record	Year
50 Yard Freestyle	Bloomfield Hills - Andover (Raffi Karapetian)	:20.37	1992
100 Yard Freestyle	Bloomfield Hills - Andover (Eric Matuszak)	:44.43	1994
100 Yard Butterfly	Lansing - Eastern (Cameron Mull)	:49.3	1994
100 Yard Backstroke	Dearborn (Jeff Neumeyer)	:49.97	1993
100 Yard Breaststroke	Ann Arbor - Pioneer (Dave Chernek)	:55.66	1981
200 Yard Freestyle Relay	Bloomfield Hills - Andover (Raffi Karapetian, Kats Ohashi, Greg Behling, Eric Matuszak)	1:23.57	1992
200 Yard Medley Relay	Birmingham - Wylie E. Groves (Bob Sala, Drew Hansz, Jim Kennedy, Steve Hansz)	1:34.33	1991
200 Yard Freestyle	Bloomfield Hills - Andover (Eric Matuszak)	1:36.73	1994
200 Yard Individual Medley	Lansing - Eastern (Ian Mull)	1:49.84	1992
400 Yard Freestyle Relay	Bloomfield Hills - Andover (Eric Matuszak, Hank Weed, Mark D'Errico, Raffi Karapetian)	3:06.10	1992
500 Yard Freestyle	Ann Arbor - Huron (Eric Bailey)	4:27.10	1988
One Meter Springboard	Ann Arbor - Pioneer (Bruce Kimball)	584.75 pts.	1981

SWIMMING (Girls)

Event	School – Competitors	Record	Year
50 Yard Freestyle	East Lansing (Heather Strang)	:23.44	1980•
100 Yard Freestyle	East Lansing (Heather Strang)	:50.31	1982
100 Yard Butterfly	Portage - Portage Northern (Suzanne Toledo)	:56.47	1992
100 Yard Backstroke	Portage - Portage Northern (Suzanne Toledo)	:55.39	1993
100 Yard Breaststroke	Okemos (Keri Reynolds)	1:02.78	1990
200 Yard Freestyle	East Lansing (Heather Strang)	1:47.58	1981
200 Yard Freestyle Relay	Zeeland (Kristen Nagelkirk, Tara Drenten, Dana VanSingel, Cara Ford)	1:35.69	1990
200 Yard Medley Relay	Birmingham - Seaholm (Carolyn Deighan, Camilla Andin, Meredith McMahon, Bonnie Benjamin)	1:47.23	1992
200 Yard Individual Medley	Ann Arbor - Pioneer (Kerri Hale)	2:04.13	1992
400 Yard Freestyle Relay	Midland - H. H. Dow (Marcie Dostal, Kathy Hoffman, Amy Bohnert, Kristy Heydanek)	3:32.48	1988
500 Yard Freestyle	Ann Arbor - Pioneer (Jennifer Jackson)	4:50.20	1986•
One Meter Diving	Bloomfield Hills - Lahser (Jennifer Dixon)	483.60 pts.	1991

• Preliminaries

TENNIS (Boys)

Most Consecutive Coaching Championships:

13 — Bob Wood, Grosse Pointe Woods - University Liggett (1972-84)

TENNIS (Girls)

Most Consecutive Coaching Championships:

11 — Stephanie Prychitko, Grosse Pointe - Grosse Pointe South (1976-86)

TRACK AND FIELD (Boys)

Consecutive Dual Meet Victories:

105 — Caledonia (1978-88)
104 — Kingsley - Kingsley Area (1975-86)

Event (Meters)	School — Competitors	Record	Year
100-Meter Dash	Bay City - Central (Micah Morris)	10.3	1994
110-Meter High Hurdles	Detroit - Central (Thomas Wilcher)	13.6	1982
200-Meter Dash	Detroit - Denby (Anthony Mahone)	21.0	1984
300-Meter Low Hurdles	Jackson (Michael Parker)	35.9	1984
300-Meter Intermediate Hurdles	Jackson (Brandon Gunn)	37.5	1994
400-Meter Relay	Detroit - Central (Michael Thomas, William White, Marc Jett, Thomas Wilcher)	41.7	1982
400-Meter Dash	Mt. Clemens (Omar Davidson)	46.6	1984
800-Meter Relay	Detroit - Cass Technical (Fred Wilkerson, Clarence Williams, Jackari Johnson, Darryl Rankins)	1:25.0	1994
800-Meter Run	Mt. Clemens - Chippewa Valley (Rick Gledhill)	1:50.63	1988
1600-Meter Relay	Detroit - Cooley (Robert Adams, David Norman, Raphael Johnson, Marco West)	3:16.05	1991
1600-Meter Run	Kentwood - East Kentwood (Brian Hyde)	4:12.74	1991
3200-Meter Relay	Monroe (Derek Bork, Matt Schroeder, Chris Brown, Tim Pitcher)	7:41.29	1988
3200-Meter Run	Walled Lake - Walled Lake Western (Brian Grosso)	8:59.20	1989
Discus	Grandville (Brett Organek)	196' 5"	1992
High Jump	Brimley - Brimley Area (John Payment)	7' 1"	1989
Long Jump	Lansing - Everett (Marcel Richardson)	23' 11½"	1988
Pole Vault	Midland - H. H. Dow (Steven Hill)	16' ½"	1993
Shot Put	Middleville - Thornapple Kellogg (Gary VanElst)	63' 7"	1968

Event (Yards)	School — Competitors	Record	Year
100-Yard Dash	Flint - Luke M. Powers (Dewayne Stozier)	9.5	1965
120-Yard High Hurdles	Detroit - Central (Thomas Wilcher)	13.5	1981
220-Yard Dash	Detroit - Northern (Marshall Dill)	20.6	1971
330-Yard Low Hurdles	Detroit - Northern (Jerome Rivers)	36.8	1980
440-Yard Relay	Detroit - Central (Marc Jett, Steve Jones, Thomas Wilcher, Demetrius Hallums)	42.1	1981
440-Yard Dash	Detroit - Kettering (Dean Hogan)	47.1	1977
880-Yard Relay	Detroit - Central (David Beasley, Steve Jones, Jeff Hardy, Demetrius Hallums)	1:26.9	1980
880-Yard Run	Drayton Plains — Waterford - Kettering (Kevin Reabe)	1:50.9	1970
Mile Relay	Detroit - Redford	3:16.4	1977
One Mile Run	Pontiac - Central (Steve Elliot)	4:08.2	1975
Two Mile Run	Birmingham - Brother Rice (Pat Davey)	9:00.4	1974
	St. Clair Shores - Lakeview (Gary Carter)	9:00.4	1977

TRACK AND FIELD (Girls)

Event (Meters)	School — Competitors	Record	Year
100-Meter Dash	Detroit - Chadsey (Vivien McKenzie)	11.70	1982
	Southgate - Aquinas (Paulette Bryant)	11.70	1984
	Ann Arbor - Pioneer (Crystal Braddock)	11.70	1988
100-Meter 33" Hurdles	Lansing - J. W. Sexton (Deanna Bouyer)	14.2	1994
200-Meter Dash	Detroit - Pershing (Angie Prince)	24.3	1984
300-Meter Low Hurdles	Benton Harbor (Carolyn Ferguson)	42.4	1984
400-Meter Relay	Detroit - Cass Technical (Stacey Randolf, Angie Jones, Cynthia Merritt, Dana McKeithen)	47.81	1985
400-Meter Dash	Detroit - Cass Technical (Julia Ford)	55.1	1994
800-Meter Relay	Detroit - Cass Technical (Shantelle Nagbe, Julia Ford, Emily Higgins, Felecia Baker)	1:38.4	1994
800-Meter Run	Bloomfield Hills - Andover (Laura Matson)	2:12.02	1985
1600-Meter Relay	Flint - Northern (Alisha Johnson, Marlene Isabelle, Carleen Isabelle, Pamela Brown)	3:49.5	1983
1600-Meter Run	Bloomfield Hills - Andover (Laura Matson)	4:45.20	1985
3200-Meter Relay	West Bloomfield (Almra Danforth, Tracy Abbott, Maureen Reed, Stacy Abbott)	9:17.46	1988
3200-Meter Run	Midland (Kayla Skelly)	10:46.3	1982
Discus	Parchment (Donna Wright)	150' 7"	1984
High Jump	Capac (Ellie Hayden)	5' 11¼"	1980
Long Jump	Flint - Central (Lorri Thornton)	19' 7"	1979
Shot Put-8 lb. 13 oz.	Temperance - Bedford (Karen Sapp)	45' 7"	1983

Event (Yards)	School — Competitors	Record	Year
100-Yard Dash	Muskegon - Mona Shores (Cathy Fitzpatrick)	10.8	1981
110-Yard Low Hurdles	Detroit - Mumford (Kim Turner)	13.6	1979
220-Yard Dash	Detroit - Central (Josephine Hobbs)	24.5	1976
	Pontiac - Waterford Mott (Molly Brennan)	24.5	1977
	Bloomfield Hills - Andover (Kori Gifford)	24.5	1980
220-Yard Low Hurdles	Flint - Northern (Tonya Lowe)	28.0	1980
440-Yard Relay	Mt. Clemens	48.2	1977
440-Yard Dash	Detroit - Mackenzie (Delisa Walton)	54.5	1978
880-Yard Relay	Detroit - Mumford (Kim Turner, Angela Sibby Darlene Johnson, Lisa Madison)	1:41.4	1979
880-Yard Run	Detroit - Mackenzie (Delisa Walton)	2:07.7	1978
Mile Relay	Ann Arbor - Pioneer (Theresa Arnold, Rhonda Lathie, Tara Cope, Barb Ellis)	3:51.3	1981
One Mile Run	Port Huron (Miriam Boyd)	4:57.4	1979
	Ludington (Missy Thompson)	4:57.4	1982
Two Mile Run	Port Huron (Miriam Boyd)	10.36.8	1978

VOLLEYBALL

Team Record:

Longest Win Streak — 92 — Flint - Holy Rosary (1974-77)

WRESTLING

Individual Records:

Season:

Falls — 52 — Matthew Brady, Flint - Kearsley (1990-91)
Falls (Consecutive) — 37 — Dan Severn, Montrose - Hill McCloy (1975-76)
Falls (Fastest) — 119 lbs. (:04) Tony Hill, Flint - Kearsley (1-26-90)
145 lbs. (:06) Rodney Nesbitt, Battle Creek - Pennfield (2-14-84)
275 lbs. (:04) Joe Sidock, Hesperia (12-6-84)
275 lbs. (:04) Michael Seelye, Lawton (12-6-85)
275 lbs. (:04) Michael Cross, Bridgeport (1-24-87)
Victories — 73 — Matthew Brady, Flint - Kearsley 73-0 (1990-91)

Career:

Falls — 146 — Matthew Brady, Flint - Kearsley (1988-91)
Four-Time State Champions: Mike Mills, Mt Pleasant — 98-112-132-138 (1976-79)
Gregory Elie, Escanaba — 98-105-112-119 (1980-83)
Robert Mariucci, Iron Mountain — 112-126-145-155 (1981-84)
Michael Murdoch, Montrose - Hill McCloy — 119-132-145-145 (1983-86)
Team Points — 1,234.0 — Gary Silva, Montrose - Hill McCloy (1978-81)
Victories — 217 — Matthew Brady, Flint - Kearsley (1988-91)

Team:

Falls — 337 — Pinconning - Pinconning Area (1986-87)
Takedowns — 1,338 — Temperance - Bedford (1990-91)

Most Dual Meet Coaching Victories:

473 — William Regnier, Temperance - Bedford (1965-94)

1994-95 MICH. HIGH SCHOOL CHAMPIONS

MID- SEASON — *Source - MI High School Athletic Association*

SPORT	CLASS	WINNING SCHOOL	HEAD COACH
Basketball Girls	A	Flint-Northern	Leteia Hughley
	B	Dearborn - Divine Child	Marylou Jansen
	C	Redford-Bishop Borgess	Dave Mann
	D	Portland-St. Patrick	Al Schrauben
Cross Country Boys	A	Ann Arbor-Pioneer	Don Sleeman
	B	Stockbridge	Jim Lister
	C	Carson City	Gordon Alrich
	D	Bath	Mel Comeau
	UP-A-B	Marquette	Dale Phillips
	UP-C	Calumet	Bruce Hannula
	UP-D	Republic-Michigamme	Kevin Pryor
Cross Country Girls	A	Troy-Athens	Debbie Zonca
	B	Caledonia	Dave Hodakinson
	C	Shepherd	Dave Burke
	D	Bear Lake	Ken Overla
	UP A-B	Marquette	Dale PHillips
	UP C	Calumet	Bruce Hannula
	UP D	Painesdale-Jeffers	Mark Ako
Football	AA	Troy	Gary Griffith
	A	Farmington Hills-Harrison	John Herrington
	BB	Monroe-Jefferson	Marc Cisco
	B	Belding-Belding Area	Irv Sigle
	CC	Orchard Lk-St. Marys Prep	George Porritt
	C	Ravenna	Dusty Fairfield
	DD	Maple City-Glen Lake	Bill Hollenbeck
	D	Mt. Pleasant-Beal City	Ben Steele
GOLF BOYS	A	Clarkston	James Chamberlair
	B	Coldwater	Roger Fuller
	C	Fenton-Lake-Fenton	Dennis Atkinson
	D	Ann Arbor- Greenhills	Chris Mile
	UP-A-B	Gladstone	Bob Davidson
	UP-C-D	Manistique	Mike Powers

Continued on page 193

1993-94 MICHIGAN HIGH SCHOOL CHAMPIONS

Sport	Class	Winning School	Head Coach
Baseball	A	– Bloomfield Hills - Brother Rice	Ron Kalczynski
	B	– Trenton	Vic Bechard
	C	– Grandville - Calvin Christian	Jay Milkamp
	D	– Hillman	David Checkley
Basketball (Boys) Page 13	A	– Detroit – Murray - Wright	Robert Smith
	B	– St. Clair Shores - Lake Shore	Greg Esler
	C	– Grandville - Calvin Christian	Tom VanderLaan
	D	– Grand Rapids - Covenant Christian	Kevin VanEngen
Basketball (Girls)	A	– Flint - Northwestern	Tonya Edwards
	B	– Dearborn - Divine Child	Mary Lou Jansen
	C	– Redford - Bishop Borgess	Dave Mann
	D	– Ann Arbor - Gabriel Richard	Tom Kempf
Competitive Cheer	A	– Rochester Hills - Rochester	Susan McVeigh
	B	– Gaylord	Gloria Packer-Berger
	C	– Pewamo – Pewamo - Westphalia	Sherry Fedewa
	D	– Webberville - Webberville Community	Jennifer Dziatczak
Cross Country (Boys)	A	– Ann Arbor - Pioneer	Don Sleeman
	B	– Fremont	Rich Tompkins
	C	– Leslie	Jim Hanson
	D	– Grass Lake	Pat Richardson
	UP A-B	– Marquette	Dale Phillips
	UP C	– Ironwood - Luther L. Wright	Bruce Beckman
	UP D	– Painesdale - Jeffers	Mark Aho
Cross Country (Girls)	A	– Troy	Kevin Spencer
	B	– Caledonia	Dave Hodgkinson
	C	– Burton - Bendle	Mike Gould
	D	– Whitmore Lake	Larry Steeb
	UP A-B	– Ishpeming - Westwood	Eric Rundman
	UP C-D	– Calumet	Bruce Hannula
Football	AA	– Dearborn - Fordson	Jeff Stergalas
	A	– Farmington Hills - Harrison	John Herringon
	BB	– Grand Rapids - East Grand Rapids	George Barcheski
	B	– Kingsford	Chris Hofer
	CC	– Hartford	James Webb
	C	– Iron Mountain	Thomas Wender
	DD	– Mendon	John Schwartz
	D	– Fowler	Steve Spicer
Golf (Boys)	A	– East Lansing	Evonne Picard
	B	– Flint - Luke M. Powers Catholic	Don VanOrden
	C	– Horton – Hanover - Horton	Rod Hardy
	D	– Grand Rapids - Baptist Acadamy	Bruce Comer
	UP A-B	– Gladstone	Bob Davison
	UP C-D	– Manistique	Mike Powers
Golf (Girls)	A	– Kalamazoo - Kalamazoo Central	Victor Callahan
	B-C-D	– Flint - Luke M. Powers Catholic	Jack Snow
	UP A-B	– Escanaba	Doug Bovin
	UP C-D	– Ontonagon - Ontonagon Area	Dennis Morin
Gymnastics (Boys)		(No Tournament Held in 1994)	
Gymnastics (Girls)	LP Open	– Holland	Tim Lont
	UP Open	– Menominee	Joe Johnson
Ice Hockey	A	– Redford - Detroit Catholic Central	Gordon St. John
	B-C-D	– Allen Park - Cabrini	Frank DeCristofaro
Skiing (Boys)	Open	– Traverse City	Jerry Stanek

1993-94 MICHIGAN HIGH SCHOOL CHAMPIONS

Sport	Class	Winning School	Head Coach
Skiing (Girls)	Open	– Petoskey	Brewster McVicker
Soccer (Boys)	A	– Warren - DeLaSalle Collegiate	Thaier Mukhtar
	B (tie)	– Beverly Hills - Detroit Country Day	Paul Bartoshuk
	B (tie)	– Richland - Gull Lake	Lee Newland
	C-D	– Riverview - Gabriel Richard	Mike Slowik
Soccer (Girls)	A	– Troy	Kevin Kelly
	B-C-D	– Madison Heights - Bishop Foley	Horst Lehrer
Softball	A	– Jenison	Jerry Hoag
	B	– Ortonville - Brandon	Don Peters
	C	– Ida	Brian Cousino
	D	– Marine City - Cardinal Mooney Catholic	Jim Benoit
Swimming (Boys)	A	– Bloomfield Hills - Brother Rice	Ron Richards
	B-C-D	– Bloomfield Hills - Andover	Mike Lane
	UP Open	– Marquette	Al Bentley
Swimming (Girls)	A	– Grand Rapids - Forest Hills Central	Tim Jaspers
	B-C-D	– Grand Rapids - East Grand Rapids	Milton Briggs
	UP Open	– Gwinn	Jo Baysore
Tennis (Boys)	A	– Okemos	Jim Powers
	B (tie)	– Bloomfield Hills - Cranbrook Kingswood	Don Brown
	B (tie)	– Mason	Dee McCaffrey
	C-D	– Grosse Pointe Woods - University Liggett	Bob Wood
	UP A-B	– Marquette	Dick Balding
	UP C-D	– Ishpeming	Erling Langness
Tennis (Girls)	A	– Okemos	Dan Stolz
	B	– Holland - Holland Christian	Tom Buursma
	C-D	– Beverly Hills - Detroit Country Day	Brad Gilman
	UP A-B	– Escanaba	Karin Flynn
	UP C-D	– Iron River - West Iron County	Brook Smith
Track (Boys)	A	– Detroit - Cass Technical	Sherrell Rowland
	B	– Comstock	Tim Cashen
	C	– New Haven	Frank Reed
	D	– Pittsford	Bruce Caswell
	UP A-B	– Menominee	Greg Langlois
	UP C	– Munising	Frances Des Armo
	UP D	– Ontonagon - Ontonagon Area	Mark Bobula
Track (Girls)	A	– Detroit - Cass Technical	Bertha Smiley
	B	– River Rouge	Robert Washington
	C	– Clare	Judy Johnson
	D	– Maple City - Glen Lake	Doug Greer
	UP A-B	– Marquette	Dale Phillips
	UP C	– Ironwood - Luther L. Wright	Dave Davis
	UP D (tie)	– Iron Mountain - North Dickenson	Paul Feak
	UP D (tie)	– Lake Linden – Lake Linden - Hubbell	Craig Sunblad
Volleyball	A	– Portage - Portage Northern	Jack Magelssen
	B	– Richland - Gull Lake	Kim Poteau
	C	– Holton	Ed Bailey
	D	– Battle Creek - St. Philip Catholic Central	Sheila Guerra
	UP A-B-C	– Iron Mountain	Tracy Beadlescomb
	UP D	– Cedarville	Mark Engle
Wrestling	A	– Warren - Lincoln	Sam Amine
	B	– Fowlerville	Dan Coon
	C-D	– New Lothrop	John Quaderer

BASEBALL CHAMPIONS – STATE - 1989--1994

Year	Class A (Coach)	Class B (Coach)	Class C (Coach)	Class D (Coach)
1989	**Harper Woods - Notre Dame** (Anthony Mardirosian)	**Harper Woods - Bishop Gallagher** (Thomas Trompics)	**Berrien Springs** (John Donley)	**Colon - Colon Community** (Dennis Hendrickson)
1990	**Sterling Heights - Ford II** (Dan Barnabo)	**Stevensville - Lakeshore** (Steve Adler)	**Saginaw - Nouvel Catholic Central** (Stephen Jaksa)	**Traverse City - St. Francis** (Craig Bauer)
1991	**Canton - Plymouth Salem** (John Gravlin)	**Chelsea** (Wayne Welton)	**Erie – Erie - Mason** (Tom McGarry)	**Waterford - Our Lady of the Lakes** (Daniel Webster)
1992	**Birmingham - Brother Rice** (Ron Kalczynski)	**Dearborn - Divine Child** (Mark Falvo)	**Blissfield** (Larry Tuttle)	**Hillman - Hillman Community** (David Checkley)
1993	**Warren - DeLaSalle Collegiate** (Brian Kelly)	**DeWitt** (Frank Deak)	**Coleman** (Joe Albaugh)	**Mt. Pleasant - Beal City** (Ron Schafer)
1994	**Bloomfield Hills - Brother Rice** (Ron Kalczynski)	**Trenton** (Vic Bechard)	**Grandville - Calvin Christian** (Jay Milkamp)	**Hillman** (David Checkley)

BASKETBALL CHAMPIONS – BOYS STATE · 1989–1994

Year	Class A (Coach)	Class B (Coach)	Class C (Coach)	Class D (Coach)
1989	**Detroit - Cooley** (Ben Kelso)	**Saginaw - Buena Vista** (Norwaine Reed)	**Birmingham - Detroit Country Day** (Kurt Keener)	**Mio – Mio - AuSable** (John Byelich)
1990	**Detroit - Southwestern** (Perry Watson)	**Birmingham - Detroit Country Day** (Kurt Keener)	**Saginaw - Nouvel Catholic Central** (Joe Ricard)	**Detroit - East Catholic** (Dave Soules)
1991	**Detroit - Southwestern** (Perry Watson)	**Birmingham - Detroit Country Day** (Kurt Keener)	**Saginaw - Nouvel Catholic Central** (Joe Ricard)	**Ann Arbor - Gabriel Richard** (Tom Kempf)
1992	**Detroit - Pershing** (Johnny Goston)	**Saginaw - Buena Vista** (Norwaine Reed)	**Detroit - St. Martin dePorres** (Ed Rachal)	**Muskegon - Western Michigan Christian** (James Goorman)
1993	**Detroit - Pershing** (Johnny Goston)	**Saginaw - Buena Vista** (Norwaine Reed)	**Southgate - Aquinas** (Ernie Price)	**Grand Rapids - Covenant Christian** (Kevin VanEngen)
1994	**Detroit – Murray - Wright** (Robert Smith)	**St. Clair Shores - Lake Shore** (Greg Esler)	**Grandville - Calvin Christian** (Tom VanderLaan)	**Grand Rapids - Covenant Christian** (Kevin VanEngen)

FOOTBALL CHAMPIONS – STATE (SINGLE CLASS) – 1989–1994

Year	Class A (Coach)	Class B (Coach)	Class C (Coach)	Class D (Coach)
1989	**Muskegon** (Dave Taylor)	**Farmington Hills - Harrison** (John Herrington)	**Schoolcraft** (Larry Ledlow)	**Mendon** (John Schwartz)
1990	**Birmingham - Brother Rice** (Albert Fracassa)	**Dearborn Heights - Robichaud** (Robert Yauck, Sr.)	**Muskegon - Muskegon Catholic Central** (Mike Holmes)	**Frankfort** (Tim Klein)
1991	**East Lansing** (Jeff Smith)	**Monroe - St. Mary Catholic Central** (Joseph Sandersen)	**Muskegon - Muskegon Catholic Central** (Mike Holmes)	**Frankfort** (Tim Klein)
1992	**Muskegon – Reeths - Puffer** (Pete Kutches)	**Marysville** (Walt Braun)	**Traverse City - St. Francis** (Larry Sellers)	**Portland - St. Patrick** (Chris Schrauben)
1993	**Farmington Hills - Harrison** (John Herrington)	**Kingsford** (Chris Hofer)	**Iron Mountain** (Thomas Wender)	**Fowler** (Steve Spicer)
1994	Farmington Hills– Harrison John Harrington	Belding–Belding 60 Area Irv Sigler	Ravenna Dusty Fairchild	Mt Pleasant– Beal City Ben Steele

FOOTBALL CHAMPIONS – STATE (DOUBLE CLASS) – 1900–1994

Year	Class AA (Coach)	Class BB (Coach)	Class CC (Coach)	Class DD (Coach)
1990	**Redford - Detroit Catholic Central** (Thomas Mach)	**Dowagiac - Dowagiac Union** (Bernard Thomas)	**Detroit - St. Martin dePorres** (Ron Thompson)	**Marion** (Thomas Cutler)
1991	**Saginaw - Arthur Hill** (Jim Eurick)	**Farmington Hills - Harrison** (John Herrington)	**Battle Creek - Pennfield** (Dave Hudson)	**Mendon** (John Schwartz)
1992	**Redford - Detroit Catholic Central** (Thomas Mach)	**Oxford** (Bud Rowley)	**Detroit - St. Martin dePorres** (Ron Thompson)	**Lake Linden – Lake Linden - Hubbell** (Ronald Warner)
1993	**Dearborn - Fordson** (Jeff Stergalas)	**Grand Rapids - East Grand Rapids** (George Barcheski)	**Hartford** (James Webb)	**Mendon** (John Schwartz)
1994	Troy Gary Griffith	Monroe–Jefferson Marc Cicso	Orchard Lake– St Mary Prep Geo.Perritt	Maple City– Glen Lake Bill Hollenbeck

BASKETBALL CHAMPIONS – GIRLS STATE – 1973 -1993

Year	Class A (Coach)	Class B (Coach)	Class C (Coach)	Class D (Coach)
1989	**Grand Rapids - Ottawa Hills** (Camilla Carter)	**Dearborn - Divine Child** (Nancy Sullivan)	**Birmingham - Detroit Country Day** (Frank Orlando)	**Carney –Carney - Nadeau** (Paul Polfus)
1990	**Detroit - Martin Luther King** (William Winfield)	**Grand Rapids - West Catholic** (Mike Braunschneider)	**Buchanan** (Bill Weaver)	**Carney – Carney - Nadeau** (Paul Polfus)
1991	**Detroit - Martin Luther King** (William Winfield)	**Flint - Luke M. Powers Catholic** (Kathy McGee)	**Burton - Bendle** (Rose Wilkins)	**Fowler** (Tom O'Rourke)
1992	**Bloomfield Hills - Marian** (Mary Lillie - Cicerone)	**Frankenmuth** (Art Pelzer)	**Carrollton** (Dennis Schumacher)	**Auburn Hills - Oakland Christian** (Ed Mehlberg)
1993	**Flint - Northwestern** (Tonya Edwards)	**Dearborn - Divine Child** (Mary Lou Jansen)	**Redford - Bishop Borgess** (Dave Mann)	**Ann Arbor - Gabriel** (Tom Kempf)
1994	Flint–Northern Leteia Hughley	Dearborn–Divine Child Marylou Jansen	Redford–Bishop Borgess Dave Mann	Portland–St Patrick Al Schrauben

1994–95 MICH. HIGH SCHOOL CHAMPIONS

continued from page 188

Skiing Boys	A	Traverse City	Jerry Stanek
Skiing Girls	A	Petoskey	Brewster McVicker
Soccer Boys	A	Canton–Plymouth Canton	Don Smith
	B	Beverly Hills Detroit	Paul Bartoshuk
	C–D	Kalmazoo–Hackett Cath.Cnt	Neil Crumpton
Swimmimg Girls	A	Grand Rapids–Forest Hills Cntrl	Tim Jaspers
	B–C–D	Zeeland	Michael Torrey
	UP Open	Gwinn	Jo Baysore

AIDS (ACQUIRED IMMUNE DEFICIENCY) MICH - U.S.

Source: Cumulative AIDS Case Statitsitcs,
Disesase Survellance, Mi Department Of Public Health

Michigan is significantly below the U.S. rate for AIDS.

The cumulative rate in Michigan for the period 1981 to Jan.1, 1995 is 68.2, compared to the U.S. rate of 161.5. Only one county (Washtenaw) exceeds the state rate, seven counties have zero cases and seven counties have had one case. Detroit, with a rate of 280.2, is above the national rate, but only a fraction of the rate of some of the nation's large cities, such as Washington, DC. (1,073.4).

The largest racial group in the U.S. with AIDS is white, followed next by black. The two groups are reversed in Michigan, however, with blacks the largest group, followed by white.

Based on rate (cases per 100,000 population), both blacks and hispanics have significantly higher numbers than whites in both the U.S. and Michigan.

Male-male sex is the leading cause of AIDS among males in Michigan, while drug injection is the primary cause among females.

More than 75% of victims are in the 25-44 years age group. None are exempt, however, with 1% of cases below the age of 5 years and 1% of cases above the age of 64.

Males outnumber females AIDS victims in Michigan 6½ to one and the total death rate is 66%.

All of these statistics are among the many on the adjoining pages.

Michigan AIDS Deaths, by Gender and Race

	MALES: NUMBER OF DEATHS					FEMALES: NUMBER OF DEATHS					
Yr. of Death	White	Black	Hisp.	Other/ Unk.	All Races	White	Black	Hisp.	Other/ Unk.	All Races	TOTAL
1978-1986	91	68	5	1	165	5	11	0	0	16	181
1987	92	67	1	0	160	5	6	0	0	11	171
1988	117	100	4	1	222	3	26	0	0	29	251
1989	170	148	6	1	325	3	29	0	0	32	357
1990	185	163	9	0	357	6	47	1	1	55	412
1991	213	185	6	1	405	13	38	1	0	52	457
1992	218	226	14	2	460	15	57	2	0	74	534
1993	253	296	14	4	567	21	76	2	0	99	666
1994	203	278	15	1	497	15	71	3	0	89	586
Unknown	7	2	1	0	10	1	0	0	0	1	11
ALL DEATHS	1,549	1,533	75	11	3,168	87	361	9	1	458	3,626

U.S. States/Territories With Most Cumulative AIDS Cases Reported to CDC as of 07/1/94

STATE	CASES	RATE[1]	STATE	CASES	RATE[1]	STATE	CASES	RATE[1]	STATE	CASES	RATE[1]
1. NY	76,345	424.4	6. PR[2]	12,845	364.7	11. MA	8,672	144.1	16. MI[3]	5,739	61.7
2. CA	72,433	243.4	7. IL	12,735	111.4	12.DC[2]	6,504	1,073.4	17. WA	5,496	112.9
3. FL	38,855	300.3	8. PA	11,375	95.7	13. LA	5,986	141.9	18. CT	5,399	164.3
4. TX	27,951	164.6	9. GA	11,001	169.8	14. OH	5,908	54.5	19. MO	5,294	103.5
5. NJ	22,496	291.0	10.MD	8,897	186.1	15. VA	5,814	94.0	20. NC	4,885	73.7

[1]Cumulative Rate per 100,000 Population, 1990 Census

[2]Abbreviations include PR for Puerto Rico, and DC for District of Columbia

[3]Michigan cumulative **annual rate per 100,000 population** ranks 36th in the U.S. as of 07/1/94.

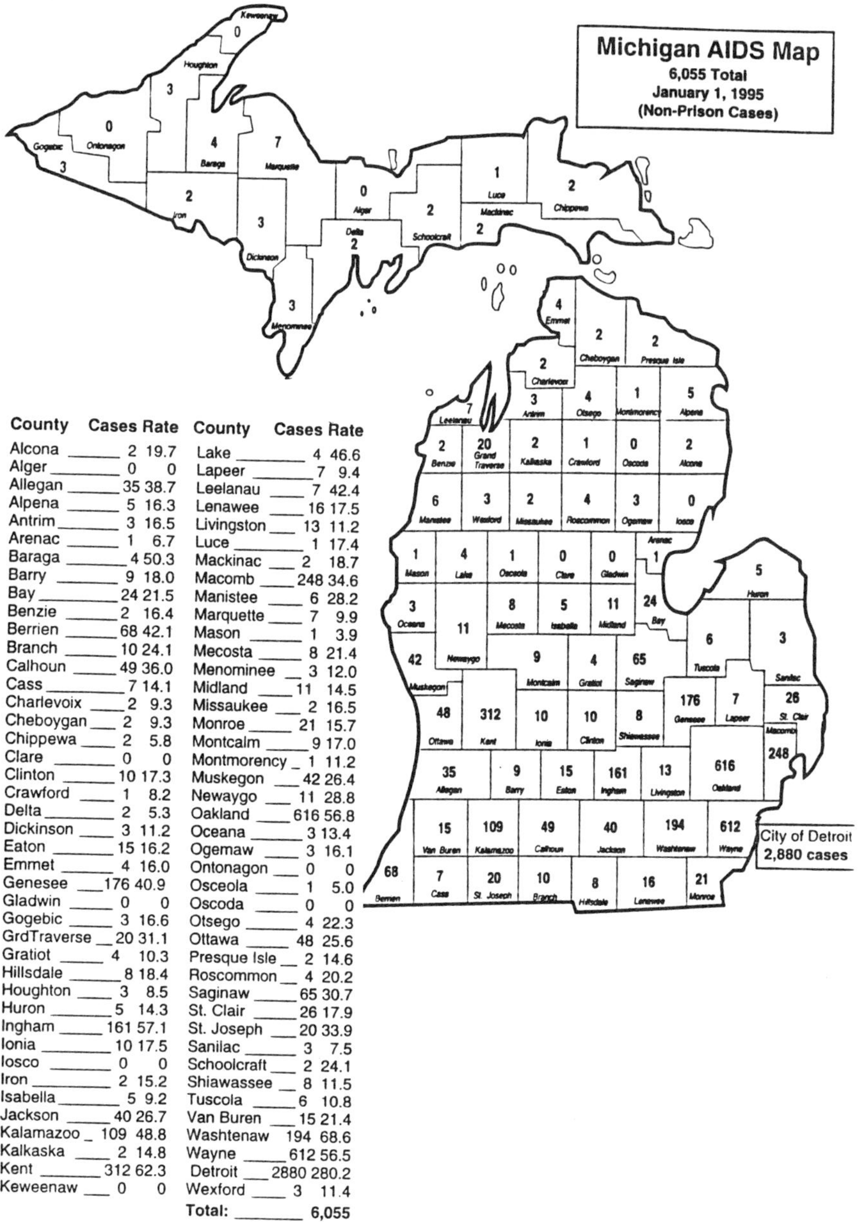

County	Cases	Rate	County	Cases	Rate
Alcona	2	19.7	Lake	4	46.6
Alger	0	0	Lapeer	7	9.4
Allegan	35	38.7	Leelanau	7	42.4
Alpena	5	16.3	Lenawee	16	17.5
Antrim	3	16.5	Livingston	13	11.2
Arenac	1	6.7	Luce	1	17.4
Baraga	4	50.3	Mackinac	2	18.7
Barry	9	18.0	Macomb	248	34.6
Bay	24	21.5	Manistee	6	28.2
Benzie	2	16.4	Marquette	7	9.9
Berrien	68	42.1	Mason	1	3.9
Branch	10	24.1	Mecosta	8	21.4
Calhoun	49	36.0	Menominee	3	12.0
Cass	7	14.1	Midland	11	14.5
Charlevoix	2	9.3	Missaukee	2	16.5
Cheboygan	2	9.3	Monroe	21	15.7
Chippewa	2	5.8	Montcalm	9	17.0
Clare	0	0	Montmorency	1	11.2
Clinton	10	17.3	Muskegon	42	26.4
Crawford	1	8.2	Newaygo	11	28.8
Delta	2	5.3	Oakland	616	56.8
Dickinson	3	11.2	Oceana	3	13.4
Eaton	15	16.2	Ogemaw	3	16.1
Emmet	4	16.0	Ontonagon	0	0
Genesee	176	40.9	Osceola	1	5.0
Gladwin	0	0	Oscoda	0	0
Gogebic	3	16.6	Otsego	4	22.3
GrdTraverse	20	31.1	Ottawa	48	25.6
Gratiot	4	10.3	Presque Isle	2	14.6
Hillsdale	8	18.4	Roscommon	4	20.2
Houghton	3	8.5	Saginaw	65	30.7
Huron	5	14.3	St. Clair	26	17.9
Ingham	161	57.1	St. Joseph	20	33.9
Ionia	10	17.5	Sanilac	3	7.5
Iosco	0	0	Schoolcraft	2	24.1
Iron	2	15.2	Shiawassee	8	11.5
Isabella	5	9.2	Tuscola	6	10.8
Jackson	40	26.7	Van Buren	15	21.4
Kalamazoo	109	48.8	Washtenaw	194	68.6
Kalkaska	2	14.8	Wayne	612	56.5
Kent	312	62.3	Detroit	2880	280.2
Keweenaw	0	0	Wexford	3	11.4
			Total:	6,055	

Cumulative rates are non-prison cases per 100,000 population. The 282 prison cases excluded from rate calculations, the table, and the map were in prison at the time of AIDS diagnosis: Jackson (240), Arenac (1), Branch (4), Chippewa (3), Gogebic (3), Ionia (5), Kent (4), Marquette (2), Muskegon (5), Oakland (2), Washtenaw (5), and Wayne (8) Counties.

MI and U.S. Cumulative AIDS Cases by Patient Group

PATIENT DESCRIPTION OR BEHAVIOR	MI AIDS : 1981 - 01/1/95			U.S. AIDS[1] : 1981 -07/1/94		
	Cases	Pct.	Rate[2]	Cases	Pct.	Rate[2]
GENDER						
Male	5,501	87%	121.9	347,767	87%	286.8
Female	836	13%	17.5	53,978	13%	42.3
Unknown	0	—	—	4	0%	—
TRANSMISSION						
Male-Male sex	3,330	53%	NA	211,779	53%	NA
Injecting Drug Use	1,569	25%	NA	98,367	24%	NA
Male-Male Sex/IDU	342	5%	NA	25,447	6%	NA
Blood Products[3]	218	3%	NA	10,514	3%	NA
Heterosexual [4]	343	5%	NA	27,281	7%	NA
Perinatal [5]	57	1%	NA	5,095	1%	NA
Undetermined [6]	478	8%	NA	23,266	6%	NA
AGE AT DIAGNOSIS						
0 - 4 years	44	1%	6.3	4,605	1%	25.1
5 - 12 years	29	0%	2.7	1,129	0%	4.0
13 - 19 years	28	0%	2.9	1,768	0%	7.3
20 - 24 years	244	4%	34.6	15,204	4%	79.9
25 - 29 years	948	15%	124.0	60,042	15%	281.7
30 - 34 years	1,374	22%	169.6	93,696	23%	428.6
35 - 39 years	1,430	23%	190.9	89,099	22%	446.3
40 - 44 years	1,075	17%	163.6	61,789	15%	350.8
45 - 49 years	566	9%	108.1	34,053	8%	245.5
50 - 54 years	299	5%	70.5	18,307	5%	161.3
55 - 59 years	141	2%	35.9	10,598	3%	100.6
60 - 64 years	83	1%	20.7	6,030	2%	56.8
65 and over	76	1%	6.9	5,427	1%	17.4
Unknown	0	—	—	2	0%	—
RACE/ETHNICITY						
White, Non-Hisp.	2,801	44%	37.1	198,130	49%	105.3
Black, Non-Hisp.	3,346	53%	259.0	130,384	32%	446.3
Hispanic	166	3%	82.3	68,903	17%	308.2
Asian	12	0%	11.4	2,706	1%	38.8
American Indian	12	0%	21.6	944	0%	52.6
Unknown	0	—	—	682	0%	—
TOTAL each group	6,337	100%	68.2	401,749	100%	161.5

[1] U.S. figures are produced by Centers for Disease Control every six months.

[2] Cumulative rates per 100,000 population are calculated using 1990 Census figures. Populations and rates are not available behaviors.

[3] Includes patients infected from coagulation disorder (158 MI; 3,618 US) or transfusion (60 MI; 6,896 U.S.) blood products.

[4] A heterosexual partner is known to be: an injecting drug user (166 MI, 14,239 US), a bisexual man (23 MI, 1,601 US), infected blood products (16 MI, 809 US), or HIV positive with unknown behavior history (138 MI, 10,632 US).

[5] Perinatal transmission is from an HIV infected mother to infant, before or at birth.

[6] Patient risks are under investigation, or no risk was identified.

Michigan AIDS Cases by Year of Report

PATIENT GROUP OR BEHAVIOR	REPORTED 1981-90		REPORTED 1991		REPORTED 1992		REPORTED 1993		REPORTED 1994	
Male	1830	89%	496	84%	672	88%	1,556	86%	947	84%
Female	215	11%	91	16%	91	12%	252	14%	187	16%
Male-Male sex	1191	58%	329	56%	400	52%	878	49%	532	47%
Injecting Drug Use	466	23%	131	22%	182	24%	512	28%	278	25%
Male-Male Sex/IDU	127	6%	24	4%	43	6%	93	5%	55	5%
Blood Products[1]	98	5%	21	4%	25	3%	51	3%	23	2%
Heterosexual [2]	69	3%	38	6%	39	5%	114	6%	83	7%
Perinatal [3]	27	1%	5	1%	10	1%	10	1%	5	0%
Undetermined [4]	67	3%	39	7%	64	8%	150	8%	158	14%
0 - 4 years	24	1%	3	1%	8	1%	6	0%	3	0%
5 - 12 years	11	1%	4	1%	6	1%	5	0%	3	0%
13 - 19 years	12	1%	3	1%	2	0%	7	0%	4	0%
20 - 24 years	86	4%	21	4%	20	3%	64	4%	53	5%
25 - 29 years	342	17%	96	16%	126	17%	255	14%	129	11%
30 - 34 years	443	22%	125	21%	164	21%	384	21%	258	23%
35 - 39 years	443	22%	139	24%	169	22%	415	23%	264	23%
40 - 44 years	312	15%	92	16%	137	18%	337	19%	197	17%
45 - 49 years	166	8%	41	7%	66	9%	172	10%	121	11%
50 - 54 years	92	4%	29	5%	34	4%	86	5%	58	5%
55 - 59 years	53	3%	17	3%	14	2%	32	2%	25	2%
60 - 64 years	32	2%	9	2%	8	1%	26	1%	8	1%
65 and over	29	1%	8	1%	9	1%	19	1%	11	1%
White, Non-Hispanic	1,022	50%	266	45%	347	45%	712	39%	454	40%
Black, Non-Hispanic	968	47%	302	51%	397	52%	1,043	58%	636	56%
Hispanic	47	2%	18	3%	19	2%	44	2%	38	3%
Asian	3	0%	1	0%	0	0%	4	0%	4	0%
American Indian	5	0%	0	0%	0	0%	5	0%	2	0%
TOTAL each year	2,045	100%	587	100%	763	100%	1,808	100%	1,134	100%

Michigan Cases: Gender by Race/Ethnicity by Transmission Behavior

MALES:	WHITE		BLACK		HISPANIC		OTHER/UNK.		TOTAL	
Male-Male Sex	1,993	76%	1,248	46%	75	50%	14	64%	3,330	61%
Injecting Drug Use	127	5%	930	34%	45	30%	0	0%	1,102	20%
Male-Male Sex/IDU	152	6%	179	7%	10	7%	1	5%	342	6%
Blood Recipient	167	6%	24	1%	2	1%	4	19%	197	4%
Heterosexual	29	1%	80	3%	5	3%	0	0%	114	2%
Perinatal	7	0%	26	1%	0	0%	0	0%	33	1%
Undetermined	142	5%	226	8%	12	8%	3	14%	383	7%
TOTAL	2,617	(48%)	2,713	(49%)	149	(3%)	22	(0%)	5,501	(100%)
FEMALES:	**WHITE**		**BLACK**		**HISPANIC**		**OTHER/UNK.**		**TOTAL**	
Injecting Drug Use	57	31%	402	64%	7	41%	1	50%	467	56%
Blood Recipient	17	9%	4	1%	0	0%	0	0%	21	4%
Heterosexual	75	41%	148	23%	6	35%	0	0%	229	27%
Perinatal	3	2%	19	3%	2	12%	0	0%	24	3%
Undetermined	32	17%	60	10%	2	12%	1	50%	95	11%
TOTAL	184	(22%)	633	(76%)	17	(2%)	2	(0%)	836	(100%)

HIV Infection Among Michigan Residents, by Patient Group (Excludes Perinatal Transmission Cases)

PATIENT GROUP OR BEHAVIOR	ESTIMATED[1] STATEWIDE HIV PREVALENCE	PATIENTS ALIVE 01/1/95 CONFIDENTIAL REPORTS[2] AIDS		HIV/Not AIDS		ANONYMOUS HIV[3] REPORTS	
		No.	Pct.	No.	Pct.	No.	Pct.
ALL MICHIGAN	10,000-15,000	2,687	100%	2,252	100%	970	100%
Male	7,700-12,900	2,319	86%	1735	77%	803	84%
Female	1,400- 3,450	368	14%	517	23%	157	16%
Unspecified[4]	Not Applicable	0	(0%)	0	(0%)	10	(1%)
Male-Male sex	4,500 - 8,400	1,349	56%	746	45%	536	68%
Inject.Drug Use	2,800 - 4,650	685	28%	522	31%	130	17%
M-M Sex/IDU	500 - 900	142	6%	88	5%	34	4%
Blood Product	300 - 450	81	3%	46	3%	8	1%
Heterosexual	700 - 2,400	160	7%	258	16%	76	10%
Undetermined[4]	Not Applicable	270	(10%)	592	(26%)	186	(19%)
0 - 12 years	< 150	7	0%	12	1%	3	0%
13 - 19 years	< 300	10	0%	52	2%	13	1%
20 - 24 years	400- 1,950	116	4%	293	13%	121	13%
25 - 29 years	1,400- 3,300	375	14%	494	22%	221	23%
30 - 34 years	2,300- 3,600	650	24%	506	23%	231	24%
35 - 39 years	1,900- 3,450	615	23%	425	19%	179	19%
40 - 44 years	1,200- 2,700	491	18%	266	12%	117	12%
45 - 49 years	500- 1,200	227	8%	121	5%	43	5%
50 - 54 years	200- 600	106	4%	47	2%	15	2%
55 - 59 years	100- 300	48	2%	21	1%	7	1%
60 - 64 years	<150	26	1%	10	0%	4	0%
65 years and over	< 150	16	1%	5	0%	4	0%
Unspecified[4]	Not Applicable	0	(0%)	0	(0%)	12	(1%)
White,Non-Hisp.	3,200- 6,450	1,161	43%	713	32%	489	52%
Black,Non-Hisp.	5,300- 9,750	1,433	53%	1,438	65%	409	43%
Hispanic	200- 450	81	3%	53	2%	45	5%
Asian	<< 150	8	0%	1	0%	3	0%
American Indian	<< 150	4	0%	6	0%	4	0%
Unspecified[4]	Not Applicable	0	(0%)	41	(2%)	20	(2%)

[1] 10,000 to 15,000 living Michigan residents are infected with HIV. The estimated prevalence for each patient group is calculated from the percentages of living, confidential HIV and AIDS cases reported in that group. The lower boundary is the smaller percentage of 10,000, and the upper boundary is the larger percentage of 15,000. Consequently, groups do not add to exactly 10,000 and 15,000.

[2] Confidential case reports were actively solicited on AIDS since 1981, and on HIV infection since April 1, 1992. HIV reports passively collected between April 1989 and March 1992 are also being added to the database. Prevalence (the number of persons living with HIV infection) is calculated using only reported cases who are alive.

[3] Anonymous HIV cases (collected actively since 4/92 and passively 4/89 to 3/92) are excluded from prevalence calculations as we cannot estimate duplicate reporting, or obtain missing or update information (e.g., AIDS diagnosis, death).

[4] Age, sex, race, and behavior percentages were calculated after excluding cases missing these data. The percentages of total cases missing these demographic information are given in parentheses.

[5] County of residence percentages were calculated after excluding persons in prison at time of diagnosis of HIV/AIDS.

HIV Infection Among Michigan Residents, by County (Excludes Perinatal Transmission Cases)

RESIDENCE AT TIME OF DIAGNOSIS	ESTIMATED[1] COUNTYWIDE HIV PREVALENCE	PATIENTS ALIVE 01/1/95 CONFIDENTIAL REPORTS[2]				ANONYMOUS HIV REPORTS[3] (01/1/95)	
		AIDS		HIV/Not AIDS			
		No.	Pct[5]	No.	Pct[5]	No.	Pct
TOTAL MICHIGAN	**10,000-15,000**	2,519	100%	1790	100%	970	100%
Alcona	1 - 15	1	<.1%	0	0%	0	0%
Alger	0 - 15	0	0%	0	0%	0	0%
Allegan	30 - 120	21	0.8%	6	0.3%	2	0.2%
Alpena	2 - 15	2	0.1%	0	0%	0	0%
Antrim	10 - 15	2	0.1%	1	0.1%	1	0.1%
Arenac	0 - 15	0	0%	0	0%	0	0%
Baraga	1 - 15	1	<.1%	0	0%	0	0%
Barry	20 - 30	4	0.2%	4	0.2%	0	0%
Bay	10- 60	9	0.4%	2	0.1%	19	2.0%
Benzie	1 - 15	1	<.1%	0	0%	0	0%
Berrien	130- 255	33	1.3%	30	1.7%	8	1.0%
Branch	20 - 90	5	0.2%	11	0.6%	4	0.4%
Calhoun	60- 180	16	0.6%	22	1.2%	6	0.6%
Cass	10 - 15	2	0.1%	1	0.1%	1	0.1%
Charlevoix	1 - 15	1	<.1%	0	0%	1	0.1%
Cheboygan	2 - 15	2	0.1%	0	0%	1	0.1%
Chippewa	3 - 15	1	<.1%	2	0.1%	1	0.1%
Clare	0 - 15	0	0%	0	0%	0	0%
Clinton	20 - 30	6	0.2%	4	0.2%	1	0.1%
Crawford	2 - 15	1	<.1%	1	0.1%	0	0%
Delta	2 - 15	2	0.1%	0	0%	1	0.1%
Dickinson	10 - 15	2	0.1%	1	0.1%	0	0%
Eaton	20 - 30	5	0.2%	4	0.2%	0	0%
Emmet	10 - 15	3	0.1%	2	0.1%	0	0%
Genesee	210 - 750	52	2.1%	89	5.0%	26	2.7%
Gladwin	0 - 15	0	0%	0	0%	0	0%
Gogebic	2 - 15	2	0.1%	0	0%	0	0%
Grand Traverse	9 - 60	9	0.4%	0	0%	15	1.6%
Gratiot	3 - 15	1	<.1%	2	0.1%	0	0%
Hillsdale	20 - 30	4	0.2%	4	0.2%	1	0.1%
Houghton	0 - 15	0	0%	0	0%	0	0%
Huron	10 - 15	2	0.1%	1	0.1%	0	0%
Ingham	220 - 810	55	2.2%	96	5.4%	14	1.4%
Ionia	10 - 15	3	0.1%	2	0.1%	1	0.1%
Iosco	1 - 15	0	0%	1	0.1%	0	0%
Iron	1 - 15	1	<.1%	0	0%	0	0%
Isabella	2 - 15	2	0.1%	0	0%	0	0%
Jackson	70- 150	17	0.7%	18	1.0%	4	0.4%
Kalamazoo	180 - 285	49	1.9%	33	1.8%	18	1.9%
Kalkaska	1 - 15	1	<.1%	0	0%	2	0.2%
Kent	310 - 735	124	4.9%	56	3.1%	199	20.5%
Keweenaw	0 - 15	0	0%	0	0%	0	0%

Michigan Estimates of HIV Prevalence,
and Reported Infections
Disease Surveillance Section, MDPH

Quarterly HIV/AIDS Analysis
January 1, 1995

HIV Infection Among Michigan Residents, by County (Excludes Perinatal Transmission Cases)

RESIDENCE AT TIME OF DIAGNOSIS	ESTIMATED[1] COUNTYWIDE HIV PREVALENCE	PATIENTS ALIVE 01/1/95 CONFIDENTIAL REPORTS[2] AIDS No.	AIDS Pct.[5]	HIV/Not AIDS No.	HIV/Not AIDS Pct.[5]	ANONYMOUS HIV REPORTS[3] No.	Pct.
TOTAL MICHIGAN	10,000-15,000	2,519	100%	1790	100%	970	100%
Lake	2 - 15	2	0.1%	0	0%	2	0.2%
Lapeer	10 - 45	2	0.1%	6	0.3%	2	0.2%
Leelanau	2 - 15	2	0.1%	0	0%	3	0.3%
Lenawee	30 - 45	7	0.3%	6	0.3%	4	0.4%
Livingston	20 - 30	4	0.2%	3	0.2%	1	0.1%
Luce	0 - 15	0	0%	0	0%	0	0%
Mackinac	2 - 15	2	0.1%	0	0%	0	0%
Macomb	270 - 660	112	4.4%	49	2.7%	35	3.6%
Manistee	4 - 30	4	0.2%	0	0%	5	0.5%
Marquette	2 - 15	2	0.1%	0	0%	1	0.1%
Mason	2 - 15	1	<.1%	1	0.1%	2	0.2%
Mecosta	10 - 30	4	0.2%	1	0.1%	0	0%
Menominee	1 - 15	0	0%	1	0.1%	0	0%
Midland	4 - 30	4	0.2%	0	0%	6	0.6%
Missaukee	1 - 15	1	<.1%	0	0%	0	0%
Monroe	10 - 30	6	0.2%	2	0.1%	3	0.3%
Montcalm	20 - 30	4	0.2%	4	0.2%	0	0%
Montmorency	1 - 15	1	<.1%	0	0%	0	0%
Muskegon	60 - 90	14	0.6%	11	0.6%	3	0.3 %
Newaygo	10 - 30	5	0.2%	1	0.1%	2	0.2%
Oakland	1,040- 1,785	263	10.4%	213	11.9%	77	7.9%
Oceana	1 - 15	1	<.1%	0	0%	0	0%
Ogemaw	10 - 15	2	0.1%	1	0.1%	0	0%
Ontonagon	0 - 15	0	0%	0	0%	0	0%
Osceola	1 - 15	1	<.1%	0	0%	1	0.1%
Oscoda	0 - 15	0	0%	0	0%	0	0%
Otsego	2 - 15	2	0.1%	0	0%	1	0.1%
Ottawa	20 - 105	18	0.7%	3	0.2%	9	0.9%
Presque Isle	0 - 15	0	0%	0	0%	0	0%
Roscommon	2 - 15	1	<.1%	1	0.1%	3	0.3%
Saginaw	80 - 165	28	1.1%	15	0.8%	17	1.8%
Saint Clair	30 - 165	8	0.3%	19	1.1%	3	0.3%
Saint Joseph	20 - 45	5	0.2%	6	0.3%	2	0.2%
Sanilac	3 - 15	1	<.1%	2	0.1%	0	0%
Schoolcraft	1 - 15	0	0%	1	0.1%	0	0%
Shiawassee	3 - 15	3	0.1%	0	0%	0	0%
Tuscola	10 - 30	4	0.2%	1	0.1%	2	0.2%
Van Buren	20 - 90	6	0.2%	11	0.6%	1	0.1%
Washtenaw	230 - 600	101	4.0%	41	2.3%	29	3.0%
Wayne	770 -1,800	301	12.0%	138	7.7%	77	7.9%
Detroit	4,580 -7,200	1153	45.8%	860	48.0%	351	36.2%
Wexford	2 - 15	2	0.1%	0	0%	2	0.2%
PRISONS[5]	over 630	168		462		0	

PUBLIC HOLIDAYS IN MICHIGAN

New Year's Day	January 1
Martin Luther King Day	Third Monday in January
Lincoln's Birthday	February 12
Washington's Birthday	Third Monday in February
Memorial or Decoration Day	Last Monday in May
Independence Day	July 4
Labor Day	First Monday in September
Columbus Day	Second Monday in October
Veterans' Day	November 11
Thanksgiving Day	Fourth Thursday in November
Christmas	December 25

MICHIGAN'S HISTORICAL MARKERS

Since 1955, the Michigan Historical Commission and the Bureau of History, Michigan Department of State, have erected over 1,100 historical markers at registered historic sites across the state. Markers commemorate Michigan's diverse history, including events such as the arrival of the British and French, industries such as mining, lumbering and agriculture, the growth of the state's educational institutions, buildings such as Michigan's newly restored, 113-year-old State Capitol and adventurous Michiganians such as early aviatrix Harriet Quimby of Coldwater. Markers can be found along Michigan's scenic highways, in roadside parks and in villages and urban centers. State historical markers are paid for with private donations.

A guide listing all the markers and their locations is available through the Bureau of History, Michigan Department of State, 1-800-366-3703.

CHRONOLOGY OF MICHIGAN HISTORY

1618 Etienne Brulé passes through North Channel at the neck of Lake Huron; that same year (or during two following years) he lands at Sault Ste. Marie, probably the first white man to look upon the Sault. The Michigan Indian population is approximately 15,000.

1621 Brulé returns, explores the Lake Superior coast, and notes copper deposits.

1634 Jean Nicolet passes through the Straits of Mackinac and travels along Lake Michigan's northern shore, seeking a route to the Orient.

1641 Fathers Isaac Jogues and Charles Raymbault conduct religious services at the Sault.

1660 Father René Mesnard establishes the first regular mission, held throughout winter at Keweenaw Bay.

1668 Father Jacques Marquette takes over the Sault mission and founds the first permanent settlement on Michigan soil at Sault Ste. Marie.

1669 Louis Jolliet is guided east by way of the Detroit River, Lake Erie, and Lake Ontario.

1671 Simon Francois, Sieur de St. Lusson, lands at the Sault, claims vast Great Lakes region, comprising most of western America, for Louis XIV.

St. Ignace is founded when Father Marquette builds a mission chapel.

First of the military outposts, Fort de Buade (later known as Fort Michilimackinac), is established at St. Ignace.

1673 Jolliet and Marquette travel down the Mississippi River.

1675 Father Marquette dies at Ludington.

1679 The *Griffon*, the first sailing vessel on the Great Lakes, is built by René Robert Cavelier, de la Salle, and lost in a storm on Lake Michigan.

La Salle erects Fort Miami at the mouth of the St. Joseph River.

1680 La Salle, with a small group, marches across the Lower Peninsula, reaching the Detroit River in ten days, the first whites to penetrate this territory.

1690 Father Claude Aveneau explores the upper reaches of the St. Joseph River; establishes mission on the present site of Niles.

1694 Antoine de la Mothe Cadillac is appointed commandant of the Michilimackinac (St. Ignace) post; remains until 1697.

1697 Fort St. Joseph is built at mission on the St. Joseph River (Niles).

1701 Detroit is founded as Fort Pontchartrain by Cadillac as a permanent settlement to protect and secure the fur trade.

Ste. Anne's Church, a log structure, is erected by Cadillac's men and dedicated two days after the founding of Detroit. Ste. Anne's is the second oldest continuously maintained Roman Catholic parish in the United States.

In the fall, Madame Cadillac and Madam Tonty arrive at the fort as the first European women in the region.

1712 British-inspired Indian raids begin, including the siege of Fort Pontchartrain.

1715 Fort Michilimackinac is reestablished on the southern shore of the Straits of Mackinac.

1756 France and England begin the Seven Years' War (also known as the French and Indian War).

1759 The French surrender to the English at Montreal; this marks the decline of French power in Michigan.

1760 British Major Robert Rogers receives the surrender of Detroit, after taking Great Lakes fortifications. About 2,000 people are within the stockade; warehouses found to contain $500,000 worth of furs.

1761 The British occupy Fort Michilimackinac.

1762 Pontiac, an Ottawa chief, plans a conspiracy against British; calls for a council near Detroit in the spring.

The English take possession of the Sault.

1763 With the ratification of the Treaty of Versailles, France loses North American mainland possessions.

Pontiac and followers enter the fort at Detroit in an abortive effort to capture it from Major Gladwin by surprise attack. Detroit endures a siege of several weeks.

1765 Pontiac signs a treaty with the British at Detroit, nearly a year after other tribes have made peace.

1775 Henry Hamilton takes command at Detroit.

1779 Nearly 3,000 persons living in the Detroit area.

1781 Spanish forces from St. Louis take Fort St. Joseph (Niles); all residents are taken prisoner; the Spanish flag is raised. Raiders depart the next day and the fort reverts to British possession.

The British transfer garrison from Michilimackinac to a new fort on Mackinac Island.

1783 The Treaty of Paris is signed, ending the Revolutionary War and including Michigan in the United States. The British control the Michigan area, however, for 13 more years.

1787 Congress enacts the Ordinance of 1787 (second Northwest Ordinance), outlining the government of the "Territory northwest of the Ohio River."

1788 The first stage of American territorial government is established under the Northwest Ordinance, except in British-occupied Michigan.

1791 The Americans under Arthur St. Clair suffer a major defeat at the hands of British-allied Indians in Ohio.

1792 Detroit, including settlements on both sides of the river, holds its first election, sending three representatives to the Parliament of Upper Canada.

1794 General Anthony Wayne decisively defeats Indians and allied British troops at the Battle of Fallen Timbers, near Toledo.

1795 The Jay Treaty is ratified by Congress. The British finally agree to relinquish all Northwest Territory lands.

The Treaty of Greenville (Ohio) is signed. The first major Indian land treaty involving Michigan, it included land on the Detroit River, the Straits of Mackinac, and Mackinac Island.

1796 The British withdraw their garrison from Detroit. The Stars and Stripes are raised for the first time on Michigan soil by Wayne's advance guard.

1798 Father Gabriel Richard (1767-1832) comes to assist at Ste. Anne's in Detroit.

1799 The Territorial Assembly convenes at Cincinnati, Ohio. The county of Wayne (embracing all of the Michigan Territory) sends one representative, elected in the first local (Michigan) election held under United States rule.

1802 Detroit holds its first election following incorporation under an act passed January 18 by the Legislative Council at Chillicothe, Ohio.

1803 Ohio is admitted to the Union, including the strip of land that 30 years later will be known as the "Toledo strip." Michigan becomes part of the Territory of Indiana.

1805 The Territory of Michigan is created, with Detroit as the capital.

Detroit is completely destroyed by fire.

General William Hull becomes the first territorial governor.

1805-6 Important commercial timbering begins, when sawmills are built on the St. Clair River to aid in rebuilding Detroit.

1807 The Treaty of Detroit is signed by Chippewa, Ottawa, Wyandot, and Potawatomi tribes meeting with General Hull.

1809 The *Michigan Essay and Impartial Observer*, the state's first newspaper, is printed by James M. Miller on a press imported by Father Richard.

1810 The Michigan Territory's population is 4,762 and includes 32 slaves, most of whom are Native Americans.

1811 A memorial to Congress stresses the defenseless position of Michigan and begs for military aid against the Indians.

1812 The United States declares war against England. Father Richard urges the population to support the American cause.

Fort Mackinac falls to the British, who know of the declaration of war earlier than the frontier post.

Hull surrenders Detroit to General Brock without firing a shot. Hull later is court-martialed.

1813 At the Battle of River Raisin at Monroe, the main body of Americans is forced to surrender and promised protection from Indian allies of British.

The massacre of the River Raisin occurs. This proves to be a powerful factor in uniting American sentiment for expulsion of the British from the west.

Commander Oliver Perry's victory on Lake Erie and William Henry Harrison's defeat of Proctor's army in Canada (in which Tecumseh is slain) end hostilities on northwestern American border.

Harrison, departing for Washington, leaves Colonel (later General) Lewis Cass as the military governor at Detroit. Cass continues, under presidential appointment, as the governor of the Michigan Territory for 18 years.

1814 The Americans make an unsuccessful attempt to recapture Mackinac Island.

The Treaty of Ghent ends the War of 1812; the British leave Mackinac Island.

1815 Governor Cass and judges adopt legislation reincorporating Detroit (city) and restoring a restricted municipal government.

1817 The Catholepistemiad, or University of Michigania, is incorporated.

John Jacob Astor establishes a trading post at Mackinac Island, centering his fur-trading activities there.

1818 Public land sales begin at Detroit; immigration from the East is under way.

Michigan's first Protestant church, the Methodist Episcopal, is erected along the banks of the River Rouge.

Walk-in-the-Water, the first steamboat on the Upper Great Lakes, arrives at Detroit on its maiden voyage.

1819 William Woodbridge is elected as the first delegate to Congress from the Michigan Territory.

With the Treaty of Saginaw, Governor Cass obtains for the United States about 6,000,000 acres of Michigan land, marking the beginning of the Indian exodus from the territory.

1820 The population of the territory is 8,096; Detroit, Mackinac, and Sault Ste. Marie are its largest towns.

The Treaty at Sault Ste. Marie is negotiated by Cass; Indians cede a 16-square-mile tract on the St. Mary's River for a fort site, but reserve fishing rights.

1821 Cass negotiates a treaty at Chicago, gaining from the Chippewa, Ottawa, and Potawatomi virtually all Michigan territory south of the Grand River that had not previously been ceded.

1823 General Hugh Brady and soldiers construct Fort Brady at the Sault, ending domination of the region by the British.

Congress advances the Territory of Michigan to the second governmental grade, authorizing the Legislative Council of 9 members presidentially appointed and 18 locally elected. Enacted laws are subject to congressional approval. The first capitol, in Detroit, is built.

Father Gabriel Richard takes office as the territorial delegate to Congress (1823-5), the only priest to serve in Congress until 1971.

1824 On motion of Father Richard, Congress appropriates $10,000 for a survey of the Great Sauk Trail (now U.S. 12) between Detroit and Chicago and makes an additional appropriation in 1825.

1825 The opening of the Erie Canal in New York facilitates settlement of Michigan and shipping of farm products to the East.

1830 Michigan's population is 31,639.

Fur trade reaches its peak. Its subsequent decline leaves some regions without commercial activity.

Michigan issues a railway charter to the Detroit & Pontiac Railway, the first incorporated railway in the limits of old Northwest Territory.

1831 General Lewis Cass, appointed secretary of war by President Jackson in July, resigns the governorship.

Stevens T. Mason, at age 19, becomes the acting governor of the Michigan Territory.

1832 A seven-week cholera epidemic devastates Detroit; Belle Isle is used for quarantine.

Father Richard, priest, legislator, and educator, dies of cholera, contracted while nursing the sick.

1834 The Territorial Legislature petitions Congress for permission to form a state government. Southern states protest the admission of another free state; Ohio protests the boundary Michigan claims. Congress refuses to grant its permission.

The second cholera epidemic at Detroit begins with the death of Governor George B. Porter. It wipes out one-seventh of the population.

1835 Pioneers in Macomb and adjoining counties discover oil.

The Ohio Legislature passes an act asserting claims to the "Toledo strip" along its northern boundary.

Governor Mason calls out the militia as the "Toledo War" begins with more anger than gunfire. Border incidents continue into September, and jurisdictional wrangling goes on through all of 1836.

A convention at Detroit drafts a state constitution in preparation for statehood.

Stevens T. Mason, who had been removed from office by President Jackson because of Mason's action on the Toledo question, is elected as the first governor of the state of Michigan at 23 years of age.

1836 Congress accepts Michigan's constitution. It agrees to admit the state upon condition that Michigan accept Ohio's boundary in return for four-fifths of the Upper Peninsula.

At the first convention of assent held at Ann Arbor in September, the conditions set by Congress are rejected.

The horse-powered Erie & Kalamazoo Railroad chartered in 1833 reaches Adrian from Toledo. The first steam locomotive in the state is put in operation on this line the following year, as the railroad is the first west of New York State to operate.

Democrats call a convention on their own initiative and assent to entry into the Union. Whig opponents take no part in this "frost-bitten" convention held in Ann Arbor in December.

Daily stages from Detroit begin carrying mail and passengers to Sandusky, Chicago, and central Michigan; a railroad between Detroit and Jackson is under construction; shipbuilding becomes important along nearby rivers and lakeshores. During seven months of navigation, 200,000 people pass through Detroit's port.

Bituminous coal mining begins in Michigan.

A Quaker preacher employs an underground railroad to bring slaves into Cass County, and movement of fugitive and freed slaves into the state begins.

1837 Detroit's population is almost 10,000.

Michigan is admitted to the Union as a free state as Arkansas is admitted as a slave state.

The Panic of 1837 strikes Michigan.

Michigan experiences its first strike as journeymen carpenters parade through Detroit streets.

1838 Detroit elects Michigan's first school board under state law.

The Grand Rapids furniture industry has its beginning.

1839 Effects of the Panic of 1837 help break Democratic monopoly, and Whigs carry state election.

1841 Dr. Douglas Houghton, the first state geologist, reports on rich copper deposits of the Lake Superior region and makes cautious mention of the possibility of iron ore in the Marquette district.

The University of Michigan, reorganized and offering college curriculum, opens at Ann Arbor.

1842 Indians cede Keweenaw Peninsula and Isle Royale, the last Indian holdings in the state.

1844 Surveyor William A. Burt (inventor of the solar compass and other important items) accidentally makes the first iron-ore discovery at Negaunee.

General Lewis Cass, former governor, former secretary of war, and ambassador to France, is elected U.S. senator from Michigan.

The first major copper operations begin in the Keweenaw district.

1846 Dr. A.C. Van Raalte, Dutch secessionist pastor, sails from Rotterdam with 53 Hollanders; they form the nucleus of western Michigan's large Dutch settlements begun the following winter.

The Jackson Mining Company begins operations on the site of Burt's 1844 discovery, first iron-ore mining in the state.

Michigan becomes the first English-speaking jurisdiction in the world to abolish capital punishment.

1847 The old capitol in Detroit is used for the last time by the state legislature, which makes Lansing the new, permanent capital of the state.

1848 King James Strang, a Mormon leader, builds a tabernacle and lays out the town of St. James on Big Beaver Island.

The state legislature meets for the first session in the new capitol at Lansing.

1849 The first annual statewide fair is held at Detroit.

The Cliff Mine pays a dividend of $60,000, the first sum of this magnitude distributed in North America on copper investment.

Michigan's manufactured goods are valued at more than $11,000,000. There are 558 sawmills operating in the state.

1850 Michigan's population is 397,654.

The second state constitution is approved.

1851 Lumber mill output of Saginaw amounts to 92,000,000 board feet.

1852 The Michigan State Normal School is dedicated at Ypsilanti. It is the first teacher-training institute west of the Alleghenies.

1854 The Republican party is formed and named at meetings held in Jackson.

1855 The Soo Ship Canal and Locks are completed by the state.

Michigan Agricultural College (Michigan State University) is established. It becomes the nation's first land grant college.

1856 Abraham Lincoln gives an antislavery address in Kalamazoo.

1857 General Lewis Cass is appointed U.S. Secretary of State and is succeeded in the U.S. Senate by Zachariah Chandler.

The Christian Reformed Church in North America is founded by Michigan's Dutch settlers, following secession from the Reformed Church.

1860 Michigan's population is 749,113.

Successful well-drilling of salt begins in Saginaw County.

1861 Thomas A. Edison erects his first electrical battery and begins experiments at Fort Gratiot (Port Huron).

The First Michigan Regiment leaves Fort Wayne. It is the first western regiment to reach Washington during the Civil War, in which 90,000 Michigan soldiers see service.

1864 First Michigan Colored Infantry is mustered in. Michigan's black troops number 1,673.

Bessemer steel is first manufactured in any appreciable amount in America, at Wyandotte.

The copper lode at Calumet is discovered. Michigan's production of copper has for 17 years exceeded that of any other state (holds first place until 1887).

1870 Michigan's population is 1,054,670.

The value of agricultural produce for the year is estimated at $88,000,000.

Annual lumber production for the state averages 3 million board feet, and is the highest in the country for a period of 20 years.

1871 Forest fires ravage the state, destroying towns and leveling thousands of acres of valuable pine, causing losses in the millions of dollars.

Calumet & Hecla Mining Company consolidates local (Calumet) mining interests, controlling one of world's richest copper districts. Calumet becomes a company town typical of the copper country.

Negaunee's average annual iron-ore production reaches 135,000 tons.

1872 Republic Mine opens; the 88 percent pure iron deposits permit continuous high-level production for 55 years.

1873 Financial panic begins early in the year.

1876 At the Centennial Exposition (Philadelphia), Detroit is given first place among world's stove-manufacturing centers and receives prizes for shoes. The best display of furniture from the United States credited to Grand Rapids. Michigan has the finest exhibit in forestry products and fruit.

An Ontonagon mine operator, after seeing Bell's invention at the Philadelphia exposition, builds the first telephone system (20 miles) in Michigan.

1877 Active operations begin in the mines of the Menominee iron district.

1879 Six years after the cornerstone was laid, the new state capitol at Lansing is dedicated and occupied, several months after completion at a cost of more than $1,500,000.

1880 Michigan's population is 1,636,937.

Iron ore is discovered in large quantities at Bessemer in the Gogebic Range.

1881 The Soo Ship Canal and Locks are taken over by the federal government.

Railroad ferry service connects Upper and Lower Peninsulas, making the Upper Peninsula readily accessible for the first time.

A permanent hydroelectric plant is erected at Grand Rapids—one of the earliest anywhere.

Another devastating series of fires scorch the state, with the newly established American Red Cross sending help in its first disaster relief.

1882 Josiah W. Begole elected governor on the Fusion ticket, interrupting an almost unbroken Republican rule that began in 1854.

1883 A compulsory school attendance law is enacted.

Half of copper mined in United States since 1847 has come from Michigan.

Cherry orchards in the upper fruit belt first begin to bear.

1884 Working of iron-ore deposits of the Gogebic Range begins, when transportation facilities are acquired.

John and Thomas Clegg build Michigan's first self-propelled vehicle, a four-wheeled steamer auto.

1885 A series of lumber strikes occur in Saginaw Valley, and the militia is called out.

The Michigan Mining School (Michigan Technological University) opens in Houghton.

The ten-hour workday law is passed.

1886 Prospecting for oil and gas and first commercial production in St. Clair and Saginaw Counties begin.

1887 Ransom E. Olds' first auto steamer appears.

Iron-ore shipments from the Menominee Range begin; at the end of the year, total shipments amount to 6,000,000 tons.

1888 Shipments of iron ore from Escanaba alone reach 1,107,129 tons.

Michigan's lumber boom peaks with the production of 4,292,000,000 board feet.

1890 Michigan's population is 2,093,889.

1891 Port Huron, Michigan, and Sarnia, Ontario, are joined by the Grand Trunk R.R. tunnel under the St. Clair River, first subaqueous railroad tunnel linking foreign countries.

1894 Hazen S. Pingree, mayor of Detroit, attracts national attention with his city-lot potato patches for feeding 1893 depression sufferers.

Fort on Mackinac Island is given to the state for a public park.

1895 Central Michigan University, founded as a private school, becomes a state normal school.

1896 Ransom E. Olds brings out a practical four-wheeled, gasoline-powered auto in Lansing.

Henry Ford's "quadricycle" is tested in Detroit.

1899 Olds Motor Works in Detroit erects the first factory built in America for the manufacture of automobiles.

Northern Michigan University is founded.

1900 Michigan's population is 2,420,982.

1902 Packard Motor Car Company and Cadillac Motor Car Company are organized.

1903 The House of David (a sect founded in 1792) is established in Benton Harbor by "King" Benjamin and "Queen" Mary Purnell.

The Ford Motor Company is incorporated in Detroit.

1904 The organization of Buick Motor Company marks the beginning of auto manufacturing in Flint on a large scale.

Western State Normal School (Western Michigan University) opens in Kalamazoo.

1906 Timbering of second-growth forests begins in the Upper Peninsula.

1907 Michigan's third constitution is drafted (approved by electorate in 1908).

The Detroit Tigers, led by Ty Cobb, win the first of three consecutive pennants.

1908 William C. Durant organizes General Motors Company as Ford introduces the most famous of the early cars, the Model T.

Fisher Body Corporation is founded.

1910 Michigan's population is 2,810,173.

1911 Durant organizes the Chevrolet Motor Car Company, when the Chevrolet brothers complete experiments on a new auto.

1913 The Western Federation of Miners calls a strike among 13,514 Upper Peninsula copper miners. Violence and bloodshed result from demands for an 8-hour day, a minimum daily wage of $3.50, and abolition of the "widow maker," a one-man drill.

The legislature passes a bill providing for ten trunkline highways. There are 60,000 autos registered in Michigan.

1914 Henry Ford announces the adoption of a $5 minimum wage for an 8-hour day.

A congressional committee arrives to investigate the copper miners' strike, which terminates shortly afterward, each side claiming victory. The union fails to gain recognition.

The first Dodge auto is produced.

Following the 1913 strike, Finns initiate cooperative stores in the copper country.

1915 *Michigan Manual of Freedmen's Progress*, showing the professional, political, religious, and educational achievements of African-American citizens of the state, is published by Freedmen's Progress Commission.

1916 Many Michigan men join Canadian units leaving for France to fight in World War I.

Annual copper production reaches a peak of 270,000,000 pounds of refined copper, while iron-ore production from the Marquette Range is 5,500,000 tons.

1917 The country's first War Preparedness Board is organized in Michigan. In the first year of war, Detroit builds 120 ships, spends $10,000,000 improving plants for the making of munitions. Auto manufacturers contract to deliver 19,000 engines.

1918 Michigan men in World War service reaches a total of 135,485.

War contracts let in Detroit now total $705,000,000.

1919 Commercial airplanes are placed on sale for the first time.

The influenza epidemic strikes the country and much of the world, killing 3,814 in Detroit.

1920 Michigan's population is 3,668,412.

Radio station WWJ in Detroit opens as a pioneer station in the broadcasting of regular daily programs.

1921 Edwin Denby, who had enlisted at Detroit as a private in the Marine Corps in 1917, becomes secretary of the navy.

Important administrative reforms in state government are legislated. The superintendent of public instruction is given supervision of all schools, private, denominational, and public, and the departments of conservation, labor, public safety, welfare, and agriculture are created.

1922 Airline service is instituted between Detroit and Cleveland.

1923 The William L. Clements Library of American History opens at Ann Arbor.

1926 The worst disaster in Michigan iron mining occurs at the Barnes-Hecker Mine, when quicksand breaks through the walls, entombing 52 men 1,000 feet below the surface. The mine is sealed and abandoned.

1927 The Cranbrook Foundation (Bloomfield Hills) is created and turned over to trustees.

1928 The first all-metal dirigible, constructed for the Navy by Detroit manufacturers, is successfully flown at Grosse Ile Airport.

1929 Some large copper mines of the Keweenaw Peninsula close; 85 percent of the Keweenaw County population goes on relief.

1930 Michigan's population is 4,842,325, an increase of more than 1,170,000 since 1920. Urban centers account for 68.2 percent of the population, almost an exact reversal of the situation in 1880.

The vehicle tunnel between Detroit and Windsor, Ontario, is opened.

1932 Governor William A. Comstock calls a statewide "banking holiday" to avoid bank runs, after disclosure of the condition of the Union Guardian Trust Company, Detroit.

The "Ford Hunger March" riot occurs at the Ford plant in Dearborn.

1933 The Michigan sales tax begins.

1935 Michigan celebrates its centennial of statehood.

One-fifth of Michigan's employables are without work; the state population has dropped 28 percent since the 1930 census.

The United Automobile Workers (UAW) is organized.

The Detroit Tigers win the World Series. With championships in this era from the Lions in professional football, the Red Wings in hockey, and Joe Louis in boxing, Detroit is known as the "City of Champions."

1936 Mass organization of labor under the CIO is strengthened by the affiliation of International Union, United Automobile Workers of America, with the CIO.

With the Flint sit-down strike leading the way, General Motors shuts down, affecting 150,000 workers and closing more than 60 plants in 14 states.

1937 The UAW strike reaches a peaceful conclusion as collective bargaining agreements are signed by General Motors and most other automotive and parts manufacturers, except the Ford Motor Company, which fought unionization until 1941.

Keweenaw Peninsula copper mining again turns upward, with production reaching 75,000 pounds.

A wave of sit-down strikes in various industries eventually leads to a breakdown of the open-shop tradition in the state.

1938 International "Blue Water Bridge," connecting Port Huron and Sarnia, Ontario, is dedicated.

1939 Frank Murphy, former governor, takes office as Attorney General of the United States. Governor Frank D. Fitzgerald dies. Luren D. Dickinson, acting governor of Michigan, appoints Matilda R. Wilson as lieutenant governor, the first woman to serve in that capacity.

1940 Attorney General Frank Murphy is appointed to the United States Supreme Court to succeed the late Associate Justice Pierce Butler.

Michigan's population is 5,256,106.

1941 Auto plants are converted to the production of war materials and Michigan becomes known as the "Arsenal of Democracy."

The United States enters World War II. By the time the war ended in 1945, 673,000 Michigan men and women had served in the armed forces.

1943 Interracial riots strike Detroit, leaving thirty-four dead and hundreds injured.

1945 Senator Arthur H. Vandenberg from Grand Rapids helps frame the United Nations Charter.

The Detroit Tigers win the World Series.

1946 Lake Superior State College is opened at Sault Ste. Marie.

1947 Walter Reuther assumes the presidency of the U.A.W.

WWJ-TV, Detroit, begins commercial television broadcasting in Michigan.

1950 Michigan's population is 6,371,766.

Ferris Institute, founded in 1884, becomes a state institution.

1952 The Detroit Lions win the first of three world championships in professional football in the decade (also 1953 and 1957).

1953 About 250,000 Michigan men and women see military service during the Korean War (1950-53).

1954 American Motors Corporation is formed by the merger of Hudson Motor Car Company and Nash-Kelvinator Corporation.

1955 During its centennial year, Michigan Agricultural College becomes a university.

1956 Wayne University in Detroit becomes a state university.

The Interstate Highway Act is passed. It provided for federal-state cooperation in highway construction.

1957 Oakland University founded.

After ages of dreams and efforts in the 1930s halted by the war, the five-mile-long Mackinac Bridge is completed, finally uniting Michigan's two peninsulas.

Professional basketball comes to Michigan when the Fort Wayne Pistons move to Detroit.

1958 G. Mennen Williams, a native of Detroit, is elected to an unprecedented sixth term as governor.

Computers are first used by state government.

1959 Detroit and the entire Great Lakes region gain access to world markets with the opening of the St. Lawrence Seaway.

1960 Cobo Hall is built as the Detroit Civic Center.

Michigan's population is 7,823,194.

1963 Grand Valley State College is opened.

Michigan's fourth state constitution, drafted in 1961-62, is approved by the voters.

1964 James McDivitt from Jackson commands the Gemini IV mission and becomes Michigan's first astronaut.

1965 State Executive Organization Act passed.

Saginaw Valley State College is chartered as a state institution.

1967 The urban unrest that has been evident in several U.S. cities strikes Detroit with a riot that leaves 45 dead.

The state income tax act is enacted.

1968 The Detroit Tigers win the World Series.

1969 Governor George Romney resigns to become the U.S. Secretary of Housing and Urban Development in the Nixon administration.

1970 Michigan's population is 8,881,826.

1972 The Michigan Lottery Bureau is created.

1973 American military involvement in Vietnam ends; over 400,000 Michigan men and women serve.

An accident in which a fire retardant containing polybrominated biphenyl (PBB) is mixed with livestock feed sets off a crisis that threatens Michigan's agriculture and public health.

1974 Gerald R. Ford, former congressman from Grand Rapids, becomes the 38th President of the United States and first Michiganian to serve in that capacity.

1975 The Pontiac Silverdome is opened.

1976 Throwaway bottles are banned as the result of an initiative requiring deposits on beer and soft drink containers.

1979 The Michigan State University Basketball Team wins the NCAA championship.

1980 Michigan's population is 9,262,078

A presidential convention (Republican) is held in Detroit for the first time.

1981 William G. Milliken becomes the state's longest-serving governor. He serves a total of 14 years.

1982 Martha Griffiths, a veteran of 20 years' service in the Congress, is the first woman in Michigan history elected to the post of lieutenant governor. (Matilda Wilson was appointed to the position in 1939.)

The movement to renovate Michigan's 103-year-old capitol begins with the organization of Friends of the Capitol.

1984 The Detroit Tigers win the World Series.

"Big Three" American automakers—General Motors, Ford, and Chrysler—report total profits for year of $9.8 billion, a new high.

1986 Republican William Lucas is the first black candidate to represent a major party in a gubernatorial election in Michigan.

1987 Michigan celebrates its sesquicentennial of statehood. The 84th legislature convenes with the highest number of women lawmakers in state history (2 senators and 20 representatives).

1989 The Michigan Library and Historical Center is dedicated in Lansing.

The University of Michigan Men's Basketball Team wins the NCAA championship and the Detroit Pistons win the first of two consecutive National Basketball Association crowns.

1984 The Detroit Tigers win the World Series.

"Big Three" American automakers—General Motors, Ford, and Chrysler—report total profits for year of $9.8 billion, a new high.

1986 Republican William Lucas is the first black candidate to represent a major party in a gubernatorial election in Michigan.

1987 Michigan celebrates its sesquicentennial of statehood. The 84th legislature convenes with the highest number of women lawmakers in state history (2 senators and 20 representatives).

1989 The Michigan Library and Historical Center is dedicated in Lansing.

The University of Michigan Men's Basketball Team wins the NCAA championship and the Detroit Pistons win the first of two consecutive National Basketball Association crowns.

1990 The restored chambers of the Senate and of the House are reopened and the lawmakers return to their traditional home after holding sessions elsewhere. The Senate becomes the first state legislative body in the nation to include microcomputers on the chamber floor.

The population of Michigan is 9,295,297.

1992 The U.S. Congress passes the Michigan Scenic Rivers Act protecting over 500 miles on 14 rivers from development.

The Twenty-Seventh Amendment to the U.S. Constitution is ratified by the vote of Michigan. The text of the amendment, which provides that no law varying the compensation of Senators and Representatives shall take effect until an election of Representatives has intervened, was originally submitted to the states as part of the Bill of Rights in 1789.

The restored Michigan State Capitol is rededicated.

1993 Chemists at the University of Michigan synthesize a gigantic ball-shaped molecule that may suggest how proteins function in living organisms. It is the largest molecule ever created in a laboratory from carbon and hydrogen atoms alone.

FORTUNE 500 COMPANIES IN MICHIGAN

Source : Fortune Magazine 4-18-94

MICHIGAN 22 Companies

RANK		500 SALES RANK	SALES $MILLIONS	PROFITS $MILLIONS	HEADQUARTERS
1	GENERAL MOTORS	1	133,621.9	2,465.8	3044 W. Grand Blvd., Detroit 48202
2	FORD MOTOR	2	108,521.0	2,529.0	American Rd., Dearborn 48121
3	CHRYSLER	8	43,600.0	(2,551.0)	12000 Chrysler Dr., Highland Park 48288
4	DOW CHEMICAL	21	18,060.0	644.0	2030 Dow Center, Midland 48674
5	WHIRLPOOL	73	7,533.0	51.0	2000 M-63, Benton Harbor 49022
6	KELLOGG	86	6,295.4	680.7	1 Kellogg Square, Battle Creek 49016
7	MASCO	132	3,886.0	221.1	21001 Van Born Rd., Taylor 48180
8	UPJOHN	139	3,611.2	392.4	7000 Portage Rd., Kalamazoo 49001
9	DOW CORNING	216	2,043.7	(287.0)	2200 W. Salzburg Rd., Midland 48686
10	MASCOTECH	244	1,774.8	47.6	21001 Van Born Rd., Taylor 48180
11	LEAR HOLDINGS	245	1,756.5	10.1	21557 Telegraph Rd., Southfield 48034
12	FEDERAL-MOGUL	267	1,575.5	40.1	26555 Northwestern Hwy., Southfield 48034
13	DETROIT DIESEL	269	1,560.1	20.7	13400 Outer Dr. W., Detroit 48239
14	TECUMSEH PRODUCTS	297	1,337.3	81.4	100 E. Patterson St., Tecumseh 49286
15	GERBER PRODUCTS	307	1,269.5	42.5	445 State St., Fremont 49413
16	INTERNATIONAL CONTROLS	377	909.3	(43.3)	2016 N. Pitcher St., Kalamazoo 49007
17	HERMAN MILLER	395	855.7	22.1	855 E. Main Ave., Zeeland 49464
18	SPX	425	756.1	(40.6)	700 Terrace Point Dr., Muskegon 49443
19	THORN APPLE VALLEY	436	729.9	13.9	18700 W. Ten Mile Rd., Southfield 48075
20	LA-Z-BOY CHAIR	460	684.1	27.3	1284 N. Telegraph Rd., Monroe 48161
21	VALASSIS COMMUNICATIONS	473	661.4	81.9	36111 Schoolcraft Rd., Livonia 48150
22	UNIVERSAL FOREST PRODUCTS	474	661.0	10.4	2801 E. Beltline N.E., Grand Rapids 49505
	TOTAL		341,703.5	4,460.1	
	MEDIAN		1,666.0	41.3	

Trivia

Q Which noted New Yorker dominated the Michigan Fur Trade ?

A John Jacob Astor.

Q When was the Soo Canal, connecting lakes Superior and Huron, opened ?

A 1855 (one of the world's busiest).

RICHEST PLACES IN MICHIGAN

Source: Bureau of the Census

Listed below are cities and towns of 2500 people or more, and $50,000 or more medium family income (1990).

Names only are cities. Townships are idenified with an asterick (*) . Villiages are idenified with a double asterick (**)

PLACE	COUNTY	MEDIAN FAMILY INCOME	PLACE	COUNTY	MEDIAN FAMILY INCOME
Ada *	Kent	$150,000	Grosse Pte Woods	Wayne	$55,687
Alaiedon *	Ingham	$51,715	Hartland *	Livingston	$50,627
Ann Arbor *	Washtenaw	$56,359	Huntington Woods	Oakland	$61,057
Atlas *	Genesee	$50,205	Independence *	Oakland	$53,233
Beverly Hills **	Oakland	$61,841	Lathrup Villiage	Oakland	$59,072
Birmingham	Oakland	$57,573	Lodi *	Washtenaw	$58,516
Bloomfield *	Oakland	$84,441	Marion *	Livingston	$52,673
Bloomfield Hills	Oakland	$150,001	Northville *	Wayne	$55,465
Bloomfield Twp	Oakland	$84,495	Oakland *	Oakland	$63,881
Brighton *	Livingston	$56,009	Pleasant Ridge	Oakland	$54,658
Cascade *	Kent	$63,301	Plymouth *	Wayne	$53,768
E Grand Rapids	Kent	$60,355	Rochester Hills	Oakland	$54,996
Farmington Hills	Kent	$51,986	Salem *	Wastenaw	$51,.948
Forest Hills	Oakland	$59,346	Southfield *	Oakland	$69,466
Franklin **	Oakland	$91,423	Texas *	Kalamazoo	$55,592
Grosse Ile *	Wayne	$62,619	Troy	Oakland	$55,407
Grosse Pointe	Wayne	$62,947	Tyron *	Livingston	$50,637
Grosse Pointe *	Wayne	$118,090	Webster *	Washtenaw	$56,815
Grosse Pte Farms	Wayne	$66,844	W Bloomfield *	Oakland	$68,654
Grosse Pte Park	Wayne	$54,586	Williamston *	Ingham	$50,277
Grosse Pte ** Shores	Wayne Macomb	$115,310	York *	Washtenaw	$55,998

MICHIGAN LOTTO

Winning Numbers– Prizes

Source: Michigan Bureau of State lottery

DATE....	NAME................	CITY................	COUNTY...	PRIZE.......
12/18/93	Claimed*	Grand Rapids	Kent	$7,000,000
01/12/94	Claimed*	Sterling Hts.	Macomb	$6,100,000
02/19/94	Lottery Club*	Farmington Hills	Oakland	$12,284,551
03/02/94	Claimed*	Tecumseh	Lenawee	$2,500,000
03/05/94	Claimed*	Wyoming	Kent	$2,000,000
04/02/94	Claimed*	Lansing area	Claimed*	$8,513,388
04/23/94	Claimed*	Shelby Twp.	Macomb	$2,600,000
05/04/94	Claimed*	Claimed*	Claimed*	$2,300,000
07/09/94	Claimed*	West Michigan*	Claimed*	$2,708,371
06/29/94	Claimed*	Wayland	Allegan	$25,060,510
08/20/94	Claimed*	Livonia	Wayne	$17,419,784
09/24/94	Claimed*	Saginaw	Saginaw	$2,000,000
09/14/94	Claimed*	Dearborn Hts	Wayne	$2,433,333
09/14/94	Claimed*	Ogemaw County*	Ogemaw	$2,433,333
09/14/94	Jean Deurwearder	Cheboygan	Cheboygan	$2,433,333
09/21/94	Claimed*	Marquette	Marquette	$2,100,000
09/21/94	Claimed*	Marquette	Marquette	$2,100,000
11/05/94	Claimed*	Detroit	Wayne	$16,628,666
11/26/94	Claimed*	Flint	Genesee	$1,933,333
11/26/94	Claimed*	North. Michigan*	Claimed*	$1,933,333
11/26/94	Claimed*	Bad Axe	Huron	$1,933,333
04/13/94	Unclaimed (1 of 1)			$2,367,495
2/14/94	Claimed*	Livonia	Wayne	$2,206,949
2/28/94	Claimed*	Detroit	Wayne	$1,850,000
2/14/94	Claimed*	Grand Rapids	Kent	$2,206,949
1/04/95	Claimed*	Brooklyn	Jackson	$1,050,000
2/28/94	Islands Lotto Club	Les Cheneaux Islands	Mackinac	$1,850,000
1/04/95	Claimed*	Grand Haven	Ottawa	$1,050,000

PRIZES WON BY FISCAL YEAR
(IN $ MILLIONS)

1984	$289.0
1985	$426.5
1986	$481.2
1987	$494.5
1988	$587.1
1989	$558.1
1990	$588.3
1991	$565.9
1992	$612.4
1993	$684.6

RETAILER COMMISSIONS BY FISCAL YEAR
(IN $ MILLIONS)

1984	$39.4
1985	$58.8
1986	$67.0
1987	$67.9
1988	$81.3
1989	$76.6
1990	$78.9
1991	$75.2
1992	$81.3
1993	$83.9

NET REVENUES TO EDUCATION BY FISCAL YEAR (IN $ MILLIONS)

1984	$236.4
1985	$359.6
1986	$414.9
1987	$401.7
1988	$488.4
1989	$483.9
1990	$489.1
1991	$456.6
1992	$474.0
1993	$427.6

TICKET SALES BY FISCAL YEAR (IN $ MILLIONS)

1984	$585.2
1985	$885.5
1986	$999.4
1987	$1,006.3
1988	$1,201.1
1989	$1,155.3
1990	$1,197.9
1991	$1,138.7
1992	$1,218.5
1993	$1,243

MICHIGAN LAKES & WATERWAYS

Source - MI Dept of State

SHORTEST RIVER:
Saginaw, 20 miles.

DETROIT RIVER handles more boat traffic than any river in the world.

SAGINAW RIVER has the largest drainage basin of any Michigan river.

FALLS: 150
Tehquamenon Falls are second only to Niagara Falls east of the Mississippi

BEACH: Metropolitan Beach, in Macomb County, is the world's largest lake man-made beach.

SAND DUNES: Sleeping Bear, 57,000 acres, is the largest hill of live shifting sand in the U.S.

PARKS & FORESTS OF MICHIGAN

Michigan has more parks and recreation places -- 2,953 -- than any other state.

52% of state land, covering 19,373,000 acres, is forest.

The state has:
STATE PARKS - 78
STATE FORESTS - 32
NATIONAL FORESTS - 5
NATIONAL CAMPGROUNDS -3
STATE GAME & WILDLIFE AREAS - 64
STATE FOREST CAMPGROUNDS - 153

HIGHEST POINT, Mt. Curwood, 1980 ft. above sea level.

GEOGRAPHIC CENTER, Wexford (near Cadillac)

GREAT LAKES
Michigan's share of the Great Lakes covers 38,575 square miles, embracing part of 4 of the 5 Great Lakes. They are:
- Lake Superior, 1,333 feet deep
- Lake Michigan, 925 feet deep
- Lake Huron, 725 feet deep
- Lake Erie, 212 feet deep

INLAND LAKES: 11,037

10 LARGEST INLAND LAKES:
Houghton, 31.3 sq. mi.
Torch, 29 sq. mi.
Burt, 28.4 sq. mi.
Charlevoix, 27.2 sq. mi.
Mullet, 25.3 sq. mi.
Gogebic, 20.4 sq. mi.
Portage, 18.3 sq. mi.
Crystal, 16.3 sq. mi.
Manistique, 16.1 sq. mi.
Black, 15.7 sq. mi.

DEEPEST INLAND LAKE:
Torch, 297 feet deep

RIVERS:
Michigan has 36,350 miles of rivers.

LONGEST RIVERS:
Grand, 300 miles
Manistee, 200 miles
Menominee, 180 miles

SWIFTEST RIVER:
Au Sable, drops 609 feet.

WIDEST RIVER:
Detroit, 2,200 feet.

MICHIGAN'S NEW TELEPHONE AREA CODE 810 AND REVISED 313

(810)

Also includes small portions of these counties:

Washtenaw
Livingston
Shiawassee
Saginaw
Wayne

(313)

Also includes small portions of these counties:

Livingston
Jackson
Lenawee

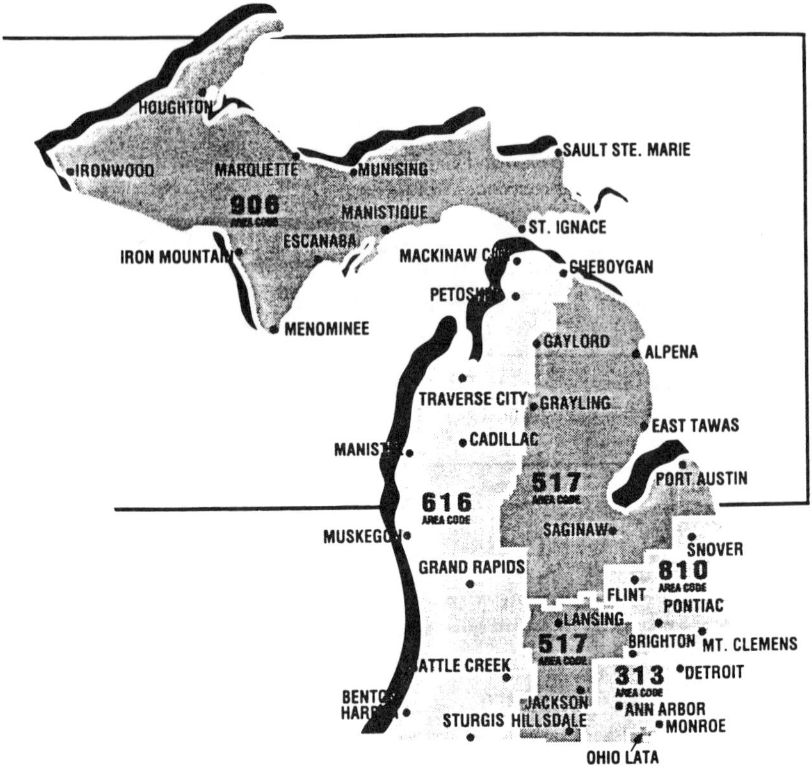
HOUGHTON
IRONWOOD
MARQUETTE
MUNISING
SAULT STE. MARIE
906
AREA CODE
MANISTIQUE
ST. IGNACE
ESCANABA
CHEBOYGAN
MENOMINEE
GAYLORD
ALPENA
TRAVERSE CITY
GRAYLING
EAST TAWAS
CADILLAC
PORT AUSTIN
517
AREA CODE
616
AREA CODE
SAGINAW
SNOVER
GRAND RAPIDS
810
AREA CODE
FLINT
PONTIAC
LANSING
517
AREA CODE
BRIGHTON
MT. CLEMENS
313
AREA CODE
DETROIT
JACKSON
ANN ARBOR
STURGIS
HILLSDALE
MONROE
OHIO LATA

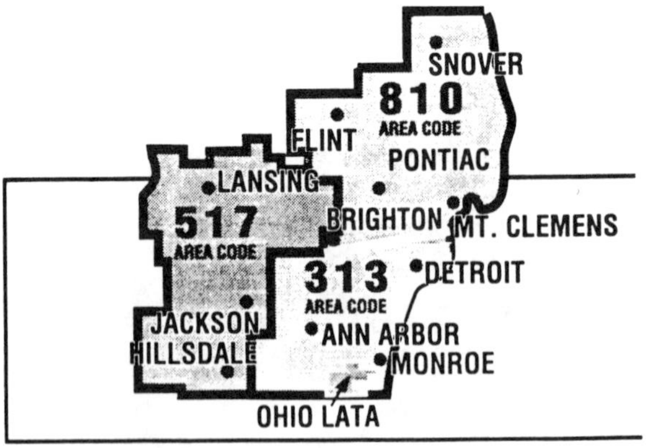
SNOVER
810
AREA CODE
FLINT
PONTIAC
LANSING
517
AREA CODE
BRIGHTON
MT. CLEMENS
313
AREA CODE
DETROIT
JACKSON
HILLSDALE
ANN ARBOR
MONROE
OHIO LATA

ZIP CODES - FIRST 3 NUMBERS - BY AREA

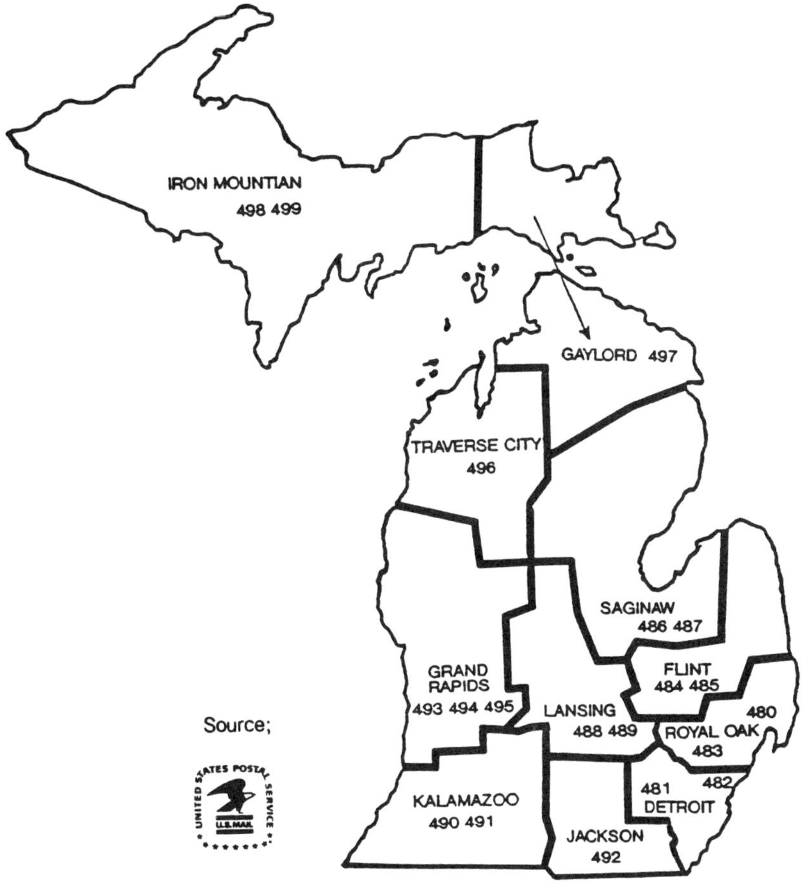

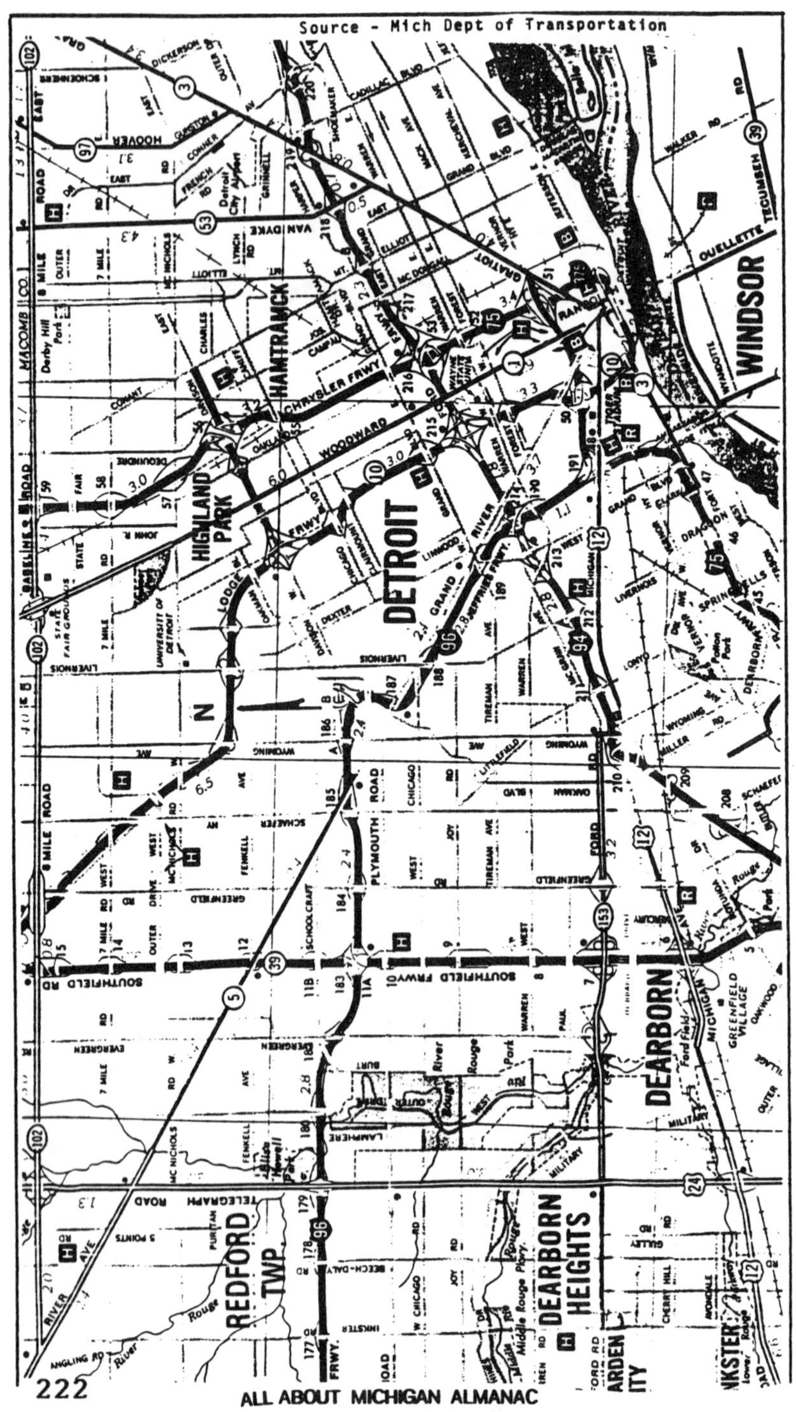
Source - Mich Dept of Transportation
DETROIT
WINDSOR
DEARBORN
DEARBORN HEIGHTS
HIGHLAND PARK
HAMTRAMCK
REDFORD TWP
GREENFIELD VILLAGE

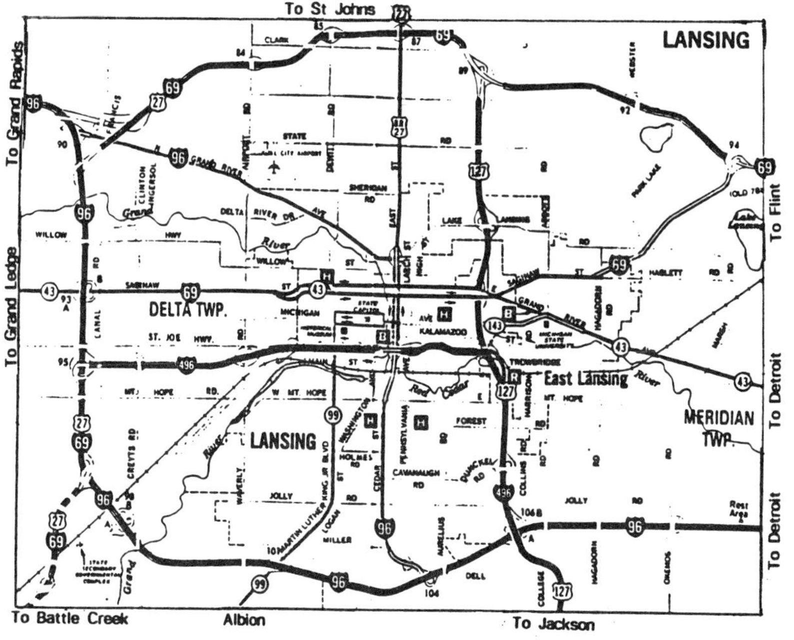

Source - Mich Dept of Transportation

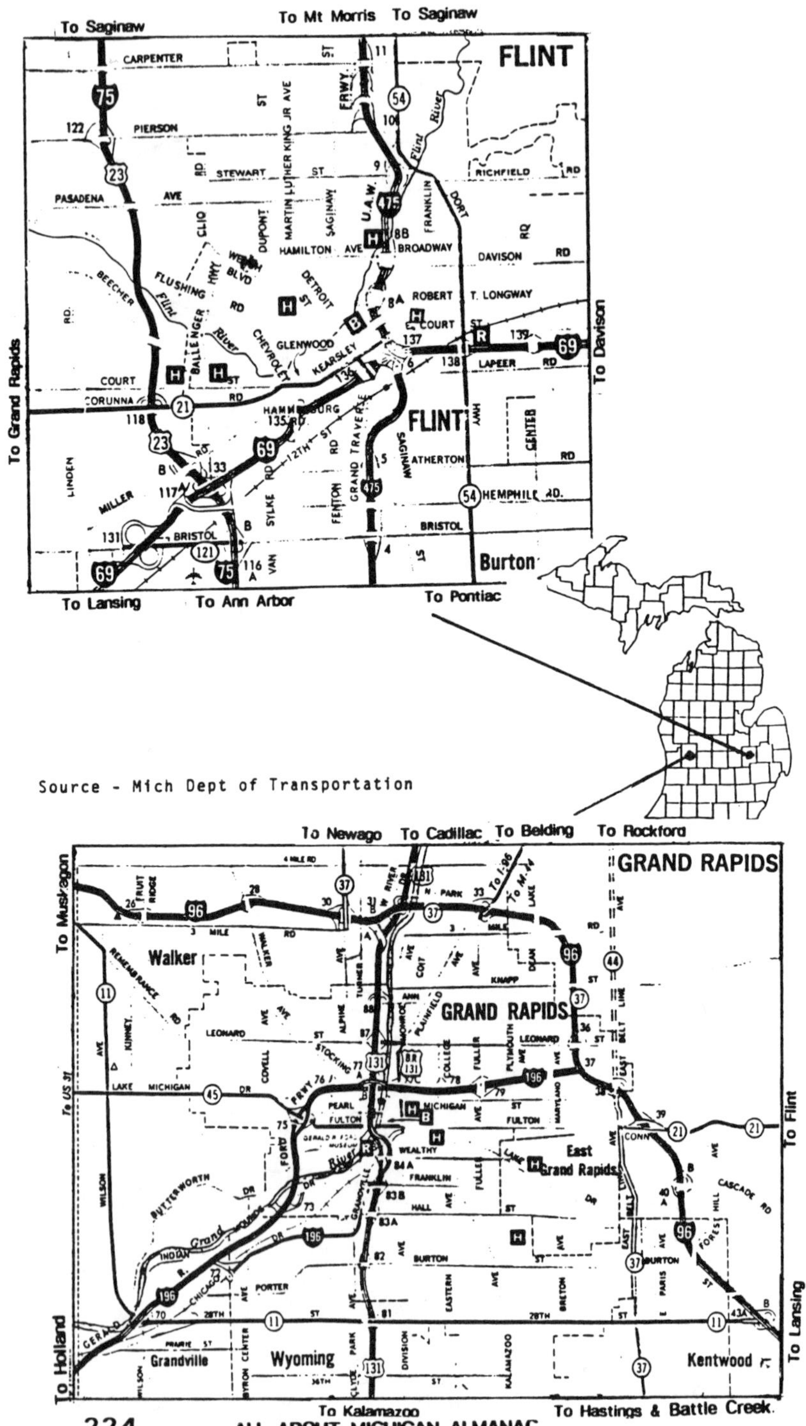

Source - Mich Dept of Transportation

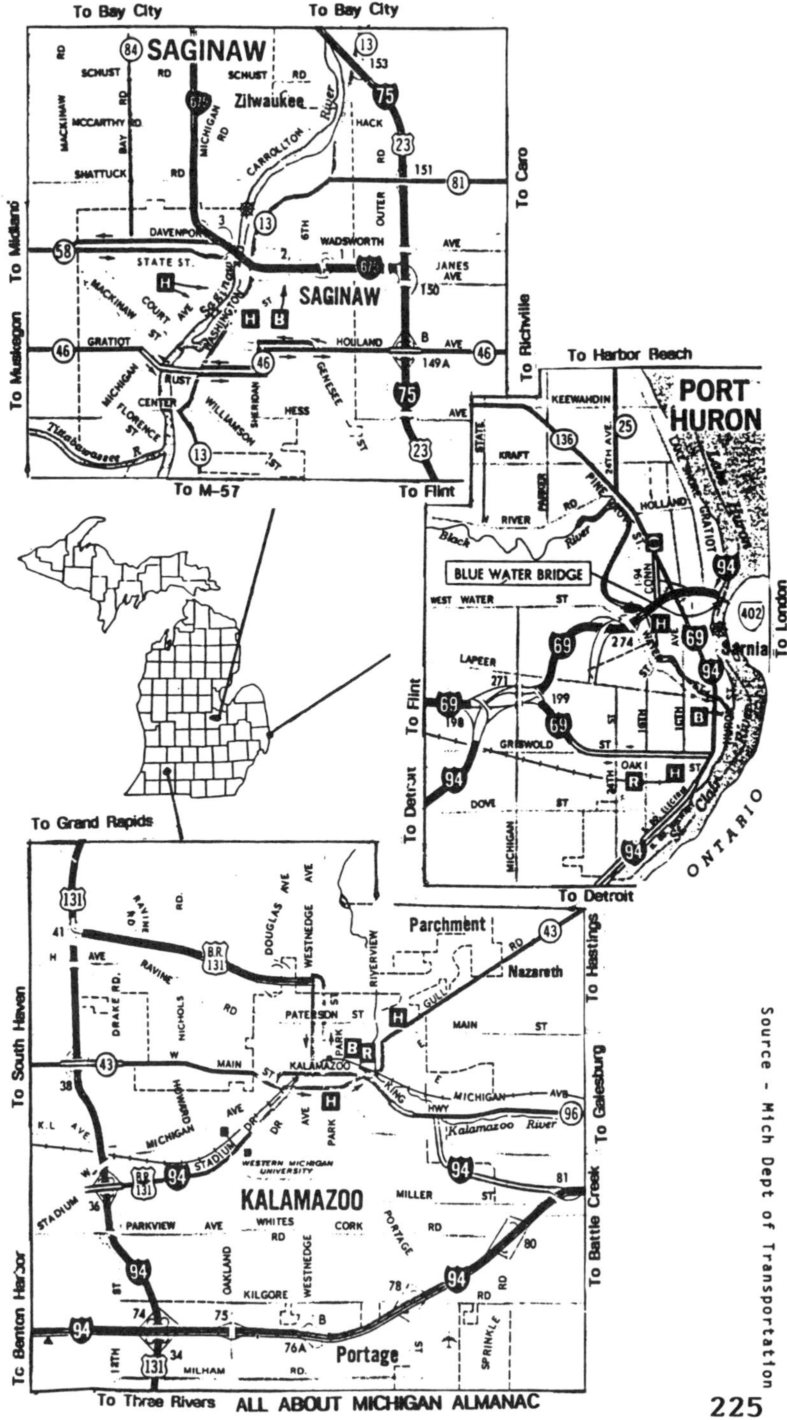

ALL ABOUT MICHIGAN ALMANAC

Source - Mich Dept of Transportation

AREA AGENCIES ON AGING

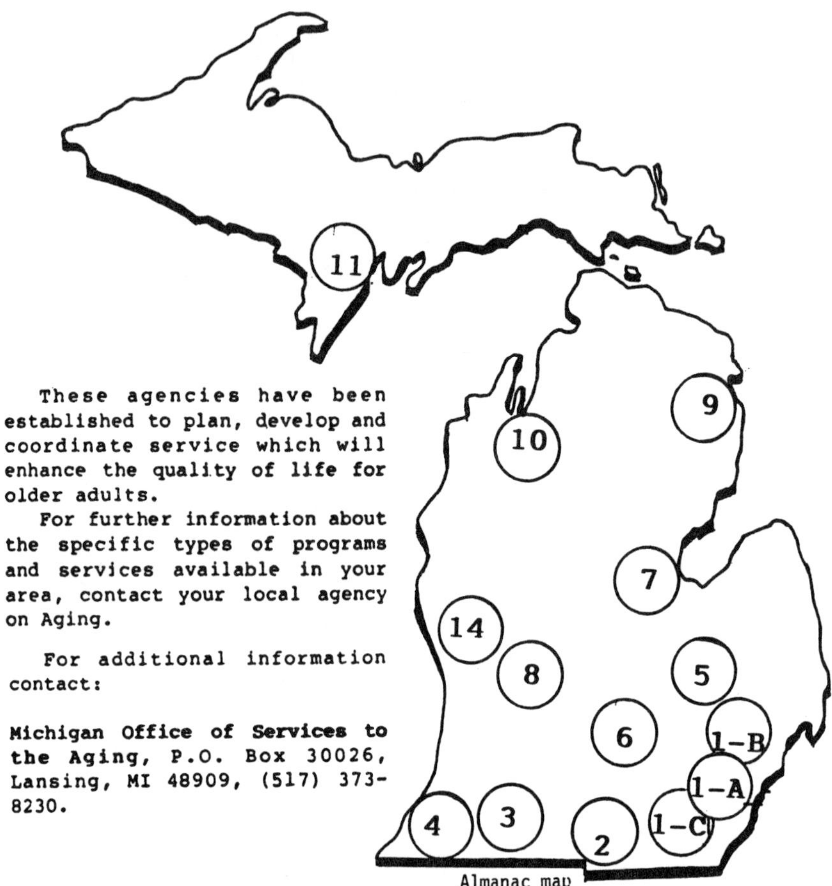

Almanac map

These agencies have been established to plan, develop and coordinate service which will enhance the quality of life for older adults.

For further information about the specific types of programs and services available in your area, contact your local agency on Aging.

For additional information contact:

Michigan Office of Services to the Aging, P.O. Box 30026, Lansing, MI 48909, (517) 373-8230.

1-A Detroit Area Agency on Aging
1100 Michigan Building
220 Bagley
Detroit, MI 48226
Phone: (313) 222-5330
Fax: (313) 222-5308
Serves: Cities of Detroit, Hamtramck, Highland Park, Grosse Pointe, Grosse Pointe Park, Grosse Pointe Shores, Grosse Pointe Woods, Grosse Pointe Farms and Harper Woods

1-B Area Agency on Aging 1-B
400 Franklin Center
29100 Northwestern Hwy.
Southfield, MI 48034
Phone: (810) 948-1640 1-800-852-7795
Fax: (810) 948-9691
Serves: Counties of Livingston, Macomb, Monroe, Oakland, Washtenaw, St. Clair

1-C The Senior Alliance, Inc.
3850 Second Street, Suite 160
Wayne, MI 48184
Phone: (313) 722-2830
Fax: (313) 722-2836
Serves: All of Wayne County excluding those communities served by Region 1-A

2 Region 2 Area Agency on Aging
P.O. Box 646
Adrian, MI 49221
Phone: (517) 265-7881
Fax: (517) 263-1069
Serves: Counties of Jackson, Hillsdale, Lenawee

3. Area Agency on Aging-Region III
8135 Cox's Drive, Suite 1-C
Portage, MI 49002
Phone: (616) 327-4321 1-800-272-1167
Fax: (616) 327-3301
Serves: Counties of Barry, Branch, Calhoun, Kalamazoo, St. Joseph

4 Region IV Area Agency on Aging, Inc.
2919 Division Street
St. Joseph, MI 49085
Phone: (616) 983-0177 1-800-442-2803
Fax: (616) 983-5218
Serves: Counties of Berrien, Cass, Van Buren

5 Valley Area Agency on Aging
711 North Saginaw, Room 325A
Flint, MI 48503
Phone: (810) 239-7671
Fax: (810) 239-8869
Serves: Counties of Genesee, Lapeer, Shiawassee

6 **Tri-County Office on Aging**
3315 S. Pennsylvania
Lansing, MI 48910
Phone: 517/887-1440
Fax: 517/887-8071
Serves: Counties of Clinton, Eaton, Ingham

7 Region VII Area Agency on Aging
126 Washington Avenue
Bay City, MI 48708
Phone: (517) 893-4506 1-800-858-1637
Fax: (517) 893-2651
Serves: Counties of Bay, Clare, Gladwin, Gratiot, Huron, Isabella, Midland, Saginaw, Sanilac, Tuscola

8 Area Agency on Aging of Western Michigan, Inc.
1279 Cedar Street, N.E.
Grand Rapids, MI 49503-1378
Phone: (616) 456-5664
Fax: (616) 456-5692
Serves: Counties of Allegan, Ionia, Kent, Lake, Mason, Mecosta, Montcalm, Newaygo, Osceola

9 Region IX Area Agency on Aging
Northeast Michigan Community
Service Agency, Inc.
2373 Gordon Road
Alpena, MI 49707
Phone: (517) 356-3474
Fax: (517) 354-5909
Serves: Counties of Alcona, Arenac, Alpena, Cheboygan, Crawford, Iosco, Montmorency, Ogemaw, Oscoda, Otsego, Presque Isle, Roscommon

10 Area Agency on Aging of
Northwest Michigan
P.O. Box 2010
Traverse City, MI 49685
Phone: (616) 947-8920 1-800-442-1713
Fax: (616) 947-6401
Serves: Counties of Antrim, Benzie, Charlevoix, Emmet, Grand Traverse, Kalkaska, Leelanau, Manistee, Missaukee, Wexford

11 Region 11 Area Agency on Aging
UPCAP Services, Inc.
P.O. Box 606
Escanaba, MI 49829
Phone: (906) 786-4701 1-800-562-4806
Serves: Counties of Alger, Baraga, Chippewa, Delta, Dickinson, Gogebic, Houghton, Iron, Keweenaw, Luce, Mackinac, Marquette, Menominee, Ontonagon, Schoolcraft

14 Region 14 Area Agency on Aging
255 West Sherman Boulevard
Muskegon Heights, MI 49444
Phone: (616) 727-8025 1-800-442-0054
Fax: (616) 727-8028
Serves: Counties of Muskegon, Oceana, Ottawa

EMPLOYMENT, BY MAJOR INDUSTRY STATE & METRO AREAS,

SOURCE: U.S. Bureau of Labor Statistics

Data below is for October,1994, not seasonally adjusted.
Cities listed include the metropolitan area.
Statistics are in 1,000.

	TOTAL	CONSTRUCTION	MANUFACTURING
MICHIGAN	4,195.5	157.4	956.1
ANN ARBOR	252.4	7.0	54.2
BENTON HARBOR	70.9	2.1	21.5
DETROIT	1,963.5	68.3	440.7
FLINT	170.9	5.9	46.8
GRAND RAPIDS MUSKEGON-HOLLAND	491.1	21.6	142.5
JACKSON	58.2	1.9	13.2
KALAMAZOO-BATTLE CREEK	204.1	7.5	50.7
LANSING-EAST LANSING	220.7	6.8	30.1
SAGINAW-BAY CITY-MIDLAND	172.7	8.6	41.4

	TRANSPORTATION & PUBLIC UTILITIES	WHOLESALE & RETAIL TRADE	FINANCE, INSURANCE & REAL ESTATE
MICHIGAN	161.7	969.0	193.8
ANN ARBOR	5.4	48.1	9.3
BENTON HARBOR	2.9	14.9	2.6
DETROIT	86.0	454.5	106.7
FLINT	4.2	40.1	6.4
GRAND RAPIDS MUSKEGON-HOLLAND	17.3	115.7	19.5
JACKSON	3.6	13.9	1.[illegible]
KALAMAZOO-BATTLE CREEK	6.3	43.9	10.[illegible]
LANSING-EAST LANSING	6.2	48.4	12.[illegible]
SAGINAW-BAY CITY-MIDLAND	6.5	43.7	6.[illegible]

	SERVICES	GOVERMENT
MICHIGAN	1,085.7	662.8
ANN ARBOR	57.8	70.6
BENTON HARBOR	17.5	9.3
DETROIT	570.5	235.9
FLINT	42.7	24.7
GRAND RAPIDS MUSKEGON-HOLLAND	120.3	54.1
JACKSON	13.3	10.2
KALAMAZOO-BATTLE CREEK	49.3	35.8
LANSING-EAST LANSING	49.4	67.2
SAGINAW-BAY CITY-MIDLAND	43.3	23.0

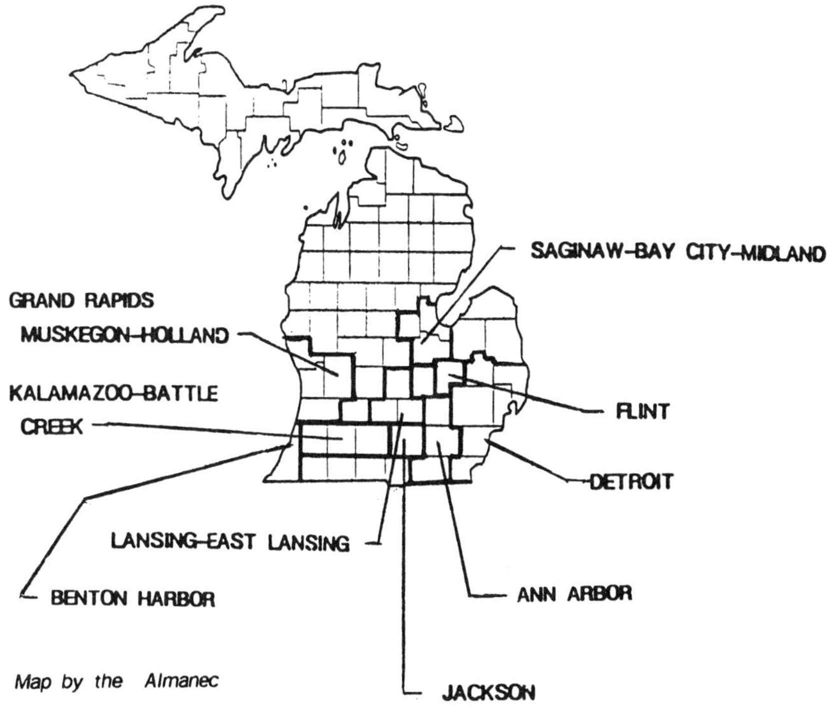

Map by the Almanec

METRO AREAS - SELECT

AGE under 18 years
65 and over
INCOME
RACE

Age	Under 18 years, % 1990	65 years & over, % 1990	Percentage chnnge 1990-1992
METRO ANN ARBOR	24.5%	11 5%	3.0%
METRO DETROIT	26.0%	11.9%	1.0%
METRO FLINT	28.0%	10.2%	0.7%
METRO GRAND RAPIDS-MUSKEGON-HOLLAND	28.6%	11.1%	2.8%
METRO KALAMAZOO-BATTLE CREEK	25.9%	11.8%	1.65%
METRO LANSING-EAST LANSING	25.6%	9.0%	0.9%,
METRO SAGINAW-BAY CITY-MIDLAND	27.5%	12.1%	0.8%
METRO DETROIT-ANN ARBOR-FLINT	26.1%	11.5%	1.1%

Metro Detroit-
Ann Arbor-Flint
Race

TOTAL POPULATION 1990	% BLACK	% AM INDIAN	% ASIAN	% HISPANIC
5,187,000	20.5%	0.4%	1.4%	2.0%

Metro Detroit-
Ann Arbor-Flint
Income

PERSONAL INCOME TOTal ($ MIL.) 1992	ANNUAL % CHANGE 1991-92	PER CAPITA PERSONAL INCOME ($ ACTUAL) 1992	% OF NATIONAL AVERAGE 1992
$112,702	5.5%	$21,484	106.9%

CITIES OF OVER 25,000 POPULATION –

Land Area
Density (People Per Sq Mile)
Population, 1992, 1990, 1980, % Change
Rank in U.S.

Source: U.S. Bureau of the Census

City	Land area,[2] 1990 (Sq. mi.)	Population: 1992 Total persons	1992 Rank	1992 Per square mile	1990	1980	Net change, 1980–1992 Number	Net change, 1980–1992 Percent
MICHIGAN	56 809.2	9 433 665	X	166	9 295 297	9 262 044	171 621	1.9
Allen Park city	7.0	30 714	914	4 388	31 092	34 196	-3 482	-10.2
Ann Arbor city	25.9	109 766	175	4 238	109 592	107 969	1 797	1.7
Battle Creek city	42.8	54 435	465	1 272	53 540	35 724	18 711	52.4
Bay City city	10.4	39 023	698	3 752	38 936	41 593	-2 570	-6.2
Burton city	23.5	27 806	997	1 183	27 617	29 976	-2 170	-7.2
Dearborn city	24.4	88 296	238	3 619	89 286	90 660	-2 364	-2.6
Dearborn Heights city	11.7	59 521	407	5 087	60 838	67 706	-8 185	-12.1
Detroit city	138.7	1 012 110	9	7 297	1 027 974	1 203 368	-191 258	-15.9
East Detroit city	5.1	35 437	775	6 948	35 283	38 280	-2 843	-7.4
East Lansing city	9.5	48 513	549	5 107	50 677	51 392	-2 879	-5.6
Farmington Hills city	33.3	76 892	295	2 309	74 652	58 056	18 836	32.4
Ferndale city	3.9	24 095	1 070	6 178	25 084	26 227	-2 132	-8.1
Flint city	33.8	139 311	132	4 122	140 761	159 611	-20 300	-12.7
Garden City city	5.9	31 464	890	5 333	31 846	35 640	-4 176	-11.7
Grand Rapids city	44.3	191 230	85	4 317	189 126	181 843	9 387	5.2
Holland city	14.2	31 494	889	2 218	30 745	26 281	5 213	19.8
Inkster city	6.3	30 341	928	4 816	30 772	35 190	-4 849	-13.8
Jackson city	11.0	38 164	717	3 469	37 446	39 739	-1 575	-4.0
Kalamazoo city	24.6	81 253	275	3 303	80 277	79 722	1 531	1.9
Kentwood city	21.0	39 479	689	1 880	37 826	30 438	9 041	29.7
Lansing city	33.9	126 722	146	3 738	127 321	130 414	-3 692	-2.8
Lincoln Park city	5.8	41 665	646	7 184	41 832	45 105	-3 440	-7.6
Livonia city	35.7	101 375	196	2 840	100 850	104 814	-3 439	-3.3
Madison Heights city	7.2	32 524	856	4 517	32 196	35 375	-2 851	-8.1
Midland city	27.6	39 012	699	1 413	38 053	37 269	1 743	4.7
Muskegon city	14.4	40 932	661	2 843	40 283	40 823	109	.3
Novi city	30.5	37 228	739	1 221	32 998	22 525	14 703	65.3
Oak Park city	5.0	30 359	927	6 072	30 462	31 537	-1 178	-3.7
Pontiac city	20.0	69 350	342	3 468	71 166	76 715	-7 365	-9.6
Portage city	32.2	41 694	645	1 295	41 042	38 157	3 537	9.3
Port Huron city	8.0	33 982	815	4 248	33 694	33 981	1	Z
Rochester Hills city	32.8	64 161	375	1 956	61 766	(6)	(6)	(6)
Roseville city	9.8	51 124	511	5 217	51 412	54 311	-3 187	-5.9
Royal Oak city	11.8	67 298	354	5 703	65 410	70 893	-3 595	-5.1
Saginaw city	17.4	70 719	335	4 064	69 512	77 508	-6 789	-8.8
St. Clair Shores city	11.5	67 363	353	5 858	68 107	76 210	-8 847	-11.6
Southfield city	26.2	81 088	277	3 095	75 728	75 568	5 520	7.3
Southgate city	6.9	30 154	934	4 370	30 771	32 058	-1 904	-5.9
Sterling Heights city	36.6	118 314	156	3 233	117 810	108 999	9 315	8.5
Taylor city	23.6	70 250	338	2 977	70 811	77 568	-7 318	-9.4
Troy city	33.5	78 719	289	2 350	72 884	67 102	11 617	17.3
Warren city	34.3	142 404	123	4 152	144 864	161 134	-18 730	-11.6
Westland city	20.5	85 524	254	4 172	84 724	84 603	921	1.1
Wyandotte city	5.3	30 542	920	5 763	30 938	34 006	-3 464	-10.2
Wyoming city	24.3	64 123	376	2 639	63 891	59 616	4 507	7.6

CITIES OF OVER 25,000 POPULATION –

White Population
Black
Am Indian
Asian
Hispanic
Language Spoken at Home

Source: U.S. Bureau of the Census

City	Population characteristics, 1990						Language spoken at home, percent speaking—	
	Race							
	White	Black	American Indian, Eskimo, or Aleut	Asian	Hispanic	Percent foreign born	Language other than English	Spanish
MICHIGAN	7 756 086	1 291 706	55 638	104 983	201 596	3.8	6.6	1.6
Allen Park city	30 465	144	66	233	986	6.1	9.1	1.0
Ann Arbor city	89 841	9 905	386	8 424	2 827	10.9	13.5	2.1
Battle Creek city	43 226	8 854	342	670	978	2.3	5.0	1.4
Bay City city	36 446	953	313	174	2 189	.9	6.3	3.1
Burton city	26 295	710	276	127	578	1.8	4.3	1.3
Dearborn city	87 099	494	297	837	2 483	16.5	25.0	1.4
Dearborn Heights city	59 214	277	252	782	1 398	9.3	15.5	1.3
Detroit city	222 316	777 916	3 655	8 461	28 473	3.4	7.5	2.8
East Detroit city	34 819	87	132	199	290	6.8	10.2	.3
East Lansing city	42 869	3 513	170	3 542	1 268	10.7	13.0	1.8
Farmington Hills city	70 073	1 429	129	2 870	887	9.7	11.5	.8
Ferndale city	24 020	348	216	358	426	6.7	8.4	1.3
Flint city	69 788	67 485	1 045	690	4 014	1.6	5.0	2.1
Garden City city	31 393	76	133	161	483	3.5	4.6	.8
Grand Rapids city	144 464	35 073	1 573	2 164	9 394	3.9	8.0	3.6
Holland city	26 971	324	103	979	4 347	6.9	16.2	10.6
Inkster city	11 118	19 199	131	206	332	2.1	3.4	1.1
Jackson city	30 020	6 615	219	153	954	1.7	4.7	1.6
Kalamazoo city	62 039	15 053	450	1 505	2 153	4.7	7.2	2.1
Kentwood city	34 522	2 113	159	740	761	4.7	6.9	2.2
Lansing city	94 135	23 626	1 295	2 263	10 112	3.1	8.7	4.7
Lincoln Park city	40 712	386	219	180	1 588	4.0	7.7	1.6
Livonia city	98 870	265	182	1 352	1 355	6.8	8.7	.7
Madison Heights city	30 878	292	159	788	399	8.0	9.4	.7
Midland city	36 362	654	135	728	638	4.4	5.5	1.2
Muskegon city	28 148	10 916	390	139	1 416	1.5	5.2	2.2
Novi city	31 690	259	108	874	372	6.2	7.7	.9
Oak Park city	19 143	10 449	37	719	444	14.9	19.7	1.4
Pontiac city	36 475	30 033	594	965	5 701	2.3	8.6	5.7
Portage city	38 704	1 139	147	846	593	3.2	5.1	1.5
Port Huron city	30 342	2 296	286	198	1 175	2.7	4.6	1.6
Rochester Hills city	58 667	844	132	1 959	875	7.2	8.0	.9
Roseville city	50 007	513	234	572	627	5.7	8.4	.7
Royal Oak city	64 035	332	163	729	695	6.4	6.2	.7
Saginaw city	36 324	28 046	375	302	7 304	1.8	7.5	5.4
St. Clair Shores city	67 201	141	229	439	646	6.6	8.9	.4
Southfield city	51 409	22 053	190	1 801	1 300	14.1	15.6	1.5
Southgate city	29 693	362	153	336	856	5.6	9.2	1.4
Sterling Heights city	113 452	475	279	3 369	1 314	9.9	15.1	.6
Taylor city	66 017	2 980	407	892	1 991	3.9	6.0	1.5
Troy city	66 701	983	115	4 943	927	11.6	14.2	.8
Warren city	140 995	1 047	669	1 942	1 583	8.1	12.9	.4
Westland city	80 197	2 829	467	831	1 594	4.4	5.9	.8
Wyandotte city	30 379	73	185	123	653	3.9	8.0	.9
Wyoming city	59 752	1 736	350	955	2 234	3.5	5.5	2.5

CITIES OF OVER 25,000 POPULATION -

Age of Population
Male - Female Ratio

Source: U.S. Bureau of the Census

City	Population characteristics, 1990—Con.											
	Age											
	Percent—											
	Under 5 years	5 to 17 years	18 to 20 years	21 to 24 years	25 to 34 years	35 to 44 years	45 to 54 years	55 to 64 years	65 to 74 years	75 years and over	Median age (Years)	Males per 100 females
MICHIGAN	7.6	18.9	4.8	6.0	16.9	15.1	10.2	8.5	7.1	4.9	32.6	94.4
Allen Park city	6.0	14.8	3.2	4.2	15.8	14.3	9.8	11.6	13.3	7.0	38.8	92.8
Ann Arbor city	5.8	11.5	13.1	14.2	20.7	14.5	7.6	5.3	4.0	3.2	27.3	97.9
Battle Creek city	8.4	19.2	4.0	5.1	16.5	14.5	9.1	8.7	8.0	6.5	33.1	88.6
Bay City city	7.9	18.4	4.2	5.9	17.4	14.1	8.6	8.2	8.9	6.5	33.0	90.4
Burton city	7.4	19.5	4.5	5.2	17.5	14.6	10.9	9.4	7.0	4.0	32.7	92.9
Dearborn city	7.2	15.9	3.7	5.1	17.3	14.0	9.4	9.4	10.6	7.3	35.5	93.6
Dearborn Heights city	6.0	14.6	3.7	5.4	17.1	13.0	10.8	12.6	11.0	5.8	37.3	92.3
Detroit city	9.1	20.4	5.1	6.2	16.5	14.2	8.6	7.9	7.2	5.0	30.8	86.5
East Detroit city	7.0	15.7	3.4	4.9	18.3	13.3	8.0	10.6	11.9	6.9	35.4	89.8
East Lansing city	3.4	7.1	32.3	24.8	12.5	7.9	4.6	2.9	2.5	2.0	21.6	94.2
Farmington Hills city	6.6	16.1	3.0	5.5	18.8	17.0	11.9	9.4	7.2	4.6	35.0	94.8
Ferndale city	8.4	17.4	3.8	6.2	22.2	14.6	8.5	6.8	6.6	5.5	31.4	96.4
Flint city	9.5	20.9	5.1	6.3	17.6	13.5	8.6	7.8	6.2	4.5	29.7	87.9
Garden City city	6.9	18.3	4.0	5.4	19.1	14.6	10.1	11.7	7.0	2.9	33.1	97.7
Grand Rapids city	9.4	18.1	5.6	7.2	19.5	13.1	7.2	6.9	6.7	6.4	29.8	90.5
Holland city	8.6	18.3	7.8	8.1	16.9	12.5	7.5	6.7	7.1	6.7	29.0	89.1
Inkster city	8.1	20.8	4.7	6.3	16.8	13.8	9.6	8.5	7.3	4.0	30.8	89.1
Jackson city	9.4	18.9	4.6	6.4	18.1	12.9	7.8	7.7	7.6	6.6	30.7	88.3
Kalamazoo city	7.5	14.5	12.6	12.1	17.6	12.1	6.9	5.9	5.5	5.3	26.8	89.2
Kentwood city	8.0	18.2	4.1	7.3	21.5	15.3	9.2	6.8	5.5	4.1	30.5	91.7
Lansing city	9.2	18.2	4.5	7.8	20.9	14.8	8.2	6.8	5.6	4.0	29.7	90.1
Lincoln Park city	7.1	17.1	4.0	5.4	18.8	14.6	8.8	9.7	9.4	5.0	33.7	93.5
Livonia city	6.6	16.5	3.7	4.8	16.1	15.6	11.8	11.8	8.2	4.9	36.3	94.5
Madison Heights city	7.2	15.6	4.0	6.7	21.5	13.7	9.9	10.0	6.8	4.7	32.6	93.5
Midland city	7.2	17.9	5.1	6.3	16.7	15.6	11.0	8.5	6.6	5.2	33.1	93.5
Muskegon city	8.8	17.8	4.8	7.2	19.1	13.5	7.2	7.0	7.6	7.0	30.8	98.0
Novi city	7.8	17.7	3.3	5.4	21.4	18.6	10.7	7.2	5.0	3.0	32.5	93.6
Oak Park city	8.2	20.0	4.0	4.9	16.8	16.1	9.3	7.8	7.9	4.9	32.8	92.1
Pontiac city	10.0	20.5	5.3	7.6	19.1	13.8	8.3	6.7	5.0	3.7	28.3	93.8
Portage city	7.3	19.7	4.0	5.3	17.2	17.7	11.7	8.6	5.6	2.9	33.1	94.1
Port Huron city	8.6	19.7	4.8	6.1	17.6	12.9	8.5	7.9	7.4	6.5	31.1	87.4
Rochester Hills city	7.2	19.2	3.7	4.6	17.0	19.3	12.5	7.8	4.8	3.9	34.1	94.7
Roseville city	7.2	16.7	4.0	5.8	20.1	13.8	8.9	9.8	8.8	4.9	33.1	92.0
Royal Oak city	6.8	13.9	2.8	5.0	22.4	15.7	8.9	8.9	9.3	6.4	34.6	89.3
Saginaw city	9.9	22.1	4.7	5.7	16.7	13.5	7.9	7.6	6.8	5.2	29.6	85.4
St. Clair Shores city	5.7	14.0	3.4	4.8	16.4	13.9	9.9	13.3	11.4	7.2	38.6	90.1
Southfield city	5.9	14.3	3.5	5.5	17.7	15.9	10.8	9.5	8.8	8.2	37.0	88.1
Southgate city	6.0	16.0	4.2	5.9	17.8	15.6	10.6	10.6	9.1	4.3	35.1	94.2
Sterling Heights city	6.5	19.4	4.9	6.3	16.3	17.3	12.8	7.3	5.7	3.5	32.9	95.3
Taylor city	8.3	19.5	4.9	6.8	18.5	14.4	10.8	8.9	5.2	2.8	30.6	94.5
Troy city	6.7	19.8	3.8	4.8	15.3	19.3	13.6	8.2	5.2	3.2	34.8	96.1
Warren city	6.2	14.7	4.0	6.5	17.7	12.3	11.7	12.1	9.4	5.5	35.7	94.6
Westland city	7.3	16.3	4.4	7.1	21.1	14.1	10.1	8.9	6.3	4.5	31.9	92.3
Wyandotte city	7.1	17.2	3.6	5.4	18.1	14.8	8.4	9.1	10.3	5.9	34.2	93.4
Wyoming city	9.0	18.8	4.1	7.1	21.4	14.0	8.3	7.6	6.1	3.6	29.8	94.2

CITIES OF OVER 25,000 POPULATION –

Educational Attainment
Median Family Income
Per Capita Income
Income From Social Security
Income From Public Assistance

Source: U.S. Bureau of the Census

City	Educational attainment, 1990: Persons 25 years and over	Educational attainment, 1990: Percent— High school graduate or higher	Educational attainment, 1990: Percent— Bachelor's degree or higher	Median family income (Dollars)	Income from— Social Security	Income from— Public assistance	Median household income: Median income (Dollars)	Median household income: Percent change, 1979–1989	Pe capi income (Dollar
MICHIGAN	5 842 642	76.8	17.4	36 652	26.7	9.6	31 020	61.4	14 15
Allen Park city	22 361	78.7	16.5	45 392	38.5	3.5	39 925	48.4	17 01
Ann Arbor city	61 122	93.9	64.2	50 192	14.4	3.2	33 344	82.0	17 78
Battle Creek city	33 977	76.6	15.8	31 115	30.3	14.2	25 306	90.5	12 96
Bay City city	24 846	70.0	9.4	28 038	33.9	15.2	21 380	37.4	10 78
Burton city	17 505	72.7	6.7	35 390	27.8	11.9	29 961	43.1	12 94
Dearborn city	60 798	75.9	21.7	42 215	35.5	5.8	34 909	57.7	16 85
Dearborn Heights city	42 800	74.1	13.7	42 433	35.4	4.0	36 771	45.3	16 49
Detroit city	612 078	62.1	9.6	22 566	28.8	26.1	18 742	34.1	9 44
East Detroit city	24 367	69.5	8.9	39 288	39.5	4.7	34 069	57.9	14 15
East Lansing city	16 425	96.6	71.2	43 125	11.9	2.2	24 716	64.8	11 21
Farmington Hills city	51 514	89.2	42.0	63 101	21.8	3.0	51 986	68.7	25 49
Ferndale city	16 200	73.8	13.0	33 934	26.7	8.2	28 964	64.6	12 7
Flint city	81 932	69.3	10.3	25 083	27.1	23.8	20 176	17.4	10 41
Garden City city	20 831	75.0	7.1	42 364	26.6	4.6	38 717	51.5	14 25
Grand Rapids city	113 374	76.4	20.8	32 049	26.0	10.7	26 809	73.5	12 07
Holland city	17 680	73.6	22.5	37 122	27.9	7.0	30 689	78.7	13 3
Inkster city	18 513	66.7	7.3	30 191	29.4	17.0	25 198	36.9	10 7
Jackson city	22 769	71.5	10.8	25 355	30.9	16.8	20 830	43.1	10 4
Kalamazoo city	42 964	79.6	29.8	29 869	23.8	13.4	23 207	58.7	11 9
Kentwood city	23 648	83.9	26.0	40 946	20.3	4.3	34 324	75.5	15 4
Lansing city	77 268	78.3	18.3	31 576	20.8	13.0	26 398	55.5	12 2
Lincoln Park city	27 784	67.6	6.8	36 016	32.9	7.2	30 638	44.2	13 3
Livonia city	68 992	84.7	23.8	53 523	27.6	2.5	48 645	61.9	19 1
Madison Heights city	21 479	72.4	11.0	38 022	24.9	6.6	31 757	47.4	14 1
Midland city	24 264	88.4	41.9	49 040	23.8	5.9	38 747	64.6	19 2
Muskegon city	24 830	68.7	8.2	23 246	34.8	19.1	18 748	55.6	8 8
Novi city	21 842	89.5	33.9	54 754	16.2	2.4	47 518	76.6	20 7
Oak Park city	19 328	80.8	22.2	39 789	25.6	7.3	36 090	62.5	14 5
Pontiac city	40 606	62.4	7.9	25 834	23.9	22.1	21 962	35.7	9 8
Portage city	26 227	88.6	31.3	44 381	19.1	3.0	39 045	72.8	17 6
Port Huron city	20 474	71.2	10.6	26 785	29.3	17.0	21 522	45.6	11 2
Rochester Hills city	40 354	89.4	39.5	62 223	17.7	2.3	54 996	(2)	23 2
Roseville city	34 044	69.4	6.9	37 516	31.4	5.8	32 337	52.8	13 4
Royal Oak city	46 865	86.0	28.4	44 446	28.4	3.1	36 835	64.9	18 0
Saginaw city	40 114	68.6	9.3	21 900	28.0	25.5	17 736	22.0	8 9
St. Clair Shores city	49 139	77.9	13.7	42 926	35.8	4.1	36 929	51.8	16 6
Southfield city	53 904	84.8	34.7	49 718	29.4	3.7	40 579	53.4	21 0
Southgate city	20 957	73.8	9.5	42 390	31.6	3.6	36 526	44.8	15 4
Sterling Heights city	74 078	80.7	18.5	51 739	21.2	3.2	46 470	68.2	17 0
Taylor city	42 936	68.2	6.8	36 244	20.7	11.2	32 659	45.9	12 9
Troy city	47 392	88.9	39.9	63 187	18.7	1.9	55 407	79.4	23 2
Warren city	99 354	71.7	10.3	41 504	31.6	5.6	35 980	50.8	15 2
Westland city	55 046	75.7	11.4	41 116	23.6	5.4	34 995	53.2	15 0
Wyandotte city	20 696	68.9	7.8	33 938	35.4	8.6	28 312	45.7	13 1
Wyoming city	39 093	78.6	13.2	35 161	21.8	4.7	31 103	66.7	13 2

CITIES OF OVER 25,000 POPULATION –

City Government Employment
City Government Revenue
City Taxes

Source: U.S. Bureau of the Census

City	City government employment, October 1991			City government finances, 1990-1991				
				General revenue				
						Taxes		
	Total full-time equivalent	Rate[3]	Payroll ($1,000)	Total ($1,000)	Per capita (Dollars)	Total ($1,000)	Per capita[5] (Dollars)	Percent property
MICHIGAN	X	X	X	X	X	X	X	X
en Park city	NA	NA	NA	NA	NA	NA	NA	NA
n Arbor city	1 101	[6]100	'2 740	111 619	1 018	40 948	374	97.1
tle Creek city	676	126	1 745	78 257	1 462	31 673	592	70.3
City city	411	106	1 038	27 297	701	9 831	252	97.7
ton city	[7]87	[7]32	[7]239	12 682	459	3 492	126	94.2
arborn city	983	110	2 655	87 022	975	45 003	504	95.2
arborn Heights city	355	58	835	31 926	525	13 486	222	96.6
troit city	19 529	[8]190	49 696	1 513 907	1 473	527 639	513	37.7
st Detroit city	194	[7]55	[7]488	15 331	435	7 720	219	97.7
st Lansing city	[8]431	[8]85	·1 127	26 279	519	8 429	166	94.1
mington Hills city	353	47	1 036	38 979	522	20 842	279	95.5
ndale city	198	79	609	16 035	639	6 724	268	97.8
t city	4 276	304	10 992	320 879	2 280	44 577	317	48.8
rden City city	NA	NA	NA	13 584	427	6 901	217	94.7
and Rapids city	1 906	101	4 957	159 695	844	55 480	293	49.7
land city	425	138	1 095	25 807	839	8 559	278	97.4
ster city	NA	NA	NA	12 045	391	5 361	174	95.9
kson city	403	108	962	28 011	748	10 777	288	50.8
amazoo city	972	121	2 594	83 847	1 044	20 804	259	97.1
ntwood city	146	39	410	13 966	369	5 645	149	89.1
nsing city	-2 425	[6]190	'6 030	124 436	977	41 725	328	48.8
coln Park city	238	57	662	23 641	565	11 181	267	93.8
onia city	818	81	2 084	66 576	660	29 083	288	93.4
dison Heights city	[8]266	[8]83	'740	24 731	768	11 934	371	95.8
lland city	430	113	772	32 377	851	14 978	394	97.7
skegon city	283	70	676	24 491	608	7 477	186	92.6
vi city	229	69	610	21 157	641	12 365	375	89.5
k Park city	239	78	657	21 747	714	10 250	336	98.1
ntiac city	'2 320	[9]326	5 305	166 395	2 338	40 755	573	73.0
tage city	293	71	760	23 613	575	10 002	244	96.4
t Huron city	426	126	1 023	41 270	1 225	13 366	397	67.9
chester Hills city	208	34	518	28 156	456	13 127	213	89.6
seville city	303	59	915	28 626	557	12 449	242	97.1
yal Oak city	438	67	1 310	37 915	580	17 786	272	94.3
ginaw city	691	99	1 744	61 117	879	19 843	285	97.6
Clair Shores city	354	52	936	33 061	485	14 941	219	96.7
uthfield city	952	113	2 469	68 149	900	40 122	530	97.3
uthgate city	'90	[8]62	[8]476	16 844	547	8 163	265	95.3
rling Heights city	673	57	2 070	53 832	457	28 691	244	95.8
ylor city	NA	NA	NA	46 990	664	22 428	317	96.7
y city	499	68	1 407	54 796	752	30 461	418	95.8
rren city	[10]926	[10]64	'2 379	78 831	544	43 423	300	97.0
stland city	'361	[6]43	771	37 238	440	18 339	216	96.7
andotte city	336	[11]109	851	48 981	1 583	8 610	278	96.9
oming city	388	61	1 008	29 561	463	10 182	159	92.6

CITIES OF OVER 25,000 POPULATION –

Housing
Owner Occupied & Median Value
Rented Occupied & Median Rent

Source: U.S. Bureau of the Census

City	Housing, 1990					
	Occupied units					
	Owner occupied				Renter occupied	
	Number	Percent of total occupied	Median value[1] Value (Dol.)	Median value[1] Percent change, 1980–1990	Number	Median gross rent[2] (Dol.)
MICHIGAN	2 427 643	71.0	60 600	55.4	991 688	423
Allen Park city	10 489	87.2	67 400	40.1	1 541	492
Ann Arbor city	17 996	43.2	116 400	67.2	23 661	568
Battle Creek city	13 494	62.9	39 300	89.9	7 963	381
Bay City city	10 506	67.5	32 600	15.6	5 064	312
Burton city	7 948	76.1	44 400	32.1	2 499	388
Dearborn city	26 358	74.4	69 600	41.8	9 084	465
Dearborn Heights city	19 746	84.3	64 500	37.8	3 686	532
Detroit city	197 929	52.9	25 600	21.9	176 128	372
East Detroit city	11 761	87.5	55 300	42.5	1 682	467
East Lansing city	4 476	33.2	97 000	47.0	9 024	451
Farmington Hills city	19 190	65.6	145 900	67.9	10 044	660
Ferndale city	6 710	68.1	38 400	39.1	3 148	467
Flint city	31 306	58.1	33 900	28.4	22 588	375
Garden City city	9 676	86.3	59 700	38.5	1 537	470
Grand Rapids city	41 349	59.9	58 300	75.1	27 680	414
Holland city	7 189	68.0	68 200	68.4	3 383	453
Inkster city	6 564	58.6	36 500	24.1	4 637	436
Jackson city	8 217	55.8	32 100	35.4	6 506	338
Kalamazoo city	13 928	47.4	48 600	48.2	15 481	403
Kentwood city	8 798	57.7	78 100	57.8	6 449	475
Lansing city	27 737	54.8	48 400	45.3	22 898	399
Lincoln Park city	12 754	78.5	44 500	29.0	3 503	432
Livonia city	31 940	88.9	94 800	47.9	3 976	606
Madison Heights city	8 936	69.5	59 800	50.6	3 914	481
Midland city	10 237	69.1	74 200	41.3	4 575	422
Muskegon city	8 070	54.6	32 400	63.6	6 700	343
Novi city	9 264	73.0	127 900	59.7	3 435	680
Oak Park city	8 032	73.8	48 000	19.1	2 853	567
Pontiac city	12 321	49.7	36 300	41.8	12 456	436
Portage city	11 077	71.6	71 800	51.2	4 390	434
Port Huron city	7 172	54.5	41 400	49.5	5 986	387
Rochester Hills city	17 363	77.7	137 900	(10)	4 990	643
Roseville city	14 571	74.6	55 400	48.5	4 966	476
Royal Oak city	19 836	70.0	75 600	68.4	8 508	497
Saginaw city	15 065	57.5	32 800	26.6	11 114	343
St. Clair Shores city	23 056	84.7	69 700	50.2	4 162	504
Southfield city	17 316	53.9	85 100	28.4	14 796	672
Southgate city	8 519	70.2	58 700	38.8	3 609	503
Sterling Heights city	31 671	77.6	97 000	47.4	9 164	533
Taylor city	16 843	67.7	48 400	30.5	8 018	457
Troy city	19 548	74.7	128 900	54.4	6 619	620
Warren city	43 415	79.5	69 500	47.2	11 187	492
Westland city	19 935	60.2	63 400	40.0	13 175	512
Wyandotte city	8 627	70.0	49 400	40.7	3 692	412
Wyoming city	16 297	67.4	57 700	67.7	7 871	429

COUNTIES & STATE -

White Population
Black
Am Indian
Asian
Hispanic

Source: U.S. Bureau of the Census

County	Population characteristics, 1990					
	Race				Hispanic origin[1]	
	White	Black	American Indian, Eskimo, or Aleut	Asian or Pacific Islander	Number	Percent of total
MICHIGAN	7 756 086	1 291 706	55 638	104 983	201 596	2.2
Alcona	10 026	27	56	26	55	.5
Alger	8 422	213	304	24	43	.5
Allegan	86 760	1 448	543	411	2 895	3.2
Alpena	30 372	35	93	85	145	.5
Antrim	17 895	23	211	24	96	.5
Arenac	14 695	10	139	38	167	1.1
Baraga	6 971	49	918	10	34	.4
Barry	49 429	104	188	144	521	1.0
Bay	107 747	1 242	726	428	3 494	3.1
Benzie	11 863	30	237	35	129	1.1
Berrien	133 259	24 872	685	1 487	2 683	1.7
Branch	40 278	705	221	156	468	1.1
Calhoun	118 737	14 383	696	1 068	2 583	1.9
Cass	44 827	3 725	469	191	651	1.3
Charlevoix	20 993	17	378	41	112	.5
Cheboygan	20 837	15	478	57	80	.4
Chippewa	28 353	2 184	3 820	152	278	.8
Clare	24 665	40	160	53	132	.5
Clinton	56 639	218	276	199	1 286	2.2
Crawford	11 802	264	145	42	79	.6
Delta	36 819	16	809	99	136	.4
Dickinson	26 532	23	135	106	116	.4
Eaton	87 549	3 310	438	559	2 199	2.4
Emmet	24 122	133	683	69	118	.5
Genesee	336 651	84 257	3 132	2 902	8 877	2.1
Gladwin	21 694	19	114	40	136	.6
Gogebic	17 486	243	283	26	67	.4
Grand Traverse	63 019	259	555	318	503	.8
Gratiot	37 827	328	144	98	1 467	3.8
Hillsdale	42 919	113	143	112	395	.9
Houghton	34 469	158	153	610	164	.5
Huron	34 627	22	89	60	372	1.1
Ingham	237 183	27 837	1 941	7 562	13 478	4.8
Ionia	53 141	3 003	221	120	1 176	2.1
Iosco	28 966	632	228	269	357	1.2
Iron	13 028	4	102	32	67	.5
Isabella	52 212	635	1 020	456	714	1.3
Jackson	135 557	11 983	655	653	2 303	1.5
Kalamazoo	197 427	19 879	1 017	3 168	3 950	1.8
Kalkaska	13 321	10	114	23	87	.6
Kent	444 112	40 314	2 756	5 380	14 684	2.9
Keweenaw	1 688	1	4	6	6	.4
Lake	7 337	1 146	81	9	60	.7
Lapeer	73 049	483	319	282	1 493	2.0
Leelanau	15 958	16	451	45	188	1.1
Lenawee	86 323	1 431	303	486	5 515	6.0
Livingston	113 566	673	705	480	974	.8

	Population characteristics, 1990					
	Race				Hispanic origin[1]	
	White	Black	American Indian, Eskimo, or Aleut	Asian or Pacific Islander	Number	Percent of total
Luce	5 418	2	331	6	27	.5
Mackinac	8 955	5	1 691	11	33	.3
Macomb	693 686	10 400	2 639	9 112	7 978	1.1
Manistee	20 851	54	189	54	323	1.5
Marquette	68 027	1 170	943	538	566	.8
Mason	24 957	155	188	75	399	1.6
Mecosta	35 739	978	258	187	389	1.0
Menominee	24 464	7	382	60	59	.2
Midland	73 466	719	334	804	1 035	1.4
Missaukee	12 015	3	74	25	67	.6
Monroe	129 421	2 339	481	574	2 077	1.6
Montcalm	51 216	960	384	157	888	1.7
Montmorency	8 861	1	48	10	60	.7
Muskegon	133 931	21 617	1 338	555	3 623	2.3
Newaygo	36 758	468	248	103	968	2.5
Oakland	970 674	77 488	3 948	25 103	19 630	1.8
Oceana	21 211	58	242	50	1 390	6.2
Ogemaw	18 489	18	140	19	104	.6
Ontonagon	8 723	4	109	15	35	.4
Osceola	19 899	57	117	43	143	.7
Oscoda	7 781	2	41	5	50	.6
Otsego	17 737	18	103	82	67	.4
Ottawa	179 675	997	638	2 451	7 947	4.2
Presque Isle	13 648	11	43	30	37	.3
Roscommon	19 597	37	101	23	94	.5
Saginaw	165 430	36 849	915	1 272	13 186	6.2
St. Clair	140 294	2 987	745	475	2 558	1.8
St. Joseph	56 661	1 600	226	258	546	.9
Sanilac	39 232	39	195	71	905	2.3
Schoolcraft	7 755	7	519	13	32	.4
Shiawassee	68 686	93	397	223	1 053	1.5
Tuscola	54 051	478	345	206	1 150	2.1
Van Buren	63 189	4 690	646	217	2 254	3.2
Washtenaw	236 390	31 720	1 076	11 724	5 731	2.0
Wayne	1 212 007	849 109	8 048	21 704	50 506	2.4
Wexford	26 040	34	178	87	153	.6

COUNTIES & STATE -

Age of Population
Male - Female Ratio

Source: U.S. Bureau of the Census

Population characteristics, 1990—Con.

	Age, percent—										
	Under 5 years	5 to 17 years	18 to 20 years	21 to 24 years	25 to 34 years	35 to 44 years	45 to 54 years	55 to 64 years	65 to 74 years	75 years and over	Males per 100 females
MICHIGAN	7.6	18.9	4.8	6.0	16.9	15.1	10.2	8.5	7.1	4.9	94.4
Alcona	5.1	16.0	2.8	3.4	11.4	11.4	11.3	14.5	14.4	9.7	99.0
Alger	6.1	18.8	3.7	4.3	13.9	15.1	10.6	10.0	10.1	7.1	105.7
Allegan	8.3	21.4	3.9	5.0	17.1	15.2	9.9	7.8	6.6	4.9	98.1
Alpena	6.6	19.8	4.0	4.0	15.1	13.9	11.2	10.4	8.6	6.4	94.2
Antrim	6.9	18.8	3.3	4.0	14.3	13.6	10.4	11.2	10.4	7.0	95.6
Arenac	6.7	20.0	3.5	4.2	14.5	13.2	10.4	11.2	9.7	6.5	95.8
Baraga	6.7	19.8	3.9	4.7	12.3	14.6	10.5	8.1	10.8	8.8	101.1
Barry	7.4	20.6	4.1	4.3	15.7	15.8	11.5	9.0	6.8	4.8	100.0
Bay	7.1	19.2	4.2	5.3	15.9	15.1	10.9	8.9	7.9	5.5	93.7
Benzie	7.0	17.3	3.3	4.2	14.5	14.2	11.2	11.2	10.3	6.9	97.4
Berrien	7.4	19.6	4.5	5.2	15.5	14.4	10.4	9.3	8.0	5.7	92.0
Branch	7.7	20.2	3.8	4.8	16.1	14.5	10.6	9.1	7.7	5.6	95.8
Calhoun	7.4	19.3	4.7	5.1	15.3	15.0	10.4	9.4	7.7	5.6	93.7
Cass	7.1	19.9	4.3	4.6	15.1	15.1	11.1	9.7	7.9	5.2	96.4
Charlevoix	7.6	19.4	3.3	4.6	15.7	15.1	10.4	9.6	8.4	6.0	96.1
Cheboygan	6.7	19.4	3.4	4.0	13.3	13.9	10.7	11.1	10.3	7.1	93.6
Chippewa	6.1	17.3	6.1	7.6	18.3	14.8	8.9	8.6	7.2	5.4	124.5
Clare	7.3	18.9	3.7	4.5	14.0	12.3	10.1	11.6	10.9	6.8	93.7
Clinton	7.5	21.3	4.2	5.2	16.4	16.2	11.9	8.0	5.4	3.9	99.1
Crawford	7.3	18.8	3.6	4.6	16.1	13.5	10.3	10.8	8.9	6.0	104.8
Delta	6.7	20.3	4.0	4.3	14.5	14.8	10.4	9.7	8.7	6.6	95.0
Dickinson	6.8	19.2	3.1	4.0	14.9	14.7	9.6	9.5	9.9	8.4	96.3
Eaton	7.1	20.5	4.6	5.4	16.1	17.0	11.5	7.9	5.7	4.2	94.4
Emmet	7.5	19.2	3.6	4.4	16.2	16.3	10.0	8.7	7.8	6.3	94.3
Genesee	7.8	20.3	4.6	5.7	16.9	15.0	10.8	8.7	6.1	4.1	91.8
Gladwin	7.2	19.2	3.6	4.4	13.3	12.3	10.4	12.3	10.9	6.5	96.9
Gogebic	5.7	16.6	4.2	4.3	12.2	12.6	9.7	10.7	12.7	11.2	96.5
Grand Traverse	7.6	19.5	4.4	4.7	17.1	17.1	9.6	7.8	6.8	5.4	94.9
Gratiot	6.9	20.2	5.7	5.6	15.0	14.1	10.2	8.4	7.3	6.4	94.6
Hillsdale	7.7	20.5	5.2	5.3	15.1	13.8	10.3	8.9	7.4	5.8	96.3
Houghton	6.0	16.4	10.4	9.1	12.2	11.7	8.7	7.7	9.1	8.8	111.5
Huron	7.0	19.9	3.5	4.5	14.1	13.3	9.4	10.1	10.5	7.8	95.9
Ingham	7.4	16.9	9.3	10.2	17.9	14.8	8.6	6.3	5.0	3.7	92.4
Ionia	7.7	20.5	6.0	7.1	17.6	14.5	9.3	7.2	5.7	4.4	114.3
Iosco	8.3	18.0	4.1	6.3	17.0	12.2	8.5	10.5	8.9	6.2	100.0
Iron	5.4	16.9	2.4	2.7	11.5	12.7	9.4	12.0	14.9	12.1	91.9
Isabella	6.5	16.4	14.5	14.1	14.3	12.0	7.5	6.3	5.0	3.4	91.6
Jackson	7.3	18.5	4.1	5.4	17.6	15.7	10.3	8.8	7.2	5.1	103.2
Kalamazoo	7.3	17.1	7.3	8.2	16.9	15.1	9.8	7.6	6.0	4.6	92.9
Kalkaska	7.7	21.6	3.5	4.4	16.0	13.9	10.0	9.5	8.2	5.1	100.4
Kent	8.7	19.5	4.5	6.3	18.8	14.9	9.0	7.4	6.1	4.7	93.9
Keweenaw	4.9	15.0	2.4	2.3	10.5	13.6	10.2	11.7	14.9	14.5	95.7
Lake	6.7	18.4	2.6	3.7	11.7	11.4	10.4	13.7	12.9	8.4	96.0
Lapeer	7.3	22.3	4.6	5.1	16.3	16.6	11.6	7.6	5.2	3.5	100.4
Leelanau	7.5	18.5	3.2	3.6	14.3	17.2	10.4	10.4	8.8	6.1	99.3
Lenawee	7.3	20.9	5.0	5.4	15.3	15.2	10.4	8.4	7.1	5.0	97.2
Livingston	7.5	21.1	4.3	4.6	16.4	18.1	12.5	7.3	5.1	3.1	102.0

	Population characteristics, 1990										
	Age, percent—										
	Under 5 years	5 to 17 years	18 to 20 years	21 to 24 years	25 to 34 years	35 to 44 years	45 to 54 years	55 to 64 years	65 to 74 years	75 years and over	Males per 100 females
Luce	6.5	20.7	3.2	3.5	12.8	14.4	10.8	10.9	9.9	7.3	96.4
Mackinac	6.8	19.1	3.1	3.9	14.0	13.5	10.6	11.9	9.9	7.1	98.0
Macomb	6.8	17.1	4.2	6.1	17.9	15.0	11.1	9.5	7.7	4.6	94.5
Manistee	6.2	17.8	3.5	3.8	13.9	14.4	10.9	11.2	10.2	8.1	93.8
Marquette	7.1	18.8	6.6	7.7	17.1	15.5	8.8	7.1	6.2	5.0	103.1
Mason	7.0	19.3	3.8	4.2	13.9	14.4	10.3	10.1	9.6	7.5	94.9
Mecosta	6.1	15.8	15.4	11.9	12.3	11.2	8.2	7.8	6.8	4.5	106.5
Menominee	6.3	20.1	3.3	4.2	14.8	14.7	9.8	9.6	9.4	7.8	97.4
Midland	7.5	19.8	4.6	5.7	16.8	15.8	11.3	8.4	5.9	4.0	97.6
Missaukee	7.7	21.9	3.4	4.1	15.2	13.0	10.2	9.5	9.0	5.9	97.3
Monroe	7.7	21.0	4.5	5.3	16.3	15.5	10.8	8.5	6.1	4.3	97.2
Montcalm	7.7	20.9	4.1	5.2	16.8	14.3	10.0	8.5	7.3	5.1	103.9
Montmorency	5.8	17.7	3.2	3.1	11.6	11.9	9.5	14.3	13.9	9.0	96.0
Muskegon	8.1	20.0	4.2	5.2	16.4	14.7	9.7	8.7	7.7	5.3	95.5
Newaygo	8.4	21.2	3.5	4.2	15.4	13.8	10.5	9.4	8.1	5.5	96.8
Oakland	7.2	17.5	3.8	5.4	18.4	16.8	11.4	8.6	6.5	4.4	94.7
Oceana	7.9	21.7	3.7	4.0	14.9	13.9	10.7	9.5	8.2	5.5	96.5
Ogemaw	6.7	19.6	3.6	3.8	13.5	12.5	10.1	12.0	11.3	6.9	97.0
Ontonagon	6.1	17.8	2.9	3.4	12.7	13.9	12.3	11.5	10.6	8.9	103.5
Osceola	7.6	22.1	3.8	4.5	14.2	13.4	10.6	9.9	8.5	5.5	98.2
Oscoda	6.8	17.2	2.8	3.9	13.2	11.0	10.5	14.0	13.0	7.6	97.1
Otsego	7.7	20.8	3.7	4.6	15.4	14.8	9.9	9.6	8.1	5.4	96.6
Ottawa	8.5	20.8	5.7	6.1	17.1	15.1	9.8	7.1	5.6	4.2	97.2
Presque Isle	6.2	19.3	3.3	3.7	12.6	12.8	9.9	12.5	11.9	7.9	97.5
Roscommon	5.4	15.7	2.8	3.2	11.8	11.2	9.7	15.3	16.1	8.8	95.7
Saginaw	7.8	20.4	4.6	5.4	15.5	14.9	10.8	8.6	6.9	5.1	91.0
St. Clair	7.6	20.2	4.4	5.3	16.2	15.0	10.5	8.5	7.2	5.1	94.8
St. Joseph	7.8	21.0	4.0	4.8	15.8	14.6	10.1	8.8	7.3	5.8	95.7
Sanilac	7.4	20.9	3.8	4.5	15.0	13.4	10.0	9.5	9.0	6.6	96.2
Schoolcraft	6.1	19.6	3.1	3.5	14.0	13.7	10.4	11.2	10.5	8.0	92.3
Shiawassee	7.4	21.2	4.7	5.0	16.0	15.4	11.1	8.1	6.6	4.6	95.2
Tuscola	7.1	21.4	4.3	4.8	15.6	15.2	11.1	8.2	7.0	5.0	98.6
Van Buren	7.7	21.4	4.0	4.5	15.3	15.4	10.3	8.8	7.1	5.5	95.5
Washtenaw	6.8	14.8	9.0	10.6	19.9	16.1	9.3	6.1	4.4	3.1	97.8
Wayne	8.1	18.9	4.5	5.8	17.1	14.7	9.5	8.7	7.6	4.9	90.1
Wexford	7.8	20.9	3.5	4.8	15.8	14.4	9.8	9.2	8.1	5.7	94.8

COUNTIES and STATE -

Educational Attainment
Social Security Beneficiaries *RATE per 1000 resident population*
SSIP Recipients

	Educational attainment, 1990				Social Security Program beneficiaries, December 1990		
		Percent—					
	Persons 25 years and over	High school graduate or higher	Bachelor's degree or higher	1989 Median family income (Dollars)	Number	Rate	Supplemental Security Income Program recipients, December 1991
MICHIGAN	5 842 642	76.8	17.4	36 652	1 490 300	160.3	151 271
Alcona	7 368	68.6	9.0	20 925	3 395	334.6	227
Alger	6 009	73.0	11.5	25 750	2 145	239.1	198
Allegan	55 740	74.4	12.0	34 498	12 605	139.3	1 032
Alpena	20 165	73.6	11.4	28 441	7 425	242.6	688
Antrim	12 185	76.4	13.7	26 307	4 350	239.2	363
Arenac	9 782	65.4	7.1	23 300	3 905	261.5	364
Baraga	5 166	70.5	8.3	23 663	1 980	248.9	235
Barry	31 892	78.3	10.8	34 126	6 700	133.8	465
Bay	71 684	74.0	11.0	34 034	19 850	177.7	1 709
Benzie	8 333	76.6	15.1	24 795	2 730	223.8	231
Berrien	102 485	74.7	16.7	32 219	31 255	193.7	3 778
Branch	26 446	73.8	10.3	29 389	7 280	175.4	570
Calhoun	86 623	76.8	13.8	32 576	24 610	181.0	2 933
Cass	31 841	72.3	9.2	31 686	7 070	142.9	736
Charlevoix	13 963	79.7	16.0	29 608	4 400	205.0	289
Cheboygan	14 207	73.5	10.0	24 396	4 795	224.1	370
Chippewa	21 848	73.6	10.8	25 384	6 010	173.7	666
Clare	16 401	66.9	6.8	20 674	6 900	276.5	736
Clinton	35 745	83.7	14.6	40 234	6 255	108.1	300
Crawford	8 057	73.2	12.6	24 688	2 265	184.7	188
Delta	24 476	76.9	11.3	28 260	7 940	210.2	728
Dickinson	17 972	78.5	13.0	30 228	6 185	230.5	369
Eaton	58 205	85.5	18.5	40 690	9 765	105.1	604
Emmet	16 448	81.5	19.2	30 657	5 105	203.9	362
Genesee	265 430	76.8	12.8	36 760	66 280	154.0	8 024
Gladwin	14 388	64.8	6.5	22 563	5 515	251.9	433
Gogebic	12 497	76.3	11.4	23 350	5 655	313.3	473
Grand Traverse	41 094	84.9	22.1	33 373	11 890	185.0	1 082
Gratiot	23 966	77.1	10.9	29 328	7 090	181.9	822
Hillsdale	26 657	75.2	11.3	30 120	7 370	169.7	706
Houghton	20 646	73.9	18.0	23 800	7 900	222.9	757
Huron	22 798	68.0	8.9	26 357	8 665	247.9	648
Ingham	158 966	83.9	29.2	37 361	36 990	131.2	4 096
Ionia	33 466	77.2	8.9	33 577	7 665	134.4	644
Iosco	19 194	76.3	10.4	23 364	6 775	224.3	367
Iron	9 594	73.0	10.0	21 235	4 420	335.5	271
Isabella	26 492	79.7	21.5	28 753	6 410	117.3	1 038
Jackson	97 049	77.7	12.9	33 967	24 915	166.4	2 477
Kalamazoo	134 684	83.4	27.1	38 397	31 285	140.0	3 314
Kalkaska	8 485	69.6	7.1	24 638	2 275	168.6	251
Kent	305 356	80.3	20.7	37 783	71 725	143.3	7 277
Keweenaw	1 287	64.3	11.1	18 459	660	388.0	42
Lake	5 931	61.3	6.6	18 333	2 700	314.6	340
Lapeer	45 437	77.6	9.3	39 036	8 305	111.1	698
Leelanau	11 127	85.1	24.1	32 323	2 830	171.2	124
Lenawee	56 323	76.3	12.9	35 210	15 870	173.5	1 384
Livingston	72 343	85.6	19.6	49 910	10 890	94.2	460

	Educational attainment, 1990				Social Security Program beneficiaries, December 1990		
		Percent—					
	Persons 25 years and over	High school graduate or higher	Bachelor's degree or higher	Median family income (Dollars)	Number	Rate	Supplemental Security Income Program recipients, December 1991
Luce	3 811	69.6	9.6	23 343	1 565	271.6	231
Mackinac	7 156	71.4	10.4	23 097	2 525	236.6	216
Macomb	472 323	76.9	13.5	44 586	115 165	160.5	5 458
Manistee	14 619	73.3	10.5	25 115	5 430	255.3	382
Marquette	42 386	81.8	20.3	30 249	10 585	149.3	863
Mason	16 796	76.1	11.8	26 271	5 295	207.3	422
Mecosta	19 005	77.7	17.9	26 719	5 815	155.9	553
Menominee	16 514	74.3	9.3	26 141	5 420	217.5	385
Midland	47 213	83.2	27.4	40 028	10 155	134.2	776
Missaukee	7 628	69.4	8.0	23 910	2 280	187.7	205
Monroe	82 291	74.1	10.5	40 532	18 830	140.9	1 477
Montcalm	32 959	73.4	8.2	27 040	9 835	185.4	1 006
Montmorency	6 279	67.6	8.7	21 090	3 325	372.1	211
Muskegon	99 720	74.2	11.1	30 152	29 940	188.3	3 661
Newaygo	23 989	71.1	10.5	26 601	6 825	178.7	735
Oakland	717 210	84.6	30.2	50 980	149 325	137.8	9 686
Oceana	14 069	73.3	10.4	25 786	4 665	207.8	406
Ogemaw	12 379	63.0	7.2	21 110	4 645	248.6	416
Ontonagon	6 198	74.6	9.2	26 663	2 285	258.1	224
Osceola	12 491	72.1	8.7	24 716	4 670	231.8	495
Oscoda	5 433	66.6	7.9	21 044	1 815	231.4	142
Otsego	11 358	79.5	13.7	30 446	3 525	196.3	252
Ottawa	110 737	79.8	18.7	40 377	24 490	130.4	1 151
Presque Isle	9 285	65.7	8.7	25 199	3 730	271.4	294
Roscommon	14 435	69.4	7.9	20 870	7 355	371.9	375
Saginaw	131 154	74.8	13.0	33 391	36 025	170.0	4 614
St. Clair	91 241	74.8	10.7	35 678	23 615	162.2	1 969
St. Joseph	36 757	73.8	10.9	32 134	10 010	169.9	812
Sanilac	25 404	72.1	8.4	26 984	8 240	206.4	581
Schoolcraft	5 643	71.6	8.9	24 066	2 155	259.6	207
Shiawassee	43 097	78.7	10.3	34 557	10 600	151.9	913
Tuscola	34 607	73.0	8.1	31 781	9 330	168.1	854
Van Buren	43 758	71.8	12.1	29 265	12 495	178.3	1 550
Washtenaw	167 214	87.2	41.9	47 308	28 090	99.3	2 621
Wayne	1 324 635	70.0	13.7	34 099	354 935	168.1	52 505
Wexford	16 597	74.6	12.6	27 328	5 270	199.9	580

COUNTIES and STATE -

Housing Owner Occupied
Median Value
Housing Renter Occupied
Median Gross Rent
Veterans - War

	Housing, 1990						Veterans, 1990	
	Occupied units							
	Owner occupied				Renter occupied			
			Median value					
	Number	Percent of total occupied	Value (Dollars)	Percent change, 1980–1990	Number	Median gross rent[2]	Number	Percent Vietnam era
MICHIGAN	2 427 643	71.0	60 600	55.4	991 688	423	1 005 699	28.9
Alcona	3 683	86.4	48 200	48.3	578	326	1 926	24.6
Alger	2 671	80.0	39 200	38.5	666	296	1 333	26.6
Allegan	25 592	80.7	59 300	60.7	6 117	377	8 923	33.2
Alpena	9 251	78.1	41 600	29.2	2 587	307	4 095	26.0
Antrim	5 648	80.9	53 000	51.4	1 332	342	2 513	23.2
Arenac	4 595	81.4	41 800	29.4	1 047	319	1 884	24.3
Baraga	2 265	73.9	37 900	30.2	800	235	1 044	29.3
Barry	14 929	84.0	54 700	65.3	2 834	366	6 121	32.6
Bay	32 424	76.9	44 100	23.2	9 764	344	12 929	29.3
Benzie	3 906	81.9	50 200	56.4	866	337	1 800	22.8
Berrien	42 452	69.6	52 800	55.8	18 573	368	18 252	28.6
Branch	11 351	76.1	40 800	35.1	3 570	346	4 505	29.3
Calhoun	36 806	71.0	42 700	42.3	15 006	374	16 084	30.0
Cass	14 399	78.9	48 600	45.9	3 840	364	6 059	28.7
Charlevoix	6 354	77.1	53 600	55.8	1 889	353	2 716	29.4
Cheboygan	6 522	79.5	47 400	45.4	1 679	315	3 043	24.1
Chippewa	8 472	73.4	37 500	47.1	3 069	323	4 976	33.1
Clare	7 604	78.4	36 800	38.3	2 094	320	3 493	21.8
Clinton	16 785	83.0	68 000	56.3	3 427	393	5 875	31.8
Crawford	3 566	80.3	44 500	41.7	875	350	1 770	27.0
Delta	11 066	76.2	43 200	29.0	3 465	297	5 364	27.4
Dickinson	8 445	79.4	42 900	34.1	2 188	347	3 855	25.0
Eaton	24 814	72.9	68 200	49.2	9 213	436	10 415	34.5
Emmet	7 057	74.2	64 700	59.0	2 459	379	3 183	33.8
Genesee	113 585	70.4	50 500	42.3	47 711	401	47 337	30.1
Gladwin	6 816	81.6	42 700	42.8	1 541	307	2 852	20.0
Gogebic	5 822	78.2	23 300	30.9	1 627	257	3 037	19.5
Grand Traverse	17 922	74.8	66 700	47.2	6 043	446	7 692	35.1
Gratiot	10 407	76.2	38 800	40.1	3 252	333	3 825	31.6
Hillsdale	12 071	77.2	41 400	36.6	3 566	321	4 727	28.5
Houghton	9 155	69.5	28 300	30.4	4 017	281	4 318	23.8
Huron	10 532	79.4	44 500	42.6	2 736	297	3 580	24.7
Ingham	59 942	58.4	61 800	55.3	42 706	422	24 364	30.7
Ionia	14 251	77.3	47 700	53.4	4 196	341	5 963	33.6
Iosco	7 923	68.4	47 400	51.4	3 665	340	4 297	26.2
Iron	4 532	80.1	30 100	24.9	1 123	269	2 200	23.0
Isabella	11 431	65.0	53 200	41.9	6 160	393	4 349	28.7
Jackson	39 528	73.7	47 900	44.7	14 132	376	17 924	28.1
Kalamazoo	53 869	64.4	62 800	53.5	29 833	417	22 107	30.6
Kalkaska	3 974	80.5	44 500	36.9	960	354	1 761	25.1
Kent	126 627	69.7	68 200	75.3	55 113	431	47 755	28.8
Keweenaw	672	86.5	19 200	33.3	105	231	267	19.5
Lake	2 856	80.8	29 800	50.5	680	303	1 392	21.6
Lapeer	19 978	81.0	62 300	46.9	4 681	407	8 273	34.4
Leelanau	5 111	81.5	73 100	50.1	1 163	414	2 174	27.3
Lenawee	23 996	75.9	54 000	47.1	7 639	382	9 650	30.0
Livingston	32 871	84.5	97 300	56.4	6 016	521	13 273	34.7

	Housing, 1990—Con.						Veterans, 1990	
	Occupied units							
	Owner occupied				Renter occupied			
			Median value					
	Number	Percent of total occupied	Value (Dollars)	Percent change, 1980–1990	Number	Median gross rent[2]	Number	Percent Vietnam era
Luce	1 704	79.1	30 800	17.6	450	306	759	24.0
Mackinac	3 222	76.0	43 900	51.4	1 018	297	1 471	21.1
Macomb	204 609	77.2	76 800	50.6	60 382	493	82 413	29.1
Manistee	6 707	78.2	40 400	31.6	1 873	287	3 136	24.5
Marquette	16 332	64.2	44 800	18.5	9 103	333	9 314	32.5
Mason	7 576	75.9	43 300	44.8	2 408	304	3 321	24.3
Mecosta	8 564	69.9	49 100	52.5	3 696	339	3 664	26.2
Menominee	7 709	78.9	37 900	26.8	2 057	293	3 278	28.8
Midland	21 383	76.9	63 300	39.7	6 408	407	8 092	29.2
Missaukee	3 641	83.0	40 500	42.6	748	340	1 423	24.6
Monroe	36 178	77.8	67 200	46.1	10 330	423	15 237	32.2
Montcalm	14 746	79.4	42 600	52.7	3 817	340	5 904	27.0
Montmorency	2 935	81.5	41 700	42.3	665	329	1 495	19.9
Muskegon	43 011	74.4	46 300	65.4	14 787	362	18 844	29.8
Newaygo	11 330	82.2	44 300	54.4	2 446	348	4 628	28.9
Oakland	298 377	72.7	95 400	64.2	112 111	557	112 416	28.7
Oceana	6 480	80.3	43 300	52.5	1 591	333	2 745	26.6
Ogemaw	5 850	81.4	39 500	40.6	1 340	327	2 645	21.8
Ontonagon	2 949	81.0	28 100	33.8	692	248	1 475	27.0
Osceola	5 870	79.9	37 500	41.5	1 477	300	2 490	25.7
Oscoda	2 588	81.9	37 400	34.5	572	317	1 209	15.6
Otsego	5 157	79.1	56 000	43.6	1 365	365	2 340	25.0
Ottawa	50 576	80.7	74 600	65.4	12 088	454	16 905	32.3
Presque Isle	4 498	83.7	44 000	38.8	878	276	1 913	23.3
Roscommon	6 978	81.9	44 500	52.4	1 538	326	3 549	18.1
Saginaw	55 304	70.7	48 100	32.9	22 952	389	21 772	28.0
St. Clair	40 015	75.7	59 400	57.1	12 867	409	16 468	29.7
St. Joseph	16 143	74.8	44 800	38.3	5 436	345	6 604	27.0
Sanilac	11 643	79.4	42 400	36.8	3 015	337	4 061	23.8
Schoolcraft	2 537	77.0	32 300	30.2	757	273	1 138	23.6
Shiawassee	19 321	77.7	47 200	34.5	5 543	363	7 773	32.3
Tuscola	15 817	81.2	46 000	29.6	3 652	358	5 909	31.6
Van Buren	19 482	76.7	48 000	44.1	5 920	343	7 915	31.3
Washtenaw	57 787	55.3	96 000	55.8	46 741	536	23 479	33.2
Wayne	498 682	63.9	48 500	48.8	281 853	406	221 434	27.3
Wexford	7 414	74.7	41 200	40.6	2 509	356	3 205	27.5

TELEVISION STATIONS IN MICHIGAN

Station	Channel	Network	Phone
ALPENA			
WBKB-TV	Ch.11	CBS	(517) 356-3434
WCML-TV*	Ch. 6		(517) 774-3105
ANN ARBOR			
WBSX-TV	Ch. 31	HSN	(313) 973-7900
BAD AXE			
WUCX-TV*	Ch. 35		(517) 686-9362
BATTLE CREEK			
WUHQ-TV	Ch. 41	ABC	(616) 968-9341
BAY CITY			
WNEM-TV	Ch.5	NBC	
CADILLAC			
WCMV*	Ch. 27		(517) 774-3105
WGKI	Ch. 33		(616) 775-9813
WPBN-TV			
WWTV	Ch. 9	CBS	(616) 775-3478
CHEBOYGAN			
WTOM-TV	Ch. 4	NBC	(616) 947-7770
DETROIT			
CBET (Windsor, ON)	Ch. 9		(519) 255-3411
WDIV	Ch. 4	NBC	(313) 222-0444
WGPR-TV	Ch. 62	CBS	(313) 259-8862
WJBK-TV	Ch. 2	FOX	(810) 557-2000
WKBD	Ch. 50	UPN	(810) 350-5050
WTVS*	Ch. 56	PBS	(313) 873-7200
WXON	Ch. 20		(810) 355-2900
WXYZ-TV	Ch. 7	ABC	(810) 827-7777

Station	Channel	Network	Phone
EAST LANSING			
WKAR-TV*	Ch. 23	PBS	(517) 355-2300
ESCANABA			
WJMN-TV	Ch. 3		(414) 437-5411
FLINT			
WEYI-TV (Saginaw)	Ch. 25	CBS	(517) 755-0525
WFUM*	Ch. 28	PBS	(810) 762-3028
WJRT-TV	Ch. 12	ABC	(810) 233-3130
WNEM-TV (Bay City)	Ch. 5	NBC	(517) 755-8191
WSMH	Ch. 66	FOX	(810) 767-8866
GRAND RAPIDS			
WGVU-TV*	Ch. 35		(616) 771-6666
WOTV	Ch. 8	NBC	(616) 456-8888
WXMI	Ch. 17	FOX	(616) 364-8722
WZZM-TV	Ch. 13	CBS	(616) 784-4200
IRON MOUNTAIN			
WIIM-TV	Ch. 8		(814) 944-8571
KALAMAZOO			
WGVK*	Ch. 52		(616) 771-6666
WLLA	Ch. 64		(616) 345-6421
WWMT	Ch. 3	CBS	(616) 388-3333
LANSING			
WILX-TV	Ch. 10	NBC	
WLAJ-TV	Ch. 53	ABC	(517) 394-5300
WLNS-TV	Ch. 6	CBS	(517) 372-8282
WSYM-TV	Ch. 47	FOX	(517) 484-7747
MANISTEE			
WCMW*	Ch. 21		(517) 774-3105

Station	Channel	Network	Phone
MARQUETTE			
WJMY	Ch. 19		(413) 337-8900
WLUC-TV	Ch. 6		(906) 475-4161
WNMU-TV*	Ch. 13	PBS	(906) 227-1300
MOUNT CLEMENS			
WADL	Ch. 38		(810) 790-3838
MOUNT PLEASANT			
WCMU-TV	Ch. 14	PBS	(517) 774-3105
MUSKEGON			
WTLJ	Ch. 54		(616) 895-4154
ONONDAGA			
WILX-TV	Ch. 10		(517) 783-2621
SAGINAW			
WAQP	Ch. 49		(517) 754-1038
WEYI-TV	Ch. 25	CBS	
WNEM	Ch. 5	NBC	
SAULT STE. MARIE			
WGTQ	Ch. 8	ABC	
WWUP-TV	Ch. 10	CBS	(906) 632-6877
TRAVERSE CITY			
WGTU	Ch. 29	ABC	(616) 946-2900
WPBN-TV	Ch. 7	NBC	(616) 947-7770
WWTV	Ch. 9	CBS	
UNIVERSITY CENTER			
WUCM-TV*	Ch. 19	PBS	(517) 686-9362

Source: Broadcasting & Cable Market Place 1992

NEWSPAPERS IN MICHIGAN

Source: *1991 Michigan Newspaper Directory*, Michigan Press Association

W, Weekly; D, Daily; D*, Daily and Sunday

Newspaper	Location	Edition
ALCONA COUNTY		
Alcona County Review	Harrisville	W
Alcona County Herald	Lincoln	W
ALGER COUNTY		
The Munising News	Munising	W
Porcupine Press	Trenary	W
ALLEGAN COUNTY		
Allegan County News & Gazette	Allegan	W
Fennville Herald	Fennville	W
The Union Enterprise	Plainwell	W
Twin Cities News	Plainwell	W
The Commercial Record	Saugatuck	W
Penasee/Globe	Wayland	W
ALPENA COUNTY		
Alpena News	Alpena	D
ANTRIM COUNTY		
Antrim County News	Bellaire	W
The Torch	Central Lake	W
Town Meeting	Elk Rapids	W
ARENAC COUNTY		
Arenac County Independent	Standish	W
BARAGA COUNTY		
L'Anse Sentinel	L'Anse	W
BARRY COUNTY		
Freeport News	Freeport	W
Hastings Banner	Hastings	W
Middleville Sun & Caledonia News	Middleville	W
Maple Valley News	Nashville	W
BAY COUNTY		
Bay City Times	Bay City	D*
Bay City Democrat & Bay County Legal News	Bay City	W
The Valley Farmer	Bay City	W
Pinconning Journal	Pinconning	W
BENZIE COUNTY		
Benzie County Record-Patriot	Frankfort	W
BERRIEN COUNTY		
The Journal Era	Berrien Springs	W
Berrien County Record	Buchanan	W
Harbor Country News	New Buffalo	W
New Buffalo Times	New Buffalo	W
Niles Daily Star	Niles	D
The Herald-Palladium	St. Joseph/Benton Harbor	D*
The Gazette	Three Oaks	W
BRANCH COUNTY		
The Bronson Journal	Bronson	W
Daily Reporter	Coldwater	D
The Register-Tribune	Union City	W
CALHOUN COUNTY		
Albion Recorder	Albion	D
Battle Creek Enquirer	Battle Creek	D*
Homer Index	Homer	W
Marshall Chronicle	Marshall	D
CASS COUNTY		
Cassopolis Vigilant	Cassopolis	W
Dowagiac Daily News	Dowagiac	D
Edwardsburg Argus	Edwardsburg	W
Marcellus News	Marcellus	W
CHARLEVOIX COUNTY		
Charlevoix County Press	Boyne City	W
Charlevoix Courier	Charlevoix	W
CHEBOYGAN COUNTY		
Cheboygan Daily Tribune	Cheboygan	D
Straitsland Resorter	Indian River	W
CHIPPEWA COUNTY		
Evening News	Sault Ste. Marie	D
CLARE COUNTY		
Clare Sentinel	Clare	W
The Review	Clare	W
Clare County Cleaver	Harrison	W
CLINTON COUNTY		
DeWitt/Bath Review	Grand Ledge	W
Clinton County News	St. Johns	W
CRAWFORD COUNTY		
Crawford County Avalanche	Grayling	W
DELTA COUNTY		
Daily Press	Escanaba	D
Delta Reporter	Gladstone	W
DICKINSON COUNTY		
The Daily News	Iron Mountain	D
Norway Current	Norway	W
EATON COUNTY		
Grand Ledge Independent	Grand Ledge	W
Delta-Waverly News Herald	Lansing	W
Sunfield Sentinel	Sunfield	W
EMMET COUNTY		
Harbor Light	Harbor Springs	W
Petoskey News-Review	Petoskey	D
GENESEE COUNTY		
Clio Messenger	Clio	Semi-W
Davison Flagstaff	Davison	Semi-W
Davison Index	Davison	W
The Independent	Fenton	Semi-W
Tri-County News	Fenton	Semi-W
Flint-Genesee County Legal News	Flint	W
Flint Journal	Flint	D*
The Suburban News	Flint/Burton	Semi-W
The West Valley News	Flint Township	Semi-W
Flushing Observer	Flushing	Semi-W
Grand Blanc News	Grand Blanc	Semi-W
Genesee County Herald	Mt. Morris	W
GLADWIN COUNTY		
Gladwin County Record & Beaverton Clarion	Gladwin	W
GOGEBIC COUNTY		
The Daily Globe	Ironwood	D
Wakefield News	Wakefield	W
GRAND TRAVERSE COUNTY		
Traverse City Record-Eagle	Traverse City	D*
GRATIOT COUNTY		
Gratiot County Herald	Ithaca	W
HILLSDALE COUNTY		
Hillsdale Daily News	Hillsdale	D
Jonesville Independent	Jonesville	W
HOUGHTON COUNTY		
Daily Mining Gazette	Houghton	D

Newspaper	Location	Edition
HURON COUNTY		
Huron Daily Tribune	Bad Axe	D
Harbor Beach Times	Harbor Beach	W
The Progress-Advance	Pigeon	W
Sebewaing Blade-Crescent	Sebewaing	W
INGHAM COUNTY		
Towne Courier	East Lansing	W
Lansing State Journal	Lansing	D*
Leslie Local Independent	Leslie	W
Ingham County News	Mason	W
The Town Crier	Stockbridge	W
The Enterprise	Williamston	W
IONIA COUNTY		
Clarksville Record	Freeport	W
Freeport News	Freeport	W
Ionia Sentinel-Standard	Ionia	D
Portland Review & Observer	Portland	W
IOSCO COUNTY		
Iosco County News Herald	East Tawas	W
Oscoda Press	Oscoda	W
IRON COUNTY		
The Diamond Drill	Crystal Falls	W
Iron River Reporter	Iron River	W
ISABELLA COUNTY		
Morning Sun	Mt. Pleasant	D
Shepherd Argus	Shepherd	W
JACKSON COUNTY		
The Exponent	Brooklyn	W
The Blazer News	Jackson	W
Jackson Citizen Patriot	Jackson	D
Jackson County Legal News	Jackson	W
The Parma News	Parma	W
Springport Signal	Springport	W
KALAMAZOO COUNTY		
Climax Crescent	Climax	W
Kalamazoo Gazette	Kalamazoo	D*
The Commercial-Express	Vicksburg	W
KALKASKA COUNTY		
Leader and Kalkaskian	Kalkaska	W
KENT COUNTY		
South Advance	Byron Center/ Caledonia	W
Advance	E. Grand Rapids	W
Cadence	Grand Rapids	W
Grand Rapids Press	Grand Rapids	D*
Northfield Advance	Grand Rapids	W
Kentwood Advance	Kentwood	W
Lowell Ledger	Lowell	W
Rockford/Cedar Springs Advance	Rockford	W
Rockford Squire	Rockford	W
Sparta/Kent City Advance	Sparta	W
Walker-Westside Advance	Walker	W
Wyoming Advance	Wyoming	W
KEWEENAW COUNTY		
Covered by newspapers in Houghton County		
LAKE COUNTY		
Lake County Star	Baldwin	W
LAPEER COUNTY		
The Tri-City Times	Imlay City	W
The County Press	Lapeer	W
LEELANAU COUNTY		
The Leelanau Enterprise & Tribune	Leland	W
LENAWEE COUNTY		
Daily Telegram	Adrian	D*
Blissfield Advance	Blissfield	W
Clinton Local	Clinton	W
Hudson Post-Gazette	Hudson	W
Morenci Observer	Morenci	W
Tecumseh Herald	Tecumseh	W
LIVINGSTON COUNTY		
Brighton Argus	Brighton	W
Livingston County Press	Howell	W
LUCE COUNTY		
Newberry News	Newberry	W
MACKINAC COUNTY		
St. Ignace News	St. Ignace	W
MACOMB COUNTY		
Armada Times	Armada	W
The Macomb Daily	Mt. Clemens	D*
Mt. Clemens, Clinton Twp., Fraser, Macomb Twp., Harrison Twp. Advisor	Mt. Clemens	W
Anchor Bay Beacon	New Baltimore	W
The Bay Voice	New Baltimore	W
Richmond Review	Richmond	W
The Romeo Observer	Romeo	W
Romeo-Washington-Bruce Twp. Advisor	Utica	W
St. Clair Shores-Roseville-East Detroit Advisor	Utica	W
Sterling Heights-Utica-Shelby Township Source	Utica	W
Warren Advisor	Utica	W
Warren Weekly	Utica	W
MANISTEE COUNTY		
Manistee County Pioneer Press	Bear Lake	W
Manistee News-Advocate	Manistee	D
MARQUETTE COUNTY		
The Mining Journal	Marquette	D*
MASON COUNTY		
Daily News	Ludington	D
MECOSTA COUNTY		
The Pioneer	Big Rapids	D
The Pioneer East	Mecosta	W
MENOMINEE COUNTY		
Menominee Herald-Leader	Menominee	D
Menominee County Journal	Stephenson	W
MIDLAND COUNTY		
Midland Daily News	Midland	D*
MISSAUKEE COUNTY		
The Waterfront	Lake City	W
MONROE COUNTY		
Monroe Evening News	Monroe	D*
The Independent	Dundee	W
The Guardian	Monroe	W
MONTCALM COUNTY		
Carson City Gazette	Carson City	W
The Daily News	Greenville	D
Lakeview Enterprise	Lakeview	W
MONTMORENCY COUNTY		
Montmorency County Tribune	Atlanta	W
MUSKEGON COUNTY		
The Muskegon Chronicle	Muskegon	D*
The Examiner	Muskegon	W
White Lake Beacon	Whitehall	W

Newspaper	Location	Edition
NEWAYGO COUNTY		
Times-Indicator	Fremont	W
OAKLAND COUNTY		
The Auburn Argus	Auburn Hills	W
Birmingham Eccentric	Birmingham	Semi-W
Clarkston News	Clarkston	W
Reminder	Clarkston	W
Farmington Observer	Farmington	Semi-W
Legal Advertiser — Oakland County	Ferndale	W
Herald Advertiser	Holly	W
The Lake Orion Review	Lake Orion	W
Milford Times	Milford	W
Milford-Highland Spinal Column Newsweekly	Milford	W
Novi-Commerce Spinal Column Newsweekly	Novi	W
Novi News	Novi	W
The Oxford Leader	Oxford	W
Pontiac-Oakland County Legal News	Pontiac	W
The Oakland Press	Pontiac	D*
Daily Tribune	Royal Oak	D*
The Rochester Clarion	Rochester	W
Rochester Eccentric	Rochester	Semi-W
South Lyon Herald	South Lyon	W
Southfield Eccentric	Southfield	Semi-W
Troy Eccentric	Troy	Semi-W
Union Lake Spinal Column Newsweekly	Union Lake	W
West Bloomfield Eccentric	W. Bloomfield	Semi-W
West Bloomfield Spinal Column Newsweekly	W. Bloomfield	W
OCEANA COUNTY		
Oceana's Herald Journal	Hart	W
OGEMAW COUNTY		
Ogemaw County Herald	West Branch	W
ONTONAGON COUNTY		
Ontonagon Herald	Ontonagon	W
OSCEOLA COUNTY		
Evart Review	Evart	W
Marion Press	Marion	W
The Herald-News	Reed City	W
OSCODA COUNTY		
Oscoda County Herald	Mio	W
OTSEGO COUNTY		
Gaylord Herald Times	Gaylord	W
OTTAWA COUNTY		
Grand Haven Tribune	Grand Haven	D
Holland Sentinel	Holland	D*
Grand Valley Advance	Jenison	W
Ottawa Advance	Jenison	W
Zeeland Record	Zeeland	W
PRESQUE ISLE COUNTY		
Onaway Outlook	Onaway	W
Presque Isle County Advance	Rogers City	W
ROSCOMMON COUNTY		
Houghton Lake Resorter	Houghton Lake	W
Roscommon Herald-News	Roscommon	W
SAGINAW COUNTY		
Bridgeport-Birch Run Weekly News	Bridgeport	W
Tri-County Citizen	Chesaning	W
Frankenmuth News	Frankenmuth	W
Saginaw News	Saginaw	D*
The Saginaw Press	Saginaw	W
The Township Times	Saginaw	W
ST. CLAIR COUNTY		
Courier-Journal/St. Clair Independent Press	Algonac	W
Times Herald	Port Huron	D*
Yale Expositor	Yale	W
ST. JOSEPH COUNTY		
The Express	Colon	W
Sturgis Journal	Sturgis	D
Commercial News	Three Rivers	D
SANILAC COUNTY		
Brown City Banner	Brown City	W
Sanilac County Jeffersonian	Croswell	W
Deckerville Recorder	Deckerville	W
Marlette Leader	Marlette	W
Official Michigan	Marlette	W
Minden City Herald	Minden City	W
Sanilac County News	Sandusky	W
SCHOOLCRAFT COUNTY		
Manistique Pioneer-Tribune	Manistique	W
SHIAWASSEE COUNTY		
Durand Express	Durand	W
The Argus-Press	Owosso	D
Shiawassee County Journal	Perry	W
Shiawassee County Independent	Owosso	W
TUSCOLA COUNTY		
Tuscola County Advertiser	Caro	W
Cass City Chronicle	Cass City	W
Mayville Monitor	Mayville	W
Millington Herald & Lakeville Aerial	Millington	W
Vassar Pioneer Times	Vassar	W
VAN BUREN COUNTY		
Decatur Republican	Decatur	W
The Courier-Leader	Paw Paw	W
South Haven Daily Tribune	South Haven	D
WASHTENAW COUNTY		
Ann Arbor News	Ann Arbor	D*
Chelsea Standard	Chelsea	W
Dexter Leader	Dexter	W
Manchester Enterprise	Manchester	W
Milan Area Leader	Milan	W
Ypsilanti Press	Ypsilanti	D*
WAYNE COUNTY		
Allen Park News-Herald	Allen Park	Semi-W
Dearborn Heights Press & Guide	Dearborn	Semi-W
Dearborn Press & Guide	Dearborn	Semi-W
Detroit Free Press	Detroit	D*
Detroit Legal News	Detroit	D
Detroit News	Detroit	D*
Legal Advertiser-Wayne County	Detroit	W
Metro Times	Detroit	W
The Ile Camera	Grosse Ile	W
Grosse Pointe News	Grosse Pte. Farms	W
The Citizen	Hamtramck	W
Canton Observer	Livonia	Semi-W
Garden City Observer	Livonia	Semi-W
Livonia Observer	Livonia	Semi-W
Redford Observer	Livonia	Semi-W
Westland Observer	Livonia	Semi-W
Northville Record	Northville	W
The Community Crier	Plymouth	W
Plymouth Observer	Plymouth	Semi-W
Belleville Enterprise	Wayne	Semi-W
Canton Eagle	Wayne	Semi-W
Inkster Ledger-Star	Wayne	Semi-W
Romulus News-Herald	Southgate	Semi-W
Romulus Roman	Wayne	Semi-W
Wayne Eagle	Wayne	Semi-W
Westland Eagle	Wayne	Semi-W
Ecorse News-Herald	Wyandotte	Semi-W
Lincoln Park News-Herald	Wyandotte	Semi-W
Melvindale News-Herald	Wyandotte	Semi-W
Riverview News-Herald	Wyandotte	Semi-W
Southgate News-Herald	Wyandotte	Semi-W
Taylor News-Herald	Wyandotte	Semi-W
Trenton News-Herald	Wyandotte	Semi-W
Woodhaven News-Herald	Wyandotte	Semi-W
Wyandotte News-Herald	Wyandotte	Semi-W
Brownstown News-Herald	Wyandotte	Semi-W
Huron Valley News-Herald	Flat Rock	Semi-W
WEXFORD COUNTY		
Cadillac News	Cadillac	D

CRIME IN MICHIGAN – Uniform Crime Report

Source – MI Dept of State Police

NOTE – 'Index Crimes' are those which indicate the state's crime experience and include murder, rape, robbery, aggravated assault, burglary, larceny, motor vehicle theft and arson. 'Non-Index Crimes' are of a less violent type, such as negligent manslaughter, non-aggravated assaults, forgery, fraud, vandalism, etc.

Statistics indicate that total crime in 1993 is down by 1.9% from last year. Violent crimes of murder and rape decreased; however, robbery and aggravated assault showed an increase over 1992 figures. The net overall increase for violent crime is 3.1%. Property crime of burglary, larceny, and motor vehicle theft decreased by 4.6% over last year. Motor vehicle theft, down 2.4% when compared to last year, is the only index crime that has shown a decrease every year for the past nine years.

Total arrests were down 3.3% in 1993. Juveniles (16 & under) accounted for 10.2% of all those arrested. – *State Police Director Michael D. Robinbson*

FFENSES	1993	1992	1991	1990	1984
urder	922	939	1003	959	865
ape	7335	7451	7248	7094	5687
obbery	22261	20731	22574	21484	27694
ggravated Assault	43659	42792	43378	42691	30806
urglary	90878	96822	109368	104292	147948
arceny	279515	293018	317248	303145	295114
otor Vehicle Theft	56670	58037	62636	65220	78006
rson	4257	4514	4739	4459	9460
otal Index Crime	505495	524304	568194	549344	595580

RRESTS	1993	1992	1991	1990	1984
urder	1709	1850	1973	1942	1024
ape	2015	2338	2278	2256	2373
obbery	4893	4937	5248	5611	5386
ggravated Assault	14678	14283	13931	14007	9641
urglary	9670	10148	11413	11793	14764
arceny	37263	42785	47324	45349	4115
otor Vehicle Theft	3335	3784	4067	4187	[illegible]
rson	684	747	603	712	
otal Index Crime	74247	80872	86837	85857	[illegible]

RENDS (+-%)	1993	1992	1991	1990
urder	-1.8	-6.4	4.6	- 2.3
ape	-1.6	2.8	2.2	9.7
obbery	7.4	-8.2	5.1	[illegible]
ggravated Assault	2.0	-1.4	1.6	16
urglary	-6.1	-11.4	4.9	[illegible]
arceny	-4.6	-7.6	4.7	
otor Vehicle Theft	-2.4	-7.3	- 4.0	
rson	-5.7	-4.7	6.3	
otal Index Crime	-3.6	-7.7	3.4	

TOTAL INDEXED CRIME, BY COUNTY

County	1992 / 1993
ALCONA	249 / 312
ALGER	18[illegible] / 132
ALLEGAN	2,695 / 2,895
ALPENA	1,152 / 1,1[illegible]8
ANTRIM	454 / 310
ARGENAC	531 / 439
BARAGA	183 / 170
BARRY	1,430 / 1,276
BAY	4,281 / 4,155
BENZIE	439 / 455
BERRIEN	11,174 / 10,816
BRANCH	1,557 / 1,435
CALHOUN	8,729 / 8,180
CASS	1,842 / 1,544
CHARLEVOIX	494 / 566
CHEYBOYGAN	739 / 591
CHIPPEWA	1,315 / 1,175
CLARE	1,227 / 625
CLINTON	1,395 / 1,315
CRAWFORD	517 / 472
DELTA	1,183 / 1,151
DICKINSON	625 / 737
EATON	4,160 / 3,743
EMMET	1,270 / 1,175
GENESEE	32,573 / 31,160
GLADWIN	650 / 747
GAGEBIC	557 / 404
GRAND TRAVERSE	2,157 / 2,134
GRATIOT	1,211 / 1,176
HILLSDALE	1,104 / 1,047
HOUGHTON	701 / 569
[illegible]URON	873 / 854
[illegible]GHAM	16,894 / 16,582
[illegible]IA	1,501 / 1,428
[illegible]CO	1,035 / 956
IRON	431 / 366
ISABELLA	2,097 / 2,129
JACKSON	6,779 / 495
KALAMAZOO	14,894 / 14,023
KALASKA	563 / 508
[illegible]NT	30,106 / 28,638
KEW[illegible]NAW	64 / 40
LAKE	441 / 376
LAPEER	1,614 / 1,572
LEELANAU	299 / 284
LENAWEE	2,805 / 2,816
LIVINGSTON	3,605 / 3,40[illegible]
LUCE	153 / 217
MACKINAC	669 / 696
MACOMB	34,000 / 31,322
MANISTEE	541 / 584
MARQUETTE	2,106 / 1,940
MASON	1,193 / 1,305
MESCOTA	1,791 / 1,655
MENOMINEE	830 / 887
MIDLAND	2,009 / 2,020
MISSAUKEE	223 / 304
MONROE	5,912 / 5,434
MONTCALM	1,998 / 1,775
MONTMORENCY	327 / 421
MUSKEGON	11,254 / 11,137
NEWAYGO	1,263 / 1,166
OAKLAND	51,656 / 48,339
OCEANA	619 / 573
OGEMAW	753 / 953
ONTONAGON	155 / 168
OSCEOLA	538 / 615
OSCODA	411 / 447
OTSEGO	624 / 579
OTTAWA	6,931 / 6,363

	1992 / 1993
PRESQUE ISLE	260 / 254
ROSCOMMON	1,216 / 918
SAGINAW	14,806 / 14,480
ST. CLAIR	5,679 / 5,572
ST. JOSEPH	1,977 / 2,151

	1992 / 1993
SANILAC	761 / 1,054
SCHOOLCRAFT	244 / 197
SHIWAWASSEE	1,774 / 1,759
TUSCOLA	1,034 / 837
VAN BUREN	3,689 / 3,653
WASHTENAW	16,995 / 15,758
WAYNE	177,283 / 175,932
WEXFORD	1,245 / 1,241

MURDER OFFENSES

	1993	1992	1988	TRENDS (+ - %) 1 Yr 93/92	5 Yr 93/88
TOTAL	922	939	1,003	-1.8	-8.1
STATE CRIME RATE	10	10	11	0.0	-9.1

WEAPON

Firearm - Type Unknown	183
Handgun	379
Rifle	49
Shotgun	70
Knife/Cutting Instrument	90
Blunt Object	41
Personal Weapon	39
Explosives, Fire, Poison, Drugs, Strangulation, Hanging or Drowning	39
Other or Unknown	32

RELATIONSHIP OF VICTIM TO OFFENDER

Spouse (Includes Common Law)	36
Parent	10
Son/Daughter	20
Brother/Sister	5
Other Family	15
Acquaintance/Neighbor	289
Boyfriend/Girlfriend	25
Other - Known to Victim	36
Homosexual Relationship	0
Stranger	130
Unknown	356

RACE OF VICTIM

White	238
Black	676
American Indian/Alaskan Native	2
Asian/Pacific Islander	3
Unknown	3

AGE OF VICTIM

16 & Under
17 - 24
25 - 39
40 & Over
Unknown

SEX OF VICTIM

Male	694
Female	228

MICHIGAN RANK IN FARMING

Source– MI Dept of Agriculture

Commodity and unit	Rank	Production	Percent of U.S.	Leading state
		1,000		
Beans, black turtle, *cwt.*	1	1,040	77.7	**Michigan**
Beans, cranberry, *cwt*	1	575	95.4	**Michigan**
Beans, dry, all, *cwt.*	1	6,080	27.8	**Michigan**
Beans, navy, *cwt.*	1	4,060	77.1	**Michigan**
Blueberries, *pounds*	1	87,000	50.4	**Michigan**
Cherries, tart, *pounds*	1	270,000	83.5	**Michigan**
Cucumbers, for pickles, *tons*	1	128	21.8	**Michigan**
Geraniums, *pots*	1	18,290	18.0	**Michigan**
Lilies, Easter, *pots*	1	1,170	13.6	**Michigan**
Potatoes, summer, *cwt.*	1	3,500	17.1	**Michigan**
Apples, *pounds*	2	1,020,000	9.4	Washington
Bedding plants, *flats*	2	9,805	11.1	California
Gladioli, *spikes*	2	42,140	26.0	Florida
Hanging flowers, *baskets*	2	2,155	8.5	North Carolina
Asparagus, *cwt.*	3	285	12.9	California
Beans, snap, for processing, *tons*	3	70	10.7	Wisconsin
Lilies, other, *pots*	3	160	10.4	Pennsylvania
Celery, *cwt.*	3	1,134	6.2	California
Carrots, *cwt.*	3	2,016	6.3	California
Cherries, sweet, *tons*	3	30	17.8	Washington
Prunes & plums, *tons*	3	7	2.1	California
Tomatoes, for processing, *tons*	3	182	1.9	California
Beans, dark red kidney, *cwt.*	4	105	13.2	Minnesota
Beans, light red kidney, *cwt.*	4	115	10.1	California
Beans, small white, *cwt.*	4	30	21.3	Idaho
Cucumbers, fresh market, *cwt.*	4	918	9.2	Florida
Grapes, all, *tons*	4	55	1.0	California
Grapes, concord, *tons*	4	46	9.5	Washington
Hay, alfalfa, *tons*	4	5,040	6.2	California
Sugarbeets, *tons*	4	3,179	12.0	Minnesota
Beans, dry, other, *cwt.*	5	45	9.4	California
Cauliflower, *cwt.*	5	91	1.4	California
Floriculture, *dollars*	5	145,574	4.7	California
Maple syrup, *gallons*	5	75	7.4	Vermont
Mohair, *pounds*	5	74	0.5	Texas
Mushrooms, *pounds*	5	15,411	2.0	Pennsylvania
Peppers, bell, fresh market, *cwt.*	5	368	2.7	California
Strawberries, *cwt.*	5	114	0.8	California
Corn, sweet, freshmarket, *cwt.*	6	863	5.1	Florida
Milk sherbet, *gallons*	6	2,147	4.2	Iowa
Peaches, *pounds*	6	48,000	3.1	California
Pears, *tons*	6	6	0.6	Washington
Poinsettias, *pots*	6	3,085	5.5	California
Spearmint, *pounds*	6	90	3.3	Washington
Trout, *fish*	6	2,986	4.3	Idaho
Corn, for grain, *bushels*	7	236,500	3.7	Illinois
Corn, sweet, processing, *cwt.*	7	44	1.6	Wisconsin
Ice milk, *gallons*	7	12,168	3.7	California
Milk, *pounds*	7	5,435,000	3.6	Wisconsin
Milk cows, *head*[1]	7	339	3.5	Wisconsin
Corn, for silage, *tons*	8	3,960	4.8	Wisconsin
Potatoes, all, *cwt.*	8	15,280	3.6	Idaho
Beans, snap, fresh market, *cwt*	9	84	2.0	Florida
Butter, *pounds*	9	20,312	1.4	California
Cantaloupes, fresh market, *cwt.*	9	99	0.5	California
Hay, all, *tons*	9	5,790	3.9	South Dakota
Oats, *bushels*	9	7,150	3.5	North Dakota
Onions, *cwt.*	9	2,201	3.9	California
Potatoes, fall, *cwt.*	9	11,780	3.1	Idaho
Rye, *bushels*	9	420	4.1	South Dakota
Soybeans, *bushels*	9	54,720	3.0	Illinois
Honey, *pounds*	10	6,930	3.0	California
Mink, *pelts*	10	56	2.2	Utah
ettuce, *cwt.*	10	75	0.1	California
abbage, fresh market, *cwt.*	11	494	2.2	New York
ogs & pigs, *head*[1]	11	1,200	2.1	Iowa
e cream, *gallons*	11	30,961	3.6	California
ash receipts from marketings, *dollars*	19	3,749,135	2.2	California

Record highs and lows in Michigan agriculture, field crops and vegetables

Commodity and unit	Year estimates started	Record	Acreage		Yield		Production	
			Harvested	Year	Per acre	Year	Total	Year
			1,000				*1,000*	
Barley, *bushels*	1866	High	303	1932	68	1985	8,400	1918
		Low	16	1974	13.5	1933	546	1866
Beans, dry, *cwt.*	1909	High	690	1930	18.5	1991	8,585	1963
		Low	185	1988	3.2	1917	1,656	1916
Corn, for grain, *bushels*	1924	High	2,800	1981	115	1990	293,180	1982
		Low	577	1929	24.5	(1)	15,637	1929
Corn, for silage, *tons*	1924	High	498	1971	14.5	1990	5,565	1977
		Low	211	1942	4.7	1930	1,542	1930
Hay, alfalfa, *tons*	1919	High	1,444	1950	4.2	1993	5,040	(2)
		Low	74	1919	1.1	1934	118	1919
Hay, all, *tons*	1866	High	2,907	1924	3.7	1990	5,790	1993
		Low	780	1866	0.6	1895	1,014	1866
Oats, *bushels*	1866	High	1,658	1918	70	1992	69,388	1946
		Low	120	(3)	18.5	1921	5,400	1991
Potatoes, *cwt.*	1866	High	374	1895	303	1993	23,256	1904
		Low	36.4	1975	26	(4)	3,557	1876
Rye, *bushels*	1866	High	913	1919	33	1989	12,143	1919
		Low	7	1866	8.8	1934	105	1866
Soybeans, *bushels*	1924	High	1,440	(5)	38	(6)	54,720	1993
		Low	1	1930	8	1927	10	1930
Spearmint, *pounds*	1935	High	8.7	1954	47	1935	280	1948
		Low	0.7	1935	20	1965	30	1965
Sugarbeets, *tons*	1906	High	187	1993	21.3	1970	3,266	1990
		Low	48	1943	5.5	1916	298	1943
Wheat, winter, *bushels*	1909	High	1,515	1953	60	1985	45,600	1984
		Low	400	1987	10.5	1912	7,350	1912
Asparagus, *cwt*	1928	High	23.5	(7)	31	1947	285	1993
		Low	1	1928	9	1981	17	1928
Beans, snap, processing, *cwt.*	1918	High	26.5	1990	3.3	1992	79,650	1990
		Low	0.8	1921	0.6	1947	600	1921
Carrots, *cwt.*	1929	High	7.5	1984	350	1930	2,278	1992
		Low	0.5	1929	150	1959	132	1936
Cauliflower, *cwt.*	1939	High	1.9	1958	141	1949	212	1949
		Low	0.7	(8)	36	1959	38	1973
Celery, *cwt.*	1928	High	7.2	1941	470	1982	1,918	1941
		Low	1.9	1960	174	1935	590	1959
Corn, sweet, fresh market, *cwt*	1949	High	15.2	1961	80	1970	1,016	1970
		Low	9	1988	42	1949	525	1949
Cucumbers, for pickles, *cwt*	1918	High	46.3	1949	6.7	1987	160,800	1987
		Low	9.3	1932	0.5	1924	17,856	1932
Lettuce, *cwt.*	1952	High	1.7	1963	300	1992	384	1967
		Low	0.28	1992	85	1953	75	1993
Onions, *cwt.*	1928	High	12.7	1935	350	1960	2,933	1984
		Low	5	1928	120	1935	852	1928
Strawberries, *cwt.*	1928	High	11.6	1957	80	(9)	45,144	1940
		Low	1.9	1993	10.8	1934	114	1993
Tomatoes, fresh market, *cwt.*	1928	High	9.4	1943	150	1993	797	1943
		Low	2.4	(10)	60	1959	204	1988
Tomatoes, processing, *tons*	1918	High	9.7	1982	32.0	1992	205	1982
		Low	1	1921	2.7	1943	5	1921

Value of production by crop, Michigan

Year	Field crops	Fruit	Vegetables
		1,000 dollars	
1993	**[2]1,822,903**	**[3]213,307**	**183,620**
1992	1,536,261	198,839	179,334
1991	1,601,528	193,045	143,164
1990	1,555,065	146,413	137,985
1989	[1]1,561,005	147,139	133,645

Record highs and lows in Michigan agriculture, fruit

Fruit	Year estimates started	Record	Trees of bearing age	Year	Production	
					Total	Year
			Thousands			
Apples, *million pounds*	1889	High	10,928	1899	1,100	1985
		Low	2,200	1960–61	53	1945
Cherries, sweet, *million pounds*	1925	High	980	1973–75	75	1978
		Low	79	1929	1	1945
Cherries, *tart, million pounds*	1925	High	3,650	1963–67	380	1964
		Low	1,339	1929	18	1927
Grapes, *tons*	1889	High	18,500	1929	77,900	1932
		Low	5,100	1989–90	4,200	1889
Peaches, *million pounds*	1889	High	12,500	1898	245	1945,46
		Low	400	1982	7	1918
Pears, *tons*	1889	High	1,319	1898	48,600	1964
		Low	140	1990	2,425	1890
Prunes & plums, *tons*	1919	High	750	1972	25,000	1971
		Low	209	1941	1,700	1945

Record highs and lows in Michigan agriculture, livestock

Livestock & livestock products and unit	Year estimates started	Record	Inventory January 1 or production	
			Total	Year
Cattle and calves, *1,000 head*	1867	High	2,036	1944
		Low	538	1867
Cattle, on feed, *1,000 head*	1930	High	250	1991
		Low	57	1931
Chickens, all, *1,000 head*	1924	High	15,512	1944
		Low	6,300	1992
Cows, beef, *1,000 head*	1920	High	239	1977
		Low	24	1925,1933
Cows, milk, *1,000 head*	1867	High	1,080	1945
		Low	225	1867
Eggs, *million eggs*	1924	High	1,697	1944
		Low	1,104	1929
Hogs & pigs, *1,000 head*	1867	High	1,397	1944
		Low	512	1935
Milk, *million pounds*	1924	High	5,758	1964
		Low	3,941	1927
Sheep, *1,000 head*	1867	High	3,100	1867
		Low	103	1992
Wool, *1,000 pounds*	1934	High	8,424	1934
		Low	722	1987

Top ten agricultural counties, Michigan, 1993

[Rankings based on 1993 County Estimates.]

Rank	Corn	Soybeans	Dry beans	All cattle	Milk cows	All hogs	Farms
1	Huron	Lenawee	Huron	Huron	Sanilac	Cass	Allegan
2	Lenawee	Saginaw	Tuscola	Sanilac	Huron	Allegan	Sanilac
3	Branch	Monroe	Gratiot	Allegan	Clinton	Ottawa	Ottawa
4	St. Joseph	Shiawassee	Bay	Ottawa	Allegan	Branch	Huron
5	Sanilac	Clinton	Sanilac	Clinton	Ottawa	Van Buren	Berrien
6	Saginaw	Sanilac	Saginaw	Ionia	Ionia	St. Joseph	Saginaw
7	Tuscola	Gratiot	Montcalm	Isabella	Kent	Hillsdale	Lenawee
8	Allegan	Hillsdale	Arenac	Kent	Isabella	Calhoun & Hillsdale	Clinton
9	Gratiot	Branch	Midland	Jackson	Missaukee	Huron	Kent
10	Hillsdale	Tuscola	Lapeer, Midland & Isabella	Lapeer & Lenawee	Missaukee & Montcalm	Ionia	Van Buren

Michigan farm numbers: Acreage, and value of farm real estate.

	Farms	Average size per farm	Total land in farms	Average value per acre of land and buildings	Total value of land and buildings	Farms rented for cash per acre	Cropland rented for cash per acre
	Number	*Acres*	*1,000 acres*	*Dollars*	*Million dollars*	*Dollars*	*Dollars*
1994	**52,000**	**206**	**10,700**	**1,212**	**12,969**	**45.40**	**49.00**
1993	52,000	206	10,700	1,130	12,807	46.00	45.60
1992	54,000	200	10,800	1,105	11,937	44.90	47.40
1991	54,000	200	10,800	1,085	11,718	52.80	45.50
1990	54,000	200	10,800	1,005	10,854	43.80	41.40
1989	55,000	196	10,800	983	10,616	42.50	44.20
1988	56,000	195	10,900	971	10,583	39.20	41.70
1980	65,000	175	11,400	1,111	12,665	46.40	49.40
1970	84,000	151	12,700	326	4,140	15.60	17.50
1960	118,000	131	15,400	194	2,989	14.10	–
1950	161,000	111	17,900	99	1,764	–	–
1940	190,000	97	18,400	51	913	–	–
1930	179,000	101	18,000	68	1,161	–	–
1920	196,447	97	19,033	75	1,437	–	–
1910	206,960	92	18,941	48	901	–	–
1900	203,261	86	17,562	33	583	–	–

Farm balance sheet: Michigan

Item	**1992**	1991	1990	1989	1988
			Million dollars		
Total farm assets	**15,567.3**	15,160.8	14,930.1	13,962.9	13,248.0
Real estate	**10,333.5**	10,238.1	10,114.9	9,308.4	8,783.9
Livestock and poultry	**1,044.0**	996.4	1,033.8	981.9	878.1
Machinery and motor vehicle	**2,481.4**	2,470.3	2,418.9	2,422.5	2,324.7
Crops[3]	**746.9**	588.5	532.8	471.5	500.8
Financial assets	**961.5**	867.6	829.8	778.6	760.6
Total farm debt	**2,601.7**	2,554.5	2,607.5	2,678.0	2,842.7
Real estate debt	**1,434.3**	1,391.0	1,447.7	1,491.9	1,620.7
Nonreal estate debt'	**1,167.4**	1,163.6	1,159.9	1,186.1	1,222.0
Equity	**12,965.6**	12,606.3	12,322.6	11,285.0	10,405.3
Debt/assets ratio	**16.7**	16.8	17.5	19.2	21.5

Number of farms and land in farms by economic sales class, Michigan

Year	Economic sales class			Total
	$1,000-$9,999	$10,000-$99,999	$100,000-and over	
		Number of farms		
1994	**27,000**	**17,000**	**8,000**	**52,000**
1993	27,500	16,500	8,000	52,000
1992	28,000	18,000	8,000	54,000
1991	28,000	18,000	8,000	54,000
1990	28,000	18,000	8,000	54,000
		1,000 acres		
1994	**1,500**	**3,100**	**6,100**	**10,700**
1993	1,500	3,100	6,100	10,700
1992	1,500	3,300	6,000	10,800
1991	1,500	3,300	6,000	10,800
1990	1,500	3,300	6,000	10,800
1989	1,500	4,300	5,000	10,800

TOTAL S.E.V. PROPERTY VALUE (REAL & PERSONAL)

CITIES AND TOWNSHIPS, BY COUNTY

1994 S.E.V. = State Equalized Value = ½ market value.
Amounts in $1,000. Source - Mich Dept of the Treasury.
Note: This list includes every city and township in state.

Alcona	383,920
TOWNSHIP:	
ALCONA	63,264
CALEDONIA	55,854
CURTIS	33,700
GREENBUSH	52,140
GUSTIN	21,789
HARRISVILLE	30,854
HAWES	34,383
HAYNES	25,853
MIKADO	15,192
MILLEN	11,063
MITCHELL	29,940
CITY:	
HARRISVILLE	9,882

Alger	149,770
TOWNSHIP:	
AU TRAIN	22,093
BURT	19,260
GRAND ISLAND	1,040
LIMESTONE	6,091
MATHIAS	8,237
MUNISING	30,853
ONOTA	11,521
ROCK RIVER	13,561
CITY:	
MUNISING	37,110

Allegan	1,773,762
TOWNSHIP:	
ALLEGAN	54,675
CASCO	61,552
CHESHIRE	23,763
CLYDE	26,142
DORR	81,210
FILLMORE	56,065
GANGES	58,951
GUN PLAIN	88,610
HEATH	47,839
HOPKINS	36,420
LAKETOWN	139,639
LEE	25,152
LEIGHTON	58,135
MANLIUS	31,790
MARTIN	34,503
MONTEREY	27,196
OTSEGO	70,946
OVERISEL	51,877
SALEM	47,172
SAUGATUCK	103,568
TROWBRIDGE	29,517
VALLEY	18,800
WATSON	22,665
WAYLAND	43,154
CITY:	
ALLEGAN	72,786
FENNVILLE	16,163
HOLLAND	223,928
OTSEGO	69,508
PLAINWELL	63,266
SAUGATUCK	51,341
SOUTH HAVEN	1,814
WAYLAND	35,602

Alpena	474,687
TOWNSHIP:	
ALPENA	166,858
GREEN	23,086
LONG RAPIDS	14,798
MAPLE RIDGE	22,497
OSSINEKE	30,792
SANBORN	30,687
WELLINGTON	7,421
WILSON	29,799
CITY:	
ALPENA	148,745

Antrim	762,367
TOWNSHIP:	
BANKS	38,059
CENTRAL LAKE	57,641
CHESTONIA	7,530
CUSTER	39,521
ECHO	13,532
ELK RAPIDS	100,978
FOREST HOME	87,414
HELENA	51,930
JORDAN	9,908
KEARNEY	51,594
MANCELONA	49,911
MILTON	127,979
STAR	17,355
TORCH LAKE	99,650
WARNER	9,359

Arenac	296,605
TOWNSHIP:	
ADAMS	7,363
ARENAC	12,159
AU GRES	25,039
CLAYTON	13,260
DEEP RIVER	25,645
LINCOLN	13,147
MASON	9,645
MOFFATT	21,534
SIMS	48,146
STANDISH	23,511
TURNER	12,223
WHITNEY	37,017
CITY:	
AU GRES	23,285
OMER	3,100
STANDISH	21,525

Baraga	99,751
TOWNSHIP:	
ARVON	13,395
BARAGA	26,434
COVINGTON	7,497
L'ANSE	44,754
SPURR	7,670

Barry	813,975
TOWNSHIP:	
ASSYRIA	22,985
BALTIMORE	20,794
BARRY	46,519
CARLTON	29,566
CASTLETON	30,067
HASTINGS	36,568
HOPE	45,870
IRVING	30,284
JOHNSTOWN	43,912
MAPLE GROVE	19,208
ORANGEVILLE	53,138
PRAIRIEVILLE	63,165
RUTLAND	49,059
THORNAPPLE	92,717
WOODLAND	31,026
YANKEE SPRINGS	94,362
CITY:	
HASTINGS	104,730

Bay	1,757,958
TOWNSHIP:	
BANGOR	284,016
BEAVER	35,130
FRANKENLUST	59,358
FRASER	50,133
GARFIELD	19,439
GIBSON	14,087
HAMPTON	360,373
KAWKAWLIN	73,076
MERRITT	31,325
MONITOR	168,018
MOUNT FOREST	16,585
PINCONNING	35,657
PORTSMOUTH	49,630
WILLIAMS	88,253
CITY:	
AUBURN	26,386
BAY CITY	367,050
ESSEXVILLE	55,961
MIDLAND	5,285
PINCONNING	18,187

Benzie	407,451
TOWNSHIP:	
ALMIRA	37,117
BENZONIA	85,358
BLAINE	16,901
COLFAX	6,117
CRYSTAL LAKE	63,520
GILMORE	12,518
HOMESTEAD	20,286
INLAND	14,222
JOYFIELD	10,258
LAKE	81,896
PLATTE	5,296
WELDON	19,162
CITY:	
FRANKFORT	34,794

(continued on next page)

(continued from preceding page)

Berrien	3,386,309
TOWNSHIP:	
BAINBRIDGE	43,064
BARODA	43,738
BENTON	245,771
BERRIEN	62,331
BERTRAND	44,662
BUCHANAN	50,541
CHIKAMING	195,255
COLOMA	86,764
GALIEN	22,624
HAGAR	79,585
LAKE	612,787
LINCOLN	285,202
NEW BUFFALO	181,020
NILES	168,984
ORONOKO	119,079
PIPESTONE	31,433
ROYALTON	89,915
SAINT JOSEPH	214,278
SODUS	33,904
THREE OAKS	43,223
WATERVLIET	53,714
WEESAW	39,953
CITY:	
BENTON HARBOR	23,236
BRIDGMAN	59,508
BUCHANAN	55,637
COLOMA	20,860
NEW BUFFALO	85,065
NILES	140,924
SAINT JOSEPH	234,746
WATERVLIET	18,491

Branch	572,902,026
TOWNSHIP:	
ALGANSEE	31,692
BATAVIA	18,739
BETHEL	15,481
BRONSON	18,361
BUTLER	16,497
CALIFORNIA	9,209
COLDWATER	51,484
GILEAD	12,079
GIRARD	30,416
KINDERHOOK	39,125
MATTESON	17,294
NOBLE	8,025
OVID	61,007
QUINCY	50,945
SHERWOOD	23,717
UNION	26,949
CITY:	
BRONSON	20,244
COLDWATER	121,627

CALHOUN	1,919,500
TOWNSHIP:	
ALBION	19,056
ATHENS	26,398
BEDFORD	98,152
BURLINGTON	22,389
CLARENCE	35,463
CLARENDON	13,900
CONVIS	22,297
ECKFORD	23,325
EMMETT	153,317
FREDONIA	26,201
HOMER	30,142
LEE	20,671
LEROY	46,030
MARENGO	27,748
MARSHALL	56,021
NEWTON	31,179
PENNFIELD	121,026
SHERIDAN	24,923
TEKONSHA	20,863
CITY:	
ALBION	82,930
BATTLE CREEK	841,321
MARSHALL	124,333
SPRINGFIELD	51,804

Cass	794,709
TOWNSHIP:	
CALVIN	29,656
HOWARD	86,704
JEFFERSON	30,739
LAGRANGE	47,904
MARCELLUS	33,315
MASON	26,494
MILTON	32,300
NEWBERG	24,899
ONTWA	87,360
PENN	66,924
POKAGON	31,470
PORTER	83,685
SILVER CREEK	93,291
VOLINIA	18,015
WAYNE	39,238
CITY:	
DOWAGIAC	62,701
NILES	6

Charlevoix	847,090
TOWNSHIP:	
BAY	55,996
BOYNE VALLEY	30,860
CHANDLER	10,218
CHARLEVOIX	84,578
EVANGELINE	29,445
EVELINE	101,093
HAYES	85,340
HUDSON	14,713
MARION	28,149
MELROSE	46,812
NORWOOD	19,098
PEAINE	28,360
SAINT JAMES	20,419
SOUTH ARM	34,668
WILSON	22,612
CITY:	
BOYNE CITY	75,766
CHARLEVOIX	123,972
EAST JORDAN	34,981

Cheboygan	602,493
TOWNSHIP:	
ALOHA	22,010
BEAUGRAND	18,518
BENTON	53,778
BURT	54,197
ELLIS	9,767
FOREST	13,963
GRANT	19,844
HEBRON	5,092
INVERNESS	43,176
KOEHLER	25,029
MACKINAW	42,482
MENTOR	10,470
MULLETT	48,911
MUNRO	21,900
NUNDA	16,030
TUSCARORA	98,147
WALKER	3,454
WAVERLY	18,768
WILMOT	8,760
CITY:	
CHEBOYGAN	68,189

Chippewa	478,737
TOWNSHIP:	
BAY MILLS	16,608
BRUCE	23,906
CHIPPEWA	3,166
DAFTER	12,721
DETOUR	22,177
DRUMMOND	47,229
HULBERT	3,513
KINROSS	26,175
PICKFORD	18,633
RABER	14,410
RUDYARD	15,393
SOO	41,415
SUGAR ISLAND	13,413
SUPERIOR	12,401
TROUT LAKE	10,063
WHITEFISH	26,998
CITY:	
S STE MARIE	170,508

Clare	484,493
TOWNSHIP:	
ARTHUR	10,134
FRANKLIN	12,862
FREEMAN	23,629
FROST	20,746
GARFIELD	39,504
GRANT	38,783
GREENWOOD	20,458
HAMILTON	29,368
HATTON	11,688
HAYES	52,138
LINCOLN	59,494
REDDING	7,789
SHERIDAN	13,427
SUMMERFIELD	12,364
SURREY	44,208
WINTERFIELD	19,129
CITY:	
CLARE	42,492
HARRISON	26,270

Clinton	964,814
TOWNSHIP:	
BATH	84,402
BENGAL	19,912
BINGHAM	42,882
DALLAS	32,413
DEWITT	172,248
DUPLAIN	32,926
EAGLE	44,890
ESSEX	23,216
GREENBUSH	31,018
LEBANON	11,637
OLIVE	36,587
OVID	43,827
RILEY	27,644
VICTOR	49,026
WATERTOWN	91,576
WESTPHALIA	33,757
CITY:	
DEWITT	75,218
SAINT JOHNS	111,626

Crawford	293,261
TOWNSHIP:	
BEAVER CREEK	37,542
FREDERIC	31,230
GRAYLING	115,945
LOVELLS	27,345
MAPLE FOREST	9,300
SOUTH BRANCH	36,935
CITY:	
GRAYLING	34,962

(continued next page)

(continued from preceding page)

Delta	519,466
TOWNSHIP:	
BALDWIN	14,168
BARK RIVER	15,237
BAY DE NOC	8,977
BRAMPTON	10,776
CORNELL	8,017
ENSIGN	11,489
ESCANABA	39,621
FAIRBANKS	8,161
FORD RIVER	26,729
GARDEN	17,605
MAPLE RIDGE	11,365
MASONVILLE	25,084
NAHMA	13,087
WELLS	115,740
CITY:	
ESCANABA	150,826
GLADSTONE	42,576

Dickinson	433,436
TOWNSHIP:	
BREEN	8,567
BREITUNG	118,341
FELCH	15,039
NORWAY	22,822
SAGOLA	22,965
WAUCEDAH	16,472
WEST BRANCH	7,344
CITY:	
IRON MOUNTAI	117,592
KINGSFORD	73,207
NORWAY	31,082

Eaton	1,617,670
TOWNSHIP:	
BELLEVUE	32,295
BENTON	40,762
BROOKFIELD	24,013
CARMEL	34,151
CHESTER	24,818
DELTA	702,035
EATON	63,748
EATON RAPIDS	54,571
HAMLIN	37,294
KALAMO	19,135
ONEIDA	65,537
ROXAND	27,908
SUNFIELD	29,832
VERMONTVILLE	22,027
WALTON	22,778
WINDSOR	100,288
CITY:	
CHARLOTTE	103,789
EATON RAPIDS	60,502
GRAND LEDGE	99,456
LANSING	31,038
OLIVET	9,004
POTTERVILLE	12,678

Emmet	1,106,072
TOWNSHIP:	
BEAR CREEK	155,181
BLISS	10,472
CARP LAKE	18,396
CENTER	8,005
CROSS VILLAGE	31,914
FRIENDSHIP	37,404
LITTLEFIELD	45,788
LITTLE TRAVERSE	111,452
MAPLE RIVER	19,727
MCKINLEY	14,398
PLEASANTVIEW	51,970
READMOND	39,251
RESORT	102,425
SPRINGVALE	32,746
WAWATAM	32,712
WEST TRAVERSE	155,811
CITY:	
HARBOR SPRINGS	103,416
PETOSKEY	134,998

Genesee	6,065,857
TOWNSHIP:	
ARGENTINE	88,401
ATLAS	123,509
CLAYTON	106,252
DAVISON	223,779
FENTON	268,739
FLINT	685,244
FLUSHING	137,321
FOREST	66,454
GAINES	78,572
GENESEE	244,938
GRAND BLANC	529,634
MONTROSE	69,552
MOUNT MORRIS	242,100
MUNDY	207,390
RICHFIELD	101,799
THETFORD	95,679
VIENNA	159,051
CITY:	
BURTON	383,152
CLIO	26,117
DAVISON	67,405
FENTON	177,837
FLINT	1,509,833
FLUSHING	132,283
GRAND BLANC	164,841
MONTROSE	16,052
MOUNT MORRIS	26,381
SWARTZ CREEK	96,301
LINDEN	37,227

Gladwin	419,700
TOWNSHIP:	
BEAVERTON	18,116
BENTLEY	9,025
BILLINGS	45,805
BOURRET	11,544
BUCKEYE	16,877
BUTMAN	56,228
CLEMENT	27,935
GLADWIN	11,979
GRIM	3,126
GROUT	19,456
HAY	23,141
SAGE	36,387
SECORD	41,612
SHERMAN	15,550
TOBACCO	40,403
CITY:	
BEAVERTON	9,565
GLADWIN	32,942

Gogebic	255,157
TOWNSHIP:	
BESSEMER	20,213
ERWIN	3,925
IRONWOOD	38,802
MARENISCO	21,841
WAKEFIELD	28,221
WATERSMEET	59,134
CITY:	
BESSEMER	16,669
IRONWOOD	53,844
WAKEFIELD	12,504

Gr Traverse	1,645,345
TOWNSHIP:	
ACME	129,763
BLAIR	72,486
EAST BAY	185,985
FIFE LAKE	18,003
GARFIELD	304,396
GRANT	18,091
GREEN LAKE	88,392
LONG LAKE	140,356
MAYFIELD	18,699
PARADISE	33,981
PENINSULA	213,787
UNION	11,477
WHITEWATER	67,635
CITY:	
TRAVERSE CITY	342,287

Gratiot	491,902
TOWNSHIP:	
ARCADA	25,575
BETHANY	22,068
ELBA	16,830
EMERSON	19,183
FULTON	30,277
HAMILTON	7,572
LAFAYETTE	15,905
NEWARK	18,125
NEW HAVEN	15,297
NORTH SHADE	13,288
NORTH STAR	17,349
PINE RIVER	35,855
SEVILLE	21,092
SUMNER	17,281
WASHINGTON	13,769
WHEELER	40,511
CITY:	
ALMA	109,646
ITHACA	25,749
ST. LOUIS	26,521

Hillsdale	649,827
TOWNSHIP:	
ADAMS	29,173
ALLEN	27,024
AMBOY	20,162
CAMBRIA	38,126
CAMDEN	23,484
FAYETTE	56,283
HILLSDALE	30,568
JEFFERSON	36,903
LITCHFIELD	16,789
MOSCOW	20,011
PITTSFORD	22,538
RANSOM	11,033
READING	35,535
SCIPIO	19,773
SOMERSET	82,009
WHEATLAND	16,357
WOODBRIDGE	14,536
WRIGHT	24,305
CITY:	
HILLSDALE	93,749
LITCHFIELD	23,665
READING	7,795

(continued next page)

(continued from preceding page)

Houghton	313,831
TOWNSHIP:	
ADAMS	18,327
CALUMET	40,699
CHASSELL	20,549
DUNCAN	5,164
ELM RIVER	6,209
FRANKLIN	10,498
HANCOCK	6,569
LAIRD	7,225
OSCEOLA	13,450
PORTAGE	37,354
QUINCY	2,521
SCHOOLCRAFT	13,159
STANTON	13,538
TORCH LAKE	28,642
CITY:	
HANCOCK	39,671
HOUGHTON	50,246

Huron	890,904
TOWNSHIP:	
BINGHAM	27,717
BLOOMFIELD	15,790
BROOKFIELD	22,146
CASEVILLE	109,014
CHANDLER	18,345
COLFAX	32,062
DWIGHT	17,473
FAIR HAVEN	21,147
GORE	5,478
GRANT	15,110
HUME	37,361
HURON	18,009
LAKE	45,020
LINCOLN	18,838
MCKINLEY	16,549
MEADE	17,490
OLIVER	34,751
PARIS	16,427
POINTE AUX BARQU	7,209
PORT AUSTIN	54,362
RUBICON	17,711
SAND BEACH	34,804
SEBEWAING	52,839
SHERIDAN	16,068
SHERMAN	34,570
SIGEL	18,320
VERONA	26,593
WINSOR	47,636
CITY:	
BAD AXE	53,026
HARBOR BEACH	39,025

Ingham	4,181,857
TOWNSHIP:	
ALAIEDON	92,608
AURELIUS	48,617
BUNKER HILL	23,448
DELHI	293,207
INGHAM	28,386
LANSING	224,143
LEROY	48,308
LESLIE	31,919
LOCKE	27,746
MERIDIAN	864,160
ONONDAGA	39,528
STOCKBRIDGE	49,869
VEVAY	60,460
WHEATFIELD	33,262
WHITE OAK	20,946
WILLIAMSTOWN	99,653
CITY:	
EAST LANSING	507,733
LANSING	1,532,048
LESLIE	18,183
MASON	94,887
WILLIAMSTON	42,735

Ionia	656,233
TOWNSHIP:	
BERLIN	34,151
BOSTON	59,587
CAMPBELL	25,918
DANBY	31,580
EASTON	27,288
IONIA	36,421
KEENE	18,641
LYONS	36,862
NORTH PLAINS	13,965
ODESSA	49,968
ORANGE	20,039
ORLEANS	27,796
OTISCO	28,098
PORTLAND	39,409
RONALD	17,351
SEBEWA	16,385
CITY:	
BELDING	58,292
IONIA	69,858
PORTLAND	44,617

Iosco	581,985
TOWNSHIP:	
ALABASTER	29,482
AU SABLE	55,448
BALDWIN	60,080
BURLEIGH	12,196
GRANT	38,251
OSCODA	142,589
PLAINFIELD	102,003
RENO	11,980
SHERMAN	11,024
TAWAS	23,088
WILBER	17,162
CITY:	
EAST TAWAS	43,450
TAWAS CITY	32,101
WHITTEMORE	3,124

Iron	219,197
TOWNSHIP:	
BATES	18,291
CRYSTAL FALLS	45,790
HEMATITE	5,029
IRON RIVER	23,264
MANSFIELD	13,434
MASTODON	28,549
STAMBAUGH	32,039
CITY:	
CASPIAN	8,444
CRYSTAL FALLS	12,961
GAASTRA	1,711
IRON RIVER	21,416
STAMBAUGH	8,265

Isabella	667,151
TOWNSHIP:	
BROOMFIELD	20,279
CHIPPEWA	43,767
COE	35,890
COLDWATER	12,063
DEERFIELD	44,668
DENVER	14,177
FREMONT	16,415
GILMORE	19,552
ISABELLA	26,291
LINCOLN	20,674
NOTTAWA	27,771
ROLLAND	13,100
SHERMAN	31,875
UNION	89,087
VERNON	18,176
WISE	13,488
CITY:	
CLARE	1,376
MOUNT PLEASANT	218,494

Jackson	2,024,195
TOWNSHIP:	
BLACKMAN	281,820
COLUMBIA	153,759
CONCORD	29,514
GRASS LAKE	69,141
HANOVER	53,082
HENRIETTA	48,847
LEONI	184,844
LIBERTY	43,863
NAPOLEON	100,000
NORVELL	54,049
PARMA	29,795
PULASKI	21,714
RIVES	45,329
SANDSTONE	50,734
SPRING ARBOR	79,261
SPRINGPORT	21,252
SUMMIT	302,431
TOMPKINS	31,213
WATERLOO	45,526
CITY:	
JACKSON	378,012

Kalamazoo	3,980,287
TOWNSHIP:	
ALAMO	55,892
BRADY	69,485
CHARLESTON	37,925
CLIMAX	31,831
COMSTOCK	263,340
COOPER	121,691
KALAMAZOO	273,658
OSHTEMO	294,025
PAVILION	81,555
PRAIRIE RONDE	37,127
RICHLAND	134,376
ROSS	139,654
SCHOOLCRAFT	122,630
TEXAS	215,012
WAKESHMA	19,429
CITY:	
GALESBURG	15,269
KALAMAZOO	1,005,446
PARCHMENT	53,562
PORTAGE	1,008,372

Kalkaska	418,289
TOWNSHIP:	
BEAR LAKE	31,405
BLUE LAKE	80,286
BOARDMAN	14,323
CLEARWATER	45,640
COLDSPRINGS	36,539
EXCELSIOR	25,248
GARFIELD	23,683
KALKASKA	102,707
OLIVER	5,368
ORANGE	12,738
RAPID RIVER	23,858
SPRINGFIELD	16,489

Kent	10,045,491
TOWNSHIP:	330,336
ADA	105,212
ALGOMA	183,917
ALPINE	49,319
BOWNE	285,045
BYRON	184,668
CALEDONIA	210,538
CANNON	690,392
CASCADE	85,361
COURTLAND	252,629
GAINES	312,325
GRAND RAPIDS	63,323
GRATTAN	73,086

(continued next page)

(continued from preceding page)

LOWELL	73,086
NELSON	47,763
OAKFIELD	58,477
PLAINFIELD	499,508
SOLON	52,376
SPARTA	123,085
SPENCER	48,054
TYRONE	52,450
VERGENNES	63,817
CITY:	
CEDAR SPRINGS	27,034
E GRAND RAPIDS	287,715
GRAND RAPIDS	2,746,810
GRANDVILLE	336,008
KENTWOOD	1,015,253
LOWELL	67,812
ROCKFORD	74,159
WALKER	461,761
WYOMING	1,257,245

Keweenaw	40,734
TOWNSHIP:	
ALLOUEZ	11,161
EAGLE HARBOR	12,356
GRANT	12,882
HOUGHTON	2,843
SHERMAN	1,490

Lake	212,679
TOWNSHIP:	
CHASE	11,195
CHERRY VALLEY	5,698
DOVER	5,402
EDEN	8,175
ELK	25,400
ELLSWORTH	9,932
LAKE	39,432
NEWKIRK	10,190
PEACOCK	13,227
PINORA	8,313
PLEASANT PLAINS	29,469
SAUBLE	10,879
SWEETWATER	6,225
WEBBER	16,209
YATES	12,926

Lapeer	1,348,591
TOWNSHIP:	
ALMONT	98,209
ARCADIA	41,716
ATTICA	66,814
BURLINGTON	18,346
BURNSIDE	28,761
DEERFIELD	68,945
DRYDEN	90,488
ELBA	93,587
GOODLAND	26,230
HADLEY	95,641
IMLAY	40,019
LAPEER	91,029
MARATHON	49,878
MAYFIELD	107,693
METAMORA	108,159
NORTH BRANCH	39,807
OREGON	85,871
RICH	20,782
CITY:	
BROWN CITY	60
IMLAY CITY	52,296
LAPEER	124,249

Leelanau	927,525
TOWNSHIP:	
BINGHAM	50,489
CENTERVILLE	24,192
CLEVELAND	29,760
ELMWOOD	85,573
EMPIRE	41,423
GLEN ARBOR	98,640
KASSON	22,442
LEELANAU	109,674
LELAND	94,026
SOLON	23,750
SUTTONS BAY	61,509
CITY:	
TRAVERSE CITY	4,046

Lenawee	1,536,017
TOWNSHIP:	
ADRIAN	86,408
BLISSFIELD	62,458
CAMBRIDGE	115,953
CLINTON	61,361
DEERFIELD	29,768
DOVER	20,605
FAIRFIELD	27,493
FRANKLIN	53,050
HUDSON	23,123
MACON	28,670
MADISON	99,827
MEDINA	18,709
OGDEN	29,152
PALMYRA	42,404
RAISIN	101,869
RIDGEWAY	26,962
RIGA	37,774
ROLLIN	78,471
ROME	22,844
SENECA	19,019
TECUMSEH	39,584
WOODSTOCK	65,611
CITY:	
ADRIAN	261,497
HUDSON	32,474
MORENCI	20,458
TECUMSEH	130,462

Livingston	3,078,331
TOWNSHIP:	467,603
BRIGHTON	56,435
COHOCTAH	38,286
CONWAY	73,802
DEERFIELD	338,890
GENOA	361,605
GREEN OAK	363,148
HAMBURG	88,371
HANDY	210,148
HARTLAND	112,492
HOWELL	41,283
IOSCO	126,515
MARION	106,349
OCEOLA	129,479
PUTNAM	178,217
TYRONE	49,328
UNADILLA	
CITY:	
BRIGHTON	168,074
HOWELL	168,298

Luce	74,257
TOWNSHIP:	
COLUMBUS	4,073
LAKEFIELD	17,520
MCMILLAN	35,450
PENTLAND	17,212

Mackinac	438,863
TOWNSHIP:	
BOIS BLANC	12,423
BREVORT	12,499
CLARK	94,320
GARFIELD	42,313
HENDRICKS	6,012
HUDSON	6,296
MARQUETTE	11,532
MORAN	50,986
NEWTON	20,062
PORTAGE	27,465
SAINT IGNACE	12,315
CITY:	
MACKINAC ISLAND	94,547
SAINT IGNACE	48,086

Macomb	14,701,705
TOWNSHIP:	
ARMADA	117,911
BRUCE	186,367
CHESTERFIELD	565,271
CLINTON	1,612,650
HARRISON	517,823
LAKE	8,091
LENOX	90,427
MACOMB	576,115
RAY	79,022
RICHMOND	62,472
SHELBY	1,259,793
WASHINGTON	346,543
CITY:	
CENTERLINE	164,986
EAST DETROIT	477,401
FRASER	330,531
MEMPHIS	11,132
MOUNT CLEMENS	269,817
NEW BALTIMORE	122,261
RICHMOND	69,938
ROSEVILLE	811,647
ST CLAIR SH	1,246,582
STERLING HTS	2,675,779
UTICA	101,320
WARREN	2,997,815

Manistee	476,015
TOWNSHIP:	
ARCADIA	22,024
BEAR LAKE	30,809
BROWN	12,859
CLEON	13,389
DICKSON	17,948
FILER	85,975
MANISTEE	50,230
MAPLE GROVE	17,633
MARILLA	5,682
NORMAN	21,769
ONEKAMA	48,351
PLEASANTON	18,097
SPRINGDALE	12,814
STRONACH	30,559
CITY:	
MANISTEE	87,868

Marquette	907,089
TOWNSHIP:	
CHAMPION	4,432
CHOCOLAY	79,069
ELY	23,947
EWING	3,991
FORSYTH	61,197
HUMBOLDT	10,345
ISHPEMING	37,252
MARQUETTE	68,853
MICHIGAMME	11,029

(continued next page)

(continued from preceding page)

NEGAUNEE	35,921
POWELL	25,908
REPUBLIC	23,862
RICHMOND	10,930
SANDS	24,152
SKANDIA	9,263
TILDEN	13,214
TURIN	2,333
WELLS	21,073
WEST BRANCH	10,506
CITY:	
ISHPEMING	56,282
MARQUETTE	333,756
NEGAUNEE	39,762

Mason	769,540
TOWNSHIP:	
AMBER	41,589
BRANCH	19,093
CUSTER	16,625
EDEN	9,705
FREESOIL	11,097
GRANT	16,220
HAMLIN	76,353
LOGAN	7,389
MEADE	4,796
PERE MARQUETTE	264,808
RIVERTON	16,357
SHERIDAN	18,521
SHERMAN	12,737
SUMMIT	89,910
VICTORY	17,381
CITY:	
LUDINGTON	132,800
SCOTTVILLE	14,152

Mecosta	566,085
TOWNSHIP:	
AETNA	18,276
AUSTIN	39,474
BIG RAPIDS	49,241
CHIPPEWA	24,930
COLFAX	29,092
DEERFIELD	13,666
FORK	18,102
GRANT	10,323
GREEN	34,220
HINTON	13,509
MARTINY	30,610
MECOSTA	29,620
MILLBROCK	15,701
MORTON	102,813
SHERIDAN	14,776
WHEATLAND	18,601
CITY:	
BIG RAPIDS	103,124

Menominee	305,342
TOWNSHIP:	
CEDARVILLE	7,482
DAGGETT	8,453
FAITHORN	4,732
GOURLEY	5,525
HARRIS	16,064
HOLMES	13,386
INGALLSTON	18,071
LAKE	11,917
MELLEN	15,505
MENOMINEE	44,467
MEYER	10,029
NADEAU	16,004
SPALDING	17,631
STEPHENSON	8,696
CITY:	
MENOMINEE	99,153
STEPHENSON	8,219

Midland	2,480,559
TOWNSHIP:	
EDENVILLE	41,334
GENEVA	12,025
GREENDALE	15,246
HOMER	55,624
HOPE	21,071
INGERSOLL	41,514
JASPER	18,650
JEROME	66,376
LARKIN	93,129
LEE	35,313
LINCOLN	29,410
MIDLAND	43,887
MILLS	19,072
MOUNT HALEY	22,686
PORTER	16,517
WARREN	26,238
CITY:	
COLEMAN	9,293
MIDLAND	1,913,164

Missaukee	258,746
TOWNSHIP:	
AETNA	9,339
BLOOMFIELD	7,636
BUTTERFIELD	13,610
CALDWELL	16,315
CLAM UNION	14,576
ENTERPRISE	10,621
FOREST	11,910
HOLLAND	8,026
LAKE	56,558
NORWICH	21,048
PIONEER	6,028
REEDER	14,311
RICHLAND	17,869
RIVERSIDE	13,274
WEST BRANCH	7,603
CITY:	
LAKE CITY	14,984
MCBAIN	15,030

Monroe	3,574,945
TOWNSHIP:	
ASH	134,327
BEDFORD	413,610
BERLIN	120,716
DUNDEE	120,573
ERIE	69,717
EXETER	57,903
FRENCHTOWN	1,139,700
IDA	78,826
LASALLE	94,952
LONDON	43,340
MILAN	37,076
MONROE	211,851
RAISINVILLE	89,720
SUMMERFIELD	56,595
WHITEFORD	90,436
CITY:	
LUNA PIER	70,422
MILAN	66,460
MONROE	667,730
PETERSBURG	10,982

Montcalm	756,707
TOWNSHIP:	
BELVIDERE	46,320
BLOOMER	17,317
BUSHNELL	14,920
CATO	36,143
CRYSTAL	40,256
DAY	16,234
DOUGLASS	32,284
EUREKA	44,204
EVERGREEN	29,933
FAIRPLAINS	18,881
FERRIS	14,888
HOME	38,505
MAPLE VALLEY	24,483
MONTCALM	40,454
PIERSON	43,999
PINE	22,822
REYNOLDS	38,222
RICHLAND	25,586
SIDNEY	30,034
WINFIELD	27,018
CITY:	
CARSON CITY	13,410
GREENVILLE	129,917
STANTON	10,865

Montmorency	251,707
TOWNSHIP:	
ALBERT	70,712
AVERY	13,638
BRILEY	36,319
HILLMAN	39,936
LOUD	12,884
MONTMORENCY	41,639
RUST	17,292
VIENNA	19,284

Muskegon	2,143,790
TOWNSHIP:	
BLUE LAKE	18,142
CASNOVIA	30,330
CEDAR CREEK	26,353
DALTON	78,208
EGELSTON	72,687
FRUITLAND	102,168
FRUITPORT	151,877
HOLTON	21,825
LAKETON	103,601
MONTAGUE	23,855
MOORLAND	16,169
MUSKEGON	178,006
RAVENNA	35,565
SULLIVAN	26,935
WHITEHALL	24,873
WHITE RIVER	41,864
CITY:	
MONTAGUE	32,945
MUSKEGON	466,384
MUSKEGON HTS	93,028
NORTH MUSKEGON	82,102
NORTON SHORES	383,392
ROOSEVELT PARK	67,512
WHITEHALL	65,960

Newaygo	632,283
TOWNSHIP:	
ASHLAND	26,302
BARTON	8,316
BEAVER	6,496
BIG PRAIRIE	34,232
BRIDGETON	17,184
BROOKS	57,804
CROTON	51,345
DAYTON	31,243
DENVER	15,122
ENSLEY	28,833
EVERETT	17,841
GARFIELD	32,828
GOODWELL	12,647
GRANT	27,325
HOME	5,657
LILLEY	13,918
LINCOLN	14,764
MERRILL	9,715
MONROE	5,258
NORWICH	8,845
SHERIDAN	37,431
SHERMAN	25,968
TROY	3,068
WILCOX	9,931

(continued next page)

(continued from preceding page)

CITY:	
FREMONT	96,561
GRANT	6,850
NEWAYGO	16,090
WHITE CLOUD	10,696

Oakland	31,180,259
TOWNSHIP:	139,668
ADDISON	2,179,316
BLOOMFIELD	221,463
BRANDON	806,349
COMMERCE	121,175
GROVELAND	339,918
HIGHLAND	136,963
HOLLY	640,966
INDEPENDENCE	237,812
LYON	392,947
MILFORD	5,698
NOVI	341,958
OAKLAND	693,468
ORION	269,313
OXFORD	112,053
ROSE	46,268
ROYAL OAK	627,502
SOUTHFIELD	243,411
SPRINGFIELD	1,373,231
WATERFORD	2,072,556
WEST BLOOMFIELD	490,940
WHITE LAKE	
CITY:	561,064
AUBURN HILLS	286,645
BERKLEY	975,050
BIRMINGHAM	521,696
BLOOMFIELD HILLS	27,485
CLAWSON	249,408
FARMINGTON	274,155
FARMINGTON HLS	2,593,603
FERNDALE	322,150
HAZEL PARK	185,971
HUNTINGTON WOOD	173,638
KEEGO HARBOR	48,868
LAKE ANGELUS	31,680
LATHRUP VILLAGE	112,767
MADISON HEIGHTS	783,512
NORTHVILLE	110,468
NOVI	1,363,812
OAK PARK	413,471
ORCHARD LAKE	186,664
PLEASANT RIDGE	69,664
PONTIAC	730,085
ROCHESTER	239,129
ROCHESTER HILLS	1,892,574
ROYAL OAK	1,306,305
SOUTHFIELD	2,295,330
SOUTH LYON	124,486
SYLVAN LAKE	55,155
TROY	3,308,095
WALLED LAKE	115,613
WIXOM	328,722

Oceana	451,104
TOWNSHIP:	
BENONA	59,327
CLAYBANK	23,595
COLFAX	10,116
CRYSTAL	7,731
ELBRIDGE	10,746
FERRY	11,412
GOLDEN	57,758
GRANT	28,824
GREENWOOD	12,586
HART	23,682
LEAVITT	10,157
NEWFIELD	27,568
OTTO	6,569
PENTWATER	81,877
SHELBY	40,310
WEARE	14,813
CITY:	
HART	24,024

Ogemaw	392,295
TOWNSHIP:	
CHURCHILL	30,934
CUMMING	15,246
EDWARDS	17,065
FOSTER	21,063
GOODAR	13,463
HILL	53,182
HORTON	15,301
KLACKING	10,153
LOGAN	12,114
MILLS	49,755
OGEMAW	17,109
RICHLAND	15,876
ROSE	23,166
WEST BRANCH	60,198
CITY:	
ROSE CITY	8,268
WEST BRANCH	29,394

Ontonagon	133,218
TOWNSHIP:	
BERGLAND	11,398
BOHEMIA	2,526
CARP LAKE	27,813
GREENLAND	8,564
HAIGHT	4,319
INTERIOR	3,960
MATCHWOOD	2,625
MCMILLAN	6,479
ONTONAGON	44,815
ROCKLAND	11,532
STANNARD	9,182

Osceola	341,421
TOWNSHIP:	
BURDELL	14,671
CEDAR	9,777
EVART	22,669
HARTWICK	11,482
HERSEY	26,193
HIGHLAND	13,186
LEROY	12,606
LINCOLN	40,503
MARION	18,807
MIDDLE BRANCH	11,573
ORIENT	17,610
OSCEOLA	12,135
RICHMOND	25,288
ROSE LAKE	22,961
SHERMAN	13,884
SYLVAN	14,015
CITY:	
EVART	28,219
REED CITY	25,835

Oscoda	176,613
TOWNSHIP:	
BIG CREEK	51,354
CLINTON	15,465
COMINS	31,780
ELMER	16,739
GREENWOOD	38,358
MENTOR	22,914

Otsego	606,726
TOWNSHIP:	
BAGLEY	116,859
CHARLTON	77,429
CHESTER	63,450
CORWITH	28,296
DOVER	22,793
ELMIRA	29,938
HAYES	53,913
LIVINGSTON	42,681
OTSEGO LAKE	83,265
CITY:	
GAYLORD	88,096

Ottawa	4,250,839
TOWNSHIP:	97,141
ALLENDALE	89,413
BLENDON	37,942
CHESTER	53,417
CROCKERY	606,929
GEORGETOWN	241,556
GRAND HAVEN	462,253
HOLLAND	78,187
JAMESTOWN	68,502
OLIVE	379,966
PARK	42,891
POLKTON	388,746
PORT SHELDON	76,414
ROBINSON	270,466
SPRING LAKE	112,948
TALLMADGE	55,139
WRIGHT	91,786
ZEELAND	
CITY:	
COOPERSVILLE	67,479
FERRYSBURG	78,142
GRAND HAVEN	280,878
HOLLAND	422,939
HUDSONVILLE	105,366
ZEELAND	142,330

Presque Isle	316,153
TOWNSHIP:	
ALLIS	13,101
BEARINGER	18,744
BELKNAP	11,508
BISMARCK	15,974
CASE	17,931
KRAKOW	25,731
METZ	6,582
MOLTKE	6,092
NORTH ALLIS	10,118
OCQUEOC	20,539
POSEN	13,971
PRESQUE ISLE	70,728
PULAWSKI	9,928
ROGERS	21,956
CITY:	
ONAWAY	8,856
ROGERS CITY	44,388

Roscommon	637,006
TOWNSHIP:	
AU SABLE	7,023
BACKUS	5,994
DENTON	134,801
GERRISH	138,680
HIGGINS	29,761
LAKE	63,206
LYON	62,807
MARKEY	57,008
NESTER	11,427
RICHFIELD	62,459
ROSCOMMON	63,834

Saginaw	3,048,947
TOWNSHIP:	
ALBEE	32,688
BIRCH RUN	99,999
BLUMFIELD	48,894
BRADY	25,755
BRANT	25,386
BRIDGEPORT	144,004
BUENA VISTA	186,044
CARROLLTON	61,352
CHAPIN	9,604
CHESANING	73,253
FRANKENMUTH	57,453
FREMONT	33,246
JAMES	29,316
JONESFIELD	24,665

(continued next page)

(continued from preceding page)

KOCHVILLE	87,112
LAKEFIELD	14,541
MAPLE GROVE	36,013
MARION	8,551
RICHLAND	58,133
SAGINAW	766,157
SAINT CHARLES	45,490
SPAULDING	26,958
SWAN CREEK	40,841
TAYMOUTH	49,021
THOMAS	230,842
TITTABAWASSEE	86,896
ZILWAUKEE	3,709
CITY:	
FRANKENMUTH	134,181
SAGINAW	586,439
ZILWAUKEE	22,389

St. Clair	3,399,190
TOWNSHIP:	
BERLIN	49,421
BROCKWAY	23,837
BURTCHVILLE	64,626
CASCO	67,767
CHINA	418,810
CLAY	263,356
CLYDE	81,263
COLUMBUS	80,997
COTTRELLVILLE	63,772
EAST CHINA	325,236
EMMETT	24,757
FORT GRATIOT	220,456
GRANT	20,933
GREENWOOD	77,672
IRA	99,746
KENOCKEE	31,396
KIMBALL	92,772
LYNN	17,530
MUSSEY	67,918
PORT HURON	129,168
RILEY	46,574
SAINT CLAIR	124,949
WALES	40,677
CITY:	
ALGONAC	66,710
MARINE CITY	73,179
MARYSVILLE	240,882
MEMPHIS	4,551
PORT HURON	437,945
SAINT CLAIR	121,891
YALE	20,385

St. Joseph	885,664
TOWNSHIP:	
BURR OAK	28,007
COLON	42,713
CONSTANTINE	58,346
FABIUS	68,030
FAWN RIVER	18,795
FLORENCE	20,570
FLOWERFIELD	21,406
LEONIDAS	16,181
LOCKPORT	47,222
MENDON	35,209
MOTTVILLE	25,061
NOTTAWA	46,077
PARK	46,357
SHERMAN	47,500
STURGIS	32,036
WHITE PIGEON	82,803
CITY:	
STURGIS	103,754
THREE RIVERS	145,587

Sanilac	729,705
TOWNSHIP:	
ARGYLE	11,867
AUSTIN	10,560
BRIDGEHAMPTON	15,560
BUEL	15,373
CUSTER	17,359
DELAWARE	30,775
ELK	19,190
ELMER	14,180
EVERGREEN	12,989
FLYNN	12,689
FORESTER	39,987
FREMONT	12,647
GREENLEAF	12,905
LAMOTTE	14,344
LEXINGTON	76,893
MAPLE VALLEY	13,622
MARION	25,438
MARLETTE	29,681
MINDEN	11,021
MOORE	18,658
SANILAC	67,951
SPEAKER	16,755
WASHINGTON	19,226
WATERTOWN	21,057
WHEATLAND	11,283
WORTH	86,935
CITY:	
BROWN CITY	12,809
CROSWELL	24,057
MARLETTE	22,216
SANDUSKY	31,665

Schoolcraft	147,451
TOWNSHIP:	
DOYLE	16,428
GERMFASK	5,061
HIAWATHA	24,292
INWOOD	14,809
MANISTIQUE	16,555
MUELLER	15,222
SENEY	4,725
THOMPSON	15,924
CITY:	
MANISTIQUE	34,431

Shiawassee	894,857
TOWNSHIP:	
ANTRIM	28,746
BENNINGTON	42,758
BURNS	40,988
CALEDONIA	76,484
FAIRFIELD	12,390
HAZELTON	33,984
MIDDLEBURY	20,716
NEW HAVEN	22,832
OWOSSO	68,547
PERRY	42,141
RUSH	23,028
SCIOTA	21,585
SHIAWASSEE	34,161
VENICE	38,546
VERNON	59,176
WOODHULL	55,901
CITY:	
CORUNNA	31,626
DURAND	41,597
LAINGSBURG	10,019
OWOSSO	166,400
PERRY	23,224

Tuscola	750,914
TOWNSHIP:	
AKRON	36,396
ALMER	39,533
ARBELA	33,464
COLUMBIA	27,862
DAYTON	24,337
DENMARK	51,095
ELKLAND	60,267
ELLINGTON	16,131
ELMWOOD	19,581
FAIRGROVE	28,910
FREMONT	33,279
GILFORD	24,618
INDIANFIELDS	75,624
JUNIATA	23,493
KINGSTON	16,436
KOYLTON	18,246
MILLINGTON	49,096
NOVESTA	16,235
TUSCOLA	36,421
VASSAR	34,454
WATERTOWN	21,280
WELLS	18,427
WISNER	14,303
CITY:	
VASSAR	31,416

Van Buren	1,185,100
TOWNSHIP:	
ALMENA	56,177
ANTWERP	127,496
ARLINGTON	23,214
BANGOR	23,760
BLOOMINGDALE	36,312
COLUMBIA	33,464
COVERT	187,444
DECATUR	39,899
GENEVA	34,697
HAMILTON	22,772
HARTFORD	31,018
KEELER	56,996
LAWRENCE	46,945
PAW PAW	120,695
PINE GROVE	36,751
PORTER	51,327
SOUTH HAVEN	66,497
WAVERLY	26,533
CITY:	
BANGOR	14,921
GOBELS	7,328
HARTFORD	16,312
SOUTH HAVEN	124,533

Washtenaw	6,717,463
TOWNSHIP:	
ANN ARBOR	249,597
AUGUSTA	81,265
BRIDGEWATER	37,413
DEXTER	127,349
FREEDOM	44,572
LIMA	80,103
LODI	143,495
LYNDON	57,208
MANCHESTER	87,079
NORTHFIELD	139,565
PITTSFIELD	506,938
SALEM	150,968
SALINE	37,050
SCIO	486,765
SHARON	39,543
SUPERIOR	220,588
SYLVAN	187,384
WEBSTER	113,774
YORK	113,408
YPSILANTI	756,710
CITY:	
ANN ARBOR	2,566,138
MILAN	50,945
SALINE	201,446
YPSILANTI	238,151

(continued next page)

WAYNE	
TOWNSHIP:	
BROWNSTOWN	298,427
CANTON	1,207,313
GROSS ISLE	351,830
GROSSE POINTE	222,501
HURON	194,502
NORTHVILLE	551,143
PLYMOUTH	884,278
REDFORD	872,786
SUMPTER	117,585
VAN BUREN	390,762
CITY:	
ALLEN PARK	660,331
BELLEVILLE	42,273
DEARBORN	3,391,457
DEARBORN HEIGHTS	968,909
DETROIT	5,895,776
ECORSE	183,886
FLAT ROCK	173,240
GARDEN CITY	429,242
GIBRALTER	86,802
GROSSE POINTE	257,312
GROSSE POINTE FARM	516,126
GROSSE POINTE PARK	377,790
GROSSE POINTE WOOD	553,196
HAMTRAMCK	121,809
HARPER WOODS	301,288
HIGHLAND PARK	164,469
INKSTER	214,845
LINCOLN PARK	485,537
LIVONIA	3,092,152
MELVINDALE	140,066
NORTHVILLE	98,261
PLYMOUTH	261,320
RIVER ROUGE	279,906
RIVERVIEW	254,248
ROCKWOOD	47,579
ROMULUS	531,027
SOUTHGATE	493,343
TAYLOR	937,309
TRENTON	597,319
WAYNE	321,657
WESTLAND	1,221,948
WOODHAVEN	305,584
WYANDOTTE	433,909
WEXFORD	433,696
TOWNSHIP:	
ANTIOCH	8,455
BOON	7,208
CEDAR CREEK	11,829
CHERRY GROVE	41,410
CLAM LAKE	36,440
COLFAX	10,108
GREENWOOD	7,498
HANOVER	13,010
HARING	51,240
HENDERSON	2,415
LIBERTY	9,213
SELMA	30,553
SLAGLE	8,424
SOUTH BRANCH	8,305
SPRINGVILLE	21,995
WEXFORD	11,138
CITY:	
CADILLAC	145,088
MANTON	9,361

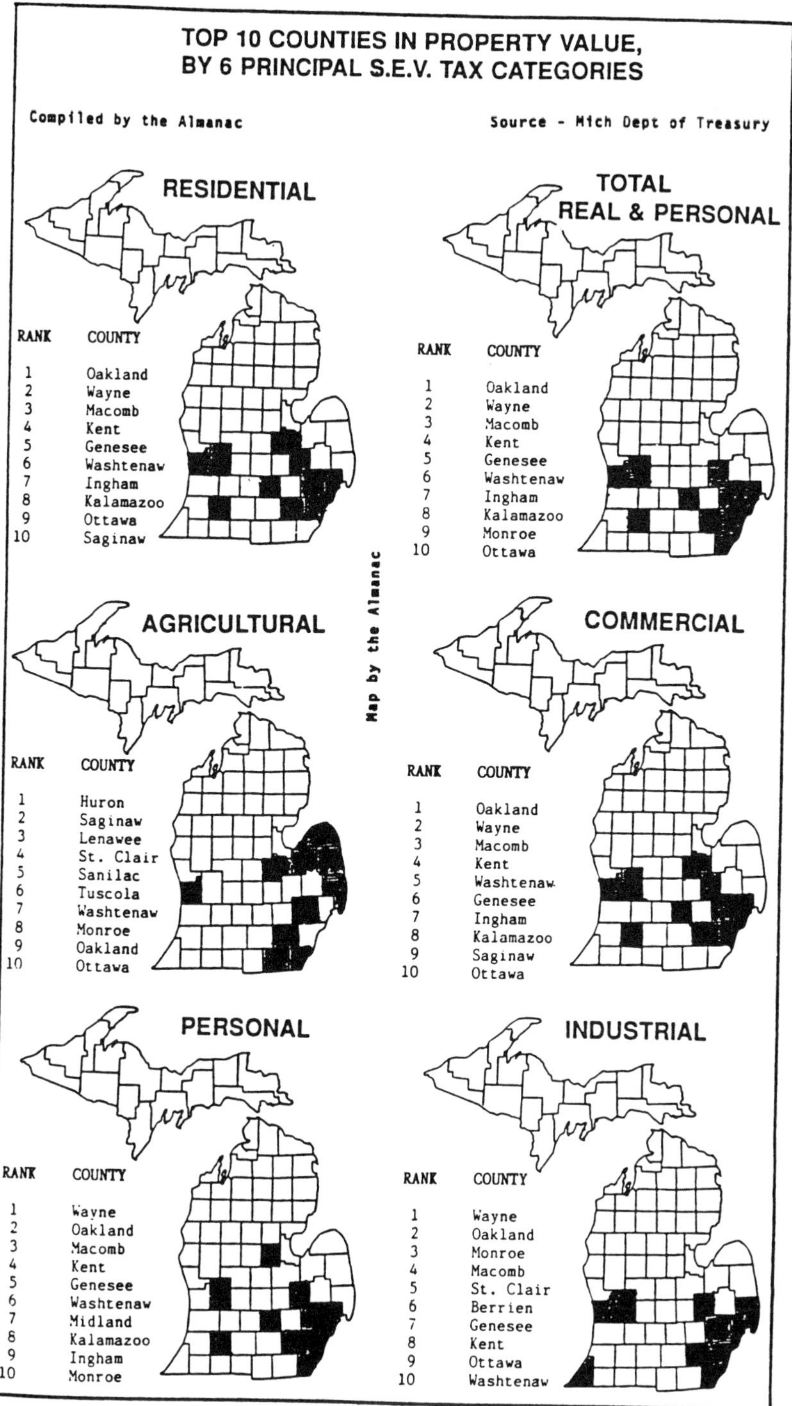
TOP 10 COUNTIES IN PROPERTY VALUE, BY 6 PRINCIPAL S.E.V. TAX CATEGORIES
Compiled by the Almanac
Source - Mich Dept of Treasury
Map by the Almanac
RESIDENTIAL
RANK COUNTY
1 Oakland
2 Wayne
3 Macomb
4 Kent
5 Genesee
6 Washtenaw
7 Ingham
8 Kalamazoo
9 Ottawa
10 Saginaw
TOTAL REAL & PERSONAL
RANK COUNTY
1 Oakland
2 Wayne
3 Macomb
4 Kent
5 Genesee
6 Washtenaw
7 Ingham
8 Kalamazoo
9 Monroe
10 Ottawa
AGRICULTURAL
RANK COUNTY
1 Huron
2 Saginaw
3 Lenawee
4 St. Clair
5 Sanilac
6 Tuscola
7 Washtenaw
8 Monroe
9 Oakland
10 Ottawa
COMMERCIAL
RANK COUNTY
1 Oakland
2 Wayne
3 Macomb
4 Kent
5 Washtenaw
6 Genesee
7 Ingham
8 Kalamazoo
9 Saginaw
10 Ottawa
PERSONAL
RANK COUNTY
1 Wayne
2 Oakland
3 Macomb
4 Kent
5 Genesee
6 Washtenaw
7 Midland
8 Kalamazoo
9 Ingham
10 Monroe
INDUSTRIAL
RANK COUNTY
1 Wayne
2 Oakland
3 Monroe
4 Macomb
5 St. Clair
6 Berrien
7 Genesee
8 Kent
9 Ottawa
10 Washtenaw

BOOKS ABOUT MICHIGAN

The many books listed here were written by many different authors, and published by many different companies. Most of them are available from bookstores, and many from libraries.

All About Michigan Almanac-1995, by Harry Shay, Pub. Instant Information, 292 pages, 17.95

STEWARTS OF THE STATE: MICHIGAN'S 43 GOVERNORS, by George Weeks, 200pp. Pub. Detroit News, $21.00
MICHIGAN, FROM THE EYRY OF THE EAGLE. by Dale Fisher. $56.
THE GREAT LAKES GUIDBOOK SERIES, George Cantor. (I) Lakes Huron & Michigan. 184pp. $7.95. (II) Lakes Erie. 216pp. $7.95.
(III) Lakes Superior & Michigan. 216pp. $7.95.
MAPBOOK OF MICHIGAN COUNTIES. Ed. McGee. 192 pp. $9.95.
BACKPACKING IN MICHIGAN. by P. $6.95.
CANOEING MICHIGAN RIVERS, by Jerry Dennis & Craig Date. 139pp. $12.95
DETROIT TIGERS, AN ILLUSTRATED HISTORY, by Joe Falls, Pub. Walker & Co. 212 pp. $24.95.
ULTIMATE MICHIGAN ADVENTURE, by Gary W. Barfknecht, Pub. Friede Publications. $13.95.
COMPLETE CITY MAPS OF MICHIGAN, by Madson, Pub. Citmap. $9.89.
MURDER, MICHIGAN, by Gary Barfknecht Pub. Friede, 272pp. $7.95.
MAIN STREET:A PORTRAIT OF SMALLTOWN MICHIGAN, by Manny Crististomo, Pub. Detroit Free Press, $19.95 and $29.95.
FAMILY FAIR:A GUIDE TO FUN IN AND AROUND MICHIGAN, by Martin Kohn, Pub. Detroit Free Press, $7.95.
MICHIGAN VOICES: OUR STATE'S HISTORY IN THE WORDS OF THE PEOPLE WHO LIVED IT, Ed. by Joe Grimm. Detroit Free Press, $18.95.
TONY SPINA, CHIEF PHOTOGRAPHER, Pub. Detroit Free Press, $47.50.
GREAT PAGES OF MICHIGAN HISTORY FROM THE DETROIT FREE PRESS, Pub.Detroit Free Press, $18.95.
MOVING PICTURES:A LOOK AT DETROIT FROM HIGH ATOP THE PEOPLE MOVER, By Manny Crisostomo. Pub:Detroit Free Press, $19.95.
MICHIGAN'S PTA'S PARENTS' ANSWER BOOK, Ed. by Alice McCarthy & Patricia Peart. 248pp. $8.95.
LAKE MICHIGAN, by John Torinus.
MICHIGAN ATLAS & GAZETTEER, DeLorme
BAD BOYS, by Isiah Thomas with Matt Dobek.
HUNTING IN MICHIGAN-THE 80'S, 192pp.Pub. The Dept. of Natural Resources, $6.95.
TEN CLASSIC TROUT STREAMS IN MICHIGAN by Garth E. Henderson,250pp.$12.95
MICHIGAN TRAIL ATLAS, by D Hansen & D Holley, 379pp. $19.95.

ADVENTUROUS EATING IN MICHIGAN, by Marjorie Winters.
AROUND THE SHORES OF LAKE MICHIGAN, by Margaret Bogue.
AROUND THE SHORES OF LAKE SUPERIOR,
CRUISING GUIDE TO THE GREAT LAKES & THEIR WATERWAYS, by Marjorie by Brazer.
FISH MICHIGAN-GREAT LAKES, by Tom Huggler, 327pp. $18.95. Ontario &
ANGLER'S GUIDE TO GREAT LAKES, 80pp. $6.95.
MICHIGAN'S TREES, by B. Barnes & W. Wagner, 355pp. $8.95. Russell
MICHIGAN TREES WORTH KNOWING, by Allen Norman F. Smith, 88pp. & G De Ruiter. 149pp. $8.95. Michigan birds), by John Ham & David Mohrardt, 160pp. $9.95. THE
BED & BREAKFAST IN MICHIGAN & SURROUNDING AREAS, by Norma Buzon.
A GUIDE TO 199 MICHIGAN WATERFALLS, by Louis Penrose.
MICHIGAN: A STATE ANTOLOGY, by David D. Anderson, 375pp. Pub. Gale Research Co. $48.00. Rusel

RESTAURANTS OF DETROIT, Ed.) by Molly Abraham, Pub. Detroit Free Press. $7.95.
UNION POWER-AMERICAN DEMOCRACY: THE UAW & THE DEMOCRATIC PARTY, 1972-83, U of M Press, 296pp.$27.
STATE OF WAR:MICHIGAN IN WORLD WAR II, by Alan Clive, Pub. U of M Press, 320pp. $24.95.
ANGLER'S GUIDE TO 10 CLASSIC TROUT STREAMS IN MICHIGAN, by Garth E. Hendrickson, Pub. U of M·Press, $12.95.
PRIMITIVE MAN IN MICHIGAN, by W. B. Hinsdale, Pub. Avery Color Studios, 229pp. $5.95.
ISLE ROYAL NATIONAL PARK, by Jim DuFresne.
MICHIGAN: OFF THE BEATEN TRACK, by Jim DuFresne.
MICHIGAN STATE & NATIONAL PARKS: A COMPLETE GUIDE, by Tom Powers.
NATURAL MICHIGAN: A NATURE-LOVERS GUIDE TO 165 MICHIGAN NATURAL ATTRACTIONS, by Tom Powers.
MICHIGAN ASSOCIATIONS DIRECTORY, Ed. by Christine Hage, Pub:Michigan Library Association.
MICHIGAN STATISTICAL ABSTRACT, Ed. David I. Verway, 733pp. $20.00.
MICHIGAN BOOKS IN PRINT (1985), Ed. Thomas L. Powers & Linda Oaklander Pub. Flint Public Library, $4.95.
MICHIGAN'S 50 BEST FISHING LAKES, 101PP. $5.95.
LADIES OF THE LAKES, maritime book by James Clary, 192pp. $27.95.

THE NORTHERN LIGHTS (150 lighthouses of the Great Lakes), by Charles K. Hyde. 208pp. $27.95.
ROAR OF THUNDER, WHISPER OF WIND, (Michigan waterfalls), by C. J. and Edna Elfant, 128pp. $24.95.
GREAT LAKES SHIPWRECKS, by William Ratigan, 400pp. $9.95.
MICHIGAN: A HISTORY OF THE WOLVERINE STATE, by W. Dunbar & G. May, 800pp. $429.95.
MACKINAC, THE GATHERING PLACE, 171pp. including a 3-D viewer, $27.95.
ATLAS OF MICHIGAN, by Lawrence M. Sommers, 256pp. $21.
MACKINAC, by Donna Winters, Pub: Bigwater Publishing, 170pp. $6.95.
A LOVE AFFAIR WITH THE UPPER PENNINSULA, by Cully Gage, Pub: Avery Color Studio, 106pp. $8.95.

THE FORDS OF DEARBORN (REV), by Ford R. Bryan, Pub: Harlo Press, 301pp. $19.95.
MICHIGAN'S TOWN & COUNTRY INNS, by Susan & Stephen J. Pyle, 232pp. $12.95.
RICHARD'S CHARTBOOK & CRUISING GUIDES: (1) Lake Erie, $39.95; Lake Huron, $47.95; Lake Michigan, $39.95.
THE LONG BLUE EDGE OF SUMMER, (Michigan coastline travel), by Doris Scharfenburg, 215pp. $9.95.
A MOST SUPERIOR PLACE (U.P.), 192pp. $24.95.
A MORAL HUNTER'S COMPANION (for Michigan), by Nancy Smith Weber, 208pp. $14.95.
HUNT MICHIGAN-HOW TO, WHERE TO, WHEN TO by Thomas Huggler, Pub. Mich Union Conservation Clubs, 350pp. $9.95.
HIAWATHA LEGENDS, by Henry R. Schoolcraft, Pub. Avery Color Studios, 272pp. $6.95.
ROAR OF 84: THE TIGER CHAMPIONSHIP SEASON, by Neal Shine, Pub. Detroit Free Press, $3.95.
50 YEARS WITH THE TIGERS, by Fred T Smith, 256pp. $9.95.
GOOD MORNIN'-THE BEST OF BOB TALBERT, S Pub. Detroit Free Press, $4.95.
AMERICAN TRAVELER, MICHIGAN, by Nancy Davies, $7.98.
BEAUTY OF MICHIGAN, Pub. LTA, $19.95.
COME EXPLORE MICHIGAN THE BEAUTIFUL-PICTORIAL HISTORY, by Tom Avery. $11.95.
COPPER COUNTRY, by John S. Penrod. Pub. Avery Colo Studios. $4.49.
DETROIT TODAY, by Dennis Cox, Pub. A&M Publishers. $22.50.
GRAND ADVENTURE TRAVERSE BAY, Pub. Michigan Bureau of History. $6.00.
HOLLAND MICHIGAN, by John Penrod, Pub Penrod/Hiawatha. $4.95.
DISTANT SHORES-PHOTOGRAPHS FROM LAKE SUPERIOR & LAKE MICHIGAN, by Richard Olsenius, Pub. Bluestream Publications. $24.95/$17.95.
IMAGES OF MICHIGAN, Pub. LTA Publications. $6.95.
IN RETROSPECT: 1960-1968, by Michigan Nature Assoc. $29.95.
LEELANAU COUNTY, by K. Scott. $32.00.
MACKINAC BRIDGE & ISLAND, by John Penrod Pub. Penrod/Hiawatha $3.95
MACKINAC ISLAND-IT'S HISTORY IN PICTURES, by Eugene T. Peterson, Pub Mackinac Island Park Commission $18.00.
MICHIGAN, A PICTORIAL GUIDE, by John Penrod, Pub. Penrod/Hiawatha. $4.49
MICHIGAN LIGHTHOUSES-COLOR PICTURES OF 8 OF MICHIGAN'S MOST SCENIC, by John Penrod, Pub. Penrod/Hiawatha. $4.95
MICHIGAN:A SCENIC VIEW OF MICHIGAN'S NORTH COUNTRY, by David Winkler, Pub. Adventure Publishing. $6.98.
NEW LEAF: A HANDBOOK FOR PRESERVING MICHIGAN'S ENVIRONMENT, by Melissa Ramsell, Pub. Michigan Conservation Clubs. $6.95.
THREE BULLETS SEALED HIS LIPS, by Ziewacz, Pub. Michigan State University Press. $13.00.
TIL DEATH DO US PART, by Paula Blanchard, Pub. A & M Publishing. $6.98.
WATER WORKS NINTEEN NINTEY-ONE: A SURVEY OF GREAT LAKES DEVELOPMENT, by Daniel K Ray, Pub. Harbor House Publishiers. $16.95.
ANIMAL TRACKS OF THE GREAT LAKE STATES, by Chris Stall, Pub. Mountaineers. $4.95.
ATLAS OF BREEDING BIRDS OF MICHIGAN, by Michigan State University Press. $39.95.
ENJOYING BIRDS IN MICHIGAN, by Michigan Audubon Society, $12.95.
FISHES OF THE GREAT LAKES REGION, by Carl Hubbs, Pub. University of Michigan. $24.95.
GUIDE TO MICHIGAN'S WILDLIFE, by David Evers, Pub. University of Michigan Press. $12.95.
MAMMALS OF THE GREAT LAKES REGION, by William Burt, Pub. University of Michigan Press. $14.95.
MAYFLIES OF MICHIGAN TROUT STREAMS, by Leonard & Leonard, Pub. Cranbrook Institute Science. $12.95.
MICHIGAN MAMMALS, by R Baker, Pub. M S U Press. $28.95.
MICHIGAN SNAKES, Michigan State University, Pub. Co-op Extension Services. $8.95.
MICHIGAN TURTLES & LIZARDS, Michigan State University, Pub. Co-op Extension Services. $9.60.
MICHIGAN WILDFLOWERS, by Helen U Smith, Pub. Cranbrook Institute of Science. $15.00.
MICHIGAN WILDFLOWERS IN COLOR, by Harry C Lund, Pub. A & M Publishing. $14.95.
MORAL HUNTERS COMPANION, by N S Weber, Pub. Michigan Natural Resources Magazine. $8.95.
MICHIGAN STATE UNIVERSITY, by John Penrod, Pub. Penrod/Hiawatha. $4.95.
MICHIGAN:A PHOTO CELEBRATION, Pub. American Geographic. $12.95.
MICHIGAN'S LAND & SONG OF HIAWATHA, Penrod/Hiawatha. $4.49.
MOST SUPERIOR LAND: LIFE IN THE Michigan Dept of Natural Resources. $24.95.
SLEEPING BEAR: YESTERDAY & TODAY, by George Weeks, Pub. A&M Publishing. $39.95/$24.95.
STILL MICHIGAN: PHOTOGRAPHS OF NORTHWEST LOWER PENINSULA, by Ken Scott, Pub. A&M Publishing. $39.50.
TRAVERSE REGION: THE MICHIGAN RIVIERA, by John Penrod, Pub. Penrod/Hiawatha. $4.95.
TEHQUAMENON IN MICHIGAN'S UPPER PENINSULA, by John Penrod, Pub. Penrod/Haiwatha. $4.49.
WILD LAKE MICHIGAN, by John & Ann Mahan, Pub. Voyageur Press. $27.95.
UPPER PENINSULA OF MICHIGAN, by John S Penrod, Pub. Penrod/Hiawatha. $4.49.
VISIONS OF THE WILD, by Michigan Natural Resources Magazine. $24.95.
ARCHITECTURE IN MICHIGAN, by Wayne Andrews, Pub. Wayne State University Press. $19.95.
ART IN DETROIT PUBLIC PLACES, by Dennis A. Nawrocker, Pub. Wayne State University. $8.95.
ARTISTS IN MICHIGAN, by Dennis Barrie, Pub. Wayne State Univerity Press. $52.50.

DETROIT INSTITUTE OF ARTS: A BRIEF by Wm. Peck, Pub. Wayne State University Press. $19.95.
LEGACY OF ALBERT KAHN, by Hawkins W. Ferry, Pub. Wayne State University. $24.95/$16.95.
MACKINAC AND THE PORCELAIN CITY, by Eugene T. Peterson, Pub. Makinac State Park. $5.00.
MARY SCHAFER AND HER QUILTS, by Marston & Cunningham, Pub. Michigan State University Press. $19.95.
MICHIGAN QUILTS, Editors MacDowell & Fitzgerald, Pub. Michigan State University Press. $24.95.
SKETCHBOOK OF MICHIGAN, by Reynold Weidenaar, Pub. Baker Book House. $15.95.
PATHWAYS TO MICHIGAN BLACK HERITAGE, Pub. Michigan Bureau of History, $2.00.
PIONEERING MICHIGAN, by Eric Freeman, Pub. Fresh Coast Books, $18.95.
ROMANCE OF MICHIGAN'S PAST, by LarryB. Massie, Pub. Priscilla Press. $8.95.
SHORT HISTORY OF MICHIGAN, by John Kern, Pub. Michigan Bureau of History. $3.00.
CALL IT NORTH COUNTRY, by John B. Martin, Pub. Wayne State University Press. $14.95.
COPPER COUNTRY, GOD'S COUNTRY, by Tom Avery, Pub. Avery Color Studios. $11.95.
DOCTOR'S SECRET JOURNAL, by George MAY, Pub: Mackinac Island State Parks Commission. $3.00.
EARLY MACKINAC, by Meade Williams, Pub. Avery Color Studios, $8.95.
FIRE SERVICE OF GRAND RAPIDS, by Carrie Jennings, Pub. Black Letter Press. $6.00.
FIRE SISTER: 299 THINGS EVERY GREAT LAKES BUFF SHOULD KNOW, by Bill Keefe, Pub. Reference Publishing. $15.95.
FROM FRONTIER FOLK TO FACTORY SMOKE, by Larry Massie, Pub. Avery Color Studios. $9.95.

AMERICAN ODYSSEY, by Robert Conot, Pub. Wayne State University. $16.95.
BETWEEN THE IRON & THE PINE by Lewis Reimaun, Pub. Avery Color Studios. $8.95.
BRIDGING THE STRAITS: STORY OF MIGHTY MAC, by Lawrence Rubin, Pub. Wayne State University Press. $12.95.
BRULE'S DISCOVERIES & EXPLORATIONS, by C W Butterfield, Pub. Black Letter Press. $8.00.
COPPER TRAILS TO IRON RAILS, by Larry Massie, Pub. Avery Color Studios. $10.95.
DEEP WOODS FRONTIER, by Theodore Karamanski, Pub. Wayne State University Press. $17.95.
DIARY OF BISHOP FREDERICK BARAGA, by Regina Walling, Pub. Wayne State University Press. $35.00.
HISTORY OF ANN ARBOR, by Jonathan Morwil, Pub. U of M Press. $12.95.
MAKING OF MICHIGAN, 1820-1860, by Justin Kastenbaum, Pub. Wayne State University Press. $17.95.
MICHIGAN: A HISTORY, by Bruce Catton, Pub. W. W. Norton. $10.95.
MICHIGAN DATE LOG, Pub. River Road. $5.95.
MICHIGAN FUR TRADE, by Ida Johnson, Pub. Black Letter Press. $17.50.
MICHIGAN IN THE WAR OF 1812, by Fred Hamil, Pub. Michigan Bureau of History. $2.00.
MICHIGAN LUMBERTOWNS, by Jeremy Kilar, Pub. Wayne State University Press. $19.95.
MICHIGAN PLACE NAMES, by Walter Romig, Pub. Wayne State University Press. $19.95.
MICHIGAN SOLDIERS ON THE CIVIL WAR, by Frederick Williams, Pub. Michigan Bureau of History. $3.00.
MICHIGAN STATE PARKS: YESTERDAY THROUGH TOMMORROW, by Claire Korn, Pub. Michigan State University Press. $10.95.
MICHIGAN: VISIONS OF THE PAST, by Richard Hathaway, Pub. Wayne State University Press. $14.00.
MICHIGAN'S WHITE PINE ERA, by Rolland Maybee, Pub. Michigan Bureau of History. $3.00.

MICHIGAN COPPER COUNTRY IN EARLY PHOTOS, by B E Tyler, Pub. Black Letter Press. $6.00.
MICHIGAN GOLD: MINING IN THE UPPER PENINSULA, by Danuel R Fountain, Pub. Adventure Publications. $12.95.
MICHIGAN PREHISTORY MYSTERIES, by Betty Sodders, Pub. Avery Color Studios, $10.95.
MICHIGAN TRIVIA, by Couch and Couch, Pub. Rutledge Hill Press. $5.95.
MICHILLANEOUS, by Gary Barfnecht, Pub. Friede Publications, $7.95.
MICHILLANEOUS II, by Gary Barfnecht, Pub. Friede Publications, $9.95.
MIGHTY MAC: A PICTURE HISTORY, by Lawrence Rubin, Pub. Wayne State University. $12.95.
MYTHS & LEGENDS OF THE MACKINACS & THE LAKE REGION, by Grace Kane, Pub. Black Letter Press, $6.50.
NOTES FROM THE NORTH COUNTRY, by O B Eustis, Pub. University of Michigan Press. $14.95.
NORTH MICHIGAN HANDBOOK FOR TRAVELERS: 1898, by J G Inglis, Pub. Black Letter Publishing, $7.95.
THE SOO, by C S Osborn, Pub. Black Letter Press, $5.00.

KNOW YOUR SHIPS-33RD ED, by Tom Manse, Pub. Marine Publications, $9.95.
LAKEBOATS 1992, by Greenwood & Dill, Freshwater Press. $7.95.
LIFE ON THE GREAT LAKES: A WHEELMAN'S STORY, Wayne State University, $29.95.
LIGHTHOUSE MAPS OF GREAT LAKES, Pub. Avery Color Studios, $9.95.
LORE OF THE LAKES, by Dan Bowen, Pub. Freshwater Press. $10.95.
MEMORIES OF THE LAKES, by Dana Bowen, Pub. Freshwater Press. $10.95.
NAMESAKES OF THE LAKES SERIES, by John O. Greenwood, Pub. Freshwater Press. $20.95.

NAMESAKES OF THE LAKES VOL. 1. $24.95.
NAMESAKES: 1900-1909.
NAMESAKES: 1910-1919.
NAMESAKES: 1920-1929.
NAMESAKES: 1930-1955.
NAMESAKES: 1956-1980.

NAMESAKES OF THE EIGHTIES(VOL. II)
NAMESAKES OF THE 90'S.
REFLECTIONS: STORIES OF THE GREAT LAKES, by Paul G Wieing, Pub. Stonehouse Publications. $19.95.
STRANGE ADVENTURES OF THE GREAT LAKES, by Dwight Boyer, Pub. Freshwater Press. $10.95.
FRESHWATER FURY, by Frank Barcus, Pub. Wayne State University Press. $29.95.
GALES OF NOVEMBER, by Robert Hemming, Pub. Contemporary Books. $12.95.
GHOST SHIPS OF THE GREAT LAKES, by Dwight Boyer, Pub. Freshwater Press. $10.95.
ISLE ROYALE SHIPWRECKS, by Fred Stonehouse, Pub. Avery Color Studios. $10.95.
LAKE SUPERIOR SHIPWRECKS, by Julious Wolff, $45.00 cl. $34.95ppr.
GREAT SHIPWRECK SURVIVALS, by William Ratigan, Pub. Eerdman Publishing. $14.95.
MUNISING SHIPWRECKS, by Fred Stonehouse, Pub. Avery Color Studios. $9.95.
SHIPWRECK CHART OF GREAT LAKES, by Tom Manse, Pub. Marine Publishing. $9.95.
SHIPWRECKS OF LAKE HURON, by Parker, Pub. Avery Color Studios, $8.95.
SHIPWRECK! A COMPREHENSIVE DIRECTORY OF OVER 3700 SHIPWRECKS, by David D. Swayze, Pub. Harbor House Publishers. $19.95.
SHIPWRECKS OF THE LAKES, by Dana Bowen, Pub. Freshwater Publishing. $10.95.
STEAMING THROUGH SMOKE & FIRE, by James Donahue, Pub. Anchor Publishing. $12.00.

COUNTRY ROADS OF MICHIGAN, by Doris Scharfenberg, $9.95.
MICHIGAN OUT-OF-DOORS, PICTURES, PROSE & POETRY, $44.95.
ON THE WATER, MICHIGAN-GUIDE TO WATER RECREATION, by Eric Freedman
ONCE UPON AN ISLE-FISHING FAMILIES ON ISLE ROYAL, by Howard Siverson, $20.95.
SHIPWRECKS OF THE STRAITS OF MACKINAC by Charles E. Feltner & Jeri Baron $17.95.
TRAVELING THROUGH TIME-GUIDE TO MICHIGAN'S HISTORICAL MARKERS, Laura R. Ashlee, Editor. $14.95. Pub. Michigan Dept of State.
MICHIGAN LIGHTHOUSES-TRAVELER'S GUIDE TO 116, $14.95.
WILD MICHIGAN, Pub. morthwood Press. $24.95.

BUTCHER'S DOZEN: 13 FAMOUS MICHIGAN MURDERS, by Lawrence Wakefield, Pub. A & M Publishing. $13.95.
DANGEROUS SOCIETY, by Carl Taylor, Pub. Michigan State University Press. $9.00.
FIX IT FAST AND EASY, by Glenn Haege, Pub. Master Handman Press. $14.95.
GEOLOGIC STORY OF THE ISLE ROYLE, by N K Huber, Pub. Avery Color Studios. $9.95.
GEOLOGY OF MICHIGAN, by John Dorr, Pub. University of Michigan Press. $32.50.

HARMONY & DISSONANCE: VOICES OF JEWISH IDENTIY IN DETROIT, by Sidney M Bolkosky, Pub. Wayne State University Press. $30.00.
JOURNEY OF JOHN ENGLER, by the Detroit News, Pub. A & M Publishing. $10.00.
LATE GREAT LAKES, by William Ashworth, Pub. Wayne State University Press. $15.95.
LIFE AFTER THE LINE, by Josie Kearns, Pub. Wayne State University Press. $17.95.
MICHIGAN MURDERS, by Gary Barnecht Pub. Friede Publications. $6.95.
MICHIGAN FOLKLIFE READER, by C. Kurt Dewhurst, Pub. Michigan State University Press. $17.00.
PRESERVATION DIRECTORY: A GUIDE TO MICHIGAN, by Chistine Hill-Rowley, Pub. Heritage Research House. $13.95.
TERRIFYING STEAMBOAT STORIES, by James L Donahue, Pub. A&M Publishing. $15.95.
WRECK OF THE EDMUND, by Fred Stonehouse, Pub. Avery Color Studios. $9.95.
BEYOND THE MODEL T: OTHER VENTURES OF HENRY FORD, by Ford R Bryan, Pub. Wayne State University Press. $24.95.
BLACKS & CHICANOS IN URBAN MICHIGAN, Michigan Bureau of History. $5.00.

GENESEE COUNTY FAIR SINCE 1850, by Stan Perkins, Pub. Briadblade Press. $8.95.
GREAT STORIES OF THE GREAT LAKES, by Dwight Boyer, Pub. Freshwater Press. $10.95.
HISTORY OF GRAND RAPIDS WITH BIOGRAPICAL SKETCHES, by Charles Tutle, Pub. Black Letter Press, $7.50.
HOLLAND AREA, by Larry Massie, Pub. Priscilla Press. $25.95.
INSIDE MACKINAC, by Peterson, Pub. Peterson Publishing. $14.95.
JOE MADDY OF INTERLOCHEN, by Norma L. Brownig, Pub. Contemporary Books. $20.00.
LORE OF WOLVERINE COUNTRY, by Stan Perkins, Pub. Broadblade Press. $17.00.
LANDLOOKER IN THE UPPER PENINSULA OF MICHIGAN, by John M. Longyear, Pub. Marquette County Historical Society. $6.95.
MICHIGAN GHOST TOWNS OF THE LOWER PENINSULA, by Roy L Dodge, Pub. Glendon Publishing. $10.95.

MICHIGAN *DRIVING* LAWS

SPEED LIMIT (All roads and highways, unless otherwise posted)

Passenger cars	55 mph (88 km/h)
except on designated, signed rural freeways	65 mph (104 km/h)
Trucks	55 mph (88 km/h)
School buses	50 mph (80 km/h)
except on freeways	55 mph (88 km/h)

Minimum 45 mph (72 km/h) for all vehicles on freeways. Motorists must reduce speeds when weather conditions are poor or where lower speed limits are posted.

SAFETY BELTS REQUIRED

To save lives and reduce injuries. Michigan law requires all drivers and all front-seat passengers to wear a safety belt. The fine is $25.

CHILD RESTRAINT

All passengers up to age 16 must also be properly buckled up, **regardless of where seated.** Infants, up to age one, must be fastened in an approved infant carrier. Up to age four, all children riding in the front seat must be in an approved child safety seat. In the back seat, children may use the vehicle safety belts. Buckle up for Life!

RAILROAD CROSSINGS

Motorists are required to stop when lights are flashing at a railroad crossing and are prohibited by state law from driving around crossing gates when they are lowered. Proceed with caution at all crossings and expect a train at any time. Trains can't stop.

Source - MI Dept of Transportation

PENALTIES THAT MAY BE ASSESSED BY COURTS FOR CERTAIN HUNTING VIOLATIONS:

VIOLATION:	PENALTY:
Violations of permits, seasons, bag limits, shooting hours and methods of taking game.	$50.00 to $500.00 fine and/or up to 90 days in jail.
Illegal taking/possession of elk.	$500.00 to $2,000.00 fine and/or 30 to 180 days in jail, and three to four year revocation of all hunting licenses, plus $1,500 restitution per elk.
Illegal taking/possession of moose.	$1,000.00 to $5,000.00 fine and 90 days to one year in jail, and three to four year revocation of all hunting licenses, plus $1,500 restitution per moose.
Illegal taking/possession of deer, bear or wild turkey.	$200.00 to $1,000.00 fine and five to 90 days in jail, and three to four year revocation of all hunting licenses, plus at least $1,000 restitution per animal.
Illegal taking/possession of all other game species.	$100.00 to $1,000.00 fine and/or up to 90 days in jail, plus restitution.
Illegal use of artificial light with bow or gun.	$100.00 to $500.00 fine and/or five to 90 days in jail and one to two years revocation of all hunting licenses.
Carrying a firearm while under influence of alcohol or drugs.	$500.00 fine and/or up to 90 days in jail.
Multiple offender - convicted two times previously within the preceding five years.	$500.00 to $2,000.00 fine and 10 to 180 days in jail and up to two years revocation of all hunting and fishing licenses, plus restitution, if applicable.

Source - MI Dept of Natural Resources

FISHING - STATE RECORD SIZE CAUGHT

MASTER ANGLER AWARDS

Master Angler Certificates are awarded to anglers who catch state record fish, or one of the top 5 fish of their kind entered during the year. Arm patches are given to all entrants whose fish meet either established weight or catch and release criteria. **To be eligible under the weight criteria, the fish must meet minimum weight standards**, be weighed on inspected scales, have signatures of two witnesses verifying weight, and pictures taken (full close-up) of the fish in color. **To be eligible under the catch and release criteria, the fish must be caught during legal seasons, meet minimum length requirements**, (measured to the nearest 1/8 of an inch), have signature of one witness verifying length, and provide a picture (full close-up) of the fish in color). For details and entry forms, contact DNR offices listed on page 3. Deadline for entries is **January 10 of the following year**.

Species	Minimum Entry Length (inches)	Minimum Entry Weight (lbs.-oz.)	Current State Record (lbs.-oz.)
American Eel	32"	3-0	7-7
Bass, Largemouth	22"	6-0	11-15
Bass, Rock	11"	1-0	3-10
Bass, Smallmouth	21"	5-0	9-4
Bass, Warmouth	9"	1-0	——
Bass, White	16"	2-0	6-7
Bass, White (Hybrid)	24"	7-0	8-3
Bluegill	10"	1-0	2-12
Buffalo, Big Mouth	32"	20-0	——
Buffalo, Black	26"	10-0	26-6
Bullhead, Black	14"	1-4	2-5
Bullhead, Brown	14"	1-8	3-10
Bullhead, Yellow	14"	1-8	3-7.25
Bowfin	27"	7-0	14-0
Burbot	26"	5-0	18-4
Carp	30"	20-0	61-8* 45-0**
Carpsucker	19"	3-0	7-8
Catfish, Channel	27"	8-0	40-0
Catfish, Flathead	29"	10-0	47-8
Crappie, Black	14"	1-12	4-2
Crappie, White	14"	1-12	2-10
Freshwater Drum	21"	7-0	26-0
Gizzard Shad	16"	1-8	3-8
Lake Herring	16"	2-8	5-6
Lake Sturgeon	50"	70-0	193-0
Longnose Gar	32"	5-0	15-0
Mooneye	12"	0-12	1-7
Musky, Great Lks.	42"	20-0	62-8
Musky, Northern	42"	20-0	45-0
Musky, Tiger	42"	20-0	51-3
Northern Pike	40"	18-0	39-0
Perch, White	10"	0-8	1-9
Perch, Yellow	14"	1-13	3-12
Salmon, Atlantic	33"	12-0	32-10
Salmon, Chinook	41"	27-0	46-1
Salmon, Coho	32"	12-0	30-9
Salmon, Pink	21"	3-0	8-9
Salmon, Pinook (Pink/King Hybrid)	30"	9-0	14-0
Sauger	21"	5-0	6-9
Smelt***	10"	None	11.8"
Splake	32"	14-0	16-4
Sucker, Longnose	17"	2-0	6-14
Sucker, N. Hog	13"	1-8	2-8
Sucker, Redhorse	22"	4-0	12-14.2
Sucker, White	20"	3-0	7-3
Sunfish, Green	9"	0-12	1-8
Sunfish, Hybrid	10"	0-12	1-7
Sunfish, P.Seed	9"	0-12	1-6
Sunfish, Redear	10"	1-0	1-13
Trout, Brook	17"	2-0	6-12
Trout, Brown	33"	16-0	34-6
Trout, Lake	34"	18-0	53-0
Trout, Rainbow (Steelhead)	34"	17-0	26-8
Trout, Tiger (Brook/Brown Hyb.)	18"	2-0	9-4
Walleye	29"	11-0	17-3
Whitefish, Lake	23"	6-0	14-4.5
Whitefish, Menominee	15"	1-0	4-0

*State Record Carp; **Largest hook and line caught Carp; ***The minimum entry requirement for Smelt is 10" for both catch and keep and catch and release entries. The Smelt State Record is by length rather than weight.

Existing Michigan Department of Transportation (MDOT) Park & Ride Lots

These are courtesy lots provided for the convenience of car and vanpool groups.

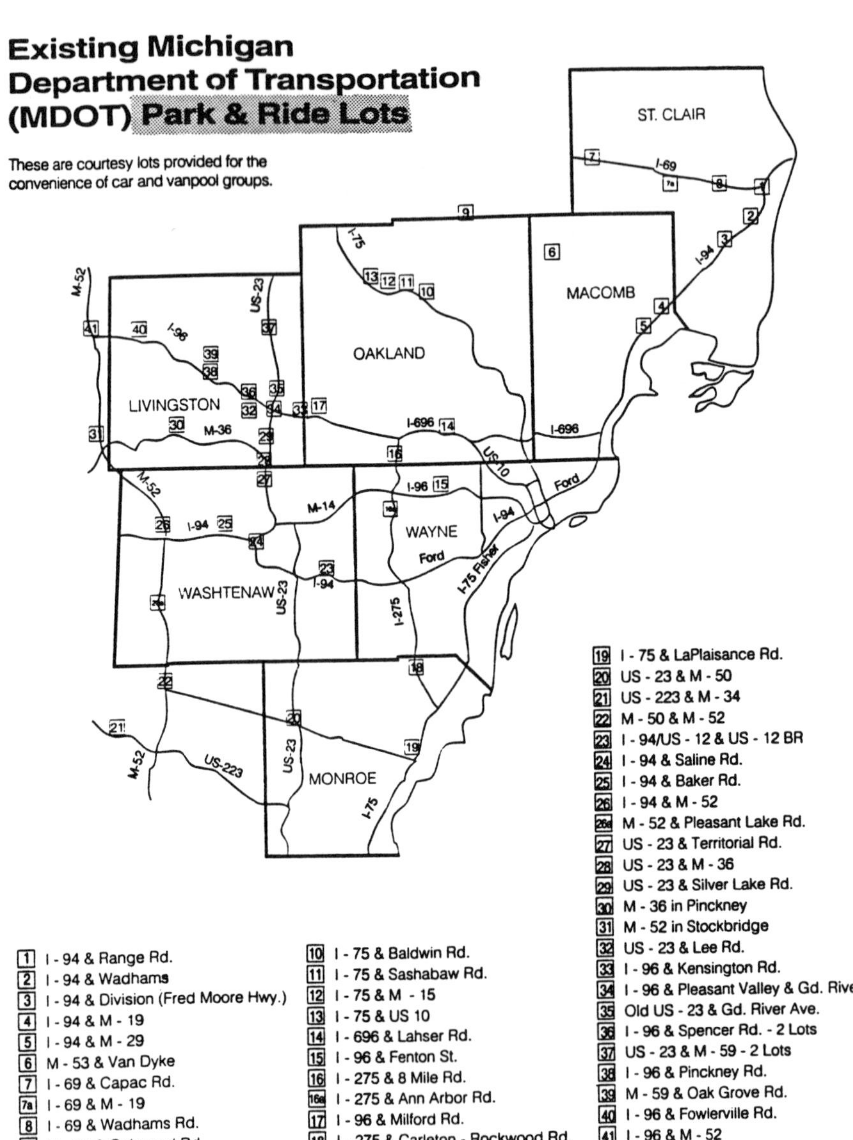

1 I - 94 & Range Rd.
2 I - 94 & Wadhams
3 I - 94 & Division (Fred Moore Hwy.)
4 I - 94 & M - 19
5 I - 94 & M - 29
6 M - 53 & Van Dyke
7 I - 69 & Capac Rd.
7a I - 69 & M - 19
8 I - 69 & Wadhams Rd.
9 M - 24 & Oakwood Rd.
10 I - 75 & Baldwin Rd.
11 I - 75 & Sashabaw Rd.
12 I - 75 & M - 15
13 I - 75 & US 10
14 I - 696 & Lahser Rd.
15 I - 96 & Fenton St.
16 I - 275 & 8 Mile Rd.
16a I - 275 & Ann Arbor Rd.
17 I - 96 & Milford Rd.
18 I - 275 & Carleton - Rockwood Rd.
19 I - 75 & LaPlaisance Rd.
20 US - 23 & M - 50
21 US - 223 & M - 34
22 M - 50 & M - 52
23 I - 94/US - 12 & US - 12 BR
24 I - 94 & Saline Rd.
25 I - 94 & Baker Rd.
26 I - 94 & M - 52
26a M - 52 & Pleasant Lake Rd.
27 US - 23 & Territorial Rd.
28 US - 23 & M - 36
29 US - 23 & Silver Lake Rd.
30 M - 36 in Pinckney
31 M - 52 in Stockbridge
32 US - 23 & Lee Rd.
33 I - 96 & Kensington Rd.
34 I - 96 & Pleasant Valley & Gd. River
35 Old US - 23 & Gd. River Ave.
36 I - 96 & Spencer Rd. - 2 Lots
37 US - 23 & M - 59 - 2 Lots
38 I - 96 & Pinckney Rd.
39 M - 59 & Oak Grove Rd.
40 I - 96 & Fowlerville Rd.
41 I - 96 & M - 52

RESIDENTIAL SALES AND PRICES
SELECT AREAS IN MICHIGAN

Source; Michigan Association of Realtors

	1993 Jan-Nov # Sales	1994 Jan-Nov # Sales	% Change	1993 Jan-Nov Ave Price	1994 Jan-Nov Ave Price	% Change
Alpena, Alcona, Presque Isle	319	311	-2.51%	$60,958	$63,326	3.89%
Ann Arbor Area	2617	2836	8.37%	$134,669	$140,033	3.98%
Battle Creek	1202	1390	15.64%	$64,503	$69,365	7.54%
Down River	2863	3207	12.02%	$75,471	$79,517	5.36%
Flint Area	3905	4307	10.29%	$73,458	$80,953	10.20%
Grand Rapids	8189	8312	1.50%	$88,097	$90,535	2.77%
Gratiot-Isabella	689	619	-10.16%	$56,495	$62,153	10.01%
Greater Kalamazoo	4245	4344	2.33%	$84,257	$88,875	5.48%
Greater Lansing	4822	5393	8.65%	$81,824	$85,878	4.95%
Holland	1583	1730	9.29%	$93,927	$102,041	8.64%
Livingston County	1467	1836	25.15%	$125,024	$131,284	5.01%
North Oakland County	3163	3875	22.51%	$108,192	$112,276	3.77%
Rochester Area	2429	1389	-42.82%	$148,485	$161,892	9.03%
Saginaw	1676	1824	8.83%	$68,968	$70,446	2.14%
Shiawassee County	290	388	33.79%	$56,732	$62,276	9.77%
South Oakland County	4901	5325	8.65%	$94,851	$106,562	12.35%
Southwestern Michigan	2237	2499	11.71%	$85,479	$87,036	1.82%
St. Joseph County	475	497	4.63%	$54,821	$62,051	13.19%
West Central	210	195	-7.14%	$57,527	$57,303	-0.39%
TOTALS	47282	50277	6.33%	$80,687	$85,690	6.20%

DEER and ELK in MICHIGAN

Deer are found in all of Michigan's 83 counties. The statewide deer population is well over one million animals.

Deer will cross roads and highways anywhere. Slow down immediately when one is sighted ahead. Motorists should be especially careful during the first 2 hours after dark and during the months of October, November and December when deer are most active.

Michigan's elk herd, numbering about 1,200 animals, ranges through parts of the Pigeon River Country and Atlanta state forests, and on adjacent private lands in Montmorency, Otsego, Cheboygan and Presque Isle counties. A recently established moose herd, though small, ranges through most of the Upper Peninsula.

Source – MI Dept of Transportation

HUNTING LICENSE FEES

RESIDENT

	(Minimum Age)	
Bear	(14)	$14.35
Archery Deer	(12)	$12.85
Junior Archery Deer	(12-16)	$6.60
Firearm Deer	(14)	$12.85
Elk	(14)	$100.35
Nonrefundable Appl. Fee Elk	(14)	$4.00
Fur Harvester's		$15.35
Junior Fur Harvester's	(up to 16)	$7.85
Small Game	(12)	$9.85
Junior Small Game	(12-16)	$5.10
Sportsperson's	(14)	$45.35
Senior Hunting	(65)	$4.00
Turkey	(12)	$9.85
Senior Turkey	(65)	$1.00

NONRESIDENT

	(Minimum Age)	
Bear	(14)	$150.35
Archery Deer	(12)	$75.35
Firearm Deer	(14)	$100.35
Fur Harvester's		$150.35
Small Game	(12)	$50.35
3-day Small Game	(12)	$20.35
Turkey	(12)	$50.35

RESIDENT & NONRESIDENT

Passbook	$1.00
Michigan Waterfowl Stamp	$3.85
Managed Waterfowl Hunt	$3.00/day
Managed Waterfowl Hunt	$10.00/ season

Nonrefundable Application Fee:
Turkey, Antlerless Deer, and Waterfowl Hunting Reservations $3.00

Source – MI Dept of Natural Resources

VITAL STATISTICS - MICHIGAN - ANNUAL 1900 - 1993

Births - Deaths - Marriages - Divorces

RATES PER 1,000 POPULATION

Source: Office of the State Registrar and Division of Health Statistics, MDPH

Year	Live Births	Deaths All Ages	Marriages	Divorces
1900	18.1	13.4	19.2	2.0
1901	17.6	13.3	19.6	2.0
1902	18.2	12.6	20.5	2.3
1903	18.1	13.1	20.5	2.3
1904	18.4	13.4	19.3	2.2
1905	18.0	13.3	20.1	2.2
1906	22.1	14.0	20.7	2.4
1907	21.9	13.6	20.7	2.3
1908	23.7	13.5	18.9	2.2
1909	23.2	13.1	19.7	2.5
1910	22.8	14.2	20.7	2.6
1911	22.7	13.1	20.6	2.8
1912	23.3	13.0	21.3	2.6
1913	23.8	13.3	21.9	2.6
1914	24.3	12.7	22.4	2.8
1915	25.0	12.5	21.9	2.9
1916	26.2	13.8	24.1	3.3
1917	26.2	13.8	25.1	3.3
1918	26.1	15.6	19.0	3.1
1919	23.5	12.7	25.4	4.2
1920	25.1	14.2	27.7	4.7
1921	25.4	11.7	21.9	4.1
1922	23.1	11.2	22.3	3.9
1923	23.1	12.3	24.7	4.4
1924	23.7	11.4	24.1	4.5
1925	23.3	11.6	21.7	4.5
1926	22.5	12.4	18.7	4.5
1927	22.3	11.3	16.2	4.7
1928	21.2	11.9	16.2	4.6
1929	20.9	11.9	15.6	5.1
1930	20.4	10.6	12.2	4.4
1931	18.5	10.1	11.8	3.9
1932	17.3	10.1	11.6	3.2
1933	16.2	9.8	13.3	3.1
1934	16.8	10.1	17.3	4.0
1935	17.3	10.1	17.9	4.3
1936	17.4	10.8	18.5	4.5
1937	17.8	10.4	18.7	4.9
1938	18.7	9.8	11.6	4.1
1939	18.1	10.0	14.5	4.4

Year	Live Births	Deaths All Ages	Marriages	Divorces
1940	18.9	9.9	17.6	4.6
1941	19.8	9.7	18.8	4.9
1942	22.4	9.5	18.6	5.1
1943	23.3	10.6	16.5	5.7
1944	21.1	10.0	15.5	6.8
1945	20.5	9.9	17.8	7.8
1946	24.3	9.6	27.6	10.2
1947	26.4	9.4	23.5	7.1
1948	24.8	9.1	20.0	5.2
1949	24.6	9.0	16.7	5.1
1950	25.1	9.0	18.3	5.0
1951	26.3	9.0	16.3	4.7
1952	26.5	8.8	15.1	4.4
1953	26.7	9.1	15.6	4.8
1954	27.3	8.6	14.6	4.6
1955	27.1	8.7	15.4	4.9
1956	27.4	8.6	15.2	4.3
1957	26.7	8.5	14.1	4.0
1958	25.8	8.4	14.0	3.6
1959	24.9	8.4	14.8	4.1
1960	24.9	8.7	15.6	4.3
1961	24.4	8.5	16.0	4.1
1962	23.0	8.8	16.4	4.4
1963	22.3	9.0	17.0	4.4
1964	21.6	8.9	18.2	4.8
1965	20.3	9.0	19.8	5.0
1966	19.9	9.0	20.2	5.2
1967	18.9	8.7	19.6	5.5
1968	18.3	8.9	21.0	5.9
1969	19.0	8.8	21.4	6.5
1970	19.3	8.6	20.7	6.7
1971	18.1	8.6	20.5	7.1
1972	16.3	8.8	20.9	7.9
1973	15.6	8.7	20.8	8.2
1974	15.1	8.4	19.3	8.8
1975	14.7	8.2	18.2	9.0
1976	14.4	8.3	18.2	9.5
1977	15.1	8.1	18.8	9.4
1978	15.1	8.1	19.2	9.8
1979	15.6	7.9	19.3	9.6
1980	15.7	8.1	18.8	9.7
1981	15.2	8.2	18.4	9.3
1982	15.0	8.2	17.9	8.6
1983	14.5	8.4	17.2	8.3
1984	15.0	8.4	17.8	8.3
1985	15.2	8.7	17.4	8.5
1986	15.1	8.8	17.0	8.7
1987	15.3	8.7	16.2	8.7
1988	15.1	8.7	16.3	8.7
1989	16.0	8.5	16.4	8.7
1990	16.5	8.4	16.4	8.7
1991	15.9	8.5	15.5	8.6
1992	15.2	8.4	15.1	8.6
1993	14.8	8.7	15.0	8.6

VITAL STATISTICS - COUNTIES

Births - Deaths - Marriages - Divorces
1993

RATES PER 1,000 POPULATION

Source: Office of the State Registrar and Division of Health Statistics, MDPH

Area	Population Estimate[1]	Live Births	Deaths	Marriages	Divorces
Michigan	9,433,666	139,560	82,286	70,771	40,470
Alcona	10,254	85	132	65	55
Alger	9,349	82	109	73	36
Allegan	93,078	1,389	811	715	433
Alpena	31,000	326	323	252	138
Antrim	18,897	274	227	179	95
Arenac	15,625	181	186	121	65
Baraga	7,828	8	121	50	17
Barry	51,196	693	411	395	257
Bay	112,131	1,451	1,032	882	573
Benzie	12,616	164	159	113	75
Berrien	161,466	2,392	1,629	1,417	762
Branch	41,871	576	382	331	258
Calhoun	138,381	1,921	1,343	1,171	804
Cass	49,112	572	463	378	236
Charlevoix	22,225	311	220	228	113
Cheboygan	21,780	283	239	204	98
Chippewa	35,640	413	302	266	128
Clare	26,384	391	350	230	154
Clinton	59,397	799	385	438	239
Crawford	12,972	167	145	107	65
Delta	38,208	445	387	334	136
Dickinson	27,014	340	309	251	132
Eaton	95,253	1,217	656	793	424
Emmet	26,057	350	251	223	133
Genesee	433,508	6,995	3,644	3,388	1,709
Gladwin	23,007	285	244	170	118
Gogebic	17,891	165	252	131	70
Grand Traverse	67,290	886	502	682	429
Gratiot	39,450	547	395	260	146
Hillsdale	44,407	607	392	319	241
Houghton	35,831	367	404	259	98
Huron	34,977	384	433	223	106
Ingham	281,798	4,056	1,854	2,362	1,205
Ionia	57,986	806	446	480	248
Iosco	30,211	291	337	199	155
Iron	13,136	125	210	99	52
Isabella	56,212	657	340	435	239
Jackson	151,740	2,106	1,376	1,257	889
Kalamazoo	225,648	3,155	1,724	1,990	1,022
Kalkaska	14,038	198	130	122	85

Area	Population Estimate	Live Births	Deaths	Marriages	Divorces
Kent	511,997	8,811	3,784	4,649	2,252
Keweenaw	1,706	17	27	15	5
Lake	9,029	120	129	76	40
Lapeer	78,526	1,137	532	638	366
Leelanau	17,292	231	166	129	76
Lenawee	94,132	1,185	827	561	459
Livingston	122,658	1,688	705	956	566
Luce	5,604	76	54	57	28
Mackinac	10,752	130	126	183	57
Macomb	728,220	9,643	6,188	6,102	2,981
Manistee	21,925	232	274	202	129
Marquette	71,428	933	598	622	266
Mason	26,420	325	271	236	149
Mecosta	38,553	470	301	279	146
Menominee	24,593	266	293	202	98
Midland	77,950	1,131	532	757	371
Missaukee	12,739	164	126	163	48
Monroe	135,962	1,608	934	843	591
Montcalm	55,445	807	472	471	289
Montmorency	9,355	85	140	63	27
Muskegon	161,980	2,389	1,537	1,357	895
Newaygo	40,756	613	386	367	240
Oakland	1,118,611	16,160	8,316	8,704	4,919
Oceana	22,954	343	220	209	115
Ogemaw	19,640	259	274	163	90
Ontonagon	8,761	85	107	64	30
Osceola	20,638	290	194	172	105
Oscoda	8,222	83	142	72	51
Otsego	19,096	289	175	164	85
Ottawa	197,297	3,152	1,229	1,572	730
Presque Isle	13,865	129	172	96	49
Roscommon	20,861	210	333	163	102
Saginaw	212,477	3,221	1,998	1,730	889
St Clair	150,085	2,112	1,361	1,055	702
St Joseph	59,388	866	559	494	380
Sanilac	40,810	557	432	289	151
Schoolcraft	8,478	108	118	74	27
Shiawassee	70,832	1,026	519	570	293
Tuscola	56,130	759	528	378	219
Van Buren	72,331	1,118	647	566	438
Washtenaw	288,025	3,944	1,591	2,088	1,190
Wayne	2,096,179	35,802	21,455	11,356	7,460
Wexford	27,099	436	254	272	128

ASSOCIATIONS & ORGANIZATIONS IN MICHIGAN

Compiled by the Almanac/multi-sources

AFL-CIO, Mich-419 S. Washington, Lansing (517) 487-5966.

Abortion Rights Action League, Mich-1314 David Whitney Bldg., Detroit 48207 (313) 965-6939.

Aging, Area Agencies On-Association of Mich-115 W. Allegan, Lansing (517) 482-4871.

Agri-Dealers Association, Mich-2500 Kerry, Lansing (517) 485-8580.

Agricultural Co-op Mktg. Assoc-7373 W. Saginaw, Lansing (517) 323-7000.

Alcohol Problems, MichInterfaith Council On-1120 E. Oakland, Lansing (517) 484-0016.

Alcoholism, Natl Council On-840 David Whitney Gldg., Detroit (313) 963-0581.

American Legion, Dept. of Mich. & Aux-212 N. Verlinden, Lansing (517) 371-4720.

American-Arab Anti-Discrimination Comm-2111 Woodward, Detroit (313) 965-7680.

Amvets, Dept. of Mich-477 Michigan, Detroit (313) 964-6920.

Amer Helenic Congress-13365 Michigan, Dearbom (313) 846-7440.

Anti-Defamation League of B'Nai B'Rith-163 Madison, Detroit (313) 962-9686.

Anti-Vivisection League, Mich-9145 Manor, Detroit (313) 931-1050.

Arabian Horse Assoc. of Mich-5201 Venorden, Webberville (517) 521-4001.

Architects, Mich. Soci. of-553 E. Jefferson, Detroit (313) 965-4100.

Arthritus Foundation-923 Beech, Lansing (517) 485--9920.

Arts, Mich Council for the-1200 Sixth, Detroit 48226 (313) 256-3731.

Assoc. Executives, Mich Assoc of 305 Abbott, E. Lansing (517) 336-4334

Athletic Assoc High School-1019 Trowbridge, E. Lansing (517) 332-5046.

Audubon Soc., Mich-6011 W. St. Joseph, Lansing (517) 886-9144.

Automobile Dealers, Mich Assoc of -1500 Kendale, E. Lansing (517) 337-3911.

Automotive Hall of Fame-3225 Cook, Midland (517) 631-5760.

Badminton Assoc., U.S.* P.O. Box 456, Waterford (313) 627-4884.

Bankers Assoc. of Mich - 222 N. Washington Sq., Lansing (517) 485-3660.

Bankers Assoc, Mich Community-2385 Delhi Commerce Dr., Holt (517) 487-9139

Baptist Churches, Am-of Michigan-4578 S. Hagadom, E. Lansing (517) 332-3594.

Bar, Mich State-306 Townsend, Lansing (571) 372-9030.

Barbers Assoc., State-214 E. Center, Alma 48801 (517) 463-5863.

Beverage Assoc., Mich Licensed-534 S. Walnut, Lansing (517) 482-0803.

Blind, Leader Dogs for the-1039 S. Rochester, Rochester 48063 (313) 651-9011.

Boat Assoc. Am Power*B-17640 E. Nine Mile Rd., East Detroit (313) 773-9700.

Bow Hunters, Assoc., Mich-14433 Parkside, Warren 48093 (313) 294-0175.

Bowling Assoc., Mich Womin's-Box 65, Ossineke 49755 (517) 471-5181.

Bowling Congress, Am-72601 Greater Mack, St. Clair Shores (313) 773-6350.

Bridge Assoc., Mich-1720 Cliffs Landing, Ypsilanti 48198 (313) 484-1321.

Broadcasters, Mich. Assoc. of-819 N. Washington, Lansing (517) 484-7444.

Builders, Mich Assoc of Home-426 S. Walnut, Lansing (517) 484-5933.

Building & Construction Trades Council, State-419 S. Washington Sq. Lansing (517) 484-8427.

Builders & Contractors of Mich, Assoc.-100 Holister Bldg., Lansing (517) 485-8020.

Business Assoc. of Mich, Small 222 N. Washington, Lansing (517) 482-8788.

Cancer Soc., Am (Mich Div) 416 Frandor, Lansing (517) 351-0430.

Catholic Conference, Mich-505 N. Capitol, Lansing (517) 372-9310.

Catholic Women, League of-120 Parson, Detroit (313) 831-1000.

Certified Public Accountants,Mich Assoc. 28116 Orchard Lake, Farmington Hills (313) 855-2288.

Chamber of Commerce, Mich-600 S. Walnut, Lansing (517) 371-2100.

Cherry Comm, Mich-7373 W. Saginaw, Lansing (517) 321-1231.

Cherry Producers, Mich Assoc of-678 Front N.W., Grand Rapids 49504 (616) 454-6196.

Child Abuse, Mich Council for Prevention of-116 W. Ottawa, Lansing (517) 485-9113.
Child & Family Agencies, Mich Fed of Private-230 N. Washington, Lansing (517) 485-8852.

Childbirth Without Pain Education Assoc*-20134 Snowden, Detroit 48235 (313) 341-3816.
Chinese Am Educational & Cultural Center of Mich-1826 Glenwood, Ann Arbor 48104 (313) 971-3516.
Chiropractic Society, Mich-6215 W. St. Joseph, Lansing (517)323-7430.
Christian Assoc. for Home Education-1320 Fairoaks Ct., E. Lansing (517) 351-6086.
Christian Church (Disciples of Christ), Mich Region-2820 Covington, Lansing 48912 (517) 372-3220.
Church of Christ Mich Confer United, 5945 Park Lk. Rd., E. Lansing 48823 (517) 332-3551.
Church of God, Gen Assembly, in Mich-4212 Alpha, Lansing 48910 (517) 393-7020.
Citizens Lobby, Mich-122 S. Grand, Lansing (517) 372-7111.
Citizens Research Council of Mich-1502 Mich Natl. Tower, Lansing (517) 485-9444.
Civil Liberties Union, Am, of Mich-1701 David Whitney Bldg., Detroit (313) 961-4662.
Civil Air Patrol-16601 Airport, Lansing (517) 321-4130.
College Assoc., Mich Community-750 Mich Natl. Tower, Lansing (517) 372-4350.
College & Universities of Mich. Assoc. of **Independent**-Mich Natl. Tower, Lansing (517) 372-9160.
College & Universities, Mich Assoc of Governing Boards-306 Townsend, Lansing (517) 372-0537.
Common Cause, Mich-109 E. Oakland, Lansing (517) 484-5385.
Community Action Agency Assoc., Mich-108 W. Allegan, Lansing (517) 484-1353.
Community Economic Development Coalition, Mich-1801 W. Main, Lansing (517) 371-4249.
Computer & Automated Systems Assoc-1 SME Dr., Dearborn (313) 271-1500.
Communist Party of Mich-908 Michigan, Detroit (313) 961-2025.
Concrete Institute, Am*-Box 19150, Detroit 48219 (313) 532-2600.
Consulting Engrg Council of Mich-1407 S. Harrison, Lansing (517) 332-2066.
Construction Assoc of Mich-1351 E. Jefferson, Detroit (313) 567-5500.
Contractors, Assoc Gen of Mich-2323 N. Larch, Lansing (517) 371-1550.
Convenience Stores, Assoc of Mich- Michigan Natl Tower, Lansing (517)487-9139.
Cosmetologist Assoc., Mich-1319 George, Lansing (517) 371-2729.
Correctional Officers, Am Assoc of*-Criminal Justice Dept., Northern Mich University, Marquette
Council of Churches, 3186 Pine Tree, Lansing (517) 887-6640.
Counties, Michigan Assoc of-935 N. Washington, Lansing (517) 482-5850.
County Officers Assoc, Mich United Hollister Bldg., Lansing (517) 371-2333.
Credit Unions, Mich Assoc of-3303 W. Saginaw, Lansing (517) 321-3068.
Crime & Delinquency, Mich Council On-300 N. Washington, Lansing (517) 482-4161.
Crippled Children, Mich League for-14946 Penrod, Detroit (313) 273-8088.
Dairy Assoc, Am-Assoc. of Mich-2163 Jolly, Okemos (5170 349-8923.
Daughters of the AM Revolution, Mich Soc-305 W. Elm, Monroe (313) 242-2184.
Democratic Party of Mich-606 Townsend, Lansing (517) 371-5410.
Dental Assoc., Mich-230 N. Washington Sq., Lansing (517) 372-9070.
Diabetes Foundation, Junior-5763 Canal, Diamdale (517) 646-8086.
Dietetic Assoc., Mich-200 N. Capitol, Lansing (517) 487-6389.
Disabilities, Learning, Assoc of Mich-200 Museum, Lansing (517) 485-8160.
Disabled American Veterans-477 Michigan, Detroit (313) 964-6595.
Domestic Violence, Mich Coalition Against-106 W. Allegan, Lansing (517) 372-4960.
Economics for Human Development-410 E. Grand River, Lansing (517) 482-5571.
Economic Alliance For Mich 150 W. Jefferson, Detroit
Education Assoc., Mich-1216 Kendale, E. Lansing (517) 392-6551.

Education Data Network Assoc., Mich-1350 Kendal, (517) 332-7679.
Education Special Services Assoc., Mich-1480 Kendale, E. Lansing (517) 332-2581
Education, Mich Assoc for Community & Adult-530 W. Ionia, Lansing (517) 484-2822.
Electronic Service Dealers Assoc. of Mich-8840 W. Warren, Dearborn
Employee Ownership Center Mich-1880 Penobscot Bldg., Detroit (313) 964-5040.
Employers Association, Mich State-Box 13158, Lansing 48901 (517) 394-5900.
Engineering Soc of Mich-100 Farnsworth, Detroit 48202 (313) 832-5400.
Engineers, Am Soc of Agricultural*-2950 Niles Rd., St. Joseph
Engineers, Soc of Mfg*-P.O. Box 930, Dearborn
Engineers, Mich Soc Professional-215 N. Walnut, Lansing (517) 487-9388.
Epilepsy Center of Mich-3800 Woodward, Detroit (313) 1222.
Episcopal Diocese of Mich-4800 Woodward, Detroit 48201 (313) 832-4400.
Fairs & Exhibitions, Mich Assoc of-P.O. Box 241, Allegan 49010 (616) 673-6050.
Farm Bureaau, Mich-7373 W. Saginaw, Lansing 48909 (517) 323=7000.
Farmers Co-operatives, Mich Assoc of-5000 Marsh, Okemos (517) 349-5660.
Farmers Union, Mich-500 E. Lansing, Potterville (517) 645-2330.
Fathers for Equal Rights-25333 Lois, Southfield (313) 354-3060.
Fed. of State, Cty. & Municipal Emp., Am-Mich Council-1034 N. Washington,Lansing (517)487-5081.
Firefighters Union, Mich State-419 S. Washington, Lansing (517) 372-6536.
Florist Transworld Delivery Assoc* (FTD), 29200 Northwestern Hwy. Southfield (313) 355-9300.
Food Dealers Assoc., Mich-221 N. Walnut, Lansing (517) 372-6800.
Forresters, Independent Order of-4467 Byron Center SW, Wyoming (517) 534-0040.
Foundations, Council of Mich-Box 599, Grand Haven 49417 (616) 842-7080.
Garden Clubs of Mich, Federated-3600 Northview, Kalamazoo 49007 (616) 344-2549.
Gen. Contractors, Assoc., -of Am, Mich Chapter-2323 N. Larch, Lansing (517) 371-1550
Golf Courses, Mich Assoc. of Public-911 Haynes NE, Comstock Park 49321 (616) 784-1355.
Governmental Employees, Mich Assoc of 6920 S.Cedar, Holt (517) 694-3123.
Grange, Mich State-1730 Chamberlain, Haslett 48840 (517) 339-2171.
Greater Mich Foundation, 809 Center, Lansing (517) 487-3616.
Grocers Assoc, Mich-221 N. Walnut, Lansing (517) 372-6800.
Handicapped Driving Aids of Mich-4020 Second, Wayne (313) 595-4440
Health Appeal, Combined of Mich-900 Long, Lansing (517) 694-1717.
Health Assoc., Mich Mental-220 N. Chestnut, Lansing (517) 485-7168.
Health Assoc., Mich Catholic-6215 W. St.Joseph, Lansing (517) 323-3993.
Health Care Assoc of Mich-7413 Westshire Dr., Lansing (517) 627-1561.
Health Council, Mich-1305 Abbott, E. Lansing (517) 337-1615.
Hearing Aid Society, Natl*-20361 Middlebelt, Livonia (313) 478-2610.
Hearing & Speech, Mich Assoc. for Better, 724 Abbott, E. Lansing (517) 337-1646.
Heart Assoc. of Mich., Am-271 Woodland Pass, E. Lansing (517) 332-0385.
Heart Fund-16310 W. Twelve Mile Rd., Southfield (313) 557-9500.
Historical Soc of Mich-2117 Washtenaw, Ann Arbor (313) 769-1828.
HMO's in Mich, Assoc.-327 Seymour, Lansing (517) 371-3181.
Hockey Assoc. Mich Amateur-2034 Clifton, Lansing (517) 484-8233.
Homemakers, Mich Assoc of Future-106 Wills House, MSU, E. Lansing (517) 355-7662.
Horatio Alger Soc*-4907 Alison Dr. Lansing
Horsemen's Assoc, Mich Harness-4650 Moore, Okemos (517) 349-2920.
Horticultural Soc, Mich State-102 Horticultural Bldg., MSU, E. Lansing 48824. (517) 355-5194.
Hospital Assoc., Mich- 6215 W. St. Joseph, Lansing (517) 323-3443.
Housing Coalition, Mich-Llansing (517) 377-0509.
Humane Society, Mich-7401 Chrysler, Detroit 48211 (313) 872-3400.
Human Services, Mich League for-300 N. Washington, Lansing (517) 487-5436.
Indian Child Welfare Agency, Mich-6425 S. Pennsylvania, Lansing (517) 393-3256.
Indian Employee & Training Services, Mich- 809 Cedar, Lansing (517) 482-3326.

Indian Services, Am-9301 Michigan, Detroit (313) 581-9011.
Infant Death Syndrome, Sudden, Mich-4201 St. Antoine, Detroit (313) 494-0222.
Insurance Agents, Mich Prof-3700 Capital City Blvd., Lansing (517) 321-0106.
Insurance Companies, Mich Assoc of -404 Kalamazoo Plaza, Lansing (517) 482-1643.
International Institute-111 E. Kirby, Detroit (313) 871-8600.
Inter-Tribal Council of Mich-405 E. Easterday, Saulte Ste Marie 49783 (906) 632-6896.
Inventors, Am Assoc of*-6562 E. Curtis, Bridgeport.
Investment Clubs, Natl Assoc of*-1515 E. Eleven Mile Rd., Royal Oak.
Investors, Natl Assoc of*-1515 E. Eleven Mile Rd., Royal Oak (313) 543-0612.
Jaycees, Mich-230 N. Washington, Lansing (517) 487-6077.
Jewish Congress, Am-163 Madison, Detroit (313) 965-3353.
Jewish Congress, Mich-300 N. Washington, Lansing (517) 485-8303.
Kidney Foundation of Mich-3378 Washtenaw, Ann Arbor. 1-800-482-1455.
Kiwanis Inter, Mich Dist-515 N. Cedar 48854 (517) 676-3837.
Knights of Columbus, Mich Council-12824 Warren, Dearborn 48126 (313) 581-3455.
Korean Hot Line Services-27075 W. Nine Mile Rd. Southfield (313) 356-4488.
Landlords Assoc., Mich-5620 S. Washington, Lansing (517) 487-4458.
Latin Assoc for Social & Economic Devel.-4138 W. Vernor, Detroit (313) 554-2025.
Lawyers Assoc, Mich Trial-501 S. Capitol, Lansing (517) 482-7740.
Leukemia Foundation of Mich-19022 W. 10 Mile, Southfield (313) 353-8222.
Library Assoc., Mich-1000 Long Blvd., Lansing (517) 694-6615.
Library Consortium, Mich-6810 S. Cedar, Holt (517) 694-4242.
Libertarian Party of Mich-11700 Merriman Rd., Livonia 1-800-343-1364.
Lion's Club of Mich 3186 Pine Tree, Lansing (517) 887-6640.
Lodging Assoc., Mich-30161 Southfield, Southfield (313) 645-5850.
Lung Assoc of Mich, Am-403 Seymour, Lansing (517) 484-4541.
Lutheran Church, Am, Mich Dist-21900 greenfield, Oak Park 48237 (313) 968-5450.
Lutheran Social Services of Mich-801 S Waverly, Lansing (517) 321-7663.
MACMA-Mich Agricultural Co-op Mktg. Assoc., 7373 W. Saginaw, Lansing (517) 323-7000.
Make-A-Wish Foundation of Mich1028 E. Saginaw, Lansing (517)372-4220.
Mfg. Engineers, Soc of*-1 SME Dr., Dearborn (313) 646-3331.
March of Dimes-3307 W. Saginaw, Lansing (517) 323-7339.
Marine Corps League-477 Michigan, Detroit (313) 964-6830.
Medical Soc., Mich State-120 W. Saginaw, E. Lansing (517) 337-1351.
Medicine, Emergency-Am Board-200 Woodland Pass, E. Lansing (517) 332-4800.
Metal Health Assoc.,in Mich. 319 W. Lenawee, Lansing (517)485-7168.
Merchants Council & Assoc., Mich-116 W. Ottawa, Lansing (517) 485-5536.
Michigan Beautiful, Keep-Box 664, Farmington (313) 477-6647.
Milk Producers Assoc., Mich-Box 5078, Southfield 48037 (313) 354-9790.
Minority Business Delv Council, Mich-2990 W. Grand Blvd., Detroit 48202 (313) 873-3200.
Motor Vehicle Mfg. Assoc*-300 New Center Bldg., Detroit (313) 872-4311.
Multiple Sclerosis Soc., Mich Chapter-1595 Cranwood, Okemos (517) 347-0888.
Municipal League, Mich-416 W. Ottawa, Lansing (517) 485-1314.
Muscular Dystrophy Assoc-10551 Allen, Allen Park (313) 381-3838.
Museums Assoc., Mich-1221 E. Kearsley, Flint 48503 (313) 762-1170.
NAACP (Natl Assoc for the Adv. of Colored People)-2990 E. Grand Blvd. Detroit (313) 871-2087.
Non-Profit Homes Assoc., Mich 1423 Keystone, Lansing (517) 393-0500.
NOW-Mich National Organization of Women, 217 Townsend, Lansing (517) 485-9687.
Numismatic Assoc., Mich-Box 2014, Livonia 48151 (313) 261-9326.
Nurses Assoc., Mich-2310 Jolly Oak, Okemos (517) 349-5640.
Nurses League of Mich, License Pratical 5900 Executive Dr., Lansing (517) 882-6657.
Oil & Gas Assoc.,Mich-1610 Mich Natl Tower, Lansing (517) 487-1092.
Optometric Assoc., Mich-530 W. Ionia, Lansing (517) 482-0616.
Organic Growers, Mich Co-op of-3086 E. Main, Benton Harbor 49022 (616) 944-5012.

Osteopaathic Physicians & Surgeons, Mich Assoc-327 Seymour, Lansing (517) 485-9600.

PTA (Parents & Teachers) Mich Congress of-1011 N. Washington, Lansing (517) 485-4345

Parents Anonymous of Mich-1553 Woodward, Detroit 1-800-482-0747.

Petroleum Industries of Mich, Assoc.,-707 Mich Natl Tower, Lansing (517) 372-7455.

Pharmacists Assoc., Mich-815 N. Washington, Lansing (517) 484-1466.

Physicians Assts., Mich Academy-1305 Abbott, E. Lansing (517) 337-9797.

Physicians, Family-Mich Academy-2164 Commons Pkwy., Okemos (517) 347-0098.

Planned Parenthood Affiliates of Mich-217 Townsend, Lansing (517) 482-1080.

Plant Guard Workers, United, of Am*-25510 Kelly Rd., Roseville (313) 772-7250.

Poles of America, Alliance of - 3514 Caniff, Hamtramck, (313) 872-8929.

Polish Legion of Am Veterans, USA-11621 Conant, Hamtramck (313) 891-7528.

Police Troopers Assoc., Mich-530 W. Ionia, Lansing (517) 374-6810.

Pork Producers Assoc., 4265 Okemos Rd., Okemos (517) 347-0850.

Pregnancy Services of Mich-Abortion Alternatives, Inc.-116 Bridge Diamondale (517) 646-6166.

Press Assoc., Mich-827 N. Washington, Lansing (517) 372-2424.

Principals Assoc., Mich Elementary & Middle School-1405 S. Harrison, E. Lansing (517) 353-8770.

Professional Employees Soc., Mich-1026 E. Michigan, Lansing (517) 482-1737.

Professors, Am Assoc of University-115 W. Allegan, Lansing (517) 482-2775.

Progressive Labor Party-10 Witherell, Detroit (313) 963-2612.

Protection & Advocacy Service, Mich 109 W. Michigan, Lansing (517) 487-1755.

Public Transit Assoc., Mich-216 N. Chestnut, Lansing (517) 374-6810.

Quarter Horse Assoc., Great Lakes-1817 Victor, Lansing (517) 485-9404.

Reading Assoc., Mich-Box 7509, Grand Rapids 49510 (616) 538-0892.

Realtors, Mich Assoc. of 720 N. Washinton, Lansing (517) 372-8890.

Recreation & Parks Assoc., Mich-2722 E. Michigan, Lansing (517) 485-9888.

Republican Heritage Groups of Mich-1665 First Natl Bldg., Detroit (313) 645-9770.

Republican Party of Mich-2121 E. Grand River, Lansing (517) 487-5413.

Restaurant Assoc., Mich-2125 University Park Dr., Okemos (517) 349-0272.

Retailers Assoc., Mich-221 N. Pine, Lansing (517) 372-5656/1-800-366-3699.

Retarded Citizens, Mich, Assoc for-333 S. Washington, Lansing (517) 487-5426.

Retired Persons, Am Assoc of-930 John R., Troy 48083. (313) 585-0027.

Right to Life of Mich-300 S. Washington, Lansing (517) 487-3376.

Right to Work Assoc., Mich-15694 N. East, Lansing (517)

Savings Institutions, Mich League of-200 N. Washington, Lansing (517) 371-2200.

School Administrators, Mich Assoc of-421 W. Kalamazoo, Lansing (517) 371-5250.

School Boards, Mich Assoc of-421 W. Kalamazoo, Lansing (517) 371-5700.

Service Station Dealers Assoc of Mich-200 N. Capitol, Lansing (517) 484-4096.

Seventh Day Adventist, Mich Confer Assoc-320 W. St. Joseph, Lansing 48933.

Sheriffs Assoc, Mich-515 N. Capitol, Lansing (517) 485-3135.

Sherrif Assoc., **Deputy**-of Mich-230 N. Washington Sq. Lansing, (517) 485-4602.

Social Service Assoc., 935 N. Washington, Lansing (517) 371-5303.

Socialist Workers Party-2135 Woodward, Detroit (313) 961-0395.

Substance Abuse Coordinators, Mich Assoc., 913 W. Holmes, Lansing (517) 393-6700

Substance AA Abuse Hotline 1-800-765-4320.

Substance Abuse Info Center, Mich-925 E. Kalamazoo, Lansing (517) 482-9902.

Synagogues of Am, Mich Region United-29901 Middlebelt, Farmington Hills 48018 (313) 855-5950.

Teachers, Mich Federation of-419 S. Washington, Lansing (517) 371-4300.

Teamsters Joint Council No 43, Mich-2741 Trumbull, Detroit 48216 (313) 961-1730.

Technology Council, Mich-2005 Bates, Ann Arbor 48109 (313) 763-9757.

Television Assoc., Mich Cable

Tenants Resource Center, Inc-300 Bailey, E. Lansing (5170 337-9795.

Townships Assoc., Mich 512 Westshire, Lansing (517) 321-6467.

Traffic Safety Assoc., of Mich-Mich Natl Tower, Lansing (5170 487-8811.
Trail Assoc., North County*-2780 Mundy, White Cloud.
Travelers Aid Society-406 David Whitney Bldg., Detroit (313) 962-6740.
Trial Lawyers Assoc., Mich-401 S. Capitol, Lansing (517) 482-7740.
Trucking Assoc., Mich-5800 Executive, Lansing (517) 393-2053.
UAW-United Automobile Workers of Am*-8000 E. Jefferson, Detroit (313) 926-5000.
United Way of Mich-300 N. Washington, Lansing (517) 371-5860.
United Nations Assoc-UNICEF Center-730 E. Michigan, Lansing (517) 485-43254.
University Professors-Am Assoc., 115 W. Allegan, Lansing (517) 482-2775.
University Women, Am Assoc of-204 Museum Dr., Lansing (517) 372-8302.
Veterans of America, Mich Paralyzed-477 Michigan, Detroit (313) 961-9583.
VFW-Veterans of Foreign Wars of US, Dept. of Mich-924 N. Washington, Lansing (517)485-9456.
Veterans of World War 1, USA-477 Michigan, Detroit (313) 964-6555.
Veterinary Medical Assoc., Mich-1405 S. Harrison, E. Lansing 48823 (517) 332-2913.
Vietnam Veterans of Am, Mich Council-14913 Heyer, Livonia 48154 (313) 873-9745.
Water Coalition, Mich Clean-300 N. Grand River, Lansing (517) 484-9710.
Women Business Owners, Natl Assoc-12606 N. Inkster, Redford (313) 937-
Women,Assoc of Career-920 Long Blvd., Holt (517) 694-2076.
Women for America, Concerned-205 Museum Dr., Lansing (517) 484-5383.
Women Political Leadership Caucus, Natl Black-4E Alexandrine, Detroit (313)833-6660.
Women Voters of Mich, League-200 Museum, Lansing 48933 (517) 484-5383.
Women's Clubs, Gen Fed of, in Mich-659 S. Gargantua, Clawson (313) 435-5767.
Women's Clubs, Mich Assoc of Colored-3260 Murray Hill, Saginaw 48601 (517) 777-5281.
Women's Economic Club of Detrit-155 W. Congress, Detroit (313) 963-5088.
Women's Studies Assoc., Mich 213 W. Main, Lansing (517) 372-9772.
World Medical Relief-11745 Twelth, Detroit (313) 866-5333.
Youth Hostel, Am, Mich Council-3024 Coolidge, Berkley 48072 (313) 545-0511.
Youth Services, Mich Network of Runaway & Homeless, 115 W. Allegan, Lansing (517) 484-5262.

Trivia

Q Which is the recorded largest species of fish ever caught in Michigan waters ?

A Lake Sturgeon, 193 lbs, 87" long. (It was caught in 1992, in Mullett Lake, Cheyboyan County by Joe Maka, Jr., of Grand Haven, Michigan).

Q What is the size of the largest recorded Trout ever caught in Michigan waters ?

A It was 34.38 lbs, 38.25" long (It was caught in 1984, in Arcadia Lake, Manistee County, by Michael Kent of Lansing, by trolling with Copy Cat bait).

Q What is the average age of Michigan farm operators?

A 51.9 years (The average age varies from a low of 48.5 in Crawforf County to a high of 57.4 in Alcona County).

Q Which radio station in Detroit became the world's first scheduled broadcaster ?

A WWJ (in 1920).

Q Who exported the first automobile ?

A Ransom Olds (1893, exported to India).

Q What was the age of Sgt John Clem, when he served with Michigan troops at Chickamauga during the Civil War (1863) ?

A Twelve

Q In which year did the Detroit Fire Dept operate it's last horse drawn fire wagon ?

A 1922

Q If only the white population of Detroit was counted, what would be the largest city in Michigan?

A Detroit (although 77% of the Detroit population is black, the 22% white population is larger than the total population of the state's second largest city, Grand Rapids).

BE FULLY INFORMED!

ALL ABOUT MICHIGAN ALMANAC

AND IT MAKES A UNIQUE AND USEFUL GIFT, TOO.

GRADUATION
BIRTHDAY
CHRISTMAS
GOODWILL
NEW NEIGHBOR

IT WILL BE RECEIVED AS AN UNEXPECTED SURPRIZE. YOUR THOUGHTFULNESS WILL BE APPRECIATED AS IT IS READ AND USED IN THE MONTHS AND YEAR(S) AHEAD.

ORDER TODAY!
$17.95 plus $2.75 S/H

INSTANT INFORMATION CO.
P.O. BOX 202
HARTLAND, MI 48353

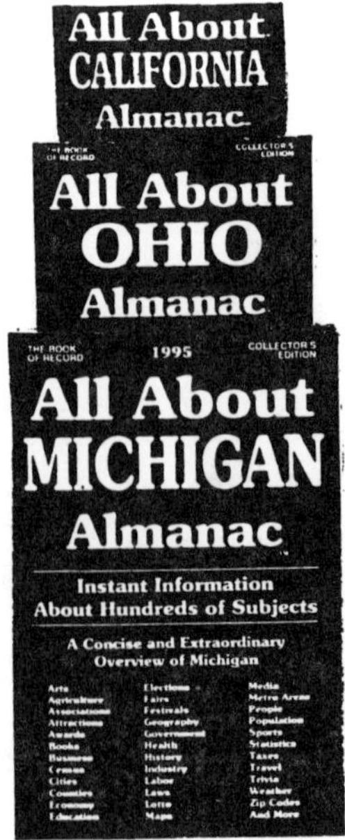